Stories of Civil War in El Salvador

A Battle over Memory

· ·

ERIK CHING

The University of North Carolina Press Chapel Hill

© 2016 The University of North Carolina Press
All rights reserved
Set in Charis by Westchester Publishing Services
Manufactured in the United States of America

The University of North Carolina Press has been a member
of the Green Press Initiative since 2003.

Library of Congress Cataloging-in-Publication Data
Names: Ching, Erik Kristofer, author.
Title: Stories of civil war in El Salvador : a battle over memory /
    Erik Ching.
Description: Chapel Hill : University of North Carolina Press, [2016] |
    Includes bibliographical references and index.
Identifiers: LCCN 2015040518| ISBN 9781469628660 (pbk : alk. paper) |
    ISBN 9781469628677 (ebook) | ISBN 978-1-4696-3041-0
    (hardback: alk. paper)
Subjects: LCSH: El Salvador—History—1979–1992. | Collective
    memory—El Salvador. | Group identity—El Salvador. | Social classes—
    El Salvador.
Classification: LCC F1488.3 .C475 2016 | DDC 972.8405/3—dc23
LC record available at http://lccn.loc.gov/2015040518

Cover illustration: Photograph of soldiers courtesy of Colección Fotográfica
del Museo de la Palabra y la Imagen, El Salvador, and used strictly by
permission of Museo de la Palabra y la Imagen.

put to press with an award
Figure Foundation
reading blueprints of belief

To Cathy

Contents

Acknowledgments

In the prologue to Rodrigo Guerra y Guerra's 2011 memoir about the 1979 coup, the Salvadoran writer and journalist Rafael Menjívar Ochoa says, in reference to the many life stories that have appeared in El Salvador since the end of the civil war, "these materials need to be processed and placed in their proper context, within the framework of history yet to be written."[1] Menjívar Ochoa has since passed away, but had he lived to read this book, I hope he would have seen it as helping to fill those absences.

I began to conceptualize this study in the late 2000s while working on other projects about recent Salvadoran history. One of those projects was the translation of *La Terquedad del Izote*, the war diary of Carlos Henríquez Consalvi, a.k.a. Santiago, the main voice of Radio Venceremos, the FMLN's clandestine radio station during the war.[2] My involvement in that project, which was translated as *Broadcasting the Civil War in El Salvador*, allowed me to discover that vast numbers of life stories were emerging from El Salvador and that they had not been subjected to rigorous academic inquiry. I also realized that the study of the historical memory of the civil war was in its infancy.[3]

Another project that helped me to conceptualize the present one was my involvement in the study of the contested memory of an earlier trauma in Salvadoran history, the peasant uprising and military massacre of 1932. In *Remembering a Massacre in El Salvador*, my coauthors and I learned that in the decades following the events of 1932, Salvadorans separated into diverse memory groups that narrated the events of 1932 differently, and that their narrations changed in accordance with contemporary exigencies. It seemed that with the end of the civil war more than two decades in the past, the time was right to investigate Salvadorans' remembrances of it.

I'm deeply indebted to many people who made this study possible. First and foremost I wish to recognize my home institution, Furman University, which granted me a full-year sabbatical leave that provided me with the time and opportunity to complete the bulk of the present book. To various colleagues who read some or all of the manuscript in various stages, or who provided me with advice, I would like to offer my thanks, especially Paul Almeida, Jeff Gould, Terry Lynn Karl, Héctor Lindo, Michael Schroeder, David Spencer, Ralph Sprenkels, and Knut Walter. The two anonymous reviewers commissioned by UNC Press proved very knowledgeable about the Salvadoran case and provided me with helpful insights that improved the final text. Colleagues in El Salvador have aided me in diverse ways throughout this project. They include, but are not limited to César Acevedo, René Aguiluz, Ricardo Argueta, Fidel Campos, Carlos Henríquez Consalvi, Carlos Gregorio López Bernal, Sister Peggy O'Neill, and Alfredo Ramírez. Maria Mayo worked with me as a research assistant during a summer thanks to funding provided by the Furman Advantage Program. The image that appears on the front cover was graciously provided by the Museum of Word and Image in San Salvador, under the direction of Carlos Consalvi. I would also like to thank the University of North Carolina Press, its editor Elaine Maisner, whose suggestions very much improved the manuscript, and her assistant editor, Alison Shay. Thanks also to Carol Noble for an outstanding copyedit, and to Carolyn Ferrick for the followup edit.

I could not have completed this project without my family's support. So to my parents, Harriette and Woody Ching, my sister Nissa Ching, and my in-laws, Matt and Carol Stevens and Rob and Jaime Stevens, and our extended family member, Blanca Castaño, I extend deep gratitude. My most heartfelt appreciation goes out to my immediate family: my spouse, Cathy Stevens, and our three children, Anders, Halle, and Evan; I owe this one to you.

Abbreviations and Acronyms in the Text

ABECAFE   Asociación Salvadoreña de Beneficiadores y Exportadores de Café (Association of Coffee Producers)

ARENA   Alianza Republicana Nacionalista (Nationalist Republican Alliance)

BIRI   Batallón de Infantería de Reacción Inmediata (Rapid Action Infantry Battalion)

BPR   Bloque Popular Revolucionario (Revolutionary Popular Block)

BRAZ   Brigada Rafael Arce Zablah (Rafael Arce Zablah Brigade)

ERP   Ejército Revolucionario del Pueblo (People's Revolutionary Army)

FAL   Fuerzas Armadas de Liberación (Armed Forces of Liberation)

FARO   Frente Agrario de la Región Oriental (Agrarian Front of the Eastern Region)

FMLN   Frente Farabundo Martí para la Liberación Nacional (Farabundo Martí Nacional Liberation Front)

FPL   Fuerzas Populares de Liberación Farabundo Martí (Farabundo Martí Popular Liberation Forces)

FRAP   Fuerzas Revolucionarias Armadas del Pueblo (Armed Revolutionary Forces of the People)

FRTS   Federación Regional de Trabajadores Salvadoreños (Regional Federation of Salvadoran Workers)

FUAR   Frente Unido de Acción Revolucionaria (United Front for Revolutionary Action)

FUSADES   Fundación Salvadoreña para el Desarrollo Económico y Social (Salvadoran Foundation for Economic and Social Development)

MERS	Movimiento Estudiantil Revolucionario de Secundaria (High School Students' Revolutionary Movement)
MNR	Movimiento Revolucionario Nacional (National Revolutionary Movement)
OLAS	Organización Latinoamericana de Solidaridad (Latin American Solidarity Organization)
ORDEN	Organización Democrática Nacionalista (Nationalist Democratic Organization)
ORT	Organización Revolucionario de Trabajadores (Revolutionary Workers Organization)
PCN	Partido de Conciliación Nacional (National Conciliation Party)
PCS	Partido Comunista Salvadoreño (Communist Party of El Salvador)
PD	Partido Demócrata (Democratic Party)
PDC	Partido Demócrata Cristiano (Christian Democratic Party)
PR-9M	Partido Revolucionario 9 de Mayo (May 9th Revolutionary Party)
PRAL	Patrullas de Reconocimiento de Alcance Largo (Long-Range Reconnaissance Patrols)
PRTC	Partido Revolucionario de los Trabajadores Centroamericanos (Revolutionary Party of Central American Workers)
PRUD	Partido Revolucionario de Unificación Democrática (Revolutionary Party of Democratic Unification)
RN	Resistencia Nacional (National Resistance)
SRI	Socorro Rojo Internacional (International Red Aid)
UCA	Universidad Centroamericana José Simeón Cañas (José Simeón Cañas Central American University)
USAID	United States Agency for International Development

Stories of Civil War in El Salvador

Introduction

Something remarkable happened in a Boston courtroom in August 2013. El Salvador's former vice minister of public safety, Colonel Inocente Orlando Montano, was held partially accountable for his actions during the civil war in El Salvador in the 1980s.[1] Unable to be tried criminally for those actions in a U.S. court, even though he was living here, Montano was found guilty of lying on his application for protected status, which granted him humanitarian status to remain in the United States after having left El Salvador in 2000. Among other falsehoods, he failed to indicate on his form that he had served in the military or received military training. In order to prove that Montano lied, the prosecution had to demonstrate not only that he falsified his application by failing to reveal his military service, but also that he had engaged in activities that would have contradicted his request for humanitarian status. Therefore, in a roundabout way, Montano's case became a public accounting of El Salvador's civil war.

The expert witness for the prosecution was Terry Lynn Karl, a professor of political science at Stanford University. She provided a painstakingly researched exposé on Montano and the Salvadoran army during the war. The cornerstone of Karl's argument was that the Salvadoran military had perpetrated heinous crimes during the war, and that it had done so under a strict chain of command. She showed that troops followed the orders of their commanding officers, and that those officers had the authority to curtail their soldier's abusive actions. One of the pivotal events under examination was the assassination by the military of six Jesuit priests in November 1989 at the Universidad Centroamericana José Simeón Cañas (UCA) in San Salvador. Karl argued that Montano was part of the military's Alto Mando (high command), which had ordered the murders, and that he was present in the meeting when the decision to execute the priests was delivered.

The key witness for the defense was retired General Mauricio Vargas, another high-ranking official in the Salvadoran army, who had both commanded troops in the field and served in the Alto Mando. The crux of

Montano Case

Vargas's testimony was that any questionable activities, which perhaps were perpetrated by some soldiers, did not occur under the orders of their commanding offices. In an ironic twist, Vargas's testimony rested upon the same premise as Terry Karl's. He claimed that the army was indeed defined by a functioning chain of command, and that Montano would not have been in position to give the orders to the unit accused of killing the Jesuits. Furthermore, Vargas claimed that any orders coming from Montano would have been given to him originally by higher authorities, so responsibility would reside with them. Technically, Vargas was correct, however the prosecution never claimed Montano gave the order, but rather that he was present when the order was given and that he had the authority to countermand it.[2]

In the end, Judge Woodlock ruled in favor of the prosecution, concluding the trial with a biting critique of Montano and his defense. In short, the judge declared that the relationship between Montano's evidence and his narrative was spurious and that the evidence and narrative presented by the prosecution were more accurate. Montano received a sentence of twenty-one months in prison, and faces the prospect of being extradited to Spain to stand trial for the murder of the Jesuits, five of whom were Spaniards by birth.

What makes Montano's trial remarkable is the fact that it did not occur in El Salvador, nor will anything like it happen there in the foreseeable future. An amnesty law passed at the end of the war makes it impossible for anyone to be prosecuted for their activities during the war. Courts, like the one in Boston, are hardly perfect arbiters of truth, as they are subject to bias and influence, but at least a courtroom is a potentially neutral setting where rivaling versions of the past can be contested. A court allows for evidence to be introduced and evaluated, and for witnesses to be cross-examined, and it allows for ostensibly dispassionate assessors—a judge or a jury—to rule on the validity of the competing narratives that rival parties present. Not only does El Salvador have an amnesty law that prevents such adjudication, it lacks anything like an ongoing truth and reconciliation commission (TRC), a "confessional space" in which people receive immunity from potential prosecution in exchange for full confessions about their activities during the conflict in question.[3] Even if a postconflict country like El Salvador had an ongoing TRC and no amnesty law, the court of public opinion would play a tremendously important role in constructing collective memories about the civil war. But because El Salvador has an amnesty law and does not have any other formal truth-telling process, the war is being tried exclusively in the court of public opinion, without a judge or jury, without peer review, simply through the citizenry's freewheeling injection of its often contradictory narratives into the postwar public sphere. The sociologist Elizabeth Jelin, who specializes in the study of historical memory in the aftermath of state repression, notes that "when the state does not develop official and legitimate institutionalized channels that openly recognize past state violence and repression, the conflict over truth and over 'proper' memories develops in the societal arena."[4] Jelin's description applies well to what has been happening in El Salvador since 1992.

This book looks at the process of memory-making in postwar El Salvador through published life stories that have appeared since the end of the war in 1992. The premise is that a narrative battle is occurring in El Salvador between four memory communities, each of which advances a distinct and mutually exclusive version of the past. The shooting war may be over, but the existence of these four communities and their rivaling narratives demonstrates that the contest for the story of the war is just getting underway.[5]

· · · · ·

The civil war in El Salvador was a brutal, twelve-year-long affair (1980–1992) that left an indelible imprint on the nation's psyche. The statistical consequences of the war testify to its devastating impact. In a country roughly the size of Massachusetts, with a population of around five million people at the time, approximately 75,000 were killed, another 350,000 or more were wounded, and around one million were displaced from their homes, many of whom fled the country and ended up in the United States. Many tens of thousands more people were tortured, incarcerated, raped, conscripted, and/or abducted.[6] The number of people suffering debilitating psychological trauma remains impossible to determine, although anecdotal evidence suggests that it is widespread.[7]

Since the end of the war, Salvadorans have responded to the trauma in diverse ways. Some are trying to forget it, aided by the existence of the amnesty law.[8] Others are trying to remember it, in hopes of making sense of it.[9] The latter are finding remembrances in diverse "memory sites," or what Oren Stier, a scholar of collective memories of the Holocaust, calls the "media of memory."[10] Memory sites include, but are not limited to, monuments, murals, museums, literature, film, music, personal testimonials, and, in the case of El Salvador, a planned television drama about the 1989 murder of Jesuits.[11] Scholars of other Latin American countries have employed these types of sources and others in their study of historical memory, with one scholar describing them as "productive sites of social meaning where societies deal with, contest, struggle over, represent and continue their journey through rupture."[12]

Of the various memory sites in El Salvador, one of the most important and commonly used is published life stories.[13] The stories come in two forms, memoirs and testimonials. The former refers to self-authored works by literate people who write their own narratives. They appear in various forms, including traditional printed books, websites, and blogs. They have also taken form as extended interviews that have then appeared in traditional print or electronic media. Testimonials refer to the life stories of illiterate or marginalized people who have no access to publishing venues. In a typical testimonial format, the narrator tells his or her story to a literate outsider, usually someone with contacts in the publishing arena, who then compiles the narrative and oversees its publication. Testimonials have appeared most commonly in traditional print format, usually as compilations of multiple life stories published together in a single volume.

The criteria used in this book to determine what qualifies as a life story follow the basic contours of life story scholarship, namely that the focus of the narrative should be the individual "I," and the goal of the story should be to reveal something about the person's life. Usually, a life story narrative is structured in the first-person voice, although occasionally narrators choose to use the third person, even though they are referring to themselves. In her foundational study, *Life Stories: The Creation of Coherence*, Charlotte Linde defines life stories as any and all of "the stories and associated discourse units" that have been "told by an individual over the course of his/her lifetime," which the narrator sees as worth sharing, or as "reportable."[14]

This definition excludes standard histories in which the author is a third-person chronicler of the past rather than a narrator of his or her own story. However, most life stories operate on a continuum between the individual "I" and these historical contexts. Most narrators, particularly Salvadorans dealing with the civil war, see their lives as bound up in broader historical and spatial contexts, and thus they often move back and forth in their narratives between the "I" and wider stories. The topics of their broader narrations are usually twentieth-century El Salvador, a particular political organization, or a community to which the narrator belongs. Sometimes the narrators go even bigger and delve into U.S. history, the history of Western Civilization, and sometimes the history of humanity as a whole. A few of the sources push their engagement with third-person abstraction quite far, to the point that the narratives might be seen as more standard histories of a generalized past rather than life story narratives per se. Two such examples are the works by General Juan Orlando Zepeda, *Perfiles de la Guerra en El Salvador*, and General Humberto Corado's *En defensa de la patria*.[15] As shown in the chapters ahead, narrators who have been accused of things like crimes against humanity tend to shy away from personal issues and avoid events that could incriminate them, and thus they tend to rely more heavily on a third-person voice and to tell a more depersonalized story. Still, those stories are valuable sources because they can reveal a lot in their depersonalized silence. In his study of collective memory in Chile, Steve Stern notes that "the making of memory is also the making of silence. . . . One group's necessary memory focus becomes another group's necessary silence."[16]

El Salvador has seen an unprecedented outpouring of published life stories since the end of its civil war in 1992. In a 2010 interview, a former activist for the centrist Christian Democratic political party, Gerardo Le Chevallier, noted the deluge, saying that "everyone seems to be writing a book; I need to write one too."[17] The number of stories that have appeared since the end of the war is notable in comparison to the paucity of life stories that existed prior to 1992. Memoirs or autobiographies were virtually non existent in El Salvador. Even testimonials were uncommon, despite the fact that El Salvador played a leading role in establishing the testimonial as a genre, and that testimonials played an important role in challenging the storyline being disseminated by the mainstream media.[18] But in an authoritarian system, in which almost anything could mark a person as someone's enemy, people justifiably kept their private lives to themselves.

It is difficult to measure the volume of stories that have emerged since 1992 because they come in such diverse formats. Roughly speaking, at least a couple hundred life story publications have appeared in one form or another, and that figure could easily be raised to multiple hundreds of stories if a person were to count each individual narrative. Among the sources are some fifty book-length publications; and new stories are appearing constantly. If measured in page numbers, the stories would consist of tens of thousands of published pages.

This outpouring of life stories resides in El Salvador's new postwar public sphere, where it sheds light on the process by which Salvadorans are constructing their postwar imagined community of national identity.[19] Postwar El Salvador provides a distinct opportunity to see a new public sphere being made. Never before in Salvadoran history has a more open environment of public exchange existed. In a country long on authoritarianism and short on democracy, postwar El Salvador, for all its problems, is experiencing an unprecedented era of open and public exchange. At least relative to their recent history, Salvadorans are not being killed, tortured, or incarcerated for speaking their minds.[20] In this newly emergent arena of discourse, Salvadorans are debating many things, including their country's future, the meaning of being Salvadoran, and the historic processes that have led them to their current situation. Life stories are proving to be one of the main venues through which this dialogue is taking place. As just one example, former President Tony Saca of the conservative Alianza Republicana Nacionalista (ARENA) party professed in a speech on the thirteenth anniversary of the peace accords in 2005 that he did not know why El Salvador had a civil war. The implication of his statement was that the guerrillas started the war and that they were unjustified in doing so because conditions did not warrant it. One way former guerrillas have responded to such professions of ignorance is to tell their life stories, which they believe explain why the war happened and how it was caused by the intransigence of Saca's ideological forbearers.[21]

One factor contributing to the relative openness of El Salvador's postwar public sphere is the fact that neither side won the war outright. The two main political parties in the postwar era, ARENA and the Frente Farabundo Martí para la Liberación Nacional (FMLN), emerged directly out of the war and represent two main antagonists from the conflict. They have been relatively evenly matched in the postwar political sphere, as evidenced by the outcome of the first five presidential elections since 1992; ARENA won the first three (1994, 1999, and 2004) and the FMLN the next two (2009 and 2014). Neither side has hegemonic control over the story of the war. In this regard, El Salvador differs from other postconflict societies, like Spain after its civil war in the 1930s, where the victor, the Franco regime, promoted an official version of the war that prevailed for the next four decades, making alternative memories dangerous to share and thus difficult to come by.[22]

The civil war in El Salvador may have been a physical contest for control over people's bodies, but it was also a battle for their hearts and minds that was fought with words as weapons. Each side employed narratives to convince the populace of the righteousness of its cause. As the literary scholar Kristine Byron puts it, "the violent context of civil war underscores the maxim that control over words is as important as control over bodies."[23] Since the war's end, Salvadorans have remained cognizant of the power of words and the important role of narratives in shaping contemporary political debates. Ricardo Paredes Osorio, author of the prologue to a memoir by the rightwing political activist Ricardo Valdivieso, claims that what conservatives should learn from the war is that military hardware is not the key to success; rather "the information in people's minds is vital."[24]

Methodological Approach

The present study is based upon a comprehensive reading of the extant body of published life stories that have emerged from El Salvador since 1992. Focusing exclusively on life stories makes this a unique methodological contribution to the field of memory studies in postconflict societies. This is not to say that other memory sites are less important. In the case of El Salvador, life stories have been a predominant, and perhaps the single most important method people have chosen to express their memories of the war. Sticking to this one site of remembrance not only provides more than sufficient material for a book-length study, it also eliminates random variables that might emerge when different types of memory sites are compared. The number of life stories is so large that future patterns of remembrance will likely adhere to the broad outlines discovered here. Even if they do not, an argumentative baseline has been established for future scholars to contest.

At first glance, relying on published life stories would seem to limit the field of analysis to a small subset of the Salvadoran population—literate, relatively affluent urbanites, who probably have access to a computer. This potentially restricted readership would be comparable to Jürgen Habermas's "bourgeois public sphere," which excluded plebian participants. Although Habermas acknowledged the existence of a plebian sphere, he saw it as separate from the bourgeois sphere.[25] Subsequent scholars have taken him to task for that assumption, insisting that the two spheres, "bourgeois and plebian, elite and popular" are not distinct entities, but rather differing components of a single sphere that interact and shape one another constantly and unpredictably.[26] Such is the case in postwar El Salvador. Even though published life stories in El Salvador are initially accessible to literate audiences, their contents do not remain confined to them. They get passed around in unpredictable ways, through music, art, drama, op-ed pieces, journalism, casual conversation, formal speeches, religious sermons, and so on. Furthermore, illiterate and marginalized people are participating actively in the process by sharing their stories in the form of testimonials, which inject their experiences directly into the broader community of remembrance. Even if illiterate and marginalized people can't read the written narratives, including their own stories in printed form, the act of opening up and sharing them facilitates community action and the raising of collective consciousness. In fact, some of the testimonial collections that have emerged in postwar El Salvador exist precisely because members of particular communities set out with the goal of sharing their stories in order to educate future generations.[27]

My main methodological approach was to engage the stories without preconceived expectations. I knew this to be an impossible goal, and unavoidably I entered the research with preconceptions, although most of them proved wrong. Nevertheless, I tried to allow the sources to speak to me and to not assume that they would exhibit particular patterns. I purposefully read the sources in a haphazard manner, as I came across them, or as they appeared in publication for the first time while I was doing my research. As I read the sources, I formulated a series of questions: Who is telling their story? What do they say about the war? What narrative styles do they employ? How do they explain the origins of the war? How do they assess its consequences? What patterns, if any, emerge from the whole of the stories? If patterns emerge, what are their markers and what does their existence reveal to us about the nature of postwar memory? If no patterns emerge, what does that reveal? As these questions coalesced in my mind, I realized I needed to base my responses on a comprehensive engagement with the sources, because only then would I know if what I was finding was actually a pattern or simply a random anomaly. Surely some sources escaped my attention, such as narratives on obscure blog sites, or interviews tucked into newspapers or online periodicals. But, for the most part, I'm confident that I have covered the overwhelming bulk of the possible sources, especially the main book-length publications.

To assist me in the process of interpreting the sources, I drew upon various studies of collective memory in postconflict societies. Among them is the work of Iwona Irwin and her concept of "memory communities."[28] A scholar of Polish descent, Irwin was inspired to study collective memory in part by a desire to come to terms with the legacy of the Holocaust in her family's native land. Irwin contends that in the process of negotiating the past, particularly a painful past defined by trauma, members of a society tend to fall into varying memory communities, the adherents of which tend to share similar renditions of the past. Irwin says that the rules that bind those members together are socially constructed, meaning they are not bound together by some universally accepted, objective rendering of the past, but rather by particular versions that make sense to them for reasons deeply embedded in their particular social arenas. In Irwin's words, "it is not the absolute weight of historical injustice that matters, but rather how people perceive those past injustices." Taking this point further, she describes the process of remembrance as a dynamic one in which some events are remembered and others are forgotten. Thus, according to Irwin, "our analytical task is to uncover the rules, the normative order of remembrance" that govern individuals' residence in differing memory groups.[29] Following Irwin's lead, I set out to determine if the remembrances of the civil war in El Salvador are coalescing into memory communities, and if so what normative orders bind each of them together.

It should be evident by now that I am not trying to offer an objective account of El Salvador's civil war, but rather an objective study of the way Salvadorans are remembering their war.[30] In so doing, I am bearing witness to the extant narratives in published life stories in order to determine what they reveal to us about how Salvadorans are debating the war's meaning. Thus, I chose not to conduct original interviews as part of my sourcebase, because I did not want to draw out private thoughts or "hidden transcripts" that do not exist in the public arena.[31] Furthermore, it matters little if the authors of my sources are lying, confused, ignorant, or simply forgetful about the past.[32] Indeed, some would seem to be blatantly lying, and others make outlandish, even morally repugnant claims. Some of them seem to be pursuing highly partisan objectives. And many of the narrators have taken artistic liberties, whether consciously or not, as exemplified by the fact that they do things like recreate from memory word-for-word dialogue that occurred decades in the past.[33] But for the purposes of the present project, all that matters is that the authors' stories exist in the public sphere where they are contributing to the narrative debate.

I approach my sources as a historian, as someone looking for evidence about a particular topic. I also approach them as a sort of literary scholar, as someone who reads various works of literature to determine if any patterns or genres exist in them, perhaps beyond the conscious intent of the authors themselves.[34] Obviously, given the volume of evidence, I cannot describe each of my sources in detail, nor can I provide comprehensive examples in the body of the text to support my claims. Instead, I rely upon representative examples and offer additional support in the endnotes.

Main finds: 4 memory comties

My main discovery is that four distinct memory communities emerge from the life story sources. Each community is defined by a distinct and coherent narrative that its members employ with remarkable consistency. Among other similarities, the narrators of each group include and exclude the same events, employ a common narrative style and structure, make roughly identical claims, approach Salvadoran history in the same way, and offer analogous assessments of certain people and organizations.

The commonalities of each groups' narratives are so pronounced that they would seem to be the result of a coordinated effort to advance a preconceived agenda, like members of a political party sticking to "talking points" that were provided to them by party leaders. But that is not what is happening in El Salvador. These four memory communities are not coordinated; they do not exist as named entities; nor are the narrators themselves necessarily aware of them. In fact, most of the narrators would be quite surprised to find out how unoriginal their narratives are. Obviously some of them know about the other published stories, and they may even know some of the authors personally. But few, if any of the narrators recognize themselves as belonging to a particular memory community, and none of them set out to tell their life story in order to defend their community's narrative against its rivals. In fact, some members detest, even hate other members of their community, and they would never consciously identify themselves as sharing a communal space with them. Yet, the textual by-products of their narrative endeavors demonstrate common patterns that allow me to group them together, like the novelists of a literary genre. In other words, some of the narrators are conscious enemies but unconscious allies. Furthermore, the narratives reveal that some former allies during the war remember the war quite differently, and that some former antagonists during the war share some uncanny memory parallels.

grouping not done by authors/ narrators themselves. Not conscious. Accidental.

Each of the four memory communities is represented disproportionately by a particular subset of the Salvadoran population, and thus I have chosen to name them accordingly: civilian elites; military officers; guerrilla commanders; and rank-and-file actors, or "testimonialists." The first community of civilian elites consists almost entirely of wealthy, politically-conservative men, many of whom were founding members or early supporters of ARENA, the rightwing political party that was established in

The 4 communities (1) civilian elites

1981. The group contains few women, politically-liberal elites or members of ARENA who identify with its more neoliberal business wing and less with the militant nationalism of its founder, Roberto D'Aubuisson.

The second community of military officers consists of a group of high-ranking officers, mostly colonels and generals, who led the war effort on behalf of the Salvadoran government. Notably, this community includes no former rank-and-file soldiers, whose narratives, few in number anyways, contrast sharply with those of the officers.

The third community, guerrilla commanders, consists of high-level leaders from each of the five guerrilla organizations that comprised the FMLN. They have been by far the most prolific narrators per capita, having produced dozens of life stories, including many book-length memoirs. The number of contributions from members of each of the five guerrilla factions corresponds roughly with their respective size, with the largest number of stories coming from members of the Ejército Revolucionario del Pueblo (ERP) and the Fuerzas Populares de Liberación Farabundo Martí (FPL), the two largest factions. Also, the number of contributions from female comandantes corresponds roughly to the percentage of them that served.

Finally, the fourth group of rank-and-file actors consists almost entirely of former guerrilla combatants and civilians who sympathized with the guerrillas, mostly poor people from rural areas. Notably, the rank-and-file actors are not included in the community of former guerrilla commanders, because although they had a common enemy during the war and share some memories with one another, their narrative divergences stand out more markedly. I include in the rank-and-file community a pair of narratives by former army soldiers, because their stories have more in common with their former guerrilla antagonists than with their former army officers.

These four memory communities are dominating the public discourse of remembrance, at least within the memory site of published life stories. The existence of these communities reveals that many important actors from the civil war are absent from the debate. They include, among others, centrist politicians, non-militant leftists, foreign-born sympathizers of the guerrillas, U.S. military and diplomatic personnel and, perhaps most importantly, army soldiers and conservative peasants who either opposed the guerrillas or at least remained nonpartisan. These various actors have either not narrated their life stories, or have done so in such small numbers that they exist as isolated outliers rather than as members of a memory community. I will describe a few of these isolated works in the conclusion, but at present they stand out for having ceded the postwar discursive floor to the members of the four groups identified above.

• • • • •

Before summarizing the four narratives, I would like to clarify three methodological issues. First, the titles that I use to identify the four memory communities can be misleading in regard to the methodology that I employed to discover them. The labels might suggest that the defining characteristic of each group is membership in a particular demographic segment of Salvadoran society, and thus anyone who fits the category should be placed in that group *a priori*. But that is not the claim I make, nor is it the methodology I employed. The titles are simply titles. And while it seems obvious that being a former army officer, for example, played a role in shaping how the members of the "officer memory community" narrate the past, the members of that group are bound together by the commonalities of their narrative, not by the fact that they were once officers in the military. If other officers share their life stories in the future, and the content of their narratives differs markedly, then the category I have discovered will need to be dismantled or amended. In fact, entering into the study I expected to see greater divisions among the officers' narratives. I suspected to see the narrators divide along ideological lines between reformists and hardliners, perhaps thereby creating narrative alliances with other non-military actors who shared common ideological views; but those patterns did not reveal themselves. Instead, all the officers, regardless of ideology, narrate in a similar way and distinct from the members of the other groups. As another example, I expected to see the guerrilla comandantes divide along the factional lines of their respective guerrilla organizations. But those divisions did not reveal themselves to be significant, even though it is obvious that the comandante narrators identify strongly with their respective organization and offer negative opinions about the leaders of rival factions.

Second, even though my research is not an objective account of the war, an important component of my methodology is to point out key absences or misrepresentations by the narrators. El Salvador's civil war remains a drastically understudied, incredibly complex series of events, but some things are known beyond a reasonable doubt, thanks to some rigorous scholarship and fact-finding investigations, including an imperfect, but highly revealing report by a UN Truth Commission at the end of the war.[35] We know, for example, that the overwhelming majority of civilian deaths and human-rights violations were perpetrated by the army and its paramilitary allies. Members of the civilian elite and officer memory communities ignore that fact or obfuscate it. For example, members of the officer community portray the events of December 1981 in the hamlet of El Mozote as something other than what it was, an army massacre of nearly 1,000 unarmed peasants.[36] Parallel to taking the officers to task for that absence, I point out the refusal of certain guerrilla commanders to discuss the purges that occurred within the FPL in the latter half of the 1980s.[37] The reason narrators commit these kinds of omissions and engage in selective telling is beside the point. In most cases it is impossible to know what motivates the narrators, or to prove if they are lying, confused, ignorant or forgetful. As the U.S. memoirist Cheryl Strayed reminds us, "Memoir is the art of subjective truth."[38] What matters for the present study is the content of each group's narrative and the fact that its members have inserted it into the public sphere.

Third, the present study treats the postwar era as a singular period of time, one too short to chart changes within any particular memory community. A common strategy in the study of collective memory is to chart the ebb and flow of interpretive trends against certain events or historic processes. Such an approach can determine if members of distinct communities have changed their interpretations over time, typically in accordance with contemporary exigencies. Studies that undertake this approach normally chart trends over many decades, or centuries.[39] El Salvador's postwar era is not yet three-decades old, and it took a few years after the end of the war for people to get their stories out. Maybe future scholars will find that certain events affected the ebb and flow of collective memory in El Salvador, like the FMLN's presidential victories in 2009 and 2014, or the Great Recession of 2007/08, or the explosion in gang-related violence in the mid 2010s. But for now, I treat the postwar era as one unified time period.

[handwritten margin note: post-war as single period; too short still to trace trends]

The Four Narratives

At the core of each of memory community is a unifying theme that drives its respective members' narratives forward. The theme of the civilian elites is that their private holdings have been threatened with expropriation; that they are a beleaguered minority; and that they have had to fight to preserve their belongings and defend their rights. As for the officers,

[handwritten margin note: Themes civs]

they are driven by the singular goal of promoting the survival of the military as an institution. To that end, they recall events through a highly flexible lens that allows them to countenance various ideologies and pursue diverse policies, however contradictory they might be, as long as they serve the goal of perpetuating the military's existence. The guerrilla comandantes believe that the elites, the military and the U.S. government constituted a hegemonic cabal that presided over an unjust society and that could only be taken down through militant action. In attacking the state, the comandantes believe they were fighting a just and defensible war as the vanguard of the masses in order to restructure society for the betterment of all. The rank-and-file actors share some of the comandantes' views, notably that the war was a justifiable act of self-defense, but they are suspicious of the comandantes' vanguardism, and they see themselves as having experienced the war and the postwar era distinctly from their comandante counterparts.

The existence of these four mutually-exclusive communities suggests that a series of potentially destabilizing fault lines runs through postwar El Salvador. With such divisive versions of the past battling for influence in the populaces' mind, how can a sense of shared purpose emerge to guide Salvadorans into the future? During the war, two main antagonistic narratives existed revolving around the question of who was defending the people from whom. The elites and the military claimed that they were defending the population from the guerrillas, who they called "terrorist delinquents" and accused of fomenting anarchy in order to create a power vacuum that they could use to seize power and establish authoritarianism. In contrast, the guerrillas claimed they were protecting the populace from the army and the elites, who they accused of having presided over a decades-long system of repressive hierarchy that denied people their voice and rights.[40] These mutually exclusive claims, and the narratives that were used to express them, have certainly influenced the ways in which memories are being narrated in the postwar era. For example, the narratives by civilian elites and military officers exhibit some commonalities, and so too do the narratives by guerrilla commanders and the rank-and-file actors. However, the life stories reveal that these two sides are full of complex and cross-cutting claims and that they have to be broken down into four groups.

For example, the officers and the elites do not remember their war-time alliance fondly. Officers hold the elites partly responsible for causing the war due to their opposition to reforms that might have alleviated the pressure on common people. In turn, the elites blame the military for enacting reforms, thereby meddling in the internal affairs of the private sector and subsequently destabilizing society in a way that created an opening for radical militants to emerge. The officers also believe that the elites sold them out at the bargaining table at the end of the war, by siding with their former antagonists, the guerrilla comandantes, in an effort to eliminate the military as a rival power.

The civilian elites more or less ignore the military and focus their memories of the war on their own political activism, as if their efforts in politics brought the guerrillas to the bargaining table, rather than twelve years of combat in the field. Another discord exists between the officers and their rank-and-file soldiers. Although the sample size of former soldiers is minute, their narratives nonetheless diverge from their former officers and instead reside closer to those of their former guerrilla rivals.

The other side of the narrative battle is marked by equally discordant memories. The rank and file members of the guerrillas and their civilian sympathizers paid some of the heaviest prices during the war and a recurrent theme running through their testimonials is an uncertainty about whether the costs were worth the rewards.[41] They certainly celebrate their role in democratizing El Salvador, but they wonder what good is democracy in the midst of ongoing economic hardship and inequality. Most rank-and-file actors consider themselves to be as bad off, if not worse off after the war than before the war. This sentiment puts them at odds with their former guerrilla commanders, who have tended to do well in the postwar era, often by retaining leadership positions within the FMLN, as it transited from guerrilla army to political party. Some former guerrilla commanders lament the lack of economic restructuring coming out the war, but that failure has not had the same repercussions for them as for their mass followers, many of whom live on the edge of subsistence. The leaders were relatively affluent, well-educated urbanites before the war, and most of them remain as such after the war. Therein, aspects of their narrative converge with their civilian elite adversaries rather than with their own rank-and-file combatants. The comandantes tend to minimize their failures and instead celebrate the political reforms, which not surprisingly benefits them disproportionately as the leaders of a political party. Some former comandantes have split with the FMLN, accusing those they left behind of authoritarianism. This split highlights fault lines within the FMLN and suggests that during the war, the FMLN may have been characterized by a greater degree of internal discord than studies have been able to show. Or, perhaps it demonstrates how people's memoires of past events amend themselves in accordance with contemporary exigencies.

As these discordant memories assume narrative form and enter into the public sphere in the form of published life stories, they mark the parameters of an ongoing discursive battle. Even though the narrators do not recognize themselves as belonging to memory communities, and even though they were not inspired to tell their life story for the sake of defending a particular community's narrative against its rivals, they are, nonetheless, serving as the foot soldiers in a narrative fight.

Narrative and Identity

The discovery of these four memory communities begs a couple questions: Where did the narratives come from, and where are they going, or rather what impact are they having on Salvadoran society? While it is not my goal to answer these questions in depth, they are worth posing because they highlight the importance of documenting the existence of these communities. I rest my response on two premises, derived from a vast and sprawling literature on memory, identity and narrative: 1) we use narratives to make sense of our social world; and 2) the narratives we use, or at least the components we use to construct our narratives are not always of our own conscious choosing.[42]

When confronted with the task of making sense of an event or a series of events, especially something as vast and complex as a twelve-year-long civil war, we are confronted with a seemingly limitless array of inputs—people, places, dates, emotions, moral judgments, etc. For these inputs to make sense, we have to see them as collective, something other than a series of random and isolated variables. The events have to become an episode, in which singular variables assume meaning because they exist in relation to others. We accomplish this task through narrative. We create a narrative by picking and choosing what to include and exclude, and we turn our selections into a plot. We situate ourselves in that plot, thereby explaining to ourselves our relationship to the events. As one of the leading scholars in the field of narrativity, Margaret Somers, says, "it is through narrativity that we come to know, understand, and make sense of the social world, and it is through narratives and narrativity that we constitute our social identities. . . . all of us come to be who we are (however ephemeral, multiple, and changing) by being located or locating ourselves (usually unconsciously) in social narratives rarely of our own making."[43]

The process by which we make our selections is the product of a dialectical relationship between our conscious intentions and unconscious influences. We explain things in a way that seems normal and proper, or the 'right way to do things,' and it seems to us that we are constructing that explanation autonomously and by our own design. But in fact, we derive our understanding of what is normal at least partly through unconscious influences from the broader contexts in which we reside. Somers calls these contexts "relational settings," and she insists that they play a decisive role in shaping how we perceive our world and how we explain that world to ourselves. These settings place limits on the range of explanatory options available to us. While it may seem that we have limitless options, we are in fact able to conceptualize only a few, because of the settings in which we reside, and those few are revealed to us in ways that we are often unaware. When we construct a narrative description of an event, we may think that we are describing it in a distinct way, but the norms we rely upon might be quite unoriginal and shared by many other people. Charlotte Linde claims that "life stories are sociocultural, as well as individual creations and that social identities are negotiated through discourse."[44] Similarly, the sociologist Jocelyn Viterna writes that "identities are both internally held by an individual and externally applied to an individual by others."[45]

In the present case, each of the memoirists and testimonialists narrate with a degree of conscious intent. They describe the civil war in a way they believe to be true, or at least in a way they want other people to believe to be true. Occasionally, they reveal the purposefulness of their narrative, or at least some portion of it. For example, both General Orlando Zepeda and Colonel Camilo Hernández make clear that they were inspired to share their stories in hopes of clearing their names in the killing of the six Jesuits in November 1989. The civilian elite Orlando de Sola seems to have been inspired to share his story to deny involvement in paramilitary death squads during the war. And the former ERP commander, Arquímedes Antonio Cañadas, seems anxious to make clear that he did not betray his former comrades after he was captured by the military early in the war. And various narrators seem to have had political aspirations when they shared their stories, or at least they coincidentally launched political careers shortly before or after their stories appeared; they include, but are not limited to Lorena Peña, Salvador Sánchez Cerén,

General Orlando Zepeda, General Mauricio Vargas and Colonel Sigifredo Ochoa Pérez.

But these narrators, like all the other memoirists and testimonialists, seem quite unaware of the ways in which their narratives have been pre-determined for them by the relational settings in which they reside. The most obvious and relevant proof of those unconscious influences is my discovery that all of the story tellers employ narratives that are shared by many other people and that place them in one of four particular memory communities.

If it were my goal to determine the origin of these narratives, then I would seek to understand the incentives that inspired any given narrator during their story telling. I would want to know what variables determined the words they chose at that moment, and how in the process of making those selections, they ended up having so much in common with other narrators. Certainly, one component of that type of research would be to look for sources that would reveal these narrators' statements or thought processes in the past and then compare them to what they are saying now in their life stories. In other words, I might be looking for what Charles Tilly calls "standard stories," versions of events told recurrently by members of a particular group that become paradigmatic and frame the identity of the groups' constituent members.[46] The sociologist Elizabeth Jelin notes that certain narrative patterns are likely to emerge from the seemingly haphazard contributions of individuals who happen to share some sort of group affiliation, because their memories are constituted collectively. "The collective aspect of memory is the interweaving of traditions and individual memories in dialogue with others. . . . The outcome is not a chaotic disorder, because there is some structure shaped by shared cultural codes and some social organization."[47]

It is a safe assumption that membership in certain groups before and during the civil war endowed members with stories that have lingered into the postwar era. In the case of officers, their commonalities might originate in their training in the military academy, or in conversations they had with one another during the war while they worked side by side in the barracks, commanded troops in the field, or sat with one another in offices in San Salvador as part of the High Command. In the case of the guerrilla comandantes, perhaps their commonalities emerge from a shared educational background, religious training, or involvement in certain political parties. Perhaps their narrative emerged from their time in the war, while they interacted with other comandantes in guerrilla en-

[margin note:] reflex on the origins of these stories

[margin note:] how common experiences may have shaped standard stories

campments, or during the training of young recruits and from the narratives they employed to get those recruits to agree with their particular interpretation of the war.[48] In the case of the rank-and-file narrators, perhaps their common narrative has origins in some aspect of the culture of martyrdom that some scholars consider to be a foundational aspect of the liberationist church in El Salvador.[49] Perhaps some of the narrators read some of the other published life stories before they wrote their own and therein found themselves inclined, consciously or unconsciously, to frame their narratives similarly. However, few of the narrators demonstrate awareness of the other life stories, to say nothing of having read them.

It is not my goal in the present study to determine precisely where the narratives of the four memory communities come from, but I can safely say that their origins reside somewhere indeterminately in the past of Jelin's "cultural codes" or Somers' "relational settings." I am similarly unable to say where the narratives are going, or the channels through which they are shaping Salvadorans' consciences. But by the same argumentative logic, I can safely say that they are going somewhere. They may become the cultural codes and relational settings for future Salvadorans who will draw upon them, probably unconsciously, when they narrate their own experiences. Thus, by documenting the existence of these memory communities at the present moment, I am catching these codes and settings at a point in time, like taking a snapshot of the ongoing discursive stream of memory. I am, thus, glimpsing into what was and what will be. The literary scholar Sylvia Molloy recognizes this ongoing cycle and the role that published life stories play within it when she says that "Autobiography is always a re-presentation, that is, a retelling, since the life to which it supposedly refers is already a kind of narrative construct."[50]

Perhaps we are witnessing with these four memory communities the birth of one or more master- or meta-narratives, interpretations so powerful and so widely accepted that they become hegemonic and push other narratives aside. As the scholar of historical memory Cillian McGratten observes, "Stories that confirm what we already know are the ones most likely to take root."[51] If one or more of these narratives of El Salvador's civil war settles into people's minds, and especially if it is backed by one or more interest groups with disproportionate access to media outlets, then it becomes difficult for contrasting perspectives to break into popular consciousness. As Margaret Somers observes, "Which kinds of narratives will socially predominate is contested politically and will depend in large part on the distribution of power."[52]

Neighboring Nicaragua offers an edifying example of master narratives operating in a public sphere. Historical interpretations of the famed guerrilla fighter in the 1920s and 1930s, Augusto Sandino, have revolved around two contrasting master narratives, one of Sandino as a bandit and the other of Sandino as a anti-imperialist hero.[53] Both narratives have strong interest groups backing them and both compete with one another for predominance in the public sphere. It's conceivable that interpretations of El Salvador's civil war could break down into two such contrasting schools.

Only time will tell if El Salvador will follow Nicaragua's example, but in say forty or fifty years, if Salvadorans are still structuring the memories of their civil war similar to today, then arguably the narrative battle that we see now will have produced one or more master narratives, which is to say that one or more of the narratives will be winning. One issue that would seem to have the potential to evolve into a master-narrative is the culpability for violence during the war. It is painfully evident that a stark contrast exists in regard to accounting for the killing and human rights violations during the war. The two memory communities of officers and civilian-elites, for all their differences, stand united on this front. Their members promote a claim of moral equivalence, saying that both sides killed during the war, so the issue of responsibility for violence is moot and should not be dwelled upon. Despite the fact that this claim runs contrary to an overwhelming preponderance of evidence, the life-story sources reveal that the members of the officer and civilian-elite communities advance their versions with relentless persistence, while the other two communities of guerrilla commanders and rank-and-file testimonialists argue the opposite. The officers and civilian elites have already established a foothold in the discursive arena around this issue, and if they were able to do so consistently, over many more years, then perhaps they would accomplish the feat of turning their claim of moral equivalence into a master narrative.

There is precedent in El Salvador for just this type of process. In regard to the insurrection and military crackdown of 1932, one of the memory communities bases its identity upon an argument of moral equivalence. Its members equate the military and the rebels, even though the former massacred thousands of people in two weeks, compared to the roughly one hundred people that the rebels killed during the three-day uprising. Over the years this claim of moral equivalency has taken on a powerful, master-narrative like foothold within certain segments of the

Salvadoran population.[54] The existence of this precedent suggests that today's officer and civilian-elite memory communities have fertile ground upon which to plant their views.

Chapter Order and Final Remarks

I have divided the book into six chapters. The first chapter sets the stage with a historical overview of the past few decades of Salvadoran history. Its main goal is to provide context for the four memory communities and to introduce their constituent members. By opening with this background material, I am able to limit the amount of information in the succeeding chapters. Chapter 1 also assists readers who lack familiarity with the Salvadoran case.

In the next five chapters, I mine the various life stories to document the existence of the four communities and their corresponding narratives. Each community is covered in a single chapter, with the exception of the guerrilla commanders, who receive two chapters because of the number of their stories and the depth of detail they provide. Chapter 2 is devoted to the community of civilian elites. Chapter 3 covers the officers. Chapters 4 and 5 are dedicated to the guerrilla commanders. Chapter 6 addresses the so-called rank-and-file narrators.

I hope the present study will contribute to the burgeoning field of memory studies in postconflict Latin American societies. No comparable study exists for Central America.[55] Other Latin American countries have produced a small, but robust body of literature on the subject of collective memory and the legacy of civil conflicts.[56] The authors of those studies have been at the forefront of Latin America's participation in a broader international arena of collective memory, where events like the Holocaust have inspired entire fields of research.[57] The present study complements their work. In particular it shares a common claim running throughout them that people's memories do not necessarily refer to past truths, but rather construct those truths and inject them with meaning in a contemporary context. Beyond offering a new and distinct case within the field, the present study makes unique contributions through its methodology of relying on a singular type of memory site, published life stories, and through its discovery of four particular memory communities with their mutually-exclusive narratives.

Current studies on memory in Latin America tend to focus on individual countries. Thus, a seemingly valuable line of future research would be comparative analyses. One of the few comparative studies, by Rachel Hatcher, compares El Salvador and Guatemala. Hatcher finds that Salvadorans and Guatemalans approach memory differently, despite the fact that both countries went through brutal civil conflicts in the 1970s and 1980s where the states' armies committed the overwhelming majority of human rights violations and killings. In Guatemala, a consensus has emerged around the importance of remembering, which means that even those sectors of society that are most opposed to actually digging up the truth about the past, nonetheless feel obligated to proclaim publically their support for remembrance. In contrast, in El Salvador, it is common to hear leading public figures celebrate the merits of forgetting and the need to move forward without dwelling on the past.[58]

These findings are ironic because El Salvador's guerrillas challenged the state more effectively than did their counterparts in Guatemala. The Salvadoran guerrilla army, the FMLN, had greater success on the field of battle and thus they came to the bargaining table with a stronger hand than did the Guatemalan guerrillas. After the war was over in El Salvador, the FMLN effectively transformed itself into a major political party, whereas nothing comparable happened in Guatemala. Thus, it would seem that El Salvador is a more likely candidate for a consensus to emerge around the merits of remembrance. Why did the consensus emerge in Guatemala instead?

Any answers at this point remain speculative, but Hatcher suggests that one explanation could be the nature of the relationship between the guerrilla armies and civil-society organizations. In Guatemala, it would appear that civil-society actors remained more independent from the guerrillas than did their counterparts in El Salvador. Thus, after the war, civil actors in Guatemala continued to operate more independently and to promote relentlessly the need to remember the past. By contrast, civil society organizations in El Salvador seem to have been more closely tied to the guerrillas and thus to the FMLN as a political party in the post-war era. If the former guerrilla leadership in El Salvador has reasons to resist remembering the past, perhaps because it too committed acts that it does not want investigated, even if its misdeeds are dramatically fewer in number than its opponents, then civil society might be more compelled to follow along.[59]

In the specific context of El Salvador, the memoir and testimonial evidence affords an unprecedented look into the thinking of social actors who avoided revealing themselves publicly in the past. Civilian elites and military officers are two such groups. They have played decisive roles in the political and economic life of modern El Salvador, but they either avoided the lime light, in the case of civilian elites, or when they presented themselves publicly before the media, as officers often had to do during the war, they did not include their life stories. The same can be said about guerrilla commanders. They often sought the public stage during the war in order to promote their cause and challenge their opponents' media dominance, but their life stories typically remained hidden, in part for security reasons.[60] Similarly, even though testimonials constituted an important part of the opposition's public-relations campaign during the war, their numbers were small. And some of the so-called testimonials from the pre-1992 era that have captured much scholarly attention were written by literate leaders, like Nidia Díaz, Ana Guadalupe Martínez and Salvador Cayetano Carpio.[61] In comparative terms, the postwar era has seen an outpouring of testimonials from poor, illiterate subaltern actors, even though the supposed urgency of civil war has passed and the so-called genre of testimonial literature has become more passé.

During the civil war, each of the rivaling sides actively promoted unity as a central component of their respective war effort. That notion of unity has survived to varying degrees in scholarship on the war, and in particular within comparative studies of revolution, which argue that the unity of the opposing sides in El Salvador set it apart as a case study and played a decisive role in shaping its revolutionary outcome.[62] I am not trying to prove or disprove the validity of that scholarship, because I'm not using life story evidence to make objective claims about the civil war. But the life stories reveal that their narrators are remembering the wartime alliances as fractured and factionalized.

I am using life stories to make objective claims about the ways Salvadorans are remembering the war. I believe the evidence reveals the existence of highly diverse and mutually-exclusive memory communities that have taken form in four distinct narratives, which comprise the rivaling sides of an evolving narrative battle. In documenting the existence of this debate, I hope to contribute to a growing body of research that highlights the messy complexities of the Salvadoran conflict, and that reveals the legacies of those complexities in the postwar political environment.[63]

1 Setting the Stage

El Salvador's Long Twentieth Century

· ·

In this chapter I set the stage for the rest of the book by offering a targeted overview of El Salvador's long twentieth century, from the 1890s to the 2010s. I have chosen the content for this chapter purposefully, to introduce readers to the main players in the story and to provide the context for their actions. As an additional aid, an appendix appears at the end of the book with a list of these protagonists and brief biographical descriptions of them.

This chapter is divided into three sections: prewar, war, and postwar. The first section explains why El Salvador ended up in civil war in the 1980s. The second section charts the trajectory of the war and describes the overarching strategies of the opposing sides. The third section discusses El Salvador's condition after the war, with a focus on political affairs. I offer the following caveat: what I say in this chapter makes no difference as to the claims in the rest of the book. My interpretation of El Salvador's recent history could be totally wrong—and indeed some of the protagonists that appear in the following pages would find my version repugnant. Nevertheless, the fact remains that four distinct communities of memory exist in the medium of published life stories and their members narrate the civil war in mutually exclusive ways.

Prewar El Salvador

Salvadorans of all stripes, scholars and laypersons alike, have long been struggling to make sense of their civil war. A common point of departure for them is the relationship between structure and agency. Some analysts insist that El Salvador's longstanding structural conditions caused the civil war in the 1980s. Such conditions include the country's natural resource endowments, the legacy of Spanish colonialism, the evolution of the state and its historic construction, the ethnographic/demographic makeup of society, unpredictable changes in the international marketplace, and the actions of foreign governments, especially the United States.

What defines each of these variables is that they reside mostly beyond Salvadorans' control.

In contrast, other analysts emphasize the role of human agency, attributing the war and its causes to individuals or particular groups of people, whose actions and decisions were not determined by structural variables. Of these agency-oriented analysts, most lay blame for the war at the feet of El Salvador's economic elites, its intransigent military officers and their collective alliance with Cold War hawks in the U.S. government. According to them, this unholy trinity of actors forestalled desperately needed reforms, employed terroristic violence against the masses, and refused to negotiate a nonviolent solution to the nation's problems. Their actions forced people to take up arms in order to defend themselves.

A small portion of agency-oriented analysts offer a contrarian view. They instead find fault with the left, especially guerrilla leaders and their international allies, whom they accuse of voluntarily adopting a militant strategy that led to violent conflict.

Yet other analysts employ a hybrid approach that combines structure and agency. I subscribe to this latter approach. In the present chapter I contend that El Salvador had certain structural preconditions that made civil war likely because they constrained the range of options available to Salvadoran actors. But structure is not destiny, and ultimately Salvadorans had to decide how they were going to live their lives and organize their society within the parameters available to them. They were not destined to end up fighting one another in a civil war in the 1980s, but they would have had to make different and difficult decisions in the preceding years to avoid it. As for the competing versions of agency-oriented scholarship, I find more legitimate the side that assigns responsibility to the elites and their allies. Nevertheless, leftist militants were partisan actors in the drama, for better or worse, and there is plenty of blame to go around for El Salvador's descent into war. The political scientist Bill Stanley shares this assessment, when he notes that "extremism on both sides helped start the war and moderation by both sides helped end it."[1]

The Problem

In the 1950s and 1960s El Salvador was standing on the edge of a precipice. Its economy was dependent on agriculture and most of the productive land was owned by a small handful of families. A 1961 agricultural census revealed that less than 1 percent of the landowners owned more than 50 percent of the arable land and that more than 80 percent of rural households owned less than four acres each. Notwithstanding some economic diversification in the form of industrialization in the 1960s, agriculture, mainly coffee, accounted for more than 90 percent of the nation's extra-regional export earnings in 1970. Meanwhile, the population was growing quickly, with an estimated birthrate of 3 percent or more per year, and there was nowhere to put more people. El Salvador had no agricultural frontier, and so with few alternatives, except to join a growing rural proletariat, many people from rural areas migrated to the cities in hopes of finding one of the few industrial jobs, or they left the country. By 1969 as many as 300,000 of El Salvador's roughly four million people were squatting across the border in Honduras, where land was more abundant.

Salvadorans faced a host of problems at home. Official statistics estimated the nation's illiteracy rate in 1950 at 50 percent; it was higher in rural areas and probably much higher overall. Access to basic services, such as schools and health clinics was uneven at best. In 1951 less than one-half of all school-age children attended school, and only a small fraction of them went beyond the third grade; barely 5 percent of all children in school were at the secondary level, and they lived only in large urban areas. Rural workers faced stagnating pressures on their wages because of the overabundance of labor. Furthermore, El Salvador was heavily reliant on imported petroleum to satisfy its energy needs. So, in addition to being dependent upon fickle international markets for its agricultural commodities, El Salvador also had to endure the threat of rapidly rising oil prices. In short, El Salvador in the 1950s and 1960s was fraught with a series of fault lines that foretold major problems if nothing was done to alter the nation's course.[2]

How did El Salvador end up in this situation? The short answer is coffee and the distinctly authoritarian manner in which Salvadorans built their coffee economy. Owing to a defining structural variable, its natural endowment of land, El Salvador boasts some of the best coffee-growing soils in the world. Despite its small size, El Salvador ended up as one of the world's top five coffee producers, and its growers became some of the most efficient in the world, having had to get maximum product from minimally available land. Coffee is grown at elevation on the sides of El Salvador's volcanic slopes. The country has three main coffee-growing highland areas. The main one is in the western part of the country, at the intersection of Sonsonate, Ahuachapán, and Santa Ana departments. The second one is in the center of the country, in and around the San Salvador volcano that serves as the backdrop to the nation's capital city, San Salvador. The third region is on the opposite side of the country, at the intersection of Usulután and San Miguel departments.

When it became apparent to investors in the late nineteenth century that El Salvador possessed the potential to become a coffee producer, an intense competition for land ensued. Of the three areas suitable for coffee cultivation, only the eastern highlands in Usulután and San Miguel was akin to a frontier, meaning that it did not have large numbers of peasants already living there on communal landholdings. Getting that land into private hands was a relatively easy process of using government power to alienate the land and put it into the marketplace. The other two areas were more complicated. In those regions, large numbers of peasant communities resided on communal landholdings, some of which they had acquired from the Spanish crown in the 1500s. Moreover, a sizeable proportion of those peasant communities were comprised of indigenous peoples, which brought ethnic tension into play.

In what would end up as one of the most decisive periods in Salvadoran history, the government passed a series of land decrees in the early 1880s that effectively abolished all forms of communal landholding and ordered any and all such parcels of communal land to be divided into lots and transferred to private hands. This process of transference was not designed to cast all the peasant residents off the land and create a class of coffee barons on one side and landless laborers on the other. Rather, the law stipulated that the residents of the land were entitled to take ownership of the property they were utilizing, with the remaining fallow lands to be alienated and sold. Indeed, many thousands of peasant agriculturalists gained title to the lands they were farming at the time, and a new class of private smallholders came into existence.

Vestiges of this smallholding peasantry from the late nineteenth century can still be found in El Salvador today. But unfortunately for the long-term stability of El Salvador, the size of the parcels that each peasant household received was not large enough to sustain multiple generations of family members. Typically, the parcels were not more than ten acres in size, which is about the minimum amount of land necessary to sustain one family in subsistence agriculture. As families increased in size, and in the absence of available frontier land, younger generations of peasants had no choice but to leave their family land in search of work on the surrounding plantations. Either they had no access to land themselves because their fathers refused to divide the land among multiple heirs, or a young peasant received such a small portion of land as inheritance that he and his family had to leave the land in search of supplementary income. Invariably many of the peasant households sold their plots, usually to land speculators or members of the emergent coffee elite. Although it took longer than scholars had originally presumed, the privatization decrees of the 1880s ultimately resulted in land concentrating in the hands of a small number of elite families and a growing number of rural proletarians fulfilling their labor needs.[3]

Tiny El Salvador emerged as an important player in the global coffee trade, and it became more reliant upon a single commodity for economic survival than did most other Latin American countries. By the eve of the Great Depression, coffee accounted for 90 percent of El Salvador's export earnings. The proceeds from coffee built family fortunes that would define Salvadoran society for decades to come. It was during the coffee boom in the late nineteenth and early twentieth centuries that the notorious Salvadoran oligarchy, the so-called *"catorce"* (fourteen families) was consolidated. Even though the number of families that qualified for membership in that select group actually numbered in the many dozens, the fact remains that the rewards from coffee went to a minute segment of the population whose members lived in an increasingly privileged and insular world.

The elites were distinguished from the masses not only by class, but also by ethnicity, especially in those regions of the country with high concentrations of Indians. In the face of racial and class distinctions, the emergent coffee elite relied increasingly upon coercive violence to maintain order and guide the system in its favor. Research by the historian Knut Walter reveals the scale of militarism in El Salvador in the early twentieth century. He shows that in the mid-1920s, in the important coffee-growing department of Ahuachapán in far western El Salvador, one out of every six adult men was involved in military service in one form or another, and much of their duties revolved around policing the local population rather than defending the nation from foreign attack.[4] Therein, El Salvador was set on a path toward a highly unequal distribution of wealth and power, a system that I have dubbed "authoritarian El Salvador."[5]

It was not all doom and gloom for those who envisioned a different El Salvador, one more egalitarian and democratic. For reasons too complex to delve into here, El Salvador experienced its first free and fair presidential election in 1931.[6] It resulted in the victory of Arturo Araujo, a reform-minded landowner who admired the British Labour Party and who promised economic and social reforms. It is no surprise that a reformist movement occurred in El Salvador, because every country in Latin America experienced some form of reformist nationalism in the early twentieth century. What is distinct about El Salvador's reformist moment is how long it took to emerge and how briefly it lasted once it arrived. Araujo was ousted by a military coup less than nine months after coming to office, and the man who became president after him, General Maximiliano Martínez, not only returned El Salvador to its authoritarian roots, but also presided over one of the most brutal episodes of state violence against a civilian population in modern Latin American history.

In late January 1932, peasants rose up in rebellion throughout western El Salvador. They attacked approximately one dozen municipalities, including the departmental capitals of Sonsonate and Ahuachapán. They targeted sites of local and state power, including military garrisons, government offices and the homes and businesses of local elites. In the process, they gained control over six towns, killed approximately one hundred people, and caused varying amounts of economic damage through looting and the destruction of buildings. The military was caught off guard by the rebellion, but it quickly regained control and ousted the rebels from the occupied towns after just two or three days. Over the next two weeks, once reinforcements arrived from San Salvador, the military embarked on a mass killing spree, murdering people indiscriminately throughout the western countryside. No one knows how many people died in what has come to be called "la Matanza" (the Massacre), but estimates range anywhere from many thousands to tens of thousands.[7]

There is still a lot that we do not know about the 1932 rebellion, such as who rebelled, how they organized themselves, and what, specifically, they hoped to accomplish. But we can make a few claims with some certainty. For many years, the emergent coffee economy had subjected the peasantry of western El Salvador to a steady degree of transformative pressures that undermined their material well-being and personal security. As the rural poor were enduring years of degradation, they suddenly confronted an acute crisis in the form of a global economic depression in 1929. Whatever else it may have been, the uprising of 1932 was a clarion call to the nation that the developmental paradigm being promoted by the coffee growers had negative consequences. And while it is far too teleological to trace the origins of the civil war in the 1980s back to the events of 1932, it is painfully obvious that the Salvadoran state's willingness to kill thousands of its own people in defense of a hierarchical system set an ignoble precedent. Structural conditions may have preconditioned El Salvador to have social conflict in its western countryside in the early twentieth century, but ultimately human beings had to make the decision to murder thousands of their countrymen in two weeks' time. The Salvadoran writer and political activist Roque Dalton captured the enduring legacy of the trauma of 1932 when he wrote, in his oft-cited poem "Todos" in the early 1970s, that "we were all born half dead in 1932. To be a Salvadoran is to be half dead."[8]

The events of 1932 represent a transitional moment in Salvadoran history. They projected the authoritarianism of the past into the future, allowing the shaky Martínez regime to consolidate power, and eventually gave rise to fifty years of military dictatorships. After 1932, El Salvador's governing system functioned according to an informal alliance between the military and civilian elites in a system that Bill Stanley calls a "protection racket state."[9] Military officers held the majority of executive-level political offices, particularly the presidency, and elites have generally eschewed public service in favor of managing their affairs in the private sector. The unspoken bargain was that elites would leave the spoils of office to military officers, who in return would keep things ordered and safe for elites to go about their business without 1932-like interruptions.

The military-elite alliance proved durable, but it was a complex relationship, more a marriage of convenience than an all-out love affair. Most military officers hailed from humble backgrounds and had little in common with their elite counterparts, and they occasionally blamed the elites for causing the social problems that inspired mass discontent. For their part, the elites recognized the crucial role that the military played in keeping order, but they distrusted the officers, even the most avowedly conservative ones, because they were willing to consider social and economic reform. Indeed, the succession of military governments after 1931 ruled according to a dichotomous nexus of reform and repression, in which they maintained public order, often through brutally violent means, but promoted reformism in both idea and practice. Even the long-time leader of the Communist Party, Schafik Hándal, who despised the military's stranglehold on government and worked throughout his life to destroy it, acknowledged the reformist impulses of the military governments when he wrote in his memoir that "the political process in this tiny country is very complex."[10] Nevertheless, El Salvador was typified by authoritarian politics and a highly exclusive economy.

The Costa Rica Comparison

El Salvador did not necessarily have to end up that way, as can be revealed by comparing it with neighboring Costa Rica.[11] Costa Rica provides an example of a country that could be heavily reliant on coffee exports but still have a relatively egalitarian distribution of wealth and a functioning democracy.[12] El Salvador and Costa Rica share much in common. They are geographically close to one another and of similar size; they were ruled by the same government throughout the colonial and early independence eras; and both of their economies depended greatly on coffee exports starting in the latter part of the late nineteenth century. However, Costa Rica followed a different developmental path, avoiding much of the conflict and social turbulence that defined its counterpart to the north. Although Costa Rica experienced its own civil war in 1948, the outcome of that conflict was the abolition of the military. As a consequence, in the 1970s and 1980s, when its neighbors were plummeting into chaos, Costa Rica remained relatively peaceful, democratic, and wealthy.[13]

CR as unique

What distinguished Costa Rica was the same thing that guided El Salvador toward civil war: a combination of structural conditions and human agency. For all its similarities with El Salvador, Costa Rica exhibited some structural differences. In the nineteenth century, it had a low population density, virtually no Indians, and few communally owned lands, so its potential coffee-growing lands existed more or less as a frontier rather than as heavily cultivated peasant plots. When the coffee economy emerged, Costa Rica did not go through the same painful process that El Salvador did, alienating land from its inhabitants, or negotiating with them through the racially charged lens of scientific Darwinism that prevailed at the time, or by resorting to violent coercion to enforce a system of rules that ultimately benefited an emergent coffee-growing elite.

early strux diff

These distinct structural conditions presented Costa Ricans with a different set of parameters when they entered into political debate with one another about their nation's future. Forward-looking policy-makers in Costa Rica were able to gain the upper hand over their more reactionary counterparts. They were able to build a consensus around directing the nation's resources toward things more productive than war, like public education and welfare. It took visionary leadership to see these things through, which requires agency, but Costa Rican policy-makers enjoyed more favorable structures. Those endowments expanded the range of options available to them, relative to the normative ideologies of the day and compared to their less fortunate neighbors in El Salvador.

The Failed Solution(s)

By the 1950s El Salvador may have been too far gone to avoid civil war in the 1980s. Perhaps the window to avoid war closed during the coffee boom in the 1880s or even earlier. But if we assume that the window was still open in the 1950s, then the ability to avoid war in the 1980s would have required Salvadorans to realize the precipice upon which they were standing and to have pulled themselves back from it. The ability to recognize El Salvador's looming crisis in the 1950s is not solely the benefit of twenty-first-century hindsight. Anyone who cared to understand the situation at the time could have done so, if they had looked upon the available evidence with dispassionate eyes. Indeed, some Salvadorans did so, including high-ranking policy-makers.

some reform-minded folks, efforts in 1950s

Take, for example, the leaders of the Partido Revolucionario de Unificación Democrática (PRUD) in the 1950s. Notwithstanding the fact that they embodied El Salvador's nondemocratic political tradition, they were a group of young, reform-minded officers and civilians who had come to power in a coup d'état in 1948 promising to enact modernizing change. In the process of deciding how best to direct their energies, they accumulated data about their country to inform their decisions. One of their most important sources came from the United Nations in the form of a technical assistance team that landed in El Salvador in 1952. The team included among its ranks Bert Hoselitz, an expert in the newly emergent field of development economics from the University of Chicago. Hoselitz and the other members of the team accumulated a wide range of data to inform their recommendations, which they delivered to PRUD leaders as a confidential report, and which Hoselitz published as a book two years later.[14]

UN tech assist team

Hoselitz's assessment more or less mimics the fault lines described above. He acknowledged that El Salvador had few natural resources beyond land and labor, so he reasoned that something needed to be done to create employment for the growing rural proletariat. Hoselitz concluded that industrialization was the solution, but notably he believed that any transformation in the Salvadoran economy was going to require an active and interventionist central government. Anticipating some of the main tenets of what would come to be called modernization theory, Hoselitz believed that market forces alone would not change El Salvador, or at least that their pace of change would be so slow that problems would pile up faster than solutions. In particular, Hoselitz claimed that the state had to play an active role because wealthy elites had little incentive to change their heavy reliance on agriculture, which was producing impressive returns on their investments, based largely on the availability of cheap labor. Hoselitz advocated for such things as a land reform, a more progressive tax code, and alterations to the nation's tariff system. Even though Hoselitz described El Salvador's problems as significant, he struck an optimistic tone, believing, as was customary among development experts of his era, that active leadership guided by sound evidence could produce positive outcomes. Colonel José María Lemus, who served as the PRUD's president between 1956 and 1960, claimed in a later interview that he and his fellow PRUD leaders considered Hoselitz's book to be their "Bible for economic modernization."[15]

Hoselitz's report embodied the modernizing ethos that governed the reformist spirit of El Salvador's PRUD leadership. However, a potentially debilitating problem lay at its core, namely its failure to take into account El Salvador's political reality, including the military's own dictatorial politics, and the elites' longstanding opposition to any type of state intervention in the economy. Admittedly, a few members of both the military and elite families saw things differently. One of the dissenters was Jorge Sol Castellaños, who hailed from a wealthy family and who served as minister of the economy under President Osorio in the early 1950s. However, Sol was an exception, and most of his fellow elites ridiculed him as an opportunist and a traitor.

Salvadoran elites were hardly retrogressive when it came to making money. They were happy to diversify their investments and seek returns in industry or commerce or any other economic arena. Indeed, they bankrolled the modest industrialization that occurred in El Salvador in the 1960s and 1970s. But where their tolerance for economic diversification began, their patience for state intervention ended. In short, most Salvadoran elites had an unrelenting opposition to any form of state intervention in the economy, and so the policies proposed by the likes of Hoselitz faced serious challenges. As Jorge Sol put it at the time, "They [the PRUD leaders] could carry out some changes within parameters, such as not touching the interests of the oligarchy."[16]

The PRUD regime produced little in the way of transformative results. Partly as a consequence of the rising expectations created by its leaders' own rhetoric, the PRUD was overthrown in another modernizing coup in October 1960, which indeed had the potential to bring about more sweeping transformations, including genuine democratization. But that coup proved short-lived, as yet another, more reactionary military faction moved in, taking advantage of its ability to paint the reformers of October 1960 as communists and to seize power in January 1961 under the guise of setting El Salvador on a more restrained path.

Despite their conservative origins, the leaders of the January 1961 coup, who eventually organized themselves into a new political machine called the Partido de Conciliación Nacional (PCN), pushed modernizing reforms to unprecedented heights, and they used a reformist rhetoric that targeted civilian elites in ways far surpassing their PRUD predecessors. They oversaw various economic reforms and infrastructural projects, such the building of the Cerrón Grande dam in the early 1970s, which they envisioned as the key to economic diversification by creating cheap, domestically produced power that would fuel the nation's nascent industrialization. They oversaw a massive education reform in 1968 that was designed to train the populace for a new industrial economy.[17] And in 1976, the then-sitting PCN president, Colonel Arturo Armando Molina, tried to implement a land reform in a former cotton-growing region in eastern El Salvador.

But for all their activities, the efforts by the PCN were either insufficient, or the manner in which they were designed and implemented created more problems than they solved. The 1968 education reform is a case in point. It ultimately alienated teachers, who at 14,000 strong were the nation's largest sector of public employees. The teachers came to interpret the education reform as misguided in design and authoritarian in implementation, and in the face of government intransigence and increasing repression, many teachers turned toward radical militancy. This process by which middle-class teachers, who had been dedicated to improving teaching as a profession in the 1960s, became radical militants by the mid to late 1970s stands as a metaphor for the failure of leadership to prevent El Salvador's spiral into war.[18]

As for their attempt at land reform in 1976, PCN leaders proved either unwilling or unable to overcome the stiff opposition from conservative landowners, so they abandoned the project. Most of all, PCN leaders refused to relent on their dictatorial politics and the use of repressive violence to control mass discontent, especially in the countryside. They oversaw the creation of a massive paramilitary force, Organización Democrática Nacionalista (ORDEN). With as many as 100,000 members, most of them peasants, ORDEN quelled dissent in the rural areas, largely through terroristic violence, throughout the 1960s and 1970s.[19]

And so it went, year after year: fifty years of military dictatorship and various attempts at reform, some of which were successfully implemented, but none of which had the staying power to quell the rising tide of opposition.[20] All the while political tensions mounted, the economic crisis became worse, and social conditions deteriorated for the vast majority of the population.

The Opposition Mobilizes

El Salvador's authoritarianism did not go unchallenged. Repeatedly, and boldly in the face of the ruling regime's intransigence and propensity for violence, social movements emerged and demanded change. One such movement arose around the candidacy of Dr. Arturo Romero in the wake of a nationwide strike that resulted in the collapse of the Martínez dictatorship in 1944. Another one came about in 1958/1959 in opposition to the presidency of José María Lemus. The fall of Lemus in 1960 ushered in a short-lived but highly impactful reformist junta that spawned a host of new civil-political organizations, including the center-left Christian Democratic Party. Other examples of oppositional social movements include the coalition of centrist and leftist parties that backed the presidential bids of José Napoleón Duarte in 1972 and Ernesto Claramount in 1977.[21]

But each of these movements, and many others not mentioned here, were repeatedly beaten back by reactionary forces. The Romero movement in 1944 was forestalled by a conservative countercoup led by General Martínez's former chief of police, Osmín Aguirre. The reformist junta of October 1960 was crushed by the countercoup in January 1961 that brought to power the PCN. And the leaders of the PCN used massive voting fraud to steal the elections from Duarte in 1972 and Claramount in 1977, and then violently repressed demonstrators in the aftermath.[22] Of all the repressive actions committed by the Salvadoran state throughout its fifty years of military dictatorship, the electoral fraud of 1972 seems to have promoted the emergence of a militant opposition more than any other event. At the least, it is the episode that former guerrillas cite most commonly in their memoirs as inspiring them to abandon electoral politics and embrace militancy.

The actions by PCN leaders in 1972 and 1977 once again reflect the relationship between structure and agency in bringing about El Salvador's civil war. Structural conditions may have set the stage for electoral fraud in 1972 and 1977. Nonetheless, it took actors with agency to decide ultimately to forestall the democratic process by stealing those two elections and using violence to quell subsequent protests. In the face of elite intransigence and military leaders' unwillingness to democratize, reformers began to radicalize and radicals found themselves emboldened as more people embraced their revolutionary message.

The origins of El Salvador's militant opposition can be traced back to the late 1920s and early 1930s, when various activist organizations and labor unions formed, including the Partido Comunista Salvadoreño (PCS), the Socorro Rojo Internacional (SRI), and the Federación Regional de Trabajadores Salvadoreños (FRTS.) All three of them had their roots in urban areas and each was making strides toward reaching out to rural workers. They experienced some success in the two or three years preceding the events of 1932. But they faced a huge setback in the government repression that succeeded the peasant uprising in 1932. Whether government officials believed that the PCS, the SRI, and/or the FRTS were responsible for the uprising in the western region is not clear, but they took the opportunity to attack them nevertheless. Two of the organizations, the SRI and the FRTS, were crushed and never returned, and the third organization, the Communist Party, barely survived. Internal documents from the party that were stored in archives in Moscow reveal that as many as half of the party's roughly five hundred members were killed during the crackdown.[23]

The repression not only shattered the Communist Party organizationally, but also it enflamed debates among surviving members over proper revolutionary strategy. The essence of the debate revolved around whether El Salvador was ready for a revolution and thus whether radical organizations should move toward the offensive, as some had done in 1932, or if they should wait and concentrate their efforts on building electoral coalitions and labor unions. In the aftermath of 1932, the latter interpretation held sway, in no small part because the Communist International (Comintern) in Russia supported it, especially after 1935 when Moscow's new United Front strategy approved alliances with noncommunists in defense against German fascism. Within El Salvador, this approach of delayed militancy became known as the "Moscow line" and it remained the party's official strategy for almost fifty years, until 1980, when party leaders finally embraced militarism on the eve of civil war. Two clear examples of the party's commitment to this approach were its participation (clandestinely, of course) in the electoral coalitions that sponsored the presidential bids of Duarte in 1972 and Claramount in 1977.[24]

The success of the Cuban revolution in 1959 reignited the debate within the party over revolutionary strategy. Some members, typically younger ones, insisted that Batista's demise in Cuba proved that the time to go on the offensive had arrived. They managed to convince their more traditional, usually older comrades to allow them to form a militant wing. That organization, the Frente Unido de Acción Revolucionaria (FUAR), survived only two years (1960–1962) and it had little to show for its efforts. However, its existence revealed that differing views coexisted within the party, foreshadowing the factional splits that would occur in the near future. Ironically, the party leader who opposed the FUAR at the time, Salvador Cayetano Carpio, was the same man who would lead a militant breakaway from the party in 1969.[25]

The event that ultimately triggered a factional split within the Communist Party was the war between El Salvador and Honduras in 1969. Swept up in the wave of nationalist fervor, and responding to the accusation against the Honduran government that it was abusing Salvadoran migrants living in Honduras, the Communist Party declared its support for the war against its neighbor. A faction within the party led by Cayetano Carpio opposed that position, arguing that the ruling regime in El Salvador was indefensible, regardless of what was happening in Honduras. Cayetano Carpio left the party and took a handful of supporters with him. Soon thereafter he announced the formation of a new militant organization, the Fuerzas Populares de Liberación (FPL), which was committed to the revolutionary overthrow of the Salvadoran state. Cayetano Carpio and the FPL adhered to a particular variant of Marxism-Leninism, one inspired by China and Vietnam, which manifested itself in a strategy known as "prolonged popular war." Its basic premise was that the proper course for a revolutionary organization was to build up a wave of mass militancy, especially among the peasantry, before striking the regime. The presumption was that mass mobilization would take time, but eventually it would be an insurmountable wave that would have staying power after victory.[26]

An axiom about the Latin American left is that it splits ideological hairs and factionalizes.[27] El Salvador adhered to that axiom. At roughly the same time that Cayetano Carpio was breaking from the Communist Party and forming the FPL in 1969/1970, another militant organization emerged, eventually calling itself El Ejército Revolucionario del Pueblo (ERP). Its founding members did not come out of the Communist Party, but instead were mostly university students from San Salvador who had acquired a radical consciousness by some combination of education, student activism, exposure to liberation theology, and/or involvement in the youth wing of the Christian Democratic Party.[28] They adopted what eventually came to be called the "insurrectionary line," believing that a revolutionary organization needed to go on the offensive sooner rather than later, even in advance of mass mobilization. The belief was that oppressed masses would see the militants on the offensive and flock to it. In this regard, ERP leaders drew inspiration from Che Guevara and the Cuban revolution, although ironically, the ERP had a strong social-democratic tendency, with many of its leaders holding a modest opinion of Marxism-Leninism.

The ERP and the FPL would emerge as the two largest and most prominent guerrilla organizations in El Salvador, and their members would do most of the fighting and dying during the war. But three other, smaller guerrilla organizations emerged alongside them in the latter half of the 1970s. The first of them, the Resistencia Nacional (RN), formed in 1975 as a result of a factional split within the ERP, triggered by the decision of some ERP leaders to execute Roque Dalton not long after he joined the organization.[29] Despite breaking from the ERP, the RN remained more or less aligned ideologically with the ERP, with most of its members being more social-democratic than Marxist-Leninist. The second organization, the Partido Revolucionario de los Trabajadores Centroamericanos (PRTC), formed in 1977. Some of its key members also came out of the ERP. Their focus was directed at the regional level, toward a pan-Central American revolution, but when the civil conflict in El Salvador intensified, its members focused their attention on home. Their ideological orientation tended to align with the RN and the ERP more than the FPL.

The fifth and final militant organization to emerge was the Fuerzas Armadas de Liberación (FAL), the armed wing of the Communist Party. Because the PCS remained loyal to its Moscow line throughout the 1970s, its leaders did not create an armed wing until late in the decade, when they finally decided that El Salvador was ready for revolution. Until that time, PCS leaders were highly critical of the various guerrilla organizations, insisting that they were being rash and were doing more harm than good by employing militant tactics. Ideologically, the PCS/FAL remained Marxist-Leninist, and thus generally closer to the FPL, even though the personal animosities between the leaders of the two factions, Schafik Hándal for the PCS and Salvador Cayetano Carpio for the FPL, remained intense.[30]

All five of these militant organizations originated in cities, largely in the capital city of San Salvador, and throughout the 1970s their strongholds remained urban areas, even the peasant-oriented FPL. All of them demonstrated an impressive capacity to survive amid the state's defensive strategies. They built ties to nonmilitant mass front organizations and capitalized on the state's repressive responses to peaceful demonstrations. But as in the rest of Latin America, El Salvador's guerrillas would have been doomed had they remained exclusively urban without ties to the countryside. The densely populated and heavily guarded urban areas provided too many opportunities for detection by security forces, and generally the state's counterinsurgency tactics proved devastatingly effective in cities. Starting in the mid-1970s each of the guerrilla organizations began making more concerted efforts to build ties with the rural populace. In fact, the decisive process in the history of popular organizing in El Salvador was the linking of these nascent urban-based guerrilla movements to the broader wave of mass mobilization in the countryside.

Substantive evidence into this aspect of Salvadoran history is largely lacking, but what is available suggests that a dialectical relationship unfolded between city and country. The urban guerrillas reached out to the peasantry, organizing and radicalizing them at about the same time that peasants in various regions of the country were ready to advance their own, preexisting mobilization into militant action. The liberationist wing of the Catholic Church played an important role in raising awareness and promoting community organizing in rural areas. This merging of urban and rural represented the coming together of two relatively distinct worlds that infused one another with their respective qualities and characteristics.[31]

The links that were established in the 1970s between the urban guerrillas and the rural masses set the geographical patterns for the civil war. For reasons too varied to go into here, each guerrilla organization established ties with masses in a particular geographic area of the country. The ERP's stronghold was the far northeast corner of the country, in northern Morazán Department. It also had a presence in the southern departments of San Miguel and Usulután. The FPL's main stronghold was north of the capital city, in Chalatenango Department, but it too had a well-established zone of control in the south-central department of San Vicente. The RN was centered around Suchitoto, and more specifically on the northern slope of the Guazapa volcano. The FAL too was based on Guazapa, mainly on the southern side, looking directly toward the capital city of San Salvador. The PRTC was confined mostly to small areas in and around Usulután Department.

The Civil War

The political scientists Scott Mainwaring and Aníbal Pérez-Liñán argue compellingly that El Salvador was not structurally determined to have a civil war, even as late as the 1970s. El Salvador is one of the case studies they use in a broad examination of Latin American politics in the late twentieth and early twenty-first centuries. They reveal that despite El Salvador's problems coming into the 1970s, the country's economic indicators were comparable to other countries that either avoided civil war or that had histories of democratic governance. For example, prior to 1978, El Salvador had a higher per capita income than Colombia and a per capita GDP roughly equal to Brazil, Costa Rica, and Chile. El Salvador also had lower indicators of economic inequality than Brazil, Chile, Colombia, and Panama. Mainwaring and Pérez interpret this data as evidence that structural and economic factors alone cannot explain El Salvador's descent into civil war. Therefore, we must also consider the agency of human actors, because ultimately it was people who had to decide to go to war with one another, and to stay at war as long as they did.[32]

The event that ultimately allowed the guerrillas to wage war against the Salvadoran state was the unification of the five militant factions into a single army, the Frente Farabundo Martí para la Liberación Nacional (FMLN), in late 1980. The process of unification occurred slowly, in a series of fits and starts, reflecting the ideological differences of the factions and the distrust between their leaders. But those leaders ultimately understood that none of them had the ability to take on the Salvadoran army alone, and so eventually they managed to set aside their differences enough to create a unified front. Indeed, one of the more impressive features of the FMLN over the next twelve years was its ability to present itself to the world as a singular entity and to subsume the divisive factionalism that had defined the Salvadoran left until then. As more information comes to light about the war and the guerrillas, it is becoming increasingly evident that factionalism continued to play an important role within the guerrilla organizations, despite their façade of unity. In addition to having their own geographic zones, each of the five guerrilla factions maintained distinct fundraising channels and supply chains. They sometimes had difficulty coordinating combat operations together, and their ideological divergences never subsided—indeed, they emerged in full bloom as soon as the war ended in 1992. Nevertheless, a defining feature of the FMLN's war effort was the ability of its five constituent factions to speak singularly and to present themselves as united in their fight against the Salvadoran government.[33]

The unification of the guerrillas was the precursor to a major military offensive in early January 1981 that would mark the formal beginning of the civil war. It would come to be known as the first "final offensive," although combat between guerrillas and the state had been occurring regularly throughout the preceding years. The basic premise of the offensive followed the examples of Nicaragua in July 1979 and Cuba in late 1958, which was that the guerrilla army would throw everything it had at the military, and in response the civilian population would rise up alongside the guerrillas and create a nationwide wave of popular rebellion that would cause the regime to collapse. The guerrillas wanted to launch the offensive before Reagan took office in late January 1981, knowing that he was likely to increase support for the regime. The strategy bore the imprint of the insurrectionist line of the ERP, and while it is not clear how much Cayetano Carpio and the other leaders of the FPL agreed with the plan, they went along with it.

Unfortunately for the guerrillas and their supporters, the January offensive failed. It became apparent within a few days that the guerrillas lacked the capacity to stand up to the military, and the mass uprising did not happen. At the time, the guerrillas were still oriented toward the cities and they did not have a widespread basis of popular support in the countryside. As a consequence of the failed offensive, the guerrillas more or less abandoned the cities and retreated to their respective territories in the countryside and prepared for a longer fight. It was in the aftermath of the 1981 offensive that the war turned into a protracted rural insurgency.

Naturally, the failure in January 1981 incited debate within the guerrilla leadership. There is not a lot of evidence about the conflict, but it seems apparent that the supporters of the ERP's insurrectionist line were on the defensive against the FPL's longer-term strategy of prolonged popular war.[34] But the ERP didn't back down and instead pressed on with attacks throughout 1981 and 1982. In fact, in 1982, the ERP ordered a second nationwide offensive, but evidently the FPL, the FAL, and the PRTC refused to join, believing that the failure of January 1981 would be repeated. Only the RN joined the fight. Not surprisingly, the offensive failed, but it delivered some stinging blows, including the near collapse of the military barracks in Usulután. In a rhetorical spin, the ERP leadership downplayed the defeat in January 1981 by referring to the roughly two-year period thereafter as the "extended offensive."[35]

Regardless of ongoing differences among the respective guerrilla leaders, each of the five factions followed a similar approach during the first three years of the war. Using the small territories they controlled as bases, they struck the armed forces in nearby zones. The goal was to keep attacking and steadily expand the zones under guerrilla control by pushing the army back toward its main barracks in the larger cities. The guerrillas targeted formal military posts as well as civilians who belonged to the paramilitaries and who were doing much of the regime's dirty work.[36] Broadly speaking, the guerrillas' strategy worked, and they gained control over increasingly large swaths of territory between 1981 and 1983. "Control," however, is a relative term, because at any time the army could enter any part of the country with overwhelming firepower. But the problem for the army was that it could not reestablish a permanent presence in those zones where it had been evicted. The guerrillas usually knew where the army was going to launch its large sweeps, because big military operations took weeks of preparation and the arrival of massive amounts of supplies in easily detectable truck caravans. In the face of that kind of onslaught, the guerrillas and their supporters simply left the zone and returned when the army withdrew.[37]

Unable to find many guerrillas, the army meted out punishment to anyone and anything it could find, including civilians, animals, and infrastructure. Its goal was to destroy the guerrillas' capacity to survive in a zone through a policy commonly described as "draining the sea to get to the fish." The army invariably had to pull back from its various offensive pushes because it couldn't afford to keep that many troops tied up in one geographic area and leave itself open to attack on other fronts. When it retreated from an area, it tried to leave behind enough troops to hold the area. This effort simply started the cycle all over again, with the guerrillas striking out from small zones of control and draining the army's troops and resources without giving the army much of anything in the way of dead guerrillas to show for its efforts. In short, the army lacked the capacity to fight the guerrillas everywhere simultaneously and thus constantly found itself in a frustrating position of advancing forward and pulling back, all the while getting hit by effective guerrilla units taking advantage of the army's overreach.[38]

According to claims made by both Salvadoran officers and U.S. advisors, the Salvadoran army was not prepared to fight a guerrilla insurgency when the war began. It had been created to fight conventional wars against foreign states, primarily Honduras, as it had done in 1969. In order to respond to this new domestic enemy, the Salvadoran military had to be restructured. First it had to grow exponentially in size. At the onset of the war, the army consisted of roughly 10,000 troops, with another 3,000 or so making up the National Guard. In time, the number of soldiers swelled to well over 50,000. Most of those new troops were conscripted teenagers who spent their time standing guard at sites deemed potential targets, like plantations, bridges, dams, and power stations.[39]

In addition to growing in size, the military improved its offensive capabilities. Largely under U.S. training in El Salvador, Panama, and the United States, the army created five new Batallónes de Infantería de Reacción Inmediata (BIRIs). These were elite fighting units comprised of roughly 1,000 men each whose goal was to go out into the field and kill guerrillas. The most notorious of these new battalions was the Atlacatl Battalion, which committed some of the most egregious human rights abuses during the war. As ominous as these new units may have been, in the first phase of the war they were not particularly effective at finding guerrillas. Thus a lot of what they did in the early years of the war was to carry out mass sweeps that resulted in massacres of civilians at places like the Sumpul River on the border between Chalatenango and Honduras in May 1980, La Quesara in the lower Lempa River region in October 1981, El Mozote in northern Morazán in December 1981, and Copapayo Viejo on the banks of Lake Suchitlán in November 1983. The numbers of displaced people stand as testament to the effectiveness of the military's tactics. Northern Morazán's population declined by roughly 50 percent, and the entire area around Lake Suchitlán was more or less depopulated by 1983.[40]

In 1982, ERP commander Joaquin Villalobos granted an interview to Marta Harnecker, a Chilean journalist and academic. The interview with

Villalobos revolved primarily around the issue of strategy in El Salvador's civil war, and Villalobos provided a frank assessment of the state of the conflict and each side's pathway to victory. Naturally, Villalobos was optimistic about his side's chances, and as a longtime advocate of the insurrectionist strategy, his ruminations centered on military affairs. He was well aware that a guerrilla victory was not imminent and that more fighting was necessary. Basically, Villalobos believed that whichever side could resupply faster than the other was going win. In making that claim, Villalobos was referring to eminently practical issues, like getting well-rested troops into the field with functional weapons and ample supplies. In his words, "The problem is who recuperates more rapidly, them or us?" As a guerrilla commander, Villalobos spent a lot of time dealing with the essential issues of supplies and logistics. At the time of this interview, the guerrillas were successfully keeping up with the Salvadoran army in the arena of resupply. The guerrillas faced logistical challenges to getting food and munitions into El Salvador in quantities large enough to sustain as many 6,000 or more armed combatants and their support personnel. But the Salvadoran army, even with its ample support from the United States, was having difficulty keeping up. "What can be derived from this situation," Villalobos summarized, "is that now the time necessary for recuperation of the FMLN forces is shorter than for the army."[41] He, along with many analysts in the United States and in the Salvadoran government, believed that if everything remained as it was at that moment, the guerrillas could win.[42]

As it turned out, Villalobos's assessment in 1982 was accurate. The guerrillas were capable of standing up to the Salvadoran army in the field and they gained control over increasing amounts of territory. In addition to standard guerrilla hit-and-run strikes, they fought the army in open combat, sometimes with battalion-sized forces. Both the FPL and the ERP created special-forces units. The ERP units were called the Rafael Arce Zablah Brigades (BRAZ) and they numbered as many as 1,500 troops. By late 1983 the guerrillas could claim roughly 25 percent of El Salvador as territory under their nominal control.[43]

But something happened in 1983 that turned the tide back toward the army. The United States under President Reagan redoubled its efforts in El Salvador and ramped up its support for the Salvadoran government. That support included increasing levels of economic support and the delivery of sophisticated weaponry, especially for the Salvadoran air force, like fixed-wing fighters and attack helicopters. Accompanying this increase in economic and material support, the United States advised the Salvadoran military to improve its record on human rights abuses. Throughout the first three years of the war, the state's counterinsurgency program and paramilitary activities killed as many as one thousand people per month. During that time, the Reagan administration was under increasing pressure from domestic opponents to end, or reduce its support for the government of El Salvador.[44] Under pressure from U.S. diplomatic officers and military advisers, including a visit from Vice President Bush in late 1983, the Salvadoran officers relented. They purged some of their most abusive colleagues from the ranks and scaled back the repression, and, as a consequence, the aid kept flowing.[45]

Particularly challenging to the guerrillas was the increased capacity of the Salvadoran air force. In 1981, the air force had only a few operational helicopters and some aging French jets. A portion of this limited arsenal was damaged or destroyed in a brazen guerrilla attack on the Ilopango airfield in 1982. But after the increased commitment by the United States in late 1983 and early 1984, the air force came to have more than fifty operational helicopters, some A-37 attack jets, and some AC-47 gunships that could hover over a battlefield for hours.[46] It would have been suicidal for the guerrillas to keep large battalion-size units on the field without a viable counter to military's command of the skies, such as surface-to-air missiles, which they would not introduce until 1990.

In response to this and other enhanced capacities by the Salvadoran military, the guerrillas changed strategy and downsized their units. The large guerrilla combat units, like the ERP's BRAZ, were more or less dismantled, and the fighters were broken down into small bands. Some of the new, smaller units would go out into the countryside for extended periods, engage with the civilian population, and monitor the enemy's movements. These smaller units tended to target infrastructure, anything that would cost the government money to rebuild or repair. In other words, the conflict turned into a war of attrition, a so-called war of movement instead of a war of position. Instead of defeating the enemy on the battlefield, the guerrillas hoped to bleed it dry by draining it of its ability to govern or to survive financially. In addition to reducing the size of its units, the guerrillas also reduced their overall number of combatants. From a high of maybe 10,000 or more fighters in the early 1980s, they hit a low of half that or less during their nadir in 1986/1987.[47]

The change in strategy did not eliminate the guerrillas' ability to mount large attacks on fixed military installations or to engage the enemy in large battles in the field, as evidenced by their attack on the Fourth Brigade in Chalatenango in 1986. But these types of events occurred less frequently and carried with them less of a sense that the army might collapse at any moment. The strategic change caused some morale problems within the guerrillas' ranks, especially in the ERP, which considered itself to be the premier fighting force. Little evidence exists currently to reveal how the debate over the strategic change played out politically among the various guerrilla leaders, but a safe assumption is that the supporters of the FPL's prolonged popular war ascended at the expense of the backers of the ERP's insurrectionary approach.[48]

Partly in response to the guerrilla's downsizing, and partly as a consequence of its new emphasis on human rights, the Salvadoran military also changed strategy in late 1983 and early 1984. No longer was it going to prioritize the massive sweeps that recurrently failed to trap guerrillas en masse. Instead, the military was going to become more nimble by similarly relying on smaller units that could enter the guerrilla's rearguard for longer periods of time. It downsized some of its special-forces battalions into smaller "*cazador*" or hunter units, which consisted of two or three hundred men, rather than the previous 900 or 1,000. It also created long-range reconnaissance patrols, or Patrullas de Reconocimiento de Alcance Largo (PRALs), small groups of soldiers trained to survive in enemy territory for days or weeks at a time with the objective of finding guerrilla encampments through surveillance or tips from civilians and then calling in fast-moving airborne strikes. One of the main objectives of this strategy was to take better advantage of the military's command over the skies.[49] Coronel John Whagelstein, the ranking U.S. commander in El Salvador in 1985, summarized the strategic change in an oral history that he gave to the U.S. Army's Military History Institute that year.

> Their [the Salvadoran army's] strategy was fundamentally centered around multi-battalion, short-duration operations, which served no useful purpose in my estimation. What we needed was saturation; we needed day and night operations; we needed long-range recon; we needed to improve the intelligence capability; we needed a better Navy, we needed an Air Force that was responsive to the ground troops that could provide close air support; and more importantly we needed mobility to move troops around the battlefield while we were trying to get battalions upgraded so that they could conduct small unit operations day and night.[50]

The military's new strategy proved effective, and many of the guerrilla memoirists talk about the devastating impact of long-range patrols and airstrikes.[51] Nevertheless, the army could not defeat the guerrillas, nor could it dent their supply chain, which stands as a testament to the guerrillas' capabilities. Even with the U.S. and Salvadoran militaries dedicating major energy to stopping the guerrillas' flow of supplies, including the use of U.S. ships off the Salvadoran coast, high-tech surveillance aircraft, and satellite imagery, the guerrillas continued to bring tons of munitions and food into the country that kept them alive and fighting. In 1988, intelligence officers in the U.S. embassy expressed dismay that after nearly a decade of fighting, not one major guerrilla supply shipment had been intercepted.[52]

After 1984, the war ground to a stalemate. The army couldn't defeat the guerrillas, nor could it make significant inroads on reoccupying the 25 percent of El Salvador that had been "liberated." Neither could the guerrillas defeat the army. Furthermore, the guerrillas' war-of-attrition affected their ability to expand their base of support throughout the civilian population. When the guerrillas destroyed infrastructure and caused people to lose water, electricity, and transportation, they sometimes found it difficult to convince those people of the merits of their cause. It should also be noted that many observers, especially U.S. military advisors in El Salvador, believed that the Salvadoran military was hindered by corruption. It seemed that some officers had been bought off by the FMLN to avoid contact with guerrilla columns in certain times and contexts. Furthermore, the military's internal structure made it virtually impossible for merit to stand out as the primary basis for promotion and assignment.[53]

In theory the war could have gone on like that for a long time, as it did in Colombia in the 1990s and 2000s. But the convergence of four events broke the stalemate and pushed both sides to the bargaining table. The first event was the "second final offensive" in November 1989. In a situation reminiscent of Vietnam prior to the Tet Offensive in 1969, both Salvadoran officers and U.S. policy-makers had been describing the guerrillas as being virtually defeated in 1988/1989. But then, in a remarkable logistical feat, the guerrillas launched a massive, nationwide offensive in November 1989 that targeted all of El Salvador's major urban areas, and in particular the capital city of San Salvador. Until that time, people living in San Salvador had hardly experienced the war directly because the fighting had been going on in the countryside. The 1989 offensive brought the war to them and disproved the army's claims that the guerrillas were losing.

It took nearly two weeks to dislodge the guerrillas from the capital's outlying neighborhoods, and although the guerrillas suffered a military defeat, they scored a major public relations victory. They exposed the military as being inept and/or dishonest, and they demonstrated their own capabilities by moving thousands of armed fighters undetected from their rearguards to the outskirts of most every major city and then launching simultaneous attacks on multiple targets. Not only did the Salvadoran military resort to carpet-bombing poor neighborhoods in the capital to dislodge the guerrillas, but they also made the fateful decision to assassinate six Jesuit priests at the Universidad Centroamericana José Simeón Cañas (UCA) a few days after the offensive began, which resulted in widespread international condemnation.[54]

The second event was the guerrillas' acquisition of surface-to-air missiles. It is not clear if the guerrillas possessed the missiles at the time of the 1989 offensive, but they introduced them into the theater of conflict shortly thereafter. Suddenly, one of the military's most valued assets, control over the skies, became tenuous as the guerrillas were able to push the air force's safety zone higher, making it possible to focus more attention on fighting on the ground, where they had a more even chance.[55]

The third event was the end of the Cold War, which took away the United States' primary justification for backing the Salvadoran military: to stop the spread of Soviet-inspired communism. U.S. diplomatic personnel in the Bush administration began pressuring their Salvadoran allies to find a negotiated solution in the absence of military victory.[56]

The fourth and final event was the electoral loss by the Sandinistas in Nicaragua in 1990, which eliminated a key ally for the Salvadoran guerrillas and took away their strategic rearguard. In the face of these four events, representatives from the two opposing sides met in various cities over a two-year period under the auspices of the United Nations and slowly hammered out a peace deal. Instances of fighting occurred back in El Salvador, but eventually the negotiators found common ground, and in early January 1992 the final accord was signed in Mexico City, bringing the war to a close.

The basic outline of the deal was that the FMLN would demobilize its fighters, surrender its weaponry, and turn itself into a political party that would be allowed to participate in provincial and national elections. The army would be downsized and certain key sectors would be eliminated, namely the BIRIs and some branches of the security forces that had been the most notorious violators of human rights, including the National Guard and the treasury police. The national police would remain, but it would be restructured and a certain portion of its officers would be drawn from the ranks of FMLN combatants. To the chagrin of the FMLN, no provisions were made to address the nation's overarching economic program, which meant that the dominant neoliberal paradigm that had been unfolding over the prior five years under ARENA would remain in place. Provisions were made, however, for some people in the FMLN-controlled zones to keep land that they had occupied during the war. Other provisions were made to establish an indemnity program that would make land available to combatants on both sides, in hopes of giving them an opportunity to return to civilian life and reintegrate into the national economy. However, the follow-through on these indemnity programs was modest.[57]

Peace Accord reforms

Postwar El Salvador

When asked to describe El Salvador after the civil war, the historian Knut Walter sometimes responds provocatively by saying that "the nation of El Salvador no longer exists." To explain his comment, he points out that the Salvadoran government is barley solvent and more or less powerless before the forces of globalization that buffet it from year to year. A good part of the state's assets were privatized, including electric power distribution, banks, and telecommunications. The country lacks a national currency, having shifted from the colón to the U.S. dollar in 2001. The country's main export is people, who travel to and remain in the United States and other countries and send back remittances, which constitute one of the largest contributions to the nation's GDP; drug money-laundering may bring in more than remittances, but nobody knows for sure. A sizable proportion of economically viable enterprises are now owned wholly or partially by multinational corporations, including the important banks, all communications (mobile phones and internet), beer, petroleum derivatives, and airlines. The country imports a lot of what it consumes, especially foodstuffs, energy, and health products, which is reflected in a chronic trade deficit that would be unsustainable were it not for remittances.[58]

Walter's sentiments are anathema to anyone with nationalist pretensions, but his overarching thesis strikes a chord. Postwar El Salvador, which another Salvadoran has described as a *"casi nación"* (an almost nation) sometimes seems like a small geographic space at the mercy of international forces that serves as a transit point for foreign-made goods, some licit others illicit.[59] The extent to which this situation differs from the past is open to debate. On the one hand, El Salvador has traditionally been heavily dependent upon external variables, especially the global market for agricultural commodities and petroleum. The people who held economic power before and during the war retained it afterward, creating a situation in which peace, in the words of one scholar who identifies with the mass base of the FMLN, is little more than "war by other means."[60]

Pessimistic assessments of El Salvador's economic future coincide with similarly dire indices about El Salvador's social conditions. The nation's crime rate remains stubbornly high, with a homicide rate that often ranks as one of the highest in the world. Indicators of other social malignancies like rape and domestic abuse are no better. Guns are cheap and ubiquitous. Delinquency is on the rise, and gangs are rampant. It is not uncommon for people in poor urban neighborhoods and in rural communities to say that when boys become teenagers they face two options, migrate to the United States or join a gang. The 2008 recession intensified the problems. This plethora of issues has resulted in some people making the seemingly outlandish claim that their lives were better before the civil war than today.[61]

This sense of pessimism contrasts with the hope that accompanied the signing of the peace accords in 1992. If nothing else, El Salvador managed to refrain from sinking back into civil war after 1992, despite lingering feelings of bitterness between the former antagonists. The reforms imposed upon the military stuck, including the disbandment of the units most responsible for human rights abuses. Political reforms have also proven resilient, with El Salvador exhibiting a relatively stable and functioning democracy, a historic precedent for the country and the region. The former guerrilla army, the FMLN, transitioned into a political party after 1992, and although it failed to win the presidency until 2009 and again in 2014, it remained a strong opposition presence in the interim, scoring many victories at the municipal and legislative levels.[62] Post-war El Salvador has also seen the emergence of numerous social movements, around such issues as privatization, health care and education, which have served as something of a check on ARENA's electoral dominance prior to 2009.[63]

The history of the two main political parties, ARENA and the FMLN, reveals a lot about the tensions that define postwar El Salvador. ARENA was founded in 1981 by Roberto D'Aubuisson and a handful of other staunch conservatives who believed that their interests were not being adequately represented by the political actors at the time. Recall that the coup of 1979 had brought to power a series of reformist juntas, and even though the members of those juntas were political centrists and anti-communists, and the militant left remained excluded from the political arena, D'Aubuisson and his adherents considered the juntas unacceptable. By that time, D'Aubuisson was known not only as a militantly anticommunist rhetorician, but also as having been instrumental, along with other ARENA founders, in assembling and directing paramilitary death squads. These types of people are known locally as *escuadroneros* (death squadders). D'Aubuisson has been identified as the architect of the assassination of Archbishop Romero in March 1980.[64]

ARENA won the legislative elections in 1982 that gave it the upper hand in choosing the provisional president who would serve for the next two years until the nationwide election in 1984. D'Aubuisson was the party's choice for president, but apparently the U.S. embassy intervened and declared that it would not accept a D'Aubuisson presidency, fearful that his reputation and record on human rights would threaten U.S. domestic support for the administration's policies in El Salvador. D'Aubuisson then ran in the 1984 election and lost a close race to the American's preferred candidate, the Christian Democrat José Napoleon Duarte. ARENA remained the main political opposition party to the Christian Democrats thereafter for the next five years.[65]

Evidently, the lesson D'Aubuisson drew from his failures in 1982 and 1984 is that ARENA had to soften its public image and put forth a candidate who would be acceptable to the United States. Thus, in the wake of the 1984 defeat, he stepped aside as party leader and promoted in his stead the businessman Alfredo Cristiani, who went on to win the presidency in 1989. The rise of Cristiani marked the ascendance of what one scholar calls the "new right" within ARENA, a wing that portrays itself as moderate and probusiness rather than militantly nationalistic and rabidly anticommunist. This transformative process coincided with the formation of the Fundación Salvadoreña para el Desarrollo Económico y Social (FUSADES), a privately funded think tank that was designed to promote market-friendly economic policies and instill a spirit of entrepreneurship among young Salvadorans. FUSADES received substantial funding from the United States Agency for International Development (USAID). Although the story of FUSADES has yet to be fully revealed, existing scholarship suggests that it interacted directly with tens of thousands of young Salvadorans throughout the mid-1980s and played a significant role in distancing conservative economic policies from the militant anticommunism that ARENA's founder had linked to them. Subsequently, a sort of rivalry emerged within the ranks of ARENA between those who identified with the founders and their militant nationalism and those who embraced the pro-business, neoliberal image embodied by the likes of Cristiani. Each of the five ARENA presidential candidates, starting with Alfredo Cristiani, had to negotiate this complicated intraparty dispute.[66]

It still befuddles many casual onlookers, both inside El Salvador and abroad, that ARENA so dominated politics after the civil war, regardless of its efforts to disassociate itself from its paramilitary foundations. After all, the party never surrendered its allegiance to its founder D'Aubuisson, who continues to receive accolades from party members as a hero and a visionary. But ARENA is a powerful political machine, with a lot of money and a savvy ability to mold public opinion through the media. Moreover, ARENA has a lot of support among residents in poor, rural areas, where a substantial portion of residents are deeply religious and conservative, and during the war many of them opposed the guerrillas.[67]

The FMLN also experienced internal tensions as it transitioned into a political party after the war. The unity that the leaders of the FMLN so avidly promoted during the war showed cracks. The basic division lay between ideological hardliners (ortodoxos), who tended to be from the FPL and the PCS, and moderate social democrats (renovadores), who were disproportionately from the ERP, the RN, and the PRTC. The first major break occurred in 1993, when the former commander of the ERP, Joaquín Villalobos, and a handful of other moderate leaders broke from the FMLN and tried to form a new political party, the Partido Demócrata (PD). Their dismal showing in the next election ended their political aspirations and resulted in Villalobos leaving El Salvador and eventually becoming a vocal critic of the FMLN, especially its hardline wing.[68] Within the FMLN, the debate between moderates and hardliners went on. Each of the FMLN's three presidential candidates between 1994 and 2004 had been a comandante during the war, and each represented one the two factions. As each of these candidates failed to win the presidency, the other faction ascended. The cycle went on until the victory of Mauricio Funes in 2009, the first FMLN candidate who had not been with the guerrillas during the war. Naturally, the leaders of the FMLN were ecstatic about their party's victory in 2009, but some of them feared that Funes took the party too far from its popular roots and had formed alliances with large business interests. The FMLN prevailed in the next election in 2014 behind Funes's vice president, Salvador Sánchez Cerén, the former ranking commander of the FPL guerrilla faction during the war, who is considered to belong to the *ortodoxo* wing.[69]

Conclusion

The above narrative contends that the history of El Salvador's civil war should be read through the lens of a dialectical relationship between agency and structure. The trajectory that set El Salvador on the pathway to war resides partly in structural variables that were beyond the conscious intent and/or purposeful choice of Salvadoran actors. Those variables include, but are not limited to the system of land tenure inherited from the Spanish colonial era, the demographic makeup and ethnic composition of the population, and the unpredictable cycles of the international marketplace. Another structural variable that played a decisive role in the civil war was U.S. foreign policy. The reasons that the U.S. government under the Reagan administration invested so heavily in the Salvadoran civil war arguably had less to do with El Salvador and more to do with events Salvadorans had no control over, such as U.S. domestic politics, the Sandinista victory in Nicaragua in 1979, and the broader context of the global cold war. While it is impossible to prove a counterfactual, it is safe to say that had the United States not involved itself so heavily in El Salvador, the story of the war would have been different; the FMLN may have won, or the war would likely have been shorter, and therein, possibly, a lot less bloody.

It might be too much to expect Salvadorans to have avoided war in the 1980s, given that most every country in Latin America experienced some sort of intensified military conflict in the second half of the twentieth century. Nonetheless, it took real people in real time making real decisions to bring the war about, and to end it. Their agency is an important explanatory variable.

In the following pages, we will see how some of those people, through the venue of published life stories, have remembered that war, or at least how they have chosen to narrate it. In their works they do much the same that I have done here—provide a historic context that explains their actions and decisions. Some of the narrators even employ primary and/or secondary sources, as I have done, but most rely exclusively on their own memories, or their own narrative selections. If those narrators were to read my version of events in this chapter, some would agree with it, others would disagree with it, and a few would probably find it personally offensive. It is irrelevant if those narrators are right or wrong, honest or dishonest, forgetful or mindful. What matters is that each of them has injected his or her version of the past into El Salvador's postwar public sphere, and in so doing they are all participating in the contest for control over the story of the war.

2 The Aggrieved Minority
Civilian Elites

Salvadoran elites are a paradoxical lot; they are at once tremendously powerful and ubiquitously present, and yet aloof and elusive. Traditionally, they have shunned the limelight of politics and public service. "The rich have always considered politics to be something dirty," says Orlando de Sola, a member of one of the nation's wealthy families. Indeed, Salvadoran elites did not have a visible or organized political presence in El Salvador's modern history, perhaps until ARENA's rise in the 1980s, and even then ARENA relied heavily on a nationalistic populism built around votes from the rural poor. Various members of elite families have held government positions, usually in economic affairs, but elites have rarely spoken with a singular, unified and public voice. And almost never have they shared their personal life stories. For all their importance, El Salvador's elites remain a mystery.[1]

Hence, the sources in this chapter possess special value. They consist of roughly one dozen book-length memoirs and extended interviews in which elite Salvadorans and their spokespersons use the context of the civil war to share their life stories, thereby opening a rare window into their self-conceptualized worldview.[2] Most elite Salvadorans are ideologically conservative, although not all of them are. Regardless, those who have narrated their stories to date and who comprise the elite memory community are uniformly conservative; consequently, the present chapter is framed around the lens of theorized conservatism.

The narrative of the civilian elite memory community rests upon the premise of theft. The members of this community see themselves under threat because they have had something taken from them, or they are about to have something taken from them. They respond to this threat with a militant self-defense. They believe they must fight to reclaim what has been taken and to prevent future loss. The memoirists naturally accuse Marxist guerrillas of being the most pernicious thieves. But they also criticize their former allies—the Salvadoran army and the U.S. government. They believe that neither the U.S. government nor the Salvadoran army had their best interests at heart, and thus they portray themselves as an isolated minority struggling for survival amid an onslaught of radicalism and reformism.

Scholars of Central America share a broad consensus that a defining characteristic of El Salvador during its civil war was the strength of its alliance between elites, the military, and the United States government, especially in comparison to Nicaragua, where elite factionalism helped doom Somoza and allow the Sandinistas to claim victory in July 1979.[3] The sources in this chapter reveal that threads of factionalism ran throughout the ruling bloc in El Salvador. The elites' sense of alienation may not have been sufficiently strong to break apart the anticommunist coalition and allow for an FMLN victory, but it reveals the complexity of that coalition, or at least the ways in which elite memoirists have come to remember it in the years since.[4]

The Conservative Narrative—Theorized and Contextualized

As a point of clarification, the term "conservative" herein refers to the modern twentieth-century variant, not its nineteenth-century counterpart. Modern conservatives advocate for economic libertarianism, small government, low taxes, and steadfast opposition to state intervention in the marketplace. In the specific context of the Cold War, it meant opposition to anything that smacked of socialism or communism. Its ideological ancestor is classical, nineteenth-century liberalism and laissez-faire economics. Admittedly, modern conservatives in El Salvador sometimes take social positions that resemble traditional, nineteenth-century conservatism, such as an appeal to Catholicism, a defense of family, and a belief in old-fashioned gender roles, but for the present purpose, this chapter will focus on their political and economic views.

The North American political scientist Corey Robin has provided an analysis of modern conservatism that helps interpret the memory community of elite Salvadorans. In his book, *The Reactionary Mind*, Robin contends that to understand modern conservatism one must move beyond the prevailing notion that conservatives want liberty and the status quo in contrast to liberals and leftists who seek social transformation. Conservatism, according to Robin, is more forward-looking and dynamic than that, albeit based on "backlash politics." What conservatives disdain, he insists, is not liberty in principal, but the extension of liberty from the higher orders to the lower orders, because in that extension they perceive the loss of their own freedom. At its most basic and fundamental level, "conservatism is a meditation on—and theoretical rendition of—the felt experience of having power, seeing it threatened and trying to win it back." It is ironic that a group like El Salvador's elites would base their sense of self upon a notion of loss, because they are and have been incredibly privileged people. Robin actually uses the word "bizarre" to describe "a ruling class [that] rests its claim to power upon its sense of victimhood." But he insists that by looking at the long arc of conservatism in the Western world, even as far back as the French Revolution, this trait reveals itself constantly.

> Some conservatives criticize the free market, others defend it; some oppose the state, others embrace it; some believe in God, others are atheists. Some are localists, others nationalists, and still others internationalists. Some, like Burke, are all three at the same time. But these are historical improvisations—tactical and substantive—on a theme. Only by juxtaposing these voices—across time and space— can we make out the theme amid the improvisations.

Because a fundamental premise of conservative thinking is that the left is always threatening to seize power, conservatives see themselves as having a right, even an obligation to fight back. This belief partly explains why conservatives have a penchant for violence, because they believe they live in a continual state of self-defense.[5]

Like any piece of provocative scholarship, Robin's work has its detractors.[6] But for the present purposes, it doesn't matter if Robin is right or wrong, because his description of conservatism describes elite Salvadorans well. The available sources show remarkable consistency in their adherence to Robin's finding. If more elites were to write their memoirs, perhaps alternative trends would emerge, but at the present moment, such divergences do not exist.

A potential problem for using Robin's study to understand Salvadoran elites is that his interpretations are based primarily on Anglo-American readings. But this issue is not much of a problem. Economic libertarians in Latin America, and especially in El Salvador, have long looked to Anglo-America as a model, going back at least as far as the canonical Argentine liberal statesman of the nineteenth century, Domingo Sarmiento, who hailed Britain and the United States and disparaged Spain and southern Europe. In El Salvador, modern conservatives have a long tradition of referencing Sarmiento, as well as associating the values of individualism and laissez faire with Anglo America.[7] Elite memoirists commonly include expositions on Western history in which they attribute individualism and laissez faire to Anglo America and seek to orient El Salvador toward its modernizing tradition. One particularly loquacious example is Mario Gómez Zimmerman's *Power to the West* (*Adelante Occidente*), a 500-page treatise on Western individualism and market economics. Another revealing example is a comment made by the elite memoirist, Ricardo Valdivieso Oriani, who was asked in 2003 by a reporter from the conservative daily newspaper *La Prensa Gráfica* if he could identify a "rightwing intellectual reference point in the country." Valdivieso responded, "In El Salvador? Conservative intellectual? Good question. I don't know. . . . Perhaps an academic that defends economic liberalism in my country, my beloved El Salvador, but no one is coming to me at the moment." The best he could come up with was Roberto D'Aubuisson and the nineteenth-century political and military leader Gerardo Barrios. Beyond that, he referenced only foreigners.[8]

Salvadoran elites have historically close ties to the United States. Many of them were born, raised, or educated there, including many of the memoirists that comprise the elite memory community. Ricardo Valdivieso, for example, is known as "El Gringo" because he was raised in New York City and speaks Spanish with an accent. Guillermo "Billy" Sol Bang was born in the United States and although his parents brought him to El Salvador as a young boy, he returned to the United States to attend college at the University of Michigan and Texas A&M. Mario Gómez Zimmerman took up exile in Miami during the civil war and stayed there after the war. And José Ramón Barahona migrated to the United States in the late 1960s and made his fortune in the Washington, D.C. area.

During the war, the United States had a heavy presence in El Salvador, and it is well-established that ARENA modeled itself on the U.S. Republican Party under the guidance of various U.S. public relations agencies.[9] Since the end of the war, the United States and El Salvador have become even more intermeshed. More than two million Salvadorans live and work in the United States, sending home billions of dollars in remittances, which typically make up at least 25 percent of the nation's annual GDP. The United States is commonly referred to in El Salvador as "*departamento quince*" (the fifteenth department), another of the country's fourteen official administrative units.

The elite Salvadoran memoirists organize their narrative almost identically to the conservatives in Robin's study. That narrative is Western in origin and consists of a classic crisis—resolution—denouement structure, or in more elaborated form, an original status quo, an initial problem, an exposition, complications, crisis, climax, denouement, and a new status quo. The specific Salvadoran version of that narrative can be summarized in three parts: 1) the creation of a right, just, and proper order, that is, the original status quo; 2) the threat to that order from liberals and leftists, that is, the crisis; and 3) the fight against those threats, which if the narrator believes conservatives have won then it's a happy ending, and if they have lost, then it's a sad ending, that is, resolution and denouement.[10]

Each elite memoirist employs a variant of this three-part narrative structure. The original status quo is the period between the early 1880s and the late 1950s. The narrators portray this period as El Salvador's golden age, when government knew its place and hardworking entrepreneurs could retain the fruits of their labor. The only hiccup during this period was the peasant uprising of 1932, when disgruntled peasants and their supposed communist leaders rose up against the established order. But the government squashed the threat and returned society to safety. Thus 1932 functions as a mini narrative, because it contains all the requisite parts of the broader narrative: a threat to the ideal status quo; a fight against that threat; and the reestablishment of a stable order. Not surprisingly, elite memoirists tend to hold a special place in their hearts for the 1950s, which they see as a kind of high moment between the crisis of the 1930s and the breakdown of the 1960s, beginning with the Cuban revolution in 1959.

Another reason that 1932 is so important to elite consciousness is that it lends itself to a storyline of personal betrayal that underlies their broader narrative schematic. As Robin notes, "one of the reasons the subordinate's exercise of agency so agitates the conservative imagination is that it takes place in an intimate setting. Every great political blast . . . is set off by a private fuse."[11] As part of their portrayal of the original status quo, conservatives describe laborers as happy and docile, thanks to the just treatment they received from landowners. So when workers rose up in rebellion, first in 1932 and then later in the 1970s and 1980s, the memoirists take it personally. In fact, starting immediately after the events of 1932, elites began framing the events around a narrative of personal betrayal, in which rebellious workers betrayed the trust elites had placed in them.[12]

The second part of the elite narrative, the threat to the original status quo, begins in earnest in the 1960s. Naturally, leftist guerrillas represent

the greatest threat to elite interests, which helps to explain why a disproportionate number of elite memoirs are captivity narratives, centered
on being kidnapped or targeted for assassination by guerrillas. But as
worried as they are about guerrillas, elites are just as worried, if not
more so, about their supposed allies, the Salvadoran army and the U.S.
government. The military governments after 1960 may have been
staunchly anticommunist and ostensibly conservative, but from the perspective of the elite memoirists, they advocated a distinct variant of
modernization that included economic reforms and state intervention in
the economy. Elite memoirists opposed that version of modernization
and disliked the growing relationship between the military governments
and international development programs, like the Alliance for Progress.
According to the memoirists, those alliances began a multidecade threat
of reformism that came to full fruition in the land, banking, and export
reforms after the 1979 military coup.

The third component of the narrative, the resolution and denouement,
consists of the war and its conclusion. Because of their antipathy for the
institutional military, elite narrators downplay the army's role during the
war and instead focus on their own organizational activities, both licit
and illicit. While elites believe they won the war and once again made El
Salvador safe for free markets and private property after 1992, they harbor resentment and a lingering feeling that something that was taken
from them has yet to be returned. That unresolved resentment provides
the foundation for a new status quo in the early twenty-first century.

As with any select body of evidence, these sources represent a particular cross section of a broader population. There are more men than
women, although the North American psychologist Michael Gorkin and
his two Salvadoran colleagues have made available valuable interviews
with three generations of women from one elite family. Founders and
early backers of ARENA are disproportionately represented, including Ricardo Valdivieso, David Panamá Sandoval, Guillermo Sol Bang, Mario
Acosta Oertel, and Orlando de Sola. In light of the claim by the political
scientist Kevin Middlebrook that "ARENA was initially dominated by
the most intransigent elements of the Salvadoran right," these founders
are likely motivated to tell history in a particular way, perhaps to absolve
them of association with human rights abuses and/or to promote their
status within ARENA circles.[13] For example, in their interviews both
Orlando de Sola and Mario Acosta Oertel deny involvement in death
squads during the war.

Additionally, most of the elite narrators belong to so-called second families, who a wealthy Salvadoran once described to a North American investigative reporter as "the American-educated managers who administer the holdings of 'the 14.'"[14] The two memoirists who do hail from wealthier families, Orlando de Sola and Luis Escalante Arce, have watched their fortunes and influence decline relative to a new class of postwar elites, whose members have not yet contributed any life stories. As for the timing of the publications, most of them appeared after the war, but two of them, Mario Gómez Zimmerman's and Luis Escalate's, first appeared near the end of the war. I include them here partly because of the paucity of elite sources, and partly because their narratives demonstrate such consistency with the memoirs published after 1992 that they support strongly my claim of the homogeneity within the elite memory community.

The Right and Proper Order of Things—1880s to 1950s

A few years after the end of the civil war, a North American psychologist, Michael Gorkin, and a pair of Salvadoran colleagues tapped into elite notions of El Salvador's bygone golden age. They did so in interviews with members of three generations of one elite family as part of an oral history project.[15] Employing pseudonyms to protect their interviewees' identities, Gorkin and his colleagues name their elite family "Nuñez" and their three interview subjects "Niña Cecilia," "Monica," and "Paulina." The first interviewee, Niña Cecilia, was born in 1923 and grew up on a plantation in the western part of the country, near Sonsonate. Her grandfather, who had come to El Salvador from Spain sometime in the nineteenth century, had acquired the original family plantation. His property wasn't the largest in the region, but Niña Cecilia recalls that "we lived in this enormous house with all these corridors and many rooms." Niña Cecilia confesses that she knows little about the history of the land or how her grandfather came to own it. All she knows is that he was "some high army officer" and during her childhood he was good friends with President Martínez (1931–1944), who, she quickly points out, "was the one who crushed a Communist-run rebellion in the area in the '30s." Niña Cecilia describes growing up on the plantation in glowing terms: "Life was carefree, just perfect." She admits that her memories are those of a child, but she insists that "everything was wonderful! Life itself was like magic. As God is my judge, it was really like that." In her view, pristine nature merged harmoniously with economic production.

You'd wake up in the morning with the roosters and robins singing to you, and the cows mooing just outside in the corral where they'd be for the morning milking. I'd look out the window to see the whole world glistening. The nights were cool, so in the morning all would be covered with dew—coffee bushes, sugarcane and fruit trees. The scent of my mother's rose bushes, planted near my room, would waft through the window. And the peasants who gathered at dawn just outside the house would be waiting there for the *mandador* [work boss] to assign them their tasks for the day. Sowing, weeding, harvesting, depending on the season.

Although life on a working plantation is never easy and revolves around constant demands, Niña Cecilia notes that she "didn't have to work, cleaning my room or sweeping up or in the kitchen. We had *muchachas* [female domestic servants] who did all that." Niña Cecilia married the son of a neighboring landowner and they moved to a large house in San Salvador. Naturally, she had domestic help in her home just as she did growing up. One servant, Virginia, worked for Niña Cecilia for many years. When Niña Cecilia describes Virginia and the various other servants from her childhood, she contrasts their loyalty with her contemporary servants and says "you can't get muchachas like her, no more loyalty as in the old days." She expresses a similar sentiment when describing laborers on her family's rural properties. Her husband "Alberto" was not interested in running the properties, so Niña Cecilia administered them, claiming that she treated the workers justly. "We've always been fair," she claims, "We paid a fair wage before the war, and now—since the war the daily wage has been raised—we pay it too. If one of our workers needs medical attention or a loan to get some *maíz* or beans, we lend them what they need. We always have." That sense of fairness sets Niña Cecilia up to feel personally betrayed when the civil war comes and rural workers joined the insurgency.[16]

Monica is Niña Cecilia's daughter, and she expresses an even stronger sense of betrayal by disloyal laborers. Monica was born in 1950, and unlike her mother she grew up in the urban environs of San Salvador, but traveled to the family's plantations on weekends. She too married into a wealthy, landowning family, and her husband invested in coffee plantations early in their marriage, but that "was only a sideline for him, a kind of hobby," she points out. "Where he's really made out well is in this business [in San Salvador] he's been building all these years." Like her mother, Monica portrays the rural workers of the past in positive terms, as being loyal and properly deferential, when they had "no venom toward the landowner." She continues on to say, "Look, when I was growing up a peasant was a simple person, and content with being part of the *finca* [plantation]." She employs a family metaphor to describe the relationship between landowner and laborer. "The landowner was a like a father to them, a patron who would look after them." She admits that there might have been a little paternalism in the relationship, but it was tempered by the landowner's close "personal involvement" in the lives of the workers, which proved mutually beneficial. As she puts it, "There was this relationship—a good one, the way I see it—but now it's gone."[17]

Niña Cecilia and Monica do not talk in abstractions, but rather as members of landowning families who have had direct relationships with the people who work for them. They speak reverentially of the countryside, as a source of both wealth and serenity. Because of those sentiments, they are particularly poised to experience the sense of loss and betrayal that will come when laborers are no longer subservient, when the rising tide of social conflict turns the countryside into a war zone.

In his book *El Salvador: Who Speaks for the People?*, Dr. Mario Gómez Zimmerman offers a more abstract description of an ideal past, but an equally vigorous defense of its righteousness. Gómez is a wealthy dermatologist who was kidnapped and held for ransom by guerrillas at the beginning of the war. After being released by an army raid on the kidnappers' safe house, he took up exile in Miami. There he became disgruntled with what he describes as the "dishonest and slanderous way the war was being reported" by the liberal international media and leftist professors. In hopes of rectifying what he was hearing and reading, he decided to set the record straight by writing a more accurate version. That project took the form of *El Salvador: la otra cara de la guerra*, part personal memoir, part national history, that was first published in 1986, and then translated in 1989 as *El Salvador: Who Speaks for the People?*[18]

In *El Salvador* Gómez goes straight to the heart of one of the most contentious matters of the civil war, the nation's highly unequal distribution of wealth. Unlike some ideologically conservative authors who ignore the issue or claim that wealth is not as badly distributed as some claim, Gómez admits readily that it is: "Ownership of the land is concentrated in a few hands." He is aware that the left used that fact to rally support to their cause, but he sees the maldistribution of wealth as a natural consequence of some people working harder than others. "Nowhere are landowners more slandered than in El Salvador," he says, where some of them are portrayed as "pathetic, savage creatures . . . even though most of their holdings have been rightfully acquired." Gómez insists that the maldistribution of wealth in El Salvador occurred as a consequence of "natural selection operating through unrestricted trade." He looks back to El Salvador before the coffee era and describes it as wallowing in poverty. Not until the onset of the coffee era in the late nineteenth century could industrious entrepreneurs apply their natural talents and transform nature into a saleable commodity. Only then was wealth created and did poverty begin to subside. Gómez acknowledges that wealthy families "got richer, but the country prospered and the middle class began to flourish." The large capitalists, he insists, "made economic development possible and allowed the construction of roads, hospitals and innumerable public works that were of benefit to all." He summarizes that "this is according to capitalist philosophy and cannot be considered exploitation." Thus, the worst thing that anyone could do for El Salvador's prospects, according to Gómez, is take away the elites' wealth and hinder their ability to create more of it.[19]

Gómez admits that a few elites abused their workers, but they were the exception. Elites as a class cannot be blamed, he insists, nor should El Salvador's cherished system of free-market production be held responsible. Furthermore, most of the perpetrators of abuse were non-elite, smaller landowners who believed they had to exploit their workers to make a living. "It was not in their [elite] interest" to abuse workers, he claims. "It would have been too obvious coming from them." In fact, he says, laborers who were lucky enough to work for elite families enjoyed special privileges, like "simple but adequate housing with running drinkable water, electricity etc.; even private schools and hospitals in some cases." Whereas Goméz's nemeses, leftwing intellectuals, claim that landowners acquired their initial properties in the late nineteenth century through usurpation and graft, he insists they did so fairly, by buying and selling in a free market.[20]

Like Mario Gómez, Luis Escalante was also kidnapped and held for ransom by guerrillas, during which time he was badly injured, requiring him to go to the United States for recuperation after his release. The Escalante family is one of the most powerful and wealthy in the country. Luis was a banker, once head of the Banco Agrícola. Whereas Gómez uses his kidnapping episode as an entrée to a lengthy exposition on Salvadoran history, Escalante wrote *Sacrificios humanos* primarily to recount his own experience and to highlight the stories of more than one dozen other elites who had been kidnapped or assassinated by guerrillas.

In the midst of recounting those kidnapping stories, Escalante describes El Salvador's proper order before the war. He draws a parallel between the United States and El Salvador to explain the origin of wealth in his country. He claims that wealth was created in his country in the same manner as in the United States, through the efforts of private enterprise in a free market that came about as a result of "the vigor of imagination and initiative backed by hard work." For those who wish to discredit this process, like Marxist activists and intellectuals, Escalante says they need to realize that El Salvador's "progress and development is the consequence of a lot of tenacious work." Although he doesn't say it as explicitly as Gómez, Escalante claims that El Salvador's wealth was created in a free market in the late nineteenth century by those same families who were being targeted by leftwing guerrillas. When he describes the victims who were assassinated, Escalante imbues their story with dramatic flair by describing their deaths as a loss of national patrimony—the entrepreneurial energy and philanthropic spirit of the cherished sons of elite families.[21]

A romantic nationalism, a la Domingo Sarmiento, permeates the elite memoirists' descriptions of El Salvador's bygone era. In his canonical treatise *Facundo* (1845), Sarmiento situated Argentina's national identity in its unique natural environment and its distinct people. He provided lengthy descriptions of Argentina's boundless pampas, towering mountains, and endless blue skies. Similarly, he celebrated the hunting and tracking capabilities of the gaucho plainsmen, inveigling his readers to honor their memory, even as he ordered their extermination in the name of civilization.[22] Salvadoran elites do much the same when describing the coffee era of the late nineteenth and early twentieth centuries. Niña Cecilia and Monica, in Gorkin's *From Grandmother to Granddaughter*, celebrate the unique flora and fauna of the Salvadoran countryside, as well as its hardworking and loyal laborers. For his part, Gómez Zimmerman doesn't concern himself too much with the natural landscape, but on repeated occasions he defines Salvadorans as a distinct people who possess a special capacity for industriousness and individualism.[23]

Ricardo Valdivieso also invokes a romantic nationalism. He is a wealthy landowner who was born in 1941 to a Salvadoran father and a North American mother of Italian descent from New York City. His father owned land in El Salvador, but he was not particularly productive. Both Ricardo and his younger brother were born and raised in the United States, which accounts for him speaking Spanish with a North American accent and his nickname "El Gringo." He was drafted into the U.S. military in the early 1960s and served in Germany before returning to El Salvador for good in 1965 to devote himself to turning his father's properties into productive enterprises. In the 1970s, Valdivieso became active in conservative political circles, and after establishing a close relationship with Roberto D'Aubuisson, he became a founding member of the ARENA party. He published his memoir *Cruzando El Imposible: una saga* in 2007.

As the title to his memoir implies, Valdivieso centers his narrative around El Imposible, a forest reserve in El Salvador's far western department of Ahuachapán. When Valdivieso was a teenager, his father worried that he was losing touch with his Salvadoran roots, so he brought him to El Salvador to trek across El Imposible. As Valdivieso describes it, his father put a .22-caliber rifle into his hands, said "don't chicken out boy," and they set off into the wilds. The year, 1954, was an appropriate moment for a future conservative to find his national identity, because Salvadoran elites harbor so much nostalgia for the 1950s. Valdivieso became enraptured with El Imposible, and he waxes poetic about its distinct flora and fauna and its primitive beauty. A comet was visible each night of their trek, like a traveling companion, and Valdivieso imagined that it was "revealing the origins of the universe." The trek ended on the beaches of the Pacific Ocean. Since the coastal highway had not yet been built, no other people were around, causing Valdivieso to feel "as if those beaches had been waiting for a thousand years for our visit." Throughout all of his descriptions of El Imposible, Valdivieso employs a classically romantic nationalist discourse, in which El Salvador was a "paradise" existing in a state of "perfect harmony." He considers El Imposible to be home to El Salvador's primordial soul, and he says he discovered his own Salvadoran identity there. He reiterates this theme in describing a return trip to El Salvador in 1964 to size up his father's properties. While walking around one of the properties he stumbled across a pre-Hispanic artifact that he interpreted as a message to him from El Salvador's ancient inhabitants.[24]

Valdivieso returned to El Salvador permanently in 1965 to transform his father's lands into productive economic enterprises. He describes the work as arduous, but ultimately rewarding, just like traversing El Imposible. Because the properties were located in an isolated region (coincidentally near El Imposible), he had to live there most of the time without the creature comforts of more established landowners who lived in the cities.

Like Mario Gómez, Valdivieso situates his story within a broad rendition of Western philosophy that hails the Enlightenment and individualism. He channels a Sarmiento-like rejection of Spain and appeals to Anglo America as the font of modern values. But in a distinctly twenty-first century update, Valdivieso celebrates racial mixing, or *mestizaje*, for creating the distinctive Salvadoran racial type, "the third race, the Salvadoran," which he then uses to promote ARENA's populist nationalism.[25]

Valdivieso's contribution to the elite narrative is somewhat distinct in that his timeframe begins later, in the 1950s, rather than in the late nineteenth century. Nevertheless, his memoir makes a paradigmatic contribution to the civilian elite narrative by establishing the original status quo, an ideal era when a hardworking man driven by individual desire could make a decent living and raise a family because of El Salvador's free-market economy. When that social order came under attack, as we are about to see, Valdivieso was one of the first to head for the barricades.

Because elites are so insistent that their wealth was derived justly through hard work, almost every one of them claims that either they personally or someone in their family started with nothing and ascended the ladder of success. They reason that if they or their family members could do it, then anyone could, and thus El Salvador's liberal era is the ideal model for national development. A paradigmatic example is provided by the airline magnate Roberto Kriete, who summarized his life story in a brief narrative published as part of a book celebrating the lives of "one hundred successful Salvadorans." His father made the initial fortune in agriculture, and he describes his father's initial property, the Hacienda La Carrera, as "frontier land where there was nothing, just jungle." But he says his father worked at it steadily and built the roads and infrastructure necessary to turn it into "one of the most productive properties in all of Central America." Kriete is then quick to point out that the property was confiscated during the 1979 agrarian reform, which frames his appeal to economic libertarianism, "Nothing comes easy. . . . And that is how capital is created in the world, only through confidence and hard work."[26]

The memoirs by Guillermo Sol Bang and José Ramon Barahona advance the elite narrative in a manner akin to Valdivieso and Kriete, even though they have divergent social origins. Barahona is from a poor family in El Salvador but he migrated to the United States in the late 1960s and made a fortune as a business owner. Sol Bang was born into one of the wealthier families in El Salvador. Both men shared their personal stories in a series of interviews with the journalist Marvin Galeas, who then edited the narratives and oversaw their publication as books. Galeas wrote introductions to each work to guide readers to the appropriately conservative lesson: that success comes from hard work and that elites have the nation's best interest at heart.[27]

It would seem difficult for Barahona's memoir to contribute to the conservative trope of the elite memory community because of his humble origins. He grew up in abject poverty in the 1940s and 1950s and had to leave El Salvador in search of a better life. But his descriptions of his youth and the landscape around the Lempa River where he grew up are infused with such positive nostalgia that they embody the romantic nationalism at the core of elite narratives—a healthy and holistic society, regardless of economic inequality. In particular, Barahona speaks about the values he was taught as a child, crediting his parents and his teachers with placing great emphasis on inculcating good behavior: "She [his teacher] taught us never to use bad words, to love our country, and to respect our elders, who we always greeted and asked for their blessing." He laments that such values and their corresponding deference for authority have been lost: "What is certain is that back then students in general treated their teachers, parents and adults with more respect." He also uses the occasion of a rare trip to the capital city of San Salvador to celebrate the era of his youth, contrasting the capital's chaos and filth of today with its cleanliness and order back then. "In those days," he says, "riding a city bus was a healthy and entertaining pastime."[28]

Barahona's description of the social inequity of his youth lacks malice. The rich are not exploiters, but rather good people who worked hard to create a better life for themselves and provide jobs for people like him. He claims that the values of his upbringing paid off when he began working for wealthy families as a boy. Even though he was hired as a laborer to do menial jobs, he demonstrated diligence and a work ethic from his upbringing that allowed him to stand out to his employers, who then rewarded him with special privileges and better jobs. These privileges in turn instilled in him a personal confidence and a vision for self-improvement that served him throughout his life. Consequently, Barahona expresses gratitude to those wealthy families for what they gave him, and while he doesn't directly disparage the poor children who grew up around him for failing to make the same connections he did, he takes a swipe at laziness by criticizing contemporary Salvadorans who won't work in the fields because they would rather sit around and "wait for the money that their families send them" as remittances from the United States. The moral of Barahona's message is clear, and he states it explicitly in case anyone is missing the point: "Poverty isn't something to be ashamed of, but rather, it's an incentive to improve one's self. I know it can be done. . . . My life proves it." Despite his poverty and his migration out of El Salvador, he reinforces the conservative narrative by celebrating a social order that allowed for personal growth and that would eventually come under attack by leftist guerrillas.[29]

Compared to Barahona, Sol Bang was born into affluence, owing to vast wealth on his mother's side of the family. But he is quick to point out his father was born into poverty and worked and saved diligently to purchase a mediocre property near Zacatecoluca. Under Sol Bang's and his brother's stewardship, that property became "El Nilo," one of the most productive rice plantations in all of Central America. Sol Bang advances the conservative narrative by celebrating his father's status as a self-made man, his own hard work on "El Nilo," and the libertarian economic environment of El Salvador that allowed their entrepreneurial skills to produce results. "That is how the free market works," he says. "The client is the final determinant of the producer's success or failure."[30]

Like Valdivieso, Sol Bang's encounter with El Salvador's natural environment as a boy evokes a romantic nationalism that frames his narrative. Sol Bang's boyhood environment was located a few miles down the coast from Valdivieso's, in the central coastal plain, which has since been developed into agricultural properties, beach homes, and tourist hotels. At that time it was still an undeveloped forest full of wildlife and adventure for a young boy. In Sol Bang's words, it was "a true paradise," which he would later describe as "the promised land" while flying over it in a plane. Typical of the civilian elite narrative, neither Sol Bang nor Valdivieso has a problem with paradoxically locating El Salvador's national soul in its undeveloped natural environment while simultaneously destroying that environment in pursuit of capital-producing agricultural development. Like Sarmiento honoring the gauchos while destroying them, elite narratives in El Salvador draw upon the memory of El Salvador's primordial nature while celebrating its transformation into ordered units of economic production.[31]

The Narrative within the Narrative: 1932

It is within the context of explaining the left's ability to establish itself in El Salvador in the 1970s that the elite memoirists draw lessons from the 1932 uprising. As far as they are concerned, what happened in the 1970s and 1980s was a repeat of 1932; an idealized social order was threatened by communist subversion and elite society fought back to restore the proper order. In this regard, the story of 1932 functions as a mini narrative in the broader narrative of twentieth-century El Salvador: the original status quo is the period from the early 1880s to 1932; the crisis is the uprising; the resolution is the defeat of the insurrection; and the denouement is the establishment of a new status quo in the 1940s and 1950s.[32]

Some elites who explained the causes of the 1932 uprising at the time turned to well-honed racial and class stereotypes. They argued that rural, poor Salvadorans, and especially indigenous Salvadorans, were congenitally flawed and contradictory to the elites' civilizing mission. As one of the more notorious and oft-cited examples from 1932, a landowner from Santa Ana editorialized that "they did well in North America to shoot them; by shooting them first, before they impeded the development and progress of that nation; first they killed the Indians because the Indians will never have good sentiments toward anything. We here have been treating them as family, with every consideration and now you have seen them in action! They have ferocious instincts."[33]

The elite memoirists find such arguments to have limited value. After all, dead peasants do not make good workers, and defining them as degenerate runs contrary to nationalist populism, wherein the countryside is a source of harmony and its poor inhabitants embody the Salvadoran virtues of industriousness and individualism.

Reynaldo Galindo Pohl (1918–2012) was the patriarch of a wealthy family from Sonsonate in western El Salvador, who wrote a memoir about his childhood that had the events of 1932 as the climactic pinnacle, evidenced by the title, *Recuerdos de Sonsonate: crónica del 32 [Memories of Sonsonate: A Chronicle of '32]*. Perhaps not coincidentally, he too was victimized by a guerrilla kidnapping; his nephew Mauricio Borgonovo Pohl was abducted and assassinated by the FPL in 1977. In his memoir, he makes it clear that he believes 1932 offers lessons for the 1980s.

The importance of this work is the fact that the region of Sonsonate charted the course of Salvadoran history for many decades in the nation's life, and the events of 1932 are a central part of that. Thus, it would be useful to locate the precise links between 1932 and the civil war of the 1980s.[34]

Galindo provides overwhelmingly positive descriptions of his home region of Sonsonate. He evokes a sort of romantic nationalism about Sonsonate, in which the region is presented as distinct and worthy of celebration. The 1932 uprising represents an unraveling of Galindo's harmonious social order, and he is hard pressed to explain how such a catastrophe could happen in the midst of holistic tranquility. He resolves this problem in the same way that other elite memoirists explain the origins of the insurrection in the 1970s and 1980s, by blaming the rebellion on outsiders, namely communist agitators from San Salvador who came to the western region and took advantage of the peasants' naïvety.

Galindo's description of 1932 contains another trope that predicts the 1970s and 1980s: a reformist government that was too soft on communism. As Galindo points out, the two governments of Pío Romero Bosque (1927–1931) and Arturo Araujo (March 1931–December 1931) tolerated mass mobilization and even allowed the Communist Party to participate in elections. Supposedly Romero and Araujo believed that such moves would forestall the advance of communism, but instead they erroneously fueled the communists by giving them an exploitable opening. The only plotline that is missing from Galindo's description that would have made his explanation of 1932 a complete metaphor for the 1970s and 1980s was a traitorous military that sided with the reformists instead of the elites. He says the military did its job correctly by putting down the rebellion quickly and decisively.

Luis Escalante's rendition of 1932 is more bombastic than Galindo's, but it makes the same point. He describes the uprising as an attempt by communist activists to transform El Salvador into a Marxist regime by way of an "unbridled subversion" that resulted in a "bloody human vortex." He celebrates the military's defeat of the insurrection, and somewhat laments the high cost in lives, which is actually atypical of most elite portrayals of the events, but he insists that the loss of life was necessary to preserve the nation. He follows the standard timeframe of the elite memory community by then celebrating the years after the uprising, and especially the 1950s, as an era of "order" and "progress," notably absent of class warfare.[35]

Like Escalante, Mario Gómez situates his description of the 1970s and 1980s in an analysis of the 1932 uprising, "an important point in our history." He first sets up the foil against which he will work, a leftist North American professor who argues that the uprising "started because the rich would not let the poor prosper." Gómez rejects that argument as standard leftwing rhetoric, saying that "the poor were poor because the country was [still] poor." Instead, the insurrection was caused by conspiratorial communist agitators who "misled" peasants and used them for "evil purposes." In what would prove to be an extension of his description of his own kidnapping, Gómez mentions the various horrors and abuses committed by the communists against "the lives, honor and property of innocent people." Fortunately, the "army's prompt actions prevented further outrages." In a rather obvious defense of the army's repression, he says that "if a horde of one thousand vandals assassinates one hundred honest people, when this horde is put down its dead may number one thousand." To that end, he insists, "we may not, therefore, say that the one who killed more of its rivals is guilty of a massacre." In short, the army did what it had to do and its actions were justified. With the uprising put down, El Salvador could return to an order in which entrepreneurs could pursue wealth in an unfettered marketplace—at least for a while. Therein, the narrative is set: a new status quo in the 1940s and 1950s; crisis in the 1970s and 1980s; hopeful resolution in the defeat of the rebels; and new status quo with the return of a free-market economy after 1992.[36]

The Crisis: 1960s to 1980s

The elite memoirists believe their ideal world of market-based accumulation was threatened by multiple and diverse enemies. Primary among them, of course, was communism. The memoirists define communism as an alien and flawed ideology; alien because it originated abroad, and flawed because it contradicted at least two natural laws, the law of supply and demand, and the law of human beings as competitive and individualistic. Thus, communist ideology could only produce authoritarianism and totalitarianism. Communism empowers the state, which in turn empowers state managers, who inevitably abuse their authority by seizing the hard-earned wealth of private citizens.

The elite memoirists recognize that the most immediate variant of communism was the militant guerrilla organizations inside El Salvador. In describing the leftist insurgency that emerged in the 1970s, they are faced with the challenge of explaining how communism came to exist in El Salvador in the first place, given that they emphasize the righteousness and justness of the social order prior to the 1960s. They find the explanation in their descriptions of the 1932 uprising—crafty communists stirring up trouble among the humble masses.

Maria D'Aubuisson Arrieta, Roberto D'Aubuisson's sister, describes the stories she heard in her home as a child about communists in 1932.

> Communists cut off the heads of businessmen. . . . They entered people's homes and raped all the women. I remember hearing these stories when I was young and being very afraid, not knowing that communists were people. I always had the image in my head that communists were like Martians or extraterrestrials, and I envisioned them to be very short, with small, beady red eyes and tails.[37]

She insists that these types of descriptions helped give rise to her brother's militant anticommunism.

When the social crisis of the 1970s spiraled toward civil war, some conservative spokespersons invoked extremist rhetoric by calling for a 1932-like solution to "save El Salvador from this tidal wave of evil," as well-known conservative columnist Sidney Mazzini put it in 1977.[38] But just as in the 1930s, elites found that portraying workers as congenitally flawed undermines their nationalistic political projects. Mario Gómez Zimmerman demonstrates his awareness of this problem when he rejects the claim that ARENA is a party of the elites and insists that it is "constituted mostly by workers and campesinos who value work and individual effort." Similarly, the memoirist and former coffee grower David Panamá insists that ARENA "was born of the people, for the people."[39] To account for the renaissance of communism in their country in the 1970s and 1980s, elite memoirists turn to alternative explanations. Echoing modernization theory, they cast communism as a virus that enters the national body and makes it sick. In the words of Ricardo Valdivieso, communism operated according to a "parasitic code," and Marvin Galeas, the one-time guerrilla turned conservative spokesperson, called Marxism-Leninism "an inherently malignant doctrine that contradicts human nature."[40] The external version of these viral agents was foreign governments, like Russia, Cuba, Vietnam, and Nicaragua. According to the memoirists, they were leading an international conspiracy to take over the world and they chose to target El Salvador in the 1970s and 1980s. The memoirists are not so foolish as to assume that Russians, Cubans, or any other foreign

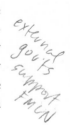

nationals were physically in El Salvador fighting against them, but they claim that those powers provided the Salvadoran communists with the necessary financial and logistical support to wage war. Guillermo Sol Bang says that the guerrillas were losing the war from the start, but they could keep fighting because of "the tons of arms and ammunition coming into the country clandestinely from Cuba by way of Nicaragua, which prolonged the war by many years." And Mario Gómez surmises that "they [the guerrillas] have great power because they have unconditional support from Cuba, Nicaragua, and, as a last resort, the Soviet Union."[41]

As part of their effort to blame foreign communists for the conflict at home, the elite memoirists sometimes avoid the term "civil war" and insist that the conflict was a war of foreign aggression. David Panamá says that "the Cuban and Nicaragua complicity with the Salvadoran terrorists . . . invalidated the claims being made by many press agencies and non-governmental organizations that tried to make the world believe that what we were experiencing in El Salvador was a civil war."[42] In a description of one of his lobbying trips to the United States in the early 1980s, Valdivieso says he portrayed the conflict as "a war of aggression, not an internal revolution." He also resents his fellow leaders in ARENA who "time and again repeat the disgraceful words that here in this country of ours we fought a civil war," which, he says, was "exactly the idea that our enemies had been trying to pass off as the truth."[43]

By focusing attention on international actors, the elite memoirists try to counter critics who hold them responsible for the war. They also stay true to the exigencies of the Cold War, which had them trying to convince U.S. policy-makers that the situation in El Salvador merited ongoing U.S. aid because the country was being targeted as a staging ground by the Soviet Union. In fact, many of the elite memoirists, including Sol Bang, de Sola, and Valdivieso, traveled to the United States during the war to lobby policy-makers about Soviet, Cuban, and Nicaraguan designs on El Salvador.

They and other elites may have been sincere in their belief about the threat to El Salvador from foreign communists, but ultimately all of them knew that their war was a local affair and that their most immediate threat was homegrown radicals, or, as they called them, "comunistas criollos." El Salvador is a small country and many of the elites knew some of their leftist adversaries personally, having grown up with them or gone to school with them. In trying to explain the comunistas criollos' willingness to embrace radicalism, the elite memoirists reveal their own, most basic interpretation of communism—that it is pathological and thus only flawed people can consciously choose to embrace it. The elite memoirists define communists as frustrated, resentful people who failed to accomplish much in their lives and thus resorted to revolution, or, in other words to ideologically sanctioned theft of rich people's hard-earned money. As Marvin Galeas once put it, the ideal recruit to the communist cause was someone with "a tormented and resentful soul." He later called people who subscribe to the statist solutions of socialism to be "mediocre men" who "always want someone else to solve their problems for them" rather than solve them "with hard work and creativity."[44] Mario Gómez describes communists simply as "social malcontents or good-for-nothings, people of ill-will."[45]

The elite memoirists insist that the most important factor motivating communists is their compulsive quest for power. "Communists seek absolute power," says Panamá.[46] The people who embraced communism in the 1970s and 1980s had been unable to obtain power or status through the extant structures of society at the time, so they resorted to revolutionary-inspired terrorism and violence. Their goal was to destabilize society to create an opening that they could use to seize power. Their models were Russia in 1917, Cuba in 1959, and Nicaragua in 1979. Mario Gómez says that the guerrillas "want the people to become hungry and desperate, and turn to vandalism, which would suit the guerrillas' purposes nicely."[47] David Panamá claims that communists would readily do things like kill 100,000 people simply to "combat a high birthrate among the population."[48]

The elite memoirists insist that the communists hid their true goals behind the veils of social justice and bettering the lives of the poor, which is what allowed them to make organizational inroads among the humble and naïve people of the countryside. "The guerrillas brought everything down for the benefit of the people," muses Gómez sarcastically.[49] Michael Gorkin's informant, Monica Núñez, says that guerrilla leaders who had studied in Russia and Cuba poisoned peasants' minds with propaganda, causing "peasants who had never thought in terms of taking their owners' land began to feel, 'Yes, that's right, the landowner is the enemy.'"[50]

The elite memoirists insist that communists were driven by sinister and selfish motives, primarily the desire to create an authoritarian dictatorship that would allow them to steal rich people's wealth for themselves. In the words of Valdivieso, communism is based on "the pretext of taking wealth, not creating it, which is nothing more than a philosophy of thieves, who, unable to create wealth . . . capture the hearts and minds of the population with jargonistic phrases uttered by their monstrous mouthpieces who lay claim to bettering society."[51] Gorkin's elite interlocutor Niña Cecilia echoes Valdivieso's sentiments, saying that "the war . . . came about through the selfish interests of the Communist leaders." She went on to accuse them of using "the peasants' hardships as a means of improving their own lives. . . . They were poor before the war and now own mansions in San Salvador and have money hidden away in Swiss banks."[52] One of the important consequences of these narrative frameworks is that the working poor can still be saved, even if they have temporarily fallen prey to the communist leaders' machinations. They can still be portrayed as a hardworking, humble people, and therein as a source of Salvadoran national identity. They have to be cast as naïve and simplistic, but honest in their failure to understand what the communist leaders are actually trying to achieve by trying to incite them to revolutionary violence.

Even though the elite memoirists consider communists to be mediocre people, they see them as dangerous because of their relentless and unbridled quest for power. While the good people of El Salvador, "the silent majority," as Gómez calls them, went about their daily routine and stayed home at night, communists busied themselves by sowing the seeds of destruction. Gómez compares them to "ants" whose work was "mostly invisible." They portray the standard communist organizational strategy as looking for ways to take advantage of openings or weaknesses in the existing social structure. In the 1980s an early ARENA activist, Mario Redaelli, told Craig Peyes, a journalist for the *Albuquerque Journal*, that he felt El Salvador's moral compass slipping away in the 1960s because of changes to the school curriculum, and "that's one of the ways communists infiltrate society."[53] Mario Gómez uses his experience at the National University in the 1960s to make a similar claim. While he and his fellow "democratic" students were innocently concentrating on their schoolwork, communists "were already hard at work taking over the University without much public awareness, and the first step was to capture the positions of leadership." He says they gained control over most of the student organizations and then used them to radicalize the student body and destabilize society. He describes the actions of the university communists as typical, in that they "do not need to hold a majority in order to manipulate a group. They scheme and maneuver to infiltrate key positions, and the rest takes care of itself when the conditions are right." He goes on to say that "they are skillful and manage to appear as genuine defenders of the group's interests, whatever their real political objectives may be." For these reasons, the elite memoirists express their view that organizations geared toward mass mobilization were really communist fronts, probably without the knowledge of its naïve members. As Gómez puts it, "Marxists are known for using respectable people and organizations to front for them while they pursue their goals. They go unnoticed while they work."[54] Maria Luisa D'Aubuisson Arrieta says in her interview that her brother Roberto D'Aubuisson "always told me that I was foolishly being used by the Communists."[55]

The classic example of a respectable but naïve person who elite memoirists believe was duped by communists is none other than Archbishop Oscar Romero. A common trope among the memoirists is that Romero unknowingly allowed himself to be manipulated by guerrillas and especially by the Jesuits of the Central American University (UCA). Romero supposedly allowed them to push him from a traditional Catholicism to liberation theology and ultimately to guerrilla militancy. The archbishop's brother, Gaspar Romero, comments on those claims in a 2006 interview, saying that they continue to bother him, because the idea that "he [Oscar Romero] was a communist who supported the guerrillas" is totally inaccurate.[56] As one example of these accusations, Mario Gómez claims "it was absolutely clear to everyone in El Salvador that Monsignor supported the guerrillas."[57]

The Traitors—Military Officers and the United States

The elite memoirists naturally hate militant guerrillas and consider them to have been the most immediate threat to their lives and livelihoods in the 1970s and 1980s. But guerrillas were hardly the lone threat they faced. The memoirists believe they were also threatened by the Salvadoran army and the U.S. government. They think that policy-makers in the United States and officers in the Salvadoran army accused them of abusing their workers and making the ground fertile for the spread of communism.

The memoirists use terms like "traitorous" and "treason" to describe military officers who supported economic reforms, especially after 1979. Luis Escalante Arce says the problems began in the 1960s, when the reigning military governments of Julio Romero and Fidel Sánchez Hernández built a close alliance with the U.S. government and international development experts, and began meddling in the economy. In Escalante's assessment, those governments "forgot their obligation to protect free enterprise" and began to "become absorbed by the socialistic and statist thinking that prevailed in most countries in the world at the time." Their actions, he says, "fomented class hatred."[58] Guillermo Sol Bang shares Escalante's skepticism of government in the 1960s, claiming that when his rice plantation, El Nilo, was at the height of its productive capability, when he and his brother were looking for wider markets throughout Central America, the Sánchez Hernández government banned rice exports, thereby destroying their ability to expand. Sol Bang claims that he and his brother responded by taking the drastic measure of abandoning rice production and converting El Nilo to cattle rather than accede to the government's demands. As a way to highlight his disregard for Sánchez Hernández and other interventionist military presidents, Sol Bang says they failed to live up to the example of the first military president, General Martínez, who he says enacted market-friendly economic reforms.[59]

Mario Gómez goes so far as to suggest that the military presidents in the 1970s were in league with communists. He points out that Sánchez Hernández and his successor Arturo Armando Molina (1972–1977) "are considered by some to be Communists or in close contact with Communists" because they wanted to dismantle the existing structures of society "beginning with free enterprise."[60] By any standard of measure, it is surprising to see the notoriously anticommunist military leaders of El Salvador being accused of communism, but according to the narrative of the civilian elite memory community, such accusations are merited. Echoing Gómez's sentiments, David Panamá says the Romero government (1962–1967) was responsible for the 1965 bombing of the offices of the daily newspaper *El Diario de Hoy* in order to silence its conservative voice. He also criticizes President Sánchez Hernández for allowing a known leftist, Dr. Fabio Castillo, to head the National University and turn it into a den of communist organizing.[61] Similarly, Gorkin's wealthy matriarch in *From Grandmother to Granddaughter*, Monica Núñez, says that "the toughest time for us during the war was not something the guerrillas did to us. It was something a *militar* [military officer] did." She claims he tried to extort wealth by forcing her husband to take him on as a business partner. Monica claims that the only way she and husband resolved the problem was to call upon wealthy friends to pressure the government to get the officer to back down. She sums up the experience by saying that she shook for weeks afterward, thinking that "we were going to wind up shot in our house, or in the street—just like so many others in this war."[62]

Valdivieso locates his criticism of the military governments in the 1950 constitution, which had been installed by the so-called revolutionary officers who came to power in the coup of 1948. The constitution empowered the state to expropriate private property in the name of social justice, although neither of the two military presidents at the time, Oscar Osorio and José María Lemus, acted on that power. Valdivieso sees the constitution as a terrible precedent that set the stage for the crippling reforms after 1979. In his opinion, the 1950 charter "destroyed the classic concept of the natural right to own property," and he goes on to say that it is "something incredible at first glance, a legislative body in a free and sovereign state lending itself to something so treasonous and low."[63]

Mario Gómez also refers to the 1950s, saying that President Osorio "started an era of large-scale corruption, [and] little by little [the army] turned against the oligarchs: and certain graduating classes, or rather, some of their members set out to grab complete political power for themselves." He goes on to say that the unity that defined conservatism in El Salvador, between the rich, the army, the church hierarchy, and the U.S. embassy, was first broken by "friction between the civilians and the military."[64]

Elite memoirists believe overall that the military did not share their core values—laissez-faire capitalism and the sanctity of private property. Military leaders may have identified with capitalism, and elites recognize that the army was the nation's frontline of defense against insurgency, but they believe that the army's main concern was its own survival and the career prospects of its ranking officers. As Mario Gómez summarizes the situation, "the military fought mostly for their survival, not to defend the interests of the rich."[65]

1979: The Great Betrayal

No events inspire more criticism by elite memoirists than the 1979 coup and the subsequent economic reforms. The coup brought together an amalgamation of actors that invokes elites' ire, including reformist military officers, the Christian Democrats, the United States under President Carter and his human rights-based foreign policy, the Jesuits at UCA, and various reformist organizations throughout El Salvador. The elite memoirists unleash some of their most vitriolic language when describing those actors and the policies they pursued after 1979.[66] David Panamá calls U.S. foreign policy-makers under Carter a bunch of "inept, deluded idiots."[67] Valdivieso borrows from 1950s-style McCarthyism to say that the U.S. State Department was infested with communists and that in the late 1970s and early 1980s Washington D.C. "was the beachhead for the entire Western hemisphere for Soviet-inspired Marxist-Leninist imperialism." He goes on to say that it is "curious that during all that time of the cold war, North Americans never perceived that the enemy was inside the bowels of their own state."[68] Monica Nuñez in Gorkin's *Grandmother to Granddaughter* blames the U.S. government for the war, saying that "the Americans were the ones who really stirred things up here." President Carter, she insists, figured that land reform "was the way to head off a revolution here. But in the end the land reform laws he and his advisers pushed on us led to our civil war. We paid for Carter's experiments. We were his guinea pigs."[69] And according to Luis Escalante Arce, the 1979 coup "highlighted a long period of corruption and decadence in El Salvador." He says the subsequent reforms were inspired by "the vigorous ideological influence of Cuban sovietism," and that the two army officers who sat on the junta were "revolutionary statists who obeyed the orders of a foreign ambassador [the United States] and certain Jesuit priests who guided them toward Marxism."[70]

Escalante's description implicitly compares the land reform to an act of sexual assault, and he uses it as a metaphor to describe what elites felt when their properties were expropriated. He refers multiple times to the defenseless, virgin-like "rustic properties" that were surrounded and seized by armed troops, while the helpless landowners "had to resign themselves to state tyranny."[71] Mario Gómez uses the analogy of enslavement to describe elites' experience as they watched the "fruits of honest labor" being taken from them.[72]

President Reagan is usually portrayed as an ally of elite Salvadorans for his militant anticommunism and his emphatic distancing from the human rights policies of his predecessor. But even he receives derision from elite memoirists for being too soft on communism. Among his faults, according to the elite memoirists, was that he continued to link military aid to human rights, refused to allow D'Aubuisson to become president in 1982 and 1984, and let the State Department be staffed by inept bureaucrats whose strategy in El Salvador was to install a "leftist" government under the auspices of the Christian Democratic Party.[73] For example, Gómez Zimmerman says he supported Reagan at first because "at the time he seemed intent on moving heaven and earth if necessary for the triumph of the democratic-capitalist ideal," but he changed his mind when Reagan's priorities shifted "to a lukewarm policy of containment of the Communist onslaught."[74]

Another irritant for elite memoirists is human rights. They despise the concept, or at least the way they perceive it to have been applied in El Salvador. They claim that human rights monitors, regardless of whether they were from the Unites States, the United Nations, or some nongovernmental organization, were looking to blame elites for every cadaver that showed up, all the while ignoring the kidnappings and assassinations being perpetrated by leftist terrorists. This sense of discrimination fuels the elite memoirists' belief that they were an isolated minority being subjected to a multidimensional assault. It explains Luis Escalante's choice of the title for his memoir, *Sacrificios humanos contra derechos humanos* [*Human Sacrifice versus Human Rights*], a cynical reference to his attempt to correct the leftist "contamination of the concept of Human Rights," because "truth is the best medicine, both for those who speak it and those who hear it."[75] As far as he and other elite memoirists are concerned, the concept of human rights was little more than a way for international socialists to hinder Salvadoran conservatives' ability to fight the enemy. Naturally, elite memoirists criticize President Carter, because his emphasis on human rights handed Nicaragua over to the communists and very nearly caused the same to happen in El Salvador. "The foreign policy of the U.S. government," writes Sol Bang, "was based on a supposed defense of human rights, which leftists throughout the world avidly supported as a way to advance their cause."[76] And echoing Valdivieso's McCarthyist theme, Luís Escalante insists that the United States' human rights policies were being directed by an "infiltration of socialists in the State Department."[77]

Nothing highlights the assault on elite interests more than attacks on them personally, which probably explains why a disproportionate number of elite memoirists were kidnap victims. Apparently, the experience of being kidnapped and/or of having a family member or friend kidnapped provides much of the motivation for elites to break their customary silence and tell their personal histories. Memoirists who are kidnap victims include Guillermo Sol Bang, Luis Escalante, and Mario Zimmerman. Mario Acosta Oertel was not kidnapped but refers to various assassination attempts on his life.[78] Galindo Pohl lost his nephew, Mauricio Borgonovo Pohl, to abduction and assassination, and Orlando de Sola had an uncle kidnapped. Even those elites whose families were not directly affected by abduction make ubiquitous references to other elite families' experiences.

Paulina, the third generation of the elite Nuñez family in Gorkin's *From Grandmother to Granddaughter*, who was fifteen years old at the time of her interview, describes the fear she felt during the war when one of her classmates at the British School was kidnapped and held for one year before being released.[79] Needless to say, when it was revealed in 1986 that some of the kidnappers were gangs of soldiers posing as guerrillas, elite-military relations degraded even further.[80]

Elite sentiments about the reforms after 1979 are so strong that they have produced a rift within conservative circles between resisters and "collaborators." Orlando de Sola says he resisted, and he contrasts his actions to the collaborationism of the first ARENA president, Alfredo Cristiani (1989–1994). De Sola describes himself as an *"agrarista,"* or coffee grower, and Cristiani as a *"beneficiador-exportador,"* or processor and exporter. Even though he has known Cristiani since childhood and their families are close, he says he opposed Cristiani's ascent within ARENA because of his response to the reforms implemented after 1979. De Sola had two properties expropriated during the land reform and he accuses Cristiani of "sacrificing the growers" and making money at their expense, because while landowners were losing land to the agrarian reform, Cristiani in his role as president of the coffee producers' association, the Asociación Salvadoreña de Beneficiadores y Exportadores de Café (ABECAFE), sold coffee to the government's new export-control board "instead of opposing it." De Sola even criticizes ARENA's founder, Robert D'Aubuisson, for being too soft on the reforms, saying that "one of the differences I had with D'Aubuisson was over the issue of agrarian reform, because I said it was a horrible thing, but he refused to say that." De Sola claims that he had a falling out with D'Aubuisson and ARENA over these issues, and especially after D'Aubuisson picked Cristiani to head ARENA after his failed presidential bid in 1984. De Sola claims that the rise of people like Cristiani sold ARENA out to the "neoliberals" as opposed to "classic liberals" like himself.[81]

David Panamá shares de Sola's sentiments, criticizing ARENA's leadership after it came under the control of people like Cristiani. He too holds Cristiani in contempt for selling coffee to the government after 1979, insisting that he tried to dissuade him at the time. Panamá claims that as a result of his opposition to the likes of Cristiani, he was marginalized within ARENA, even though he had been one of the party's founders. The new leaders, he insists, took the party in an erroneous direction, away from its core nationalist populism, and turned it into what de Sola decries as "a neomercantilist party."[82] Unlike de Sola, Panamá withholds criticism of D'Aubuisson, choosing instead to hail him as a visionary and a hero. But as a way of distinguishing himself from the new leadership of ARENA, both he and de Sola employ a rhetoric that is hardly distinguishable from their leftist enemies. Panamá repeatedly criticizes the "big oligarchic capitalists" and the "businessmen" who initially opposed ARENA, and who pursued their own selfish interests, wanting to keep El Salvador as a land of "privileges, monopolies and cronyism."[83] For his part, de Sola says that El Salvador has become a land where "a monopoly exists over public opinion that has endeavored to install a mercantilist, privileged system."[84]

Skeptical readers will certainly see plenty of reasons to view these populist-sounding claims by de Sola and Panamá as pure rhetoric, motivated by any number of self-serving factors, such as the desire to distance themselves from accusations of death squad activities, or to settle political scores with the new elites who have done better financially in the postwar economy than they have. The skeptics might be right. Nevertheless, the rhetoric being emitted by de Sola and Panamá highlights the degree to which the reforms of 1979 serve as fodder for the conservative narrative, even to the point of allowing some elite memoirists to accuse their brethren in ARENA of collaborating with the reformist enemy.

The Defense

In the face of numerous and overwhelming threats to their lives and livelihoods, elite memoirists believe that a military response was necessary. They all share de Sola's insistence that the civil war was an act of self-defense, because the left attacked them first and therefore they were justified to respond. Mario Gómez sums up that view when he says that "nobody ever won a war by running away from it."[85] In light of this view, one would assume that elite memoirists would hail the military for defending them over twelve years of fighting, and indeed they sometimes do. Mario Gómez, for example, says the members of "the Salvadoran military have distinguished themselves above all for their courage and patriotism."[86] Orlando de Sola essentially hails the army and criticizes politicians for negotiating an end to the war instead of pushing on to complete victory when he says, "I said win the war first and negotiate afterwards."[87]

However, these nods of support for the army are exceptions to the rule. Elite memoirists never got over the army's decision to back the reforms in 1979, and most of the time they deride the military and treat it with suspicion. Mario Gómez says that some military officers wanted to prolong the war because they found it suited their own purposes.[88] Gómez's critique notwithstanding, the rest of the elite memoirists withhold criticism of the military's conduct during the fighting, and certainly they do not reference the various massacres and human rights abuses. They hail individual military officers who joined forces with them, like D'Aubuisson, who also suffered in 1979, having been purged from the army as a reactionary by the new military establishment. More commonly, elite memoirists simply ignore the army all together, acting as if the many battles and the billions of dollars in U.S. military aid were irrelevant, or nonexistent. Sometimes they even take an avowedly antimilitary stance. Orlando de Sola does so when he says that "people think that we (the rich) consider the military to be our allies. I, for one, do not consider them allies. . . . I never involve myself in military affairs, ever." He claims that his family has a tradition of antimilitarism, dating back to his father's involvement in the political movements to end the Hernández Martínez dictatorship in 1944, saying that "my family has avoided getting involved in military affairs. If anything, we are antimilitary."[89]

The elite memoirists celebrate militancy, but primarily in regard to their own activities in unofficial paramilitaries rather than the formal structure of the military. Although they are anxious to deny having been an *escuadronero* (sponsor or member of a paramilitary death squad), they are willing to describe paramilitary activities positively through indirect references and veiled language. On various occasions they defend the right of civilians to take matters into their own hands when no one else will defend them. David Panamá, for example, says that dedicated army officials and civilians stood by repeatedly in the 1970s as assassins and terrorists walked free from prison because the judicial system was flawed or complicit. Tired of watching that happen, some of them "began to take the law into their own hands—an eye for eye and a tooth for a tooth." It was "painful," he says, but necessary.[90] Similarly, Mario Gómez discusses paramilitarism as a citizen's right: "Every honest man can take the law into his own hands when the government cannot handle matters and when defeat of the enemy is imperative for survival." Like Panamá, he describes paramilitarism as "a sad though legitimate necessity," and says that what the "anticommunist squads" did was neither "praiseworthy nor good." But he defends their right to exist because "the just sometimes need to avail themselves of these things as a last resort."[91]

While the elite memoirists are willing to refer to paramilitary activities, they prefer to focus attention on their political activities and lobbying organizations. Naturally, the ARENA political party dominates this conversation, and the memoirists portray its founding as their great achievement. They also celebrate ARENA's precursors, like the Frente Agrario de la Región Oriental (FARO), the civilian lobbying organization that landowners created in 1976 to oppose President Molina's land reform. The memoirists take particular joy in the success of their coreligionists in FARO who forced Molina to back down from his reformist designs and to eat his famous words that he would "not take one step backwards" (*ni un paso atrás*) in advancing land reform. Their description of ARENA portrays its founders as hardworking entrepreneurs who were isolated and under attack. With his customary hyperbole, Ricardo Valdivieso says that ARENA was "for me, not just a party, it was the beginning of a journey to civilization."[92] A key moment in the ARENA story is D'Aubuisson's arrest in May, 1980 under the orders of Colonel Majano, one of the five members of the governing junta at the time and the leader of the moderate young officers' wing of the army. Elite memoirists take pride in recounting the demonstrations and mass marches they organized to demand D'Aubuisson's release. Once out of prison, D'Aubuisson went into exile in Guatemala, where he and a few close advisors began laying the foundation for what would become ARENA. Those present during the days of exile, like Valdivieso, describe themselves as the rightwing equivalent of guerrillas, living pecuniary lives, working constantly on organizing and fundraising, and building their party from scratch.[93] The people who were in ARENA from the beginning, sometimes known as "the founders," give themselves a special place in the history of the movement, like visionary entrepreneurs who founded a small company and built it into a mighty corporation.

The memoirists who narrate the story of ARENA take particular pride in how fast their work paid off. From its modest and seemingly doomed foundations in Guatemala, ARENA soon became the most successful civilian-based conservative political party in Salvadoran history. After returning to El Salvador in late 1980, D'Aubuisson and the other founders oversaw the establishment of ARENA as a formal political party in September 1981. They then went about acquiring the requisite signatures to enter the party in the Assembly elections scheduled for the following March. Seemingly against all odds, they achieved their goal, which set up another legendary episode in the ARENA narrative. When ARENA activists, including Valdivieso and Sol Bang, were carrying the boxes of signatures into the government's election office, a guerrilla commando squad ambushed them in a machine-gun attack. Both Valdivieso and Sol Bang were wounded, but they got the materials into the office anyway, and they take pride in saying that the official inscription of ARNEA was done with their blood on its pages. ARENA's success in the March 1982 elections allowed it to form a coalition majority in the National Assembly and catapult D'Aubuisson from alienated outsider to chairman of the National Assembly. The conservative defense was underway.[94]

Resolution and Denouement: 1980s to the Present

When the elite memoirists look back on the long arc of the war and its aftermath, they find much cause for celebration. They preserved the things that were most important to them: a market economy and the sanctity of private property. Sol Bang's postwar experience as head of Comisión Hidroeléctrica del Río Lempa (CEL), the government's energy commission, provides a vivid example of their success in advancing the cause of privatization. President Cristiani placed him in charge of CEL after the war with the objective of modernizing and streamlining its operations. That assignment translated into a massive privatization of state-owned energy facilities. Sol Bang fired nearly 90 percent of CEL's employees, over their union's objections, and transferred massive amounts of state-owned energy assets to the private sector.[95] In light of the fact that what was happening in CEL was also taking place in other sectors of the national economy, including land, banks, telecommunications, and healthcare, among others, it is safe to say that the economic libertarians succeeded in dismantling the byproducts of state intervention, thereby fulfilling their most sought-after goal in the war.[96]

Nevertheless, a pall hangs over the elite memoirists' assessment of postwar El Salvador. For all their victories, the elite memoirists still express a sense of having lost something. Monica Núñez, in Gorkin's *From Grandmother to Granddaughter*, expresses this sentiment when she says that laborers never returned to being deferential after the war. "The FMLN, the civil war, ruined all that," she bemoans. Both she and her mother, Niña Cecilia, refer to another topic that inspires elite melancholy, the loss of personal security amid the crime and gangs of the postwar era. "We were free back in those days!" Núñez laments, "Not like today, when parents are afraid and wouldn't let kids like us go roaming through the hills." Pressing on, she says, "Anything can happen today, kidnapping or god knows what." Niña Cecilia offers a similar complaint about not being able to go about San Salvador freely like she used to because of crime.

> At night, even here in San Salvador, we hesitate to go out. If we're invited to a party or wedding these days, we don't go if it means traveling at night because anything can happen to you in the streets now. So more and more, we stay at home. That's how it's been since the war. The country has been set back. El Salvador is no longer the place it was before.[97]

For their parts, David Panamá and Orlando de Sola don't fear for their personal safety, or at least they don't express it in their memoirs, but their assessments of postwar El Salvador reveal a despondency similar to that of the Núñez's. Their personal fortunes are diminished, at least relative to the new "neoliberal" elites who now run the show, and the political party they helped found has pushed them aside as irrelevant "dinosaurs." In fact, Panamá employs his nationalistic populism to say that the war wasn't worth fighting because El Salvador in 2008 has more poverty and lower indices of development than before the war.[98]

despondent

The specific cause of the elites' feeling of loss varies from one individual to the next. But collectively, their somber descriptions of the postwar era imbue their narratives with an overarching sense that something has been taken away from them and has yet to be returned. The existence of that sentiment should be no surprise, according to the aforementioned scholar of conservatism, Corey Robin, who argues that conservatives need a sense of loss to fuel their endeavors. The angst that comes with the feeling that something has been taken unjustly provides a raw passion to inspire action. Conservative elites need that anxiety in reserve, where it can be drawn upon in the future if the battle for survival begins anew.

A Selective History of Death

Elite memoirists assign responsibility for death during the civil war in a highly selective manner. It is an undisputed fact that the overwhelming majority of deaths and human rights abuses during the war were committed by the right, either by the formal military or the informal paramilitaries and death squads.[99] But the memoirists give exactly the opposite impression, that the left did most of the killing and the right was

blame left

comprised of innocent victims. At best the memoirists ignore killings by the right and overstate those by the left; at worst they rely upon serpentine conspiracy theories to blame the left for the right's atrocities.

Rarely do elite memoirists mention atrocities by the right, and when they do so, they either dismiss them as leftist propaganda or discuss them within the context of killings by the guerrillas in an attempt to make them seem equal in scale. Barahona, for example, notes that "between the 1970s and 1980s eighty thousand Salvadorans were kidnapped or killed by guerrillas or by death squads." That statement confuses the matter because it fails to distinguish between the two sides' highly divergent degrees of responsibility. It also fails to mention the army at all, which carried out most of the large-scale massacres of civilians. When Barahona does mention one of those atrocities, the Sumpul River massacre of 1980, he doesn't identify the perpetrator (the army), and he diminishes its scale by mentioning it alongside the guerrilla attack on off-duty U.S. marines in San Salvador's Zona Rosa neighborhood in 1986.[100] Mario Gómez simply dismisses the massacre of the Sumpul River as "exaggerated" and suggests that perhaps the victims were "a band of guerrillas in disguise who had hid their weapons."[101]

Another strategy that elite memoirists use to deflect responsibility for killings during the war is to use the passive voice when referring to victims of rightwing terror. For example, Barahona discusses the assassination of Father Rutulio Grande, noting that his family was a great supporter of the priest. But when it comes to assigning responsibility for Grande's death, Barahona uses a passive reference to the accusations made by "the catholic church and many human rights organizations [that] didn't hesitate to place blame on the national police."[102] He offers no indication that he believes those accusations to be correct.

On various occasions the memoirists simply dispense with subtlety and defend known killers, such as when Sol Bang describes Roberto D'Aubuisson as "never violent. Since the first time I met him, despite his career in the military, he was clearly driven by a civic, political struggle."[103] An ARENA party apparatchik and business owner, Adolfo Torrez echoes Sol's sentiments about D'Aubuisson in a 2006 interview, describing him as "one of El Salvador's greatest sons."[104] David Panamá is similarly direct when claiming that "the accusations directed against ARENA, such as in regard to death squad activities, have no credibility because the people who make them are enjoying the protection of North American justice." He presses on by insisting that the left created those stories to deflect criticism from its own activities: "It was the terrorists' priority to bring these stories to life, in order to justify before public opinion, both nationally and internationally, their assassinations, kidnappings, purges and other such acts that are intrinsic to them."[105] Torrez advances much the same claim about the existence of the death squads in general, saying that "they could be an invention of the left."[106]

Most of the elite memoirists employ conspiracy theories to absolve the right of mass killings or human rights abuses, with David Panamá serving as the standard bearer. He blames the left for various high-profile atrocities that were committed by the right, including the killing of the human rights ombudsman Mario Zamora, the killing of Archbishop Romero, the attacks on mourners at Romero's funeral, the killing of the UCA Jesuits, and the bombing of the FENASTRAS labor union's office. He says the motive for all of these crimes was leftist factionalism, with one wing exacting retribution on another. He extends this type of conspiratorial criticism to President Duarte and the Christian Democrats, whom Panamá considers to have been socialists. He claims that the kidnapping of President Duarte's daughter in 1985 was a conspiracy between him and the guerrillas in order to provide Duarte with the political cover to release dozens of guerrilla prisoners. When he searches for an explanation as to why the United States chose to back Duarte and the Christian Democrats in the 1984 presidential election rather than D'Aubuisson and ARENA, Panamá says that it was to prolong the war so that the United States would have a guaranteed market for its leftover armaments from Vietnam and so that Salvadorans would continue to migrate to the United States to provide cheap labor. Panamá encapsulates his conspiratorial claims by attributing the more than 10,000 deaths per year in the early stages of the war to "the USSR's war for global domination, manifested by Cuba's Organización Latinoamericana de Solidaridad (OLAS)." Panamá's accusations are outlandish in the face of overwhelming evidence to the contrary, but the difference between him and the other elite memoirists is a matter of scale rather than of kind.[107]

Non-Elite Members of the Elite Memory Community

It is within the context of conservative critiques of communism that non-elites, especially former guerrillas who have embraced conservatism after the war, or at least who have become ardent critics of the FMLN, became de facto members of the elite memory community. In his analysis of conservatism, Robin observes that elite conservatism has always "appealed to and relied upon outsiders."[108] In the context of contemporary El Salvador, those outsiders take the form of former leftists and people from modest economic backgrounds who have become vocal spokespersons for conservative causes, especially libertarian economics. Marvin Galeas is a classic example. He comes from a modest background and spent the majority of the war in northern Morazán as an ERP militant working on the Radio Venceremos team. Galeas admits that he was never an ideologue and that he joined the guerrillas as much out of a spirit of youthful adventure as anything, but he was with the guerrillas for a long time, forming friendships, enduring hardships, and working to advance the guerrilla cause.

After the war Galeas entered a period of self-reflection that led him to embrace ideological conservatism. An articulate and productive writer, who worked as a journalist after the war, Galeas emerged as one of the most visible public spokespersons for conservative causes, and, therein, as one of the most ardent propagators of the core narrative of the elite memory community. His contributions to the narrative have come in diverse forms, including his memoir, *Crónicas de guerra*, published in 2008, and his role in bringing to life the stories of civilian elites, namely Guillermo Sol Bang and Marvin Barahona. Galeas conducted extended interviews with the two of them and turned their narratives into first-person biographies, *Sol y acero* and *El Sueño possible*, published in 2011 and 2006 respectively.[109]

Galeas charts his transition to ideological conservatism, saying that after the war "I entered into a painful and serious period of reflection about the events in which I participated." He says that through his own readings and self-study he eventually embraced the economic theories of Adam Smith and Friedrich von Hayek. Galeas is respectful of some individual guerrillas whom he befriended during his time in the mountains, but generally he looks back upon the guerrillas as a whole with harsh criticisms. He says guerrilla leaders were sectarian and ideologically inflexible and that if they had come to power they would have created an authoritarian society that would have trampled individual liberties. He cites the various critiques he received from his guerrilla superiors during the war as proof of his claim, saying they accused him of being "a bourgeois reformist and a free thinker." He responds by saying "They were right." He also claims that guerrilla leaders directed internal purges and killed fellow combatants on spurious evidence that the accused were enemy collaborators. Galeas reminds his readers of those same leaders' sins prior to the war, such as assassinating the famed poet Roque Dalton in 1975 and kidnapping and assassinating elites, like Ernesto Regalado Dueñas in 1971 and Roberto Pomo in 1977. He also employs a classic criticism that military and political leaders used throughout the war, namely accusing guerrilla leaders of living in air-conditioned luxury in foreign lands while ordering their rank-and-file members to fight and die for them back in El Salvador. One of Galeas's strongest assets as a conservative spokesperson is his claim of having turned to conservatism specifically because of his time with the guerrillas. If he turned his back on them, it was because he knew them and had a first-hand opportunity to learn of their deep limitations and flaws.[110]

Galeas assigns responsibility for death during the war just like the civilian elite memoirists. He either ignores it, uses passive language to describe it, or relies upon an argument of moral equivalence to downplay it. In his memoir, *Crónica de guerra*, Galeas mentions the El Mozote massacre and comments on the impact it had on him as a guerrilla, especially when he walked through the region one year later and saw the lingering evidence, where "everything smelled of death." But he gets to that point by first accusing the guerrillas of various wrongdoings, including the "execution of a poor boy," and prefacing his descriptions of them with descriptions of global atrocities like the dropping of the atomic bombs on Japan in 1945 and the concentration camps of the Holocaust, thereby making those events discursively similar to the guerrillas' actions. Throughout his memoir, Galeas rarely mentions atrocities by the army or the paramilitaries, but he mentions victims of the guerrillas individually and by name. Toward the end of his book, he employs the classic trope, an argument of moral equivalence, by which the right should be absolved of its crimes because the left killed people too.

> All kidnappings are contemptible, regardless of whether it is the right kidnapping a humble worker or the left kidnapping a wealthy businessman, Human rights are not a question of quantity or quality. They are either respected or violated. It is wrong to suggest that some deaths are more important than others.

What Galeas fails to recognize is that he betrays that notion throughout his memoir by disproportionately mentioning guerrilla killings and thereby making its victims seem more important than the victims of the army and paramilitaries.[111]

In assessing the postwar era, Galeas echoes the pathos of the elite memoirists, not so much by referring to a loss of personal freedom, but rather by describing society's broader disorientation. He describes violent crimes that have occurred since 1992 in gruesome detail, but without contextualization, such that his readers have no alternative but to feel a kind of apocalyptic pall hanging over their country. Galeas may celebrate some achievements of the war, like freedom of speech and the dismantling of the death squads, but as a former guerrilla who blames the left for starting the war, he has no alternative but to say emphatically that the war was not worth it, "definitely not." In his worldview, something about El Salvador is not quite right.[112]

Marvin Galeas is an example of a small, but influential number of former guerrillas and one-time leftist sympathizers who now serve as conservative spokespersons, or who at least advance the narrative cause of the elite memory community in various ways, particularly by criticizing the current leadership of the FMLN. Examples include, but are not limited to Berne Ayalá, Joaquín Villalobos, Salvador Samaoya, Paulo Lüers, and Marvin Galeas's brother, Geovani Galeas.[113]

As a team, Marvin and Geovani Galeas have succeeded particularly well in establishing themselves as roving conservative commentators. Like Marvin, Geovani Galeas was a guerrilla working with Radio Venceremos and after the war he too worked as a journalist, including as a columnist for a conservative newspaper, *La Prensa Gráfica*. The Galeas brothers have pursued an aggressive and successful strategy to get their message out. They founded an editorial company and have created websites and blogs to disseminate their writings. The content of their work varies widely, and some of it is of questionable quality, such as Geovani Galeas's hagiographic biography of Roberto D'Aubuisson, which appeared as a lengthy insert in *La Prensa Gráfica* in 2004.[114]

Some of their work is of high quality, however, even as it serves their ideological agenda. A notable example is Geovani Galeas's collaboration with another disaffected former guerrilla, Berne Ayalá, on an exposé of the purges that occurred within the FPL in the latter half of the 1980s, *Grandeza y miseria de una guerrilla*. In an impressive act of investigative journalism, Galeas and Ayala conducted interviews with various witnesses and victims to expose the dirty secret that many former guerrilla leaders knew about but had chosen to keep quiet, namely that a faction within the FPL used the pretext of defending the organization against spies to torture and kill many hundreds of civilians and FPL activists in the region of San Vicente between roughly 1986 and 1990. In fact, FPL leaders eventually executed the principle architect of the purges, a long-time figure within the FPL, Mayo Sibrián, in 1990. Galeas and Ayala insist that the main leadership of the FPL, most notably Salvador Sánchez Cerén, was complicit in the purges, and they portray the assassination of Sibrián as a cop-out and an attempt to suppress the story. They have aggressively tried to undermine Sánchez Cerén's political aspirations with websites, blogsites, and op-ed pieces, in addition to the book.[115] Another impressive work in a similar vein by Geovani Galeas is his critique of the early founders of his former guerrilla organization, the ERP, *Héroes bajo sospecha*.[116]

El Salvador offers limited economic rewards for writers, and there is a long tradition of conservative elites bankrolling middle- and lower-class spokespersons who espouse their causes. As just one example, according to the reporter Craig Pyes, early ARENA leaders planned to promote their fledgling party by "getting close to journalists, paying them, [and] exploiting their professional ambitions."[117] This fact helps to explain the commotion that ensued when it was revealed in June 2009 that for the previous five years Marvin Galeas had been receiving $2,000 per month as a consultant to the ARENA government's Ministry of Medio Ambiente. He publicly rejected the accusation that he had been given the consultancy as a payoff for his service as a conservative mouthpiece.[118] But even the likes of Paulo Lüers, another former guerrilla and editorialist for the conservative newspaper *El Diario de Hoy*, who himself has faced accusations of switching sides after the war, and who had defended the Galeas brothers previously, distanced himself from Marvin Galeas on this issue. Lüers addressed himself directly to Marvin Galeas on his blog, saying that his actions make it too easy for their critics to call them sellouts to the right: "Our detractors always accuse us of being 'rightwing sellouts,' because it is the only way they can understand how someone can criticize the left. And now, unfortunately, you've given them reason to think they are correct." He continues, saying that "while you can't understand it either, Marvin, a person can criticize the left without being bought off to do so, and without being paid for ghost consultancies."[119]

Paulo Lüers differs from the Galeas brothers in that he continues to self-identify as an ideological leftist. He left his native Germany in 1981, joined the ERP during the war, and spent most of his time working for Radio Venceremos. He defends his decision to work for *El Diario de Hoy* starting in 2007 on the grounds that the ownership promised him total editorial freedom, although he admits that as a former guerrilla "I never imagined I would be writing for this newspaper, much less that I would be part of the editorial advisory board at the behest of the latest generation of the Altamirano family [the notoriously conservative founders of the paper]." Interestingly, just two years before accepting his job with *El Diario de Hoy*, Lüers had written a scathing critique of the newspaper's ownership for being authoritarian and spying on its reporters. Even if he is writing with total freedom, as he claims, it's clear why a staunchly conservative newspaper like *El Diario de Hoy* would want to hire him. Despite the fact that he honors the ERP's conduct during the war, Lüers is a relentless critic of the postwar left for having been taken over by hardliners from the PCS and the FPL. Not surprisingly, he considers Geovani Galeas's and Edwin Ayalá *Grandeza y misería* to be an excellent work, and he constantly harangued Sánchez Cerén, then vice president, to respond to their findings. In addition, Lüers attacks almost every other leftist government throughout Latin America, claiming that all of them are similarly demagogic and antidemocratic. His sweeping condemnations of Chávez's Venezuela, Morales's Bolivia, and Castro's Cuba are indistinguishable from past conservative commentary coming out of El Salvador, which obsessed about Cuba and described it as exemplary of all things evil in the world. As one example, Lüers traveled to Venezuela in 2011 as an investigative reporter for *El Diario de Hoy*, where he wrote harsh critiques of the Chávez regime and later used those as a launching pad for criticisms of the FMLN back home. Lüers is aware of his caustic voice and he describes himself in one of his blog entries as a "sharpshooter that works alone." Indeed, the FLMN president, Mauricio Funes, who once tried to deflect Lüers's criticisms by dismissing him as a mere "bartender," seems to have embodied the axiom that with friends like Lüers, who needs enemies?[120]

Conclusion

El Salvador's elite memoirists share a common narrative about the past that has as its foundational element a sense of loss or injustice. Elite memoirists feel that they and their fellow elites were subjected to an onslaught of attacks by both revolutionaries and reformers. Their enemies' goal was to steal their wealth and distribute it to less deserving people, either communists or the poor, both of whom could have made more of themselves in El Salvador's free-market economy if only they had tried.

The memoirists argue that they made their fortunes by nurturing their entrepreneurial skills and applying them to the task of creating saleable commodities in the marketplace, so anyone who failed to do that and who then advocates for revolutionary or reformist policies is a lazy thief at best, and a power-hungry communist conspirator at worst.

El Salvador's elites have traditionally kept a low profile, or at least they have chosen not to inject their personal stories into the public sphere. Thus, the publication of some of their memoirs and interviews since 1992 represents a rare opportunity to gain insight into how some of them think and how they situate their families' lives in the context of recent Salvadoran history. The overall number of them who have chosen to tell their stories remains small and they tend to hail from a distinct subset of the population—ideologically conservative men who were early supporters of the conservative ARENA political party and its founder Roberto D'Aubuisson. Furthermore, they have disproportionately been kidnapped or assaulted by the guerrillas. If a larger number of elite Salvadorans were to share their life stories, perhaps the collective whole of the elite narrative would become more complicated and diversified. But in the meantime, those who have chosen to write and tell their stories, including Sol Bang, Valdivieso, Gómez Zimmerman, de Sola and Panamá, among others, offer narratives that are remarkably consistent with one another in both content and style, and that define the elite civilian voice in El Salvador's postwar public sphere.

The Republic Will Live as Long as the Army Lives

Military Officers

· ·

Compared to the more reclusive elites, El Salvador's military officers have maintained public profiles. They are, after all, public servants, and during the civil war they were the face of the government's campaign against the guerrillas. They frequently stood before the media to explain the military's activities and defend its actions. Nevertheless, their personal stories were not part of the equation. They did not write memoirs, nor did they inject much of their personal lives into their public personae. In the words of one of those officers, who is a memoirist, Coronel Adolfo Majano (ret.), the Salvadoran military is a notoriously "faithful representation of militaries throughout Latin America—hard and closed."[1]

The life stories some officers decided to publish after 1992 are a rare and valuable contribution to public discourse. Officers have produced roughly twice as many life stories as their counterparts in the elite memory group. Still, the overall number remains modest in comparison with the hundreds of officers who served during the war. One lower-ranking memoirist suggests that the reason more of his counterparts have not gone public with their stories is because they fear "the negative reactions or criticisms that their writings might generate."[2]

As with the sources in the previous chapter, the life stories examined in this chapter are not grouped together because their authors share a demographic statistic. They constitute a memory community because of the similarities in their recollections and the distinct style and content of their narratives. The members of this community are diverse; they adhere to competing ideological camps, belong to rival graduating classes from the military academy, and some of them do not like one another personally. But their narratives exhibit a high degree of uniformity.

The theme that binds the officer memoirists together is an overwhelming desire to defend the survival of the military as an institution. To that end, the narrators exhibit distinct characteristics, such as a highly flexible, pragmatic approach to decision-making that lacks rigid ideological paradigms. All of the officer memoirists self-identify as procapitalist and pro-Western, and therein as anticommunist. They also celebrate social and economic reforms as good things if they benefit the military's prospects, but they are just as willing to disparage reformism if they deem it a threat. Naturally, the officers recall with disdain the militant leftists who targeted the military for destruction during the war, but neither do they celebrate civilian elites. In the same way that the elites distrust the military, so too do the officers frame their narratives around suspicions of the elites and their fickle commitment to the military's survival.

The Salvadoran Military Contextualized

Almost every memoirist in this chapter graduated from El Salvador's four-year military academy, which was the only avenue to rank above second lieutenant. Prior to the restructuring of the military after the peace accords in 1992, graduates of the academy received assignments in one of the various branches of the military, including the army, the navy, the air force, or one of the various branches of security forces, including the National Guard. Most of them went into the army, which was the largest branch, and which came to include the five elite combat battalions that were created at the beginning of the war, the Batallónes de Infantería de Reacción Inmediata (BIRIS). The first and most notorious of them was the Atlacatl Battalion.

The sources in this chapter include memoirs or extended published interviews with a handful of high-ranking officers who served in key positions throughout the war. They include, but are not limited to General Orlando Zepeda Herrera, academy class of 1966 and vice minister of defense in the late 1980s; General Mauricio Vargas, academy class of 1966, combat commander in eastern El Salvador, and negotiator of the peace accords; General Humberto Corado Figueroa, academy class of 1969 and minister of defense between 1993 and 1995 (notwithstanding the complexities of his book—see introduction); Colonel Adolfo Majano, academy class of 1958 and member of the governing juntas between 1979 and 1980; Colonel Sigifredo Ochoa, academy class of 1966 and brigade commander during the war; and Colonel Jaime Abdul Gutiérrez, academy class of 1957 and member of the governing juntas between 1979 and 1982.

The sources also include narratives from some lower-ranking officers who graduated from the military academy in the middle of the war and thus ended their service at the rank of captain when the war was over. They include Captain Herard Von Santos and Captain Abraham Marín, both of whom belonged to the Atlacatl Battalion. A memoir by a sergeant, René Flores Cruz, represents the lone source from someone who did not attend the military academy. Captain Carlos Balmore Vigil offers a few personal reflections in his *Soldados en combate,* published in 2013, but his main purpose in that work is to provide more than two dozen of his fellow mid-level officers with the chance to share war stories. In addition, I draw upon a few published interviews from the 1980s, which provide, as in Chapter 2, an opportunity to see some continuity in subjects' thinking over time. Memoirs by officers who abandoned the military and joined the guerrillas, such as Captain Mena Sandoval and Captain Marcelo Cruz Cruz, as well as a pair of narratives by soldiers, are examined in later chapters because their narratives are more consistent with different memory communities.

In his 1986 autobiography, *Duarte: My Story,* President José Napoleón Duarte offered his opinion on what motivated the Salvadoran officer corps. Duarte, the Christian Democratic president and long-time antagonist of the army, ended up working alongside officers almost every day of his presidency (1984–1989), and in the process he believes he learned a lot about them. He insists that military leaders were guided more by pragmatism than ideology, because "they do not fit neatly into political categories. . . . They change. . . . They lack an ideological foundation." He admits that he was prejudiced against the military and "I regret not having learned how to analyze the philosophy of the military much earlier." What he did learn, however, is that "it is hard to categorize officers. They move along the spectrum of political thought, responding to a particular issue or to whom they last spoke."[3]

My reading of the officers' memoirs suggests that Duarte was on to something. In their life stories, the officers demonstrate little or no commitment to any specific ideological position, especially in comparison with their elite counterparts, or with their guerrilla adversaries. They offer nothing equivalent to the elites' economic libertarianism, with its requisite appeals to Adam Smith, Friedrich Hayek, or Ludwig von Mises, or to guerrilla insurgents' appeals to the likes of Marx and Lenin. Rather, they offer a generalized appeal to capitalism because it is Western and therefore somehow better than socialism, which they presumed to be somehow nonwestern in origin. A clear expression of this absence of ideological rigidity is provided by a low-ranking field commander of the Atlacatl Battalion, who explains to an interviewer what he recalls saying to a captured guerrilla, "We are an armed institutional force operating under the auspices of the Constitution of the Republic; you guerrillas are an armed insurgent force fighting for your ideals against the system, we are with the system."[4] The commander doesn't clarify what he means by "the system," but in that brief statement he effectively delineates the broad outlines of the officers' sense of self.

Throughout their careers, beginning with their four years of training in the military academy, every officer in El Salvador had drilled into him a quote by the independence hero General José Manuel Arce: "The Army will live while the Republic lives." What this really came to mean to the officers was the opposite, namely that the nation would live as long as the army lives, a belief reinforced by the fact that military officers controlled the offices of government throughout most of the twentieth century and thus almost every officer came into service seeing the military as synonymous with government.[5]

In their quest to defend the military as an institution, the officers reveal in their narratives that they employed an ideological flexibility and an ability to bend with the political winds, even to the point of residing in a recurrent state of contradiction. For example, the narrators simultaneously celebrate the United States for aiding El Salvador and criticize it for trampling El Salvador's national sovereignty; they advocate for social reforms and human rights, and oppose them for hindering the armed forces' ability to fight the war; they criticize elites and economic libertarianism, and celebrate them as fonts of capitalism and development. The officers portray themselves as belligerents in a straightforward fight for institutional survival and they demonstrate a willingness to adopt almost any position at any moment if they believe it will advance that cause.

In their pursuit of preserving the military as an institution, the officer memoirists might be motivated by selfishness, idealism, or some combination of the two. Selfishly, some officers might want to save the military in order to preserve their salaries, pensions, and prestige, and sometimes their ability to perpetrate graft and corruption. Other officers might be more motivated by idealism, or a sense of honor and mission, a commitment to a shared cause, a desire to save the nation from its enemies, or a hope to reform the imbalanced and unfair structures of Salvadoran society. After all, most of the officers came from humble backgrounds and they neither identified with, nor received acceptance from society's upper crust. Whatever their motivations, each officer memoirist demonstrates a dogged commitment to the idea that he fought to preserve the armed forces from various threats, whether from the right or the left, foreign or domestic. In fact, the officers are quite unable to disguise their institutional incentive, not only in their postwar memoirs, but even in interviews they granted during the war, when idealism was supposed to trump selfishness and pragmatism.

One such example is provided by Eugenio Vides Casanova, minister of defense between 1984 and 1988, in an interview with Max Manwaring in 1987, which appears in the publication by the National Defense University Press, *El Salvador at War: An Oral History*. At a time when heavy debates were taking place in the United States over the future of U.S. funding to El Salvador, Vides admits that he supported the U.S.-backed reforms after 1979 only "as a necessity but not necessarily as a vocation." He goes on to say that "as Minister of Defense I was going to make sure that every word behind these nine [reformist] points was to be accomplished, not only because I thought of it as something basic, but because I knew it was the only way to save this country and our own institution—the Army."[6] Similarly, Mauricio Vargas reveals that during the peace accord negotiations the overwhelming majority of the negotiators' time was spent discussing the future of the armed forces. The guerrillas wanted the military more or less dismantled and the officers wanted it preserved intact. Vargas says that his priority was to get as much as he could, but above all to ensure the military's survival. The final settlement, which resulted in a significant reduction in the scale and scope of the armed forces, has led some officers to call Vargas a traitor.[7] Notably, almost no discussion during the negotiations addressed the issue of the postwar economy, meaning that the free market status quo under the then-incumbent ARENA party prevailed. Both the elites and the guerrillas got something they wanted, which has led some officers to feel that the military was sold out at the bargaining table by a civilian alliance. General Orlando Zepeda Herrera writes in his book that the FMLN and ARENA banded together at the end of the war in hopes of "demilitarizing society."[8]

Colonel Jaime Abdul Gutiérrez's speech in the National Stadium on October 15, 1981, in commemoration of the second anniversary of the 1979 coup, provides a vivid example of the complications of military politics at the time. Gutiérrez is widely recognized as the point man for the conservative backlash against the reformist impulse after the 1979 coup. He is perhaps best known for overseeing the release of Roberto D'Aubuisson after his coreligionist on the governing junta, Colonel Adolfo Majano, ordered D'Aubuisson's arrest on the grounds of plotting a rightwing coup. Famously, D'Aubuisson was found with incriminating documents that pointed to his involvement in paramilitary death squads, including the one that killed Archbishop Romero. But rather than allow a judicial process to handle D'Aubuisson's case, Gutiérrez arranged for his release and then oversaw the steady suppression of Majano and the reform-minded youth wing of the military. Majano eventually went into exile in late 1980. Meanwhile, Gutiérrez presided over a security situation in which approximately 1,000 people were dying each month, mostly at the hands of security forces and paramilitary bands. Ironically, Gutiérrez owed his positions at the time, vice president of the junta and commander in chief of the armed forces, to the 1979 coup and all of its reformist inspirations, including the purging of officers like D'Aubuisson, who were considered too reactionary to remain in the ranks.

In his 1981 speech, Gutiérrez came across as every bit the reformist firebrand, accusing the rightwing, in both its civilian and military guises, of being the problem and calling for society to be structurally reformed. Before an audience in the National Stadium he declared that "we leaders of the liberation movement of October 15 decided this time to set forth with determination the need for structural change as measures leading to an equal distribution of the national wealth." He had preceded that claim with a brief historical narrative that identified as national heroes those military reformers who preceded him in the coups of 1931, 1948, and 1961. The only faults of those leaders, Gutiérrez insisted, was that they didn't take reformism far enough. But at least they began the process by which the era of "government by the great families came to an end . . . [when] government institutions had been conceived and managed as private interests."9

A cynical reader might dismiss Gutiérrez's populist tone as empty propaganda, and such a criticism is justified.10 But his rhetoric can't be ignored entirely. It was dangerous stuff to be throwing around if it was not backed up by something. Indeed, for all his conservatism and conspiracies against the progressive wing of the military, Gutiérrez tolerated a coalition government with the Christian Democrats, participated in a purge of reactionary officers after the October 1979 coup and supported the military serving as the armed enforcer of the economic reforms ordered by the junta. Regardless of his personal politics or what he actually thought about the reforms, Gutiérrez exemplifies an officer's adherence to the internal customs of the military and a willingness to do or say whatever was necessary to preserve the military's long-term survival. After all, as General José Garcia, the new minister of defense after the 1979 coup put it in a 1987 interview, the left's "objective [in 1979] was the destruction of the armed forces. I knew the problem was serious and my mission was to defend the armed institution to avoid its collapse."[11]

It is apparent that officers at the time feared for their futures, and they took the victory of the Sandinistas in Nicaragua in July 1979 as a warning. Somoza's once powerful officer corps fled its country destitute and without prospects, and the Salvadoran officers wanted to avoid suffering the same consequences.[12] In his 1986 memoir, President Duarte says that Nicaragua inspired even conservative officers to trump ideology with pragmatism and embrace the cause of reform.

> The officers were afraid the armed forces might not be able to put out the fires of revolution. To save the armed forces, they would have to break their alliance to the oligarchy and realign with political forces that could win popular support. Many officers vacillated over this political choice until the Nicaraguan revolution convinced them. After Salvadoran officers watched the Nicaraguan people celebrate in the streets the defeat and dismemberment of Somoza's National Guard, the conspiracy against [President] Romero gained firm adherents—even among normally conservative officers.[13]

An anonymous official in the psychological operations sector of the Salvadoran army concurred with Duarte, claiming in a 1987 interview that U.S. advisors presented the commanding officers with "improvement in human rights . . . as a way of getting more military aid, which they needed. It was a reasonable proposition and they accepted it. I think they saw what happened to Somoza, when everybody in the world turned their backs."[14]

Notwithstanding these clear expressions of pragmatism and ideological flexibility, some genuine ideological disagreements existed among the officers. Contemporary observers and later scholars insist that three or more distinguishable ideological trends were present among the officers, especially leading up to the tumultuous coup of 1979. These trends ranged from hardcore reactionaries who wanted to ally with equally strident elites and engage in a scorched-earth campaign, to more "pragmatic mainstreamers," as the CIA called them, to progressive reformers like Colonel Majano, and even to revolutionaries who abandoned the army and joined the guerrillas.[15]

Two of the better-known examples of the latter are Emilio Mena Sandoval and Marcelo Cruz Cruz. They claim in their life stories that they developed a progressive ideology steadily during their time in the army, because of the injustices they saw or experienced during their service, including human rights abuses during the 1969 war with Honduras (Cruz Cruz) and corruption within the military hierarchy (Mena Sandoval).[16] General Mauricio Vargas served with Mena Sandoval in Santa Ana in the late 1970s and describes him as having held "liberal" views.[17] But for all their opposition to the status quo, neither Mena Sandoval nor Cruz Cruz advances a particularly clear ideological position. They certainly didn't convert to Marxism-Leninism. Rather they seem to have believed that the existing system was corrupt and needed to be changed, but also that it was resilient and so only military attack could defeat it. They seemed to believe that the guerrillas had the only real chance of accomplishing that feat. Their decision to join the ERP rather than any of the other guerrilla factions seems to have been a consequence of the fact that the ERP, more than the other four guerrilla factions, recruited military officers in advance of the first offensive in 1981, which ironically had the effect of tipping off the military as to the date of the rebellion and causing many of the prospective recruits to be arrested, transferred, or otherwise neutralized.[18]

Colonel Adolfo Majano provides a similar example to Mena Sandoval and Cruz Cruz. He did not join the guerrillas; if fact he has remained a staunch anticommunist throughout his life. But he exemplifies the progressive wing of the military youth that struggled to hold back the reactionaries within the military after 1979. Among his many actions, he ordered the arrest of D'Aubuisson and strongly supported the post-1979 economic reforms. According to U.S. State Department records, by the middle of 1980 he and fellow junta-mate Gutiérrez could hardly sit in the same room together owing to their intense differences of opinion and personal animosity for one another.[19] In his memoir, Majano calls Gutiérrez "el Diablo" (the devil) and maligns the "conservative line" within the officer corps that he and the other members of the military youth opposed.

Nevertheless, true to the narrative form of his memory community, Majano comes across as more pragmatic than ideological. His opposition to President Romero in 1977–1979, and therein his justification for participating in the 1979 coup, does not center on ideology, but rather on the belief that Romero and his circle of senior officers had lost control of the situation and thus were allowing the "chaos" of the radical left to expand unchecked. His defense of economic reforms comes across as a pragmatic attempt to avoid the collapse of the military and "the kind of catastrophe that occurred in Nicaragua." He says that he and the military youth were driven by a practical desire to "remedy the critical situation of the nation" and to create a "new Armed Forces that would be conscientious, capable, patriotic, reorganized and respectable." Admittedly, Majano appeals to social justice and the plight of the poor, but without any well-developed ideological reasoning, other than his desire to prevent the left from coming to power in a revolution. So if it is true that that he was ready to support the guerrillas during the 1981 offensive, as a pair of leading commanders of the Communist Party, Schafik Hándal and José Luís Merino, claim in their memoirs, then it would certainly seem that he was doing so out of pragmatism or opportunism rather than out of a genuine regard for the guerrillas and their ideological mission.[20] My point here is not to question the motives of officers who advocated reformism and change, but rather to show that in their narratives ideology takes a back seat to pragmatism in the quest for institutional survival.

The Not-Quite-Right, Not-Quite-Proper Order of Things

The officers' narrative resembles the elites' narrative in one generalized way: they had something they wanted to preserve (their institution). They perceived it to be under threat or attack and so they fought for its survival. But beyond that similarity, the officers' narrative diverges from that of their elite counterparts in significant ways, including the portrayal of El Salvador before the war. Whereas members of the elite memory community believe that an ideal period in Salvadoran history existed between the 1880s and the 1950s, when markets were free, government stayed out of peoples' affairs, workers were passive and happy, and private accumulation occurred in accordance with entrepreneurial capacity, the members of the officer memory community find themselves in a more complicated and paradoxical position. On the one hand, the military was in charge of government for nearly fifty years, and thus at some level its members were responsible for the way things were. To that end, the officer memoirists have an incentive to portray the past in a celebratory fashion, like their elite counterparts.

However, two countervailing trends compel military officials to find flaws in the past order of things. The first trend is the *tanda*-based system of military advancement. Each graduating class from the military academy was called a "*tanda*," and the members of each *tanda*, usually around twenty of them, tended to be steadfastly loyal to one another. Their loyalty originated partly in a curious feature of the Salvadoran military, namely that many strategic and institutional decisions were made by a vote rather than handed down from upon high. The military implemented this policy in the wake of the fall of General Martínez in 1944 in hopes of preventing any one officer from becoming too powerful. Thus *tandas* were voting blocks and the more unified they were the more powerful they could be. The members of each *tanda* tended to ascend through the ranks as a group and the hierarchy that was established during their time at the academy typically remained in place throughout the officers' careers. During the era of military rule in El Salvador (1931–1979), coups tended to be inter-*tanda* disputes, in which coup plotters normally belonged to a junior *tanda* that was trying to dislodge an entrenched senior *tanda* from power. Because the young plotters needed to publicly legitimize their actions, beyond selfishly wanting to promote themselves, they accused their predecessors of failing to meet the needs of the population and promised to fix the ills through social and economic reforms.[21]

The second motivation for officer memoirists to find problems with El Salvador's past emerges from a genuine desire on the part of some of them to effect change. Few memoirists of any memory community deny that El Salvador was a poor country struggling to climb the ladder of development. Even elites recognize this; they simply insist that laissez-faire economics was the proper way to do it. Many military officials disagree with them. Whereas the elites consider reforms to be tantamount to ruin, some military officers believe the opposite, seeing the failure to reform as risking societal collapse, and, therein, the military's future.

A unifying theme running throughout the officers' memoirs is a sort of ill-defined modernization theory dating back to the late 1950s and 1960s. As articulated by one of its main architects, the MIT economist W. W. Rostow, modernization theory is a highly formalized prescription for how poor nations can develop and therefore avoid falling prey to communist revolution. The most basic premises of modernization theory are that nations advance from premodern underdevelopment to modern capitalist development through a series of stages, and that government has a role to play leading the nation through those stages. Government should not sit on the sidelines and watch the process unfold haphazardly. Rather it should use its powers of intervention to enact necessary reforms to advance the nation from one stage to the next. While doing this, the government has to defend the nation against those who would oppose the modernization process, including reactionary elites who benefit from the status quo, and opportunistic communists who hope to take advantage of the growing pains of transition to incite social revolution.[22]

In El Salvador, some variation of modernization theory was embraced by the PRUD administrations in the 1950s and the PCN administrations in the 1960s and 1970s. It inspired the leaders of those regimes to promote an array of reformist programs, such as dam building, education reform, banking reform, tax reform, and even land reform.[23] Most of the officer memoirists embraced this call for reform at the time, either as active leaders or as cadets in the military academy. Accordingly, in their memoirs they celebrate the concept of modernization and the reformist endeavors of the military regimes. However, they do so vaguely. They do not refer to modernization theory explicitly, nor do they employ anything resembling its formal analytical framework. Instead they make generalized appeals to the nation's need for reform and portray the military as the stakeholder that has been willing to roll up its sleeves and get the job done. Waldo Chávez Velasco, a civilian apparatchik in the PCN governments, captures the modernization-theory sentiment in his 2006 memoir *Lo que no conté* when he claims that until the military took over government in 1931, "El Salvador was living in the Middle Ages, both socially and economically."[24] Similarly, in his memoir, Colonel Adolfo Majano describes the opponents of reform as "opposing new ways of thinking, stalwarts of tradition, conservatism and ignorance."[25]

General Jaime Abdul Gutiérrez echoes Majano's modernization sentiments in his 2013 memoir, *Testigo y actor*, even though he despises Majano personally and considers him to have been a naïve dupe for the guerrillas. Gutierrez criticizes the elites for presiding over an unequal society and draws upon the reformist tradition of the military regimes dating back to 1931 as setting the stage for the 1979 coup. He insists that the reforms after 1979 had the potential to bring about the necessary changes in society and prevent civil war by "immunizing society against violent revolution." But, he says, the reforms were blocked by "an ultraconservative minority," whom he accuses of "blind vindictiveness."[26]

General Humberto Corado Figueroa does much the same in the 2008 work *En defensa de la patria.* He offers a case-by-case look at each military government since 1931 and celebrates their reformist endeavors. For example, he says that the first military government under General Martínez (1931–1944) enacted beneficial policies like establishing the Banco

Central de Reserva (The Central Reserve Bank), which centralized the distribution of currency under government control, a standard feature of modern capitalist nations. He hails Martínez for helping the poor by building cheap housing, buying and redistributing agricultural land, and passing a law that outlawed landowners from paying workers in *fichas* (coupons) rather than legal currency. "The Salvadoran population began to see," he writes, "how, little by little, government was working on its behalf." He showers similar accolades on the subsequent military-led governments, and especially the PCN administrations of presidents Rivera and Sánchez Hernández in the 1960s. He credits them for embracing the Alliance for Progress as part of their modernizing reforms. "Those populist political innovators, backed by the liberal North American President Kennedy . . . gave rise to the economic modernization that charted El Salvador's course since the 1970s." This reformist impulse culminated in October 1979, when the military, faced with "the frightful prospect that extremists would take power by force of arms," stepped in to "reorient political affairs and take the wind out of the sails of the insurgency by way of the military proclamation of October 15, 1979."[27]

While heralding the military's historic embrace of reform, Corado fails to explain why reforms were needed in the first place. Naturally, he casts communists as the villains, saying that ever since the late 1920s they had been conspiring to take control of the state and destroy the military in the process. But he struggles to explain why communists were able to organize. At one point he says vaguely that the problem was ineptitude and insufficient compliance with the true spirit of the liberal reforms begun in the late nineteenth century. That statement would seem to accuse landed elites and government officials of somehow letting the nation down, but he never identifies who was inept or what constituted their failure. When he explains communists' ability to organize in El Salvador, he says simply that they "ably took advantage of structural weaknesses in Salvadoran society," but once again he doesn't define those "structures" or identify the parties responsible for creating them. On one occasion Corado identifies landed elites as the culprits and criticizes them saying, "The insurgents' activities were aided and abetted by some isolated historic events and by some feudal-like attitudes that some landowners and bosses inherited from the nineteenth century. El Salvador was one of those countries where the leading families, descendants of preindependence Spanish elites, treated their workers like servants." Admittedly, that accusation is clear and strong, but it comprises two lines buried in the middle of a four-hundred-page book. It's as if Corado calls for reform in the passive voice, never identifying the subject(s) who caused the problems that military leaders had to resolve. It seems that El Salvador's need for modernization was just a typical evolutionary process that all nations went through.[28]

General Mauricio Vargas also leaves unanswered questions in his explanation of the war. As a military commander in Morazán during the war, Vargas was a favorite of the U.S. embassy because he was supposedly willing to embrace counterinsurgency programs designed to win over the peasants' hearts and minds, even though his actual record on human rights was indistinguishable from his peers. Both during and after the war, Vargas referenced the structural issues that caused the war. In an interview with a North American reporter in 1987, for example, he said that "the structural problems are used by the Marxists to foment violence. If you take that away, you take away their appeal." Similarly, twenty years later, in an interview with El Faro, he said that the war had "structural causes" and that the guerrillas "used them to promote political violence in hopes of taking power." But he does not identify the origin of those structural problems or assign responsibility to anyone for creating them, not even with a pair of brief sentences like Corado.[29]

The vice minister of defense between 1984 and 1987, Colonel Carlos López Nuila offers a classic example of the esoteric rhetoric that military officials commonly use to celebrate the reformist endeavors of the military regimes. Writing in the prologue to Corado's book in 2008, López credits the military governments between 1931 and 1979 with creating a harmonious society presided over by beneficent officers.

> Rejecting both Marxist and fascist totalitarianism, the military-led governments of El Salvador refused to impose their militarism upon Salvadoran society, despite some initial attempts to do so. The system functioned in such a way that the government and those who ran it had a military orientation, and the head of the government was "the commander" who gave orders to uniformed subordinates and civilians alike. But a symbiosis of ideological and national interests guided the process, such that the political always guided the functioning of the state rather than the other way around.[30]

López's statement exemplifies military leaders' self-conceptualization as moderates standing in between the extremes of left and right, prudently advancing the cause of modernizing reform. But he leaves himself stuck in a paradox. If things were so good under the military's watchful eye, then why was there so much need for reform? For example, López celebrates the military's reformist impulses after the 1979 coup as an attempt to resolve an escalating "crisis," but he does not clarify the cause or nature of that crisis. Interestingly, he was willing to be more explicit in the 1980s while serving as vice minister of defense during the Duarte presidency. He said the reforms "fulfilled structural changes of a social character" and undermined the guerrillas' need to fight because "there was no longer an oligarchy or a dictatorship or violations of human rights."[31] With hyperbolic rhetoric like that, it's no wonder that Duarte wanted to promote him to the rank of general.

Orlando Zepeda is less enthusiastic about the 1979 reforms in his 2008 book, *Perfiles de la guerra en El Salvador*, because he was a strong supporter of the PCN governments of the 1960s and 1970s and thus he begrudges the 1979 coup for ousting the last PCN president, General Romero. But as a supporter of the military-led governments and their reformist endeavors, Zepeda embraces the spirit of modernization. He critiques elites and the "monopolies and privileges enjoyed by the wealthiest of them" and says that El Salvador's "true problems derived from the unjust distribution of wealth produced by agricultural production, which remained in the hands of the few people who owned most of the land." That claim would certainly seem to accuse the elites of being the problem, but then he immediately says that "despite these conditions, the Salvadoran peasant lived a relatively happy and tranquil life" until the Marxists showed up and exposed them to "the ideology of class struggle." His solution to these problems is an active, vigilant government looking out for the common person and keeping extremism at bay by enacting market-friendly policies such as agricultural subsidies to poor farmers. Therein, he insists, "private initiative remains the engine for economic development," and state intervention is necessary only when it plays "a genuinely equilibrating role."[32]

To summarize, the officer memoirists don't have an ideal era in the past that provides a model for structuring society. They differ from elites in this regard, who perceive that era to be the period between the 1880s and the late 1950s. Instead, officers think something was wrong that needed fixing. They rely on an ill-defined notion of modernization to guide their narratives, but then find themselves caught in paradoxes—at once faulting the past and celebrating it, criticizing capitalist elites but celebrating capitalism, and questioning past military leaders' effectiveness while heralding them as standard bearers of reform. A consequence of these paradoxes is a lingering sense of confusion and vagueness in their narratives. But in general they appeal to an actively engaged military working to modernize society and make it safe from communism.

The Threat

The officers are unequivocal when it comes to identifying their main enemy as communism. They believe that communists wanted to destroy the thing most precious to them, the institution of the armed forces. Perhaps more than anything else, this fear of communism explains the officers' descriptions as to why the military seized control of government in the first place in 1931 and retained it thereafter. The civilian apparatchik, Waldo Chávez Velasco, who captures military thinking effectively, as he did throughout his career, says "one of the main reasons for the creation of military governments was the threat—starting in 1932—of a communist regime."[33]

The officers stress the foreign nature of the communist threat, which is to be expected because it legitimizes the military's role as defending the nation from foreign attack, but also because it plays to the logic behind the United States sending aid during the war. As an example of this view, an Atlacatl officer, Abraham Marín, says that "our nation was being threatened by foreign powers," and that "starting in the 1960s, terrorist activities sowed the seeds of conflict in every corner of every country and region [in Latin America]." It was because of that threat, and only out of the need for self-defense, that the military "created the renowned Immediate Reaction Infantry Battalions, the first of which was the Atlacatl."[34] Similarly, Orlando Zepeda defines the war as "an internal war provoked by Marxist nationals, aided by the Soviet Union . . . which wanted to bring El Salvador into the orbit of international communism, like Cuba and Nicaragua."[35] For his part, Humberto Corado says the war was caused by "aggression by international communists, within the context of the East-West conflict, which provoked an internal conflict that carried such grave repercussions for all Salvadorans."[36]

But like their elite counterparts, the officer memoirists are well aware that whatever the origins of the communist threat, its immediate manifestation in El Salvador was domestic militants, who were conspiring to destabilize society and to arm themselves for a fight. When it comes to describing communists and their ideology, the officers' views converge closely with the elites. They consider communism to be a pathology that runs contrary to human nature. In the words of Humberto Corado, "communism . . . uses people to advance a utopian vision that has failed in every country that it has been tried; it has to resort to violence, because it can't solve peoples' problems, but only exacerbate them, because, ultimately, it is contradictory to human nature."[37] When he was serving as vice minister of public security in the late 1980s, Colonel Carlos López Nuila claimed simply that communists harbor a decrepit moral framework.

> Marxists have their own moral standards. They are different morals. They are their own morals. They are neither your morals nor mine. They are not the morals of a good man. They are not the morals of the church. They are not the ethics by which we base our studies, and a lot of time, our own professional institutions. The Marxist moral states that one must utilize whatever the means in order to achieve power.[38]

The Atlacatl officer, Abraham Marín, echoes López's sentiment in his 2007 memoir, claiming that the FMLN command utilized morally repugnant strategies throughout the war. He claims, for example, that in February 1986 near the Guazapa front, guerrillas held more than 300 people "against their will and under constant threat as human shields to protect themselves from the army's troops." He also says that the guerrilla high command "considered the civilian population to be a military target," and that "the victims of mines planted by the FMLN were a consequence of intentional plans by the guerrilla leadership." He refers to the guerrillas with the terminology used by military leaders throughout the war: "*delicuentes terroristas*" (terrorist delinquents, or DT).[39]

General Jaime Gutiérrez makes similar claims, saying that the guerrillas had to forcibly recruit "children from the countryside" to fill out their ranks, because they and their message were insufficient to convince people of the worthiness of their cause. He says the guerrillas used naïve civilian allies, like members of the teacher's union in the 1960s and 1970s, as "cannon fodder." He says that throughout the war, the guerrillas used "civilians as shields," a claim echoed by Colonel Sigifredo Ochoa Pérez.[40]

Other officer memoirists join Gutiérrez, Ochoa, and Marín in focusing on supposed guerrilla wrongdoings. Some of them present the elite victims of guerrilla kidnappings and assassinations as a pantheon of martyrs, referring to each victim individually by name, and/or devoting

multiple pages of their text to elaborate charts identifying them, the perpetrators, and the crime.[41] Almost all of the officer memoirists describe
the various acts of destruction caused by the guerrillas, once again sometimes in elaborate charts showing such statistics as the number of acts of
sabotage against the electricity grid. The memoirists insist that these various acts of destruction were designed to accomplish one thing: to sow
the seeds of chaos in order to make society vulnerable to a revolutionary
takeover. For example, Waldo Chávez Velasco says the guerrillas' terrorist activities in the late 1970s destroyed the budding tourist industry and
thereby undermined a promising development initiative by the government. He also says that guerrilla acts of destruction chased foreign in-
vestment out of the country and cost poor Salvadorans their jobs.[42]

The officers insist that only people with decrepit moral frameworks
could knowingly employ such policies. They demonstrate a rhetorical
willingness to forgive peasants who joined the rebellion as humble people
who were duped by communist agitators. According to Zepeda, peasants
"were inspired by revolutionary proposals." But the officers give no such
reprieve to leftist leaders. They define them as flawed people who were
driven by a thirst for power that they could not quench through legitimate channels because of their mediocre characters and limited skill
sets. Zepeda characterizes them as "extremely violent irrational people,
blinded by their political ambitions and fanatical to the extreme"[43] When
describing guerrilla commander Joaquín Villalobos, Humberto Corado
says "he was motivated to acquire power day-to-day in the name of defending the interests of the masses."[44] And General Mauricio Vargas notoriously claimed that Salvador Sánchez Cerén, former head commander
of the FPL, vice president in the Funes administration (2009–2014), and
president of the republic (2014–), would never have made it above the rank
of private had he served in the army because of his limitations as a person.[45] Another reason the officers portray communists as pathologically
flawed is because they describe the army as having implemented reforms
for decades, especially after 1979, and thus the guerrillas had no justification to incite an insurgency, except out of a self-interested quest for
power.

The officers describe the communists' organizational strategy as sur-
reptitiously gaining control over individuals and organizations, and then
guiding them, usually without their members' awareness, to destructive
ends. In this regard, they sound resoundingly similar to their elite counterparts. According to Marín, the guerrilla "terrorists . . . sought to under-

mine the principles of democracy and liberty . . . upon the pretext of social redemption."[46] Corado uses the example of the teachers' strikes in the late 1960s and early 1970s. He almost comes out in support of the teachers, saying that their demands for educational reform and better salaries "profoundly affected society's conscience" even if he opposes their tactics. But then he says that the rank and file of the teachers "was manipulated by a group of militant educators who went on to become comandantes in the FMLN."[47]

Like the elites, the officers focus attention on Archbishop Oscar Romero as an emblem of someone who fell prey to communists' machinations. Waldo Chávez Velasco says the Jesuits at UCA brainwashed Romero causing him to "change his thinking," which Chávez describes as "a criminal act."[48] Humberto Corado is even more critical of Romero, portraying him less as a victim of the Jesuits and more as a conscious advocate for leftist terrorists. In his words, Romero "played a decisive role developing communism in El Salvador."[49]

Even General Jaime Gutiérrez, who appeals to Romero and portrays him in a sympathetic light in his memoir, even including a photograph of him and his wife with Romero, follows the standard narrative of his memory community. He says that Romero was surrounded by "people [presumably the Jesuits at UCA] who didn't want him to listen and much less speak and who manipulated him in his interviews." He calls Romero's assassination "cowardly," but assigns no responsibility for it, saying simply, in the passive voice, that "Romero was . . . assassinated." Such obfuscation is hardly surprisingly from Gutiérrez, who is perhaps best-known for releasing Roberto D'Aubuisson from prison, the man most likely responsible for Romero's killing. In fact, Gutiérrez makes no mention of D'Aubuisson in his entire memoir, even in the chapter dedicated to maligning his fellow junta-mate, Colonel Adolfo Majano, who ordered D'Aubuisson's arrest.[50]

The uprising of 1932 naturally functions as a key event in the officers' conceptualization of the communist threat. Like the elites, they see it as a decisive moment in their nation's history, when the first communists gained a foothold and began their decades-long quest for power. When describing the events of the uprising, the officers stick to the standard conservative narrative of gullible peasants being manipulated by crafty communist organizers from the cities, like Farabundo Martí, who in turn were tied to international communism through organizations like the Comintern. But the defeat of the insurrection creates a complication for the officers that the elites do not address. On the one hand, the officers hail the decisive action of the government under the command of one of their own, General Martínez, for quickly ending the rebellion and suppressing the growth of communism. But the cost of repression was high: thousands of innocent peasant lives. The wonton massacre of poor people does not correlate well with the officers' portrayal of the military as the reform-oriented defender of the common person. They resolve this problem in much the same way they would deal with accusations of human rights abuses in the 1970s and 1980s—they simply ignore it. Instead, they focus on Martínez as a social reformer who worked on the behalf of the poor, or they blame the communists for having made such actions necessary. Humberto Corado admits that "thousands of Salvadorans paid with their lives," but he blames "the insane fanaticism that attacked the stability of the state and its republican, democratic and representative regime." Thus, he says, "the governments' forces were obligated to stop the excesses being committed by the communists." The government enjoyed the support of the people, who "supported his [Martínez's] actions," and who "never considered . . . Martínez to be a tyrant, but rather the savior of the nation."[51]

Even Adolfo Majano, the leading military reformer after 1979, who is more willing to document military abuses than any of his counterparts, describes the Martínez regime as both "an iron fist and a social reformer." He accuses the military of "overestimating their [the rebels'] capabilities," and being "convinced or self-deceived" about their ties to international communism. Thus, Martínez "could have acted differently . . . and avoided the tragedy." But Majano admits that hindsight is often 20-20, because the communists did try to gain adherents inside the military barracks and divide the army during the uprising. And he says the peasants who joined in the uprising were essentially duped, with a "large quantity of peasants participating without knowing what they were doing. They were ignorant of the movement's ideological scope." Nevertheless, during the uprising "the rebel forces acted uncontrollably, and their acts of pillage and abuse discredited them." Majano's message is clear: something had to be done to stop it.[52]

When it comes to sizing up the United States, the officers find themselves in a paradox similar to that of their elite counterparts: they celebrate the United States as a benefactor and a leader in the fight against global communism, but they criticize it for emphasizing human rights, which they believe hindered their ability to fight the communist enemy at home. However, the officers approach this paradox from a less-hyperbolic position than the elites. Notably absent are the conspiracy theories in the memoirs of David Panamá and Ricardo Valdivieso, who claim the U.S. State Department was riddled with communists and that human rights monitors were part of an international communist conspiracy. Elites condemn all reformism, and by defining human rights as a type of reform, they dismiss it categorically. The officers, by contrast, embrace reforms, and sometimes even portray human rights efforts as meritorious. The consequence is that elite memoirists tend to be more consistently strident and argumentatively consistent, whereas the officers' memoirs exhibit many more contradictions and paradoxes.

Almost every officer hails the United States for coming to the aid of El Salvador during the war. In the words of Humberto Corado, "The United States of America was a strategic ally of our country; the Alliance was based on a set of shared values. . . . Its participation, in terms of economic and military aid, was fundamental and crucial to prevent El Salvador from falling victim to international communism."[53] Orlando Zepeda says that "we must recognize that its [U.S.] aid to our nation was decisive, and without it the conflict would have been much worse and longer lasting; we must also recognize that this country, the U.S., headed the global fight to stop Marxist expansionism."[54] The minister of defense between 1984 and 1988, General Eugenio Vides Casanova, summarized these sentiments pithily in an interview with Max Manwaring in 1987, saying "thank God we've been able to count on the support and aid from the United States."[55]

Hail US aid.

But just as quickly as they celebrate the United States, they criticize it for making their task of defending El Salvador more difficult. Naturally, the Carter administration and its emphasis on human rights is a particular target for their ire. Humberto Corado, for example, criticizes the United States for withdrawing military aid from the Romero regime and leaving the Salvadoran military isolated and with antiquated weaponry just as the guerrillas were increasing their armaments and striking capacity. The Carter administration "implemented a confused policy toward the region, emphasizing the spiritual over the structural," he says, but "President Romero confronted the subversive movement relentlessly, regardless of the total lack of military assistance from the U.S." He dismisses the accusations of human rights abuses by the army as "acts of common delinquency that were maliciously attributed to the police."[56] Orlando Zepeda, almost on the same page that he celebrates the United States for shortening the duration of the war with its military and economic

But US also made FFAA task more difficult

aid, says that "the results of its ill-defined strategy [of human rights, etc.] . . . prolonged the conflict and consequently degraded the moral and economic life of the republic throughout the twelve years of war."[57]

Zepeda extends his criticism of the United States to the United Nations and the various international organizations that created and supported the refugee camps in Honduras during the war. He claims that those camps became guerrilla rearguards, where combatants could recoup and recruit safely out of the army's reach. As he puts it, "We knew that the guerrillas were there [in the camps], that they were taking refuge there and we couldn't do anything about it because they were under international protection." On the one hand he uses this claim to criticize the guerrillas for being typical communist conspirators who "manipulated the civilian population in those infamous guerrilla encampments." But he also uses the claim to criticize international refugee and human rights organizations for their naivety.[58]

Sentiments like these from Zepeda and Corado are fully evident in interviews with high-ranking officers in the 1980s, such as those appearing in *El Salvador at War*. For example, Zepeda was interviewed for that collection in 1987 when he was serving as of one of the six brigade commanders. He complained that the army was under constant scrutiny from international monitors, while no one monitored the guerrillas. "They [the

guerrillas] don't have to account for their actions to anyone," he said, "especially where violations of human rights are concerned." He went on to say that "we [the armed forces] are being supervised by international entities such as the international Red Cross, the Commission for Human Rights, the United Nations, the U.S. Congress, the Senate, the Democrats, everybody." Similarly, Jaime Abdul Gutiérrez, who was interviewed in 1986 and who by that time had retired from service, said that upon looking back at the 1979 coup, he felt that due to pressure from the United States, a primary problem with the new junta was that it had to take a hands-off approach to criticizing the left: "We had to declare the Right as our only enemy." General José Garcia, who had been minister of defense between 1979 and 1984 and was interviewed in 1987, claimed that after the first junta fell apart in January 1980, "international opinion was highly critical of us [the armed forces], because those who had left the government had already begun spreading twisted and slanted rumors about us, and attacking the institution. . . . We had no support from the United States nor from anyone else. We were alone."[59]

The Carter administration and its emphasis on human rights represent a complication for the officers. After all, Carter backed the 1979 coup and the subsequent reforms, and most of the officers who have gone on to write their memoirs rose to prominence in its wake. That generation of officers, many of whom belonged to the so-called *tandona* class of 1966, and who rose to power in the 1980s during the Reagan administration, owe their position to a human rights-based purge of the officer corps in 1984, after Vice President Bush's visit in December 1983.[60] The 1984 purge was preceded by a strategic shift within the army, partly imposed by the United States. Whereas the prior focus had been on fighting the enemy in combat-only operations, some of which resulted in the mass killing of civilians, the military began to conduct civic action campaigns designed to win the hearts and minds of the population.

One result of these twists and turns is a series of contradictory positions in the officers' memoirs. Take the example of General Orlando Zepeda. He is a critic of the 1979 coup, because as a supporter of the PCN he opposes the coup for ousting the last PCN president. Thus he is quick to disparage the coup and its U.S. backing by saying that "behind the coup against Romero was the sinister hand of Ambassador Robert White, who played an important role in supporting the FMLN during the war."[61] But as a member of the *tandona*, Zepeda survived the purge in 1979 and the next one in 1984, and eventually rose to serve as vice minister of defense in 1987. So even though he is an unrelenting critic of human rights monitors and international observers, he quickly celebrates the strategic changes after 1983/1984, which he helped to implement and which were based on the presumption that the military had been committing too many human rights violations and was losing the war as a consequence. In his 2008 interview in *El Faro*, Zepeda hails the creation of the Departamento de Operaciones Sicológicas (Psy-Ops Department), because it was a centerpiece of the "changing mentality about the struggle" and the need to "win the hearts and minds of the population." To embrace that strategic shift, however, Zepeda has to accept that the prior strategies were flawed, which leads him to accept that human rights violations occurred: "I don't deny that there were excesses. . . . When battling against these forces of anarchy and insurgency violence is unavoidable and excesses are likely to occur."[62]

A contemporary example is provided by a 1987 interview with General (then a colonel) Emilio Ponce, the top-ranking member of the *tandona,* who eventually went on to serve as minister of defense (1990–1993), but who at that time was serving as commander of the Third Brigade. "We must face the fact," he said, "that we were, at one time, responsible for the brutalities and ill treatment imposed on the citizens of this country. I repeat, the support and impetus given to the democratic process and the socio-economic reforms were essential."[63]

The Defense

The officers have every confidence that the military was obligated to defend itself and the nation from the guerrilla insurgency. "The government's right to defend the nation," says Zepeda, "caused the deaths of many thousands of Salvadorans, great suffering and the destruction of many millions of dollars of resources that hindered the nation's development."[64] Whereas the elites almost ignore the armed component of the war, with the exception of their own paramilitary defenses, the officers highlight it. They are proud of the military's commitment to the war, its sacrifices, and its willingness to press on for twelve long years of combat. "The opportunity to fight beside these men," says Sergeant René Flores Cruz, referring to some of his soldiers, "was a great pleasure and privilege, and I will be eternally proud of it." For Flores, the soldiers who fought were "heroes," and "brave men," the majority of them "people from the lower classes [who] made history defending our beloved El Salvador."[65]

Captain Carlos Vigil's collection of war stories, *Soldados en combate*, exudes a similar sense of pride and an esprit de corps. The book is based on interviews that Vigil conducted with more than two dozen mid-level officers, most of whom, like him, belong to the so-called Toyota Promotion, a particularly large class of cadets who graduated from the military academy in 1985. Because there were so many of them, they were compared to a ubiquitous advertisement that Toyota was running at the time that touted its vehicles' reliability and cross-country capabilities. The members of this "Toyota" class entered the service after the strategic shift in 1983 and the purges of abusive officers in 1984, so they see themselves as having fought an honorable fight against an armed opponent. Indeed, many of them were heavily involved in combat operations throughout their careers, and their narratives in Vigil's collection focus almost exclusively on combat, which they describe not only in great detail, but also with pride in their accomplishments, comportment, sacrifice, and comradeship.[66]

The older officer memoirists take particular pride in having held back the guerrillas before and during the first "final" offensive in January 1981, when the military was, by its leaders' own admission, ill equipped, improperly trained, and internationally isolated. Humberto Corado says the armed forces successfully "defended the nation and its institutions before the revolutionary commandos," despite the fact that the army "could only count on three thousand soldiers armed with outdated weapons lacking any training from North American advisors."[67] General Eugenio Vides Casanova expressed this same view in an interview in 1987, when he was then serving as minister of defense. In describing the 1981 final offensive, he said the guerrillas underestimated the armed forces, "even though we only had 14,000 to 15,000 men . . . and were not aware of what was really coming and what we were about to face on 10 January 1981 . . . the armed forces with their own resources were able to go ahead and defeat the insurgents."[68]

Generally, the higher-ranking officers do not provide detailed descriptions of combat in their memoirs, even those who served as line officers commanding troops in the field, like General Vargas. They tend to leave the descriptions of combat to the lower-ranking officers who did the day-to-day fighting and who have chosen to share their stores, like captains Marín and Von Santos, and Captain Vigil's interviewees. Instead, the more senior officers stick to discussions of strategy and the war's broader contours.

Captain Von Santos's memoir offers rare details of combat experiences, especially in San Salvador during a roughly two-week stretch during the second final offensive in November 1989. A 1988 academy graduate who commanded an Atlacatl platoon, Von Santos had trained to be a soldier almost his entire life, and describes his years in the military academy as "allowing me to discover the best in myself." After spending four years in the academy, which included additional training at the School of the Americas in Fort Benning, Georgia, "all of us were anxious to get into combat with the guerrillas." He was happy to have been assigned to the premier combat unit, the Atlacatl Battalion. His memoir offers no ideological discussion about the war; he simply portrays himself and his men as soldiers with a valiant duty to perform—defend the nation from its enemies. He doesn't glorify combat and he speaks bluntly about its rigors and sacrifices, such as the pain of injury and the sadness of death. There is nothing glamorous in his descriptions of the grinding, house-to-house fighting that characterized the urban setting of the final offensive. "Urban warfare is particularly difficult," he says, as he describes bullets, hand grenades, and rocket-propelled grenades flying about. He speaks with pride of his unit's performance, and he takes satisfaction in his own abilities, such as the time he surprised a guerrilla in a house and killed him in hand-to-hand combat with a knife.[69] That type of descriptive detail from an officer is rare.

Regardless of the level at which they focus their attention, the officers face a major challenge when negotiating the accusations that they and/or their predecessors committed massive human rights violations. The military killed and tortured tens of thousands of noncombatants during the war, some of them in blatant mass executions. Notwithstanding the rare admissions of culpability, the officers avoid responsibility in much the same manner as the elites, by using rhetorical strategies that either ignore the abuses, dispute them, or describe them in a way that lessens their significance.

A highly revealing example as to why officers might want to avoid defending morally questionable actions is provided by Colonel Camilo Hernández, one of the nineteen officers accused by a Spanish court of being responsible for the murder of the Jesuits in November 1989. He granted an extensive interview to the journalist Carlos Dada of the online newspaper El Faro in June 2011. He states explicitly that his motive for coming forward after twenty-two years of silence is to counter the accusations leveled against him by the court and gain "absolution in Spain." He admits to involvement in the conspiracy, but insists that it was much less than the Spanish court claims. In the process of explaining his actions to Dada, he sheds rare insight on the thinking of an officer who knowingly participated in a human rights violation, and he doesn't come out of the interview looking very good.

Hernández was serving as an instructor in the military academy when the 1989 final offensive broke out. He claims that he was ordered by Colonel Guillermo Benavides, commander of the military academy, to order the Atlacatl commando unit to assassinate the Jesuits. Hernández insists that Benavides was acting on higher orders, because neither he nor Hernández had jurisdiction over the Atlacatl Battalion and its commandos would never have taken orders from them under normal circumstances. Hernández insists that he refused Benavides's command to give the order to the commandos because he disagreed with the decision to kill the Jesuits. He claims that his reasoning extended from the fact that he had come to know and respect Father Ellacuría during the 1979 coup. Hernández claims to have been a member of the progressive youth wing of the military in 1979 and a supporter of Colonel Majano. He admits that normally a solider cannot refuse an order, but because everyone involved knew that the assassinations were criminal, Benavides ignored Hernández's insubordination and gave the order to the commandos himself. Hernández says he then retired to his personal quarters. Soon thereafter one or more of the commandos came to him asking him to loan them an AK-47 rifle that he kept as a war trophy. He says he knew that the commandos intended to use the rifle to kill the Jesuits so that the evidence of the shell casings could be used to frame the guerrillas. He gave them the rifle and waited. Approximately four hours later Benavides informed him "it's done," or mission accomplished. Dada asks Hernández what he then did, and Hernández says "I went to sleep."

Dada presses Hernández: "How could you go to sleep knowing what had just happened?" In responding to those questions, Hernández first deflects responsibility by saying that "I didn't give the order." He then goes on a circuitous tangent saying that because he was posted to the military academy he was an educator, not a murderer.

> You journalists do not understand the role of the military academy. It was educational. We had no relation with any of the units that were posted there, nor did we have any jurisdiction beyond our four walls. Neither the director nor anyone else commanded those units, and those units know us. . . . Our responsibilities were limited to sentry duty, patrols, administration and guaranteeing the security of the school. To us the war did not really exist. We were the only ones who got to go home and see our families. None of us were in charge of them [the commandos], not even Colonel Benavides.

Unsatisfied with that response, Dada pushes Hernández more, asking him how he can deflect responsibility when he willingly gave the rifle to the assassins knowing their intensions. Hernández responds by saying, "Well, because they asked me, but I wasn't involved. Moreover, it wasn't my armament." When Dada insists, "But it [the AK-47] was yours!" Hernández distinguishes between the rifle as a war trophy and his personal sidearm, which had been officially issued to him: "Everyone has rifles simply for the sake of having them. I'm not going to give my pistol to anyone; it had been assigned to me. . . . I am solely responsible for my pistol."[70]

Hernández's interview offers an incredibly rare look into how a Salvadoran officer rationalizes an extralegal assassination. A similar, but less revelatory example was also secured by Carlos Dada and *El Faro* in an interview with Captain Alvaro Saravia, a member of the hit squad that murdered Archbishop Romero in March 1980. Dada caught up with Saravia living on the lam in an undisclosed location in 2008. Saravia was more guarded than Hernández and sheds little insight into his personal thinking while providing details about the assassination[71] The other officer memoirists are more like Saravia than Hernández. When they address the issue of human rights violations and mass murder at all, they do so at a remove, and with the intention of deflecting responsibility away from themselves and the military.[72]

Take the example of General Mauricio Vargas, the supposedly more open-mined peace accord negotiator and former combat officer in Morazán. He employs a classic conservative trope to downplay the military's violation of human rights by insisting that both sides committed crimes during the war, and thus neither side should be scrutinized distinctly. In a 1997 interview with the North American political scientist Jean Krasno, he suggests, metaphorically, that "you commit a grievance against me, I commit one against you; ok, pardon me, no problem, it's over."[73] Vargas refuses to acknowledge that the military committed many more "grievances" than its adversary. In an interview in January 2010 with a journalist for *El Faro*, he is once again asked about human rights violations, especially about his role as a special forces commander in the highly contentious eastern zone. He responds by admitting that "I don't want to say that everyone of us was an angel," but he insists that he personally did nothing wrong and that the army as a whole did not have a deliberate strategy of killing civilians: "I spent 32 years in the armed forces . . . and as part of our institutional mission we have an ethical code that guides our conduct. The idea that we had a scorched-earth policy . . . well, I never received any order to carry out scorched-earth tactics." Even if Vargas's statement about orders he received is accurate, which it may not be, it still leaves room for a scorched-earth policy to have been carried out, simply without a specific order, or under the leadership of other officers. When the interviewer asks him if "massacres of civilians occurred," Vargas responds by saying "a massacre could have happened." But then he downplays the possibility that such acts did occur because any such deaths that people point to could have been the result of collateral damage caused during combat when soldiers were defending themselves:

"I was a special forces battalion commander and when you enter into a little village, or a neighborhood or a house, they begin shooting at you. Adrenaline allows you to instinctively defend yourself." When asked about the infamous example of El Mozote and why else the military would have stayed there for three days except to murder civilians en masse, Vargas insists that "it still has to be fully investigated," which blatantly ignores the overwhelming evidence—forensic and eyewitness—of a military massacre. He presses on by saying that something else could have caused the troops to slow down and stay there for so long: "The only entrance into El Mozote is a bottleneck and a single sharpshooter can stop progress entirely."[74]

The Atlacatl officer Abraham Marín at least admits that the Atlacatl Battalion killed civilians in El Mozote, but he too insists that they were caught in crossfire rather than purposefully targeted. During the firefight, he says, "a lot of casualties occurred among the civilian population as a result of the combat and air support." He then uses the passive voice to say that the soldiers' actions "have been characterized as an act of violence and one of the greatest errors committed by the Battalion." Later he acknowledges that a commando unit of the Atlacatl killed the Jesuits in 1989, referring to it as a "horrendous crime." But those two references to El Mozote and the Jesuit killings comprise the totality of Marín's discussion of human rights violations or crimes by the Atlacatl Battalion, or by any other military unit during the entire war. The remainder of his book is a celebration of the Atlacatl, its mission and his role in helping to fulfill that mission.[75] At one point, after hailing the Atlacatl's record of causing guerrilla casualties, he claims the Battalion's soldiers always respected the dignity of their prisoners, who "were treated according to the established rules of war and in accordance with the principals of universal Human Rights."[76] For his part, Captain Vigil's interviewees in *Soldados en combate* provide 450 pages of stories about combat and make no mention of abusive behavior by soldiers. The first interviewee accuses guerrilla leaders of raping young women in front of their family members, and guerrilla medics of mistreating a wounded soldier in one of their clandestine health clinics, and then contrasts them with his own comportment in regard to a captured guerrilla, saying we "made the rules of the game clear, telling him that we would not mistreat him at any time and that he would eat the same food we eat."[77]

Humberto Corado similarly makes few references to the cases of human rights violations and extralegal killings, and when he does so he absolves the military of responsibility. He admits that the army tortured people, but he classifies such actions as "excesses" rather than standard policy, and furthermore he blames the guerrillas for causing such excesses because they started the war and put the military in the position of having to fight them: "Such is war: an action provokes a reaction." That same logic guides his description of El Mozote, saying that "no one has the full story to know whether or not this action came about as the result of an action against us."[78]

He follows another standard procedure of his memory community by describing assassination victims, like Father Rutilio Grande and Archbishop Romero, in the passive voice: "Rutilio Grande was assassinated," he writes, and similarly "Monseñor Romero was assassinated the 24th of March, 1980." He even implies that the guerrillas may have killed Romero because "he had betrayed some communist groups and the Marxist-Leninist cause, and in communist discipline, such actions are punishable by death." He accuses the guerrillas rather than the security forces of causing the deaths during Romero's funeral procession, and he also says the left bombed the FENASTRAS labor union office in 1986 as part of a purge caused by an internal dispute over finances. When discussing the killing of the Jesuits, Corado basically characterizes the priests as legitimate military targets because "the UCA [Central American University] was heavily involved in the Salvadoran subversion; under the Jesuit priests' leadership, the university had a center of pro-Marxist theological reflection. Father Ellacuría was a victim of his own political activism." He admits that the Atlacatl commandos committed the murders, but then quickly directs his attention to the left and criticizes it for accusing President Cristiani of being complicit in the murders, who he says, did not deserve such treatment because he had expressed a willingness to dialogue with the FMLN. When Corado addresses the paramilitary organization ORDEN, one of the most notoriously terroristic elements of the government's security apparatus in the 1960s and 1970s, he insists that it was a humanitarian aid organization that did good work for poor people in the countryside. In fact, he insists, the reason western El Salvador saw such limited guerrilla activity during the war was because of "the social work carried out by local leaders of the organization." He at least admits that members of ORDEN "committed abuses" in the northern and eastern regions, but he's much more critical of the left for unjustifiably killing members of ORDEN, who were "members of the humble masses" engaged in "development projects" who "fell victim to the fanatical hatred of the left."[79]

Adolfo Majano represents something of an exception to this pattern of ignorance and avoidance. As part of his self-identification as an enlightened reformer within the military, he assigns direct responsibility to the security forces and/or paramilitary death squads for the crimes mentioned above, such as the killing of Archbishop Romero, and he mentions many other events during that critical period of 1979–1981 that his counterparts ignore. They include, but are not limited to the mass killing of a dozen peasants on the San Vicente volcano in June 1980, the torture and murder of the FDR leadership in November 1980, the torture and murder of the American nuns in December 1980, and the assassination of the two American aid workers, Mark Pearlman and Michael Hammer, in the Sheraton Hotel in January 1981. But he still offers a modest accounting, and furthermore, he is quick to balance these references to rightwing crimes with episodes of leftist terrorism, such as the assassination of Mauricio Borgonovo Pohl by the FPL in 1977. He concludes his memoir with a harsh critique of the radical left, saying it was just as much the problem, if not more so, as the reactionary right: "To put it very simply, they [socialism and communism] are genuine aberrations. . . . Prevalent within the left is dogmatism and sectarianism that is never able to admit to being wrong."[80] In this regard, even Majano is advancing the trope of moral equivalence, claiming that both sides committed atrocities and thus they effectively cancel one another out.[81]

The Assessment: Did We Win?

The officers are universally proud of the fact that the military prevented the guerrillas from accomplishing their primary objective of overthrowing the government. In that regard, they feel as though they won, and they frequently express satisfaction about it. In the words of Colonel Carlos López Nuila in the prologue to General Humberto Corado's book, "Before the strategic objective of the FMLN, taking power by way of a Prolonged Popular War to establish a populist totalitarianism, the Armed Forces supported the government's strategy, achieving the objective of insuring the existence of an open and participatory democracy in the western tradition."[82] Corado then follows López in saying that "with professionalism, dedication, discipline and bravery, the armed forces complied honorably with its responsibility to defend the institution of the republic."[83]

The fact that the war ended through negotiation rather than victory on the battlefield needles the officers. Most of them express the belief that the military would have won the war outright if only they had been allowed to press on. As General Orlando Zepeda puts it, "The military defeat of the FMLN was only a matter a time," but magnanimously, he says, the armed forces "decided to accept a negotiated political solution to the conflict, because it was the fastest way to end the war and less painful than the military route, and moreover the people wanted it to happen."[84] Even the peace negotiator General Mauricio Vargas agrees with Zepeda, saying that "the guerrillas could have been defeated militarily." He justifies his participation in the peace negotiations with the confusing claim that "never could peace have been obtained by military means."[85]

The officers also struggle with accepting the massive changes imposed upon the military as a result of the peace accords.[86] Many units of the armed forces were dismantled and the overall size of the military was cut in half. Some of the justification for these changes came from the simple fact that the war was over and the military needed less troops. But some of changes came about because the guerrillas had enough strength at the negotiating table to impose their view that the military had committed massive numbers of human rights violations before and during the war, and thus any negotiated settlement depended on the armed forces being overhauled. Given that the officers refuse to acknowledge those violations or take responsibility for them, it is no surprise that they remain skeptical of the accord-induced restructuring of the military. As one typical example, when General Mauricio Vargas is asked by Jean Krasno in 1997 why the police forces needed to be restructured after the war, he responds vaguely about how "they had been configured during the cold war," and that because the war was over "they had to change, and we believed that public security was going to be best served by stability and so we did it." Notably, he offers no hint that the police had been responsible for some of the most blatant acts of torture and human rights violations and that the guerrillas targeted them for reform during the peace negotiations as a result.[87]

Another consequence of the war was the depoliticizing of the military and its removal from government, which challenges the officers' celebration of the military's accomplishments when it held power between

1931 and 1979. Thus, the officer memoirists employ some rhetorical gymnastics to portray the changes imposed on the military by the peace accords as a victory rather than a defeat. For example, the officers commonly portray the 1992 peace accords as the culmination of the 1979 coup, which supposedly was the moment when the military decided voluntarily to transition El Salvador back to civilian rule. As López Nuila describes it, in accepting the peace accords "in conformity with its spirit of service and its commitment to institutionally, embodied by the proclamation of October 15, 1979, the armed forces accepted a reduction in its troops and of its past constitutional role."[88] Corado says that "after the end of the conflict, the armed forces dedicated itself to an internal reorganization in the spirit of modernization in order to effectively adapt to the new reality of peace time."[89]

For some officers, the peace accords and the changes imposed upon the military remain sore spots. Mauricio Vargas acknowledges that some of his fellow officers consider him a traitor for signing the accords, not only because it denied them the opportunity to win the war militarily, but also because it forced major changes upon their institution. "There are a lot of them," he says, referring to those who see him as a traitor, "who believe that these changes should never have occurred."[90] Even Vargas is disgruntled with some aspects of the peace accords, in particular its truth commission component, which blamed the military for the overwhelming majority of human rights abuses. In his 1997 interview with Krasno, he accuses the U.N. personnel who oversaw the accords of being too ignorant about El Salvador to do an effective job. He disputes the rigor of the truth commission and accuses its members of being biased toward the FMLN: "They never made a real attempt to strike an honest balance between the government forces and the FMLN." He continues on to say that "they took a heavy hand to the government's forces but were complicit with the forces of the left. They left out a lot of things about the FMLN."[91]

General Zepeda is even more emphatic in his opposition to the changes imposed upon the military by the peace accords. He celebrates the fact that the Salvadoran military at least survived the accords and thereby resisted those "voices in the national and international press that were trying to develop in popular consciousness that the nation should follow Costa Rica's example and abolish the military." Even though that drastic action was avoided, he insists that of all the participants at the accords, "the military was the most affected." He characterizes the forced retirements and decommissioning of nearly two hundred officers in the wake of the accords as "an unjust and humiliating process of being decommissioned." He says that out of respect for those officers he refuses to name them in his book, and instead insists that "history will be the true judge of those who were involved in this process." Not surprisingly, he is one of those decommissioned officers. He goes on to agree with López Nuila and Corado that the peace accords were a natural outgrowth of the 1979 coup, but because he opposes many aspects of that coup, he sees the peace accords as more of a long-term conspiracy against the military. He insists that the 1979 coup grew out of the U.S. government's desire to impose upon El Salvador its view that militaries should stay out of politics, which Zepeda says "is what caused many governments throughout the world to fall to the communists." Ultimately, Zepeda feels that the FMLN won big at the negotiation table, evidenced by its ability to force the dismantling of the National Guard and the treasury police, which "represented a highly symbolic victory, because those bodies had led the charge against crime, anarchy, and disorder."[92]

For his part, Colonel Sigifredo Ochoa Pérez, even though serving as a deputy in the National Assembly on the behalf of the ARENA political party, accuses some of the highest leaders of ARENA of wanting to "damage the Armed Forces" during and after the peace accords. He singles out for criticism the first three ARENA presidents, Alfredo Cristiani (1989–1994), Armado Calderón Sol (1994–1999), and Francisco Flores (1999–2004).[93]

A common theme among the officers is that postwar society still has many problems that will necessitate a strong and vigorous military in the future. López Nuila says, "the dangers are far from over," describing them as "terrorism, drug trafficking . . . the protection of the nation's natural resources, the migration of labor, and the inevitable natural disasters."[94] Zepeda provides his list of "threats to national security: delinquency, gangs, organized crime, drug addiction, prostitution, homosexuality and lesbianism."[95]

Conclusion

The officers have something very precious to them: the institution of the armed forces. They believe that it was threatened and they fought vociferously to save it. Some of them may have been driven by selfish motivations—protecting their own careers, salaries, pensions, and prospects. Some may have been incentivized by higher ideals—improving the nation and bettering the lives of a broader swath of the population. Whatever their motivations, they debated heavily among themselves over the proper course of action. Exhibiting a highly flexible, even self-contradictory approach to ideology, they pursued diverse policies to achieve their shared goal of institutional survival: they took control of government, they surrendered control of government, they promoted social and economic reforms, they purged many of their own, they fought an enemy on the battlefield, they supported a negotiated peace, and, of course, along the way, they killed, tortured, and maimed many tens of thousands of people—most of them innocent civilians.

In telling their life stories, and the stories of their institution and the nation, the officers employ a shared narrative structure that bears some similarity to that of the civilian elites—a status quo existed that was worth defending, a crisis emerged in the form of communists wanting to destroy that status quo, and a resolution occurred in the form of a militant resistance to that leftist threat. However, the officers' narrative diverges from the elites' narrative in significant ways. One way in particular is in regard to the descriptions of the prewar era and the role of the elites in causing the crises that led to war. Elites describe the prewar period between the 1880s and the 1950s as sort of golden age, when private accumulation could occur unhindered in a marketplace. For the officers, most of who came from humble backgrounds, laissez-faire economics and private property were one means to a desired end, not independent ideals worth defending in and of themselves. So if pursuing their goal of institutional survival meant implementing economic reforms that ran contrary to elite interests, then so be it. In the officers' opinions, the idealized status quo was an actively involved military seeking to prevent elite selfishness from opening the door to communism. To those who portray the military as simply the praetorian guard of the nation's elites, or "plantation guards," Mauricio Vargas says, "No. We had an institutional and constitutional mission."[96] Similarly, Humberto Corado defines the army as the "peoples' armed wing," reiterating a piece of rhetoric that the Salvadoran military had used for nearly fifty years to legitimize its presence in government.[97]

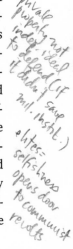

4 The Awakening

Guerrilla Comandantes before the Civil War

General Orlando Zepeda Herrera (ret.) claims that his incentive to write about the civil war was a desire to counter the left's control over the story. He insists that "almost all of the words that have been written about the war have been biased in favor of the left."[1] He later expands on this theme, claiming that "communists are very adept at managing information and utilizing their resources, including you journalists. One proof . . . is the large number of books authored by leftists."[2] Zepeda's claims are part of a longstanding conservative trope in El Salvador that bemoans the media's treatment of the political right. On the one hand, the claim is spurious. The media in El Salvador was and is controlled by a small coterie of wealthy, conservative stakeholders.[3]

Nevertheless, Zepeda's comments reflect the fact that the Salvadoran left, both its militant and nonmilitant variants, demonstrated an astute ability to build a media distribution system from scratch and disseminate their version of events. Even before the war, the incipient guerrilla organizations produced printed material in underground presses.[4] During the war they created diverse media outlets, including two radio stations, Radio Venceremos and Radio Farabundo Martí, and news agencies, like SALPRESS, which sent news reports from the frontlines in El Salvador to international audiences.[5] Before and during the war, guerrilla leaders, including Salvador Cayetano Carpio, Ana Guadalupe Martínez, and Nidia Díaz, wrote memoirs detailing their detention and torture at the hands state security forces.[6]

Whereas elites and officers have been reticent to tell their stories, seemingly wanting to avoid thorny issues, the guerrillas have been the opposite, and they have proven effective at getting their message out. The more open environment of the postwar era has resulted in many former guerrilla commanders telling their life stories in a diverse range of formats, including formal, book-length memoirs, blogs, websites, and extended interviews. Overall, the number of published life stories by former guerrilla commanders is at least twice that of the officers and elites combined.

This chapter and the next are dedicated to the memory group of former guerrilla commanders (*comandantes*). The two chapters are divided chronologically, with the onset of the civil war in 1980/1981 serving as demarcation point. The present chapter is devoted to the era prior to the outbreak of the war and includes the comandantes' youth, their decision to join the guerrillas, and their various activities during the formative 1970s when they built their militant organizations and turned them into challengers to the state. The next chapter picks up with the outbreak of civil war and follows through to the postwar era.

The unifying premise in the comandantes' narratives is that El Salvador was so structurally flawed and deeply controlled by an entrenched coterie of self-interested elites and officers that only militant revolutionary action could produce meaningful change. Once the guerrillas removed those stakeholders and gained control over the state, they, the leaders, would be best positioned and qualified to create a more just and inclusive society. As one guerrilla memoirist put it, citing an earlier assertion by his comrades in the FPL, we were obligated to "take power and construct the basis for setting up a new society."[7]

The comandante memoirists rely upon a variation of that unifying theme and follow a common pattern. They typically begin with descriptions of their childhood and the raising of their political consciousness as young adults. They then tell the parallel stories of the growth of mass social movements and their own decisions to join the militant left and enter the clandestine life of the guerrillas. Thereafter, they unfold a series of expositions and complications, including the factionalism within the guerrilla organizations, their fears of detention and torture, the joys of collective action, the cost of political activism on their personal lives, and the relationships between them and the rank and file fighters. All of these expositions and complications converge at the culminating moment in late 1980 when the guerrilla factions unite and prepare to launch their "final" offensive in January 1981.

The Narrative

Of the five top-ranking commanders at the end of the war, four have provided some form of their life story, including book-length memoirs by Schafik Hándal of the PCS/FAL, Eduardo Sancho of the RN, and Salvador Sánchez Cerén of the FPL, and an interview-length narrative by Francisco Jovel of the PRTC. Only Joaquín Villalobos of the ERP has to yet share his life story, although he has been a prolific contributor to the postwar debate through numerous newspaper columns and op-ed pieces from his post in London. Of secondary-level commanders, we have book-length memoirs by Carlos Rico Mira of the RN, Jose Luis Merino of the FAL, Juan Ramon Medrano Guzmán of the ERP, Lorena Peña of the FPL, Medardo González of the FPL, and Raul Mijango of the ERP, among others. We also have published interviews with Marisol Galindo of the ERP, Gersón Martínez of the FPL, Dagoberto Gutiérrez of the FAL, Eduardo Linares of the FPL, and Nidia Díaz of the PRTC, to name just a few. Two of the sources are by former army officers who joined the guerrillas: Francisco Mena Sandoval, who wrote a book-length memoir just as the war was ending and who gave a later interview, and Marcelo Cruz Cruz, who granted a lengthy interview three years after the war ended. Thus, the available sources offer a representative cross section of the five different guerrilla organizations and the diversity within each organization in terms of both gender and rank—ranging from combat commanders who led troops on the ground, to top-ranking commanders who spent long stretches of time abroad dealing with logistics and diplomacy.

The comandante memoirists employ a narrative structure that resembles elements of their officer and elite counterparts, in that it consists of a typical crisis–resolution–denouement format, or in more elaborated form, an original status quo, an initial problem, expositions, complications, crises, climax, denouement, and a new status quo. The elites' narrative, although multifaceted and complex, can be broken down into three basic parts: the existence of a right and proper social order between the 1880s and the 1950s (the original status quo); the threat to that order from liberals and leftists in the 1960s and 1970s (the crisis); and the fight against those threats in the 1980s, which if conservatives believe they won then is a happy ending and if they believe they lost is a sad sending (the climax, resolution, and denouement). The comandantes' narratives can also be broken down into three basic periods: the construction of an improper and unjust social order between the 1880s and 1950s (the status quo); the creation of militant opposition and the beginning of the fight back against the military and the elites in the 1960s and 1970s, culminating in the civil war of the 1980s (the crisis); and the conclusion to the war in a negotiated settlement in 1992 and the creation of a new postwar society, which if the author in question believes to have achieved desired results, is a happy ending, and if the author sees it as having failed to accomplish much, a sad ending (climax, resolution, and denouement).

The more elaborated version of this narrative adheres to some variation of the following. The original status quo is the hierarchical society that elites and officers established in the late nineteenth century with the onset of the coffee economy. The initial problem in the narrative is the individual narrator's awakening to the realities of that system. The exposition consists of the author's decision to become a political activist and eventually join a militant guerrilla organization. That decision then leads to a variety of complications, such as the negative impact on one's family life, the ideological factionalism of the organizing left, and the violent repression by the state's security forces and paramilitary death squads. Those complications usually come in serial form, consisting of numerous crises that more or less trace the individual's and/or the guerrilla organization's growth. All of the narratives culminate in the formal outbreak of war in the final offensive of January 1981.

Salvador Sánchez Cerén, top-ranking commander of the FPL for most of the war, offers a prototype of this narrative structure in his memoir. He has ten chapters with more than fifty subheadings. He begins with pleasant descriptions of his youth, which sets up his original status quo. He then moves on to the initial problem, the moment at which he discovered the troubling issues with his country and the fact that he now had to decide what to do with that information. That section, titled "Awakening of Political Consciousness," leads to the exposition of Sánchez's decision to become a political activist in "Activism as a School of Values," and then to join the FPL as a clandestine militant in "Initial Involvement in the FPL." Along with various other expositions, he describes crisis and complications, one of which was the need to leave behind his wife in order to protect her identity, which he describes in a chapter of her name, "Margarita." The other comandante narrators tend to adhere to this same pattern, although with variations. For example, some narrators deemphasize their childhood and focus more attention on the years of guerrilla ascendency in the 1970s; others provide few personal details and instead focus their stories on their militant organizations.[8]

Childhood: Precursor to the Original Status Quo

Although the comandante memoirists disagree with the civilian elite memoirists about prewar El Salvador, their narratives share a distinct commonality: they describe an era in history when things were right and proper.[9] Many of the guerrilla commanders hail from urban, educated backgrounds, and while they are hardly a uniform lot, most of them grew up in relative comfort in lower middle-class or middle-class households, removed from the grinding poverty of the typical Salvadoran rural laborer. Thus, in relating their life stories, most of them do not begin with descriptions of repression and the crushing burden of work. Rather, they describe happy and innocent upbringings surrounded by family and relative affluence. In this regard, their stories converge with the elites, who also grew up in comfortable surroundings. Whereas the elite memoirists consider the right and proper era to have existed prior to the outbreak of reformism in the 1960s, the comandante memoirists do not celebrate a particular period in Salvadoran history, but rather phases in their personal lives, mostly when as children or young adults they enjoyed innocence, before the harsh realities of El Salvador's social condition become known to them. By describing that period of youthful innocence in glowing terms, their narratives demonstrate an implicit sense of embitterment by the loss of that innocence. Herein the comandantes' narratives share an ironic parallel with elites: they seem to be inspired to fight, at least partly, because they lost something precious to them.[10]

Lorena Peña of the FPL provides one example. She grew up in a middle-class family in San Salvador in a comfortable home where "we had employees who did the domestic labor." She describes her family as loving and supportive, consisting of her mother, father, two sisters, and a brother. It was "a magical childhood . . . privileged," she says. She was the youngest of the four children and she portrays her older siblings as supportive and loving. She also mentions other family members who were present in her life and facilitated her development, including her maternal grandmother and her great uncle, who used to make her sit and listen to Beethoven. She summarizes her youth by saying "We lived in a responsible, progressive family without domestic violence and we were taught that a priority in our lives was to educate ourselves so that we could develop our own distinct characters and personalities."[11]

A similar tale is told by Eduardo Sancho, the ranking commander of the RN. He isn't quite as effusive as Peña in describing his upbringing, but it's evident that he came from a relatively privileged background of private-school education and international travel. As he puts it, "I was born neither poor nor rich, but in a comfortable middle-class position." He speaks reverentially of his family and their international ties to Costa Rica and the United States. Sancho was born in Costa Rica; when he was young his family immigrated to El Salvador, where his father taught hematology in the medical school. He refers to his parents as his "beloved parents," who lived in the exclusive neighborhood of Colonia Escalón in San Salvador. Sancho traveled to Costa Rica and Spain during his youth, and he was educated in El Salvador's exclusive Jesuit high school, the Externado de San José. From there he entered the main public university, La Universidad Nacional de El Salvador (UES) in 1965 and became involved in a variety of intellectual endeavors. He says the leftist students who controlled the student organizations at the university were suspicious of him, who "hailed from the middle class, son of a hematologist, a poet, a writer and ultimately someone who thinks with his own mind!"[12]

Humberto Centeno of the FPL similarly says, "We were a middle-class family. . . . I was a privileged child." His father was a judge in a small town and a cattle merchant. He says that he and his sisters had many responsibilities around the house growing up, but it was comfortable and happy. "I come from a family where no one ever went hungry," he says. He honors his parents by saying that while growing up "my father and mother never fought. . . . My father was a good man and my mother was a hard-working woman."[13] Almost every guerrilla comandante describes him- or herself in similar terms, such as Dagoberto Gutiérrez of the FAL, whose family was "middle class," Salvador Samayoa of the FPL, who came from a "relative affluent family," and Schafik Hándal, who hailed from a relatively prosperous family of Palestine merchants in the eastern city of Usulután and who was sent to San Salvador for school because his hometown didn't have a secondary school.[14] Gutiérrez published a short essay 2012 entitled "Letter to My Father," which exemplifies the nostalgia felt by a former comandante as he looks back on the years preceding his entrance into political activism. In the essay, Gutiérrez recalls fetching the newspaper from the corner store for his "beloved and remembered" father, to whom his words are addressed: "Later we passed the time reading, you in the hammock, I know you remember that hammock, and I in a small chair, suited to my size and age, reading the news sharing your insights with me."[15]

Some guerrilla commanders come from more modest backgrounds, but even they tend to describe their upbringing in positive terms, crediting their family environment as a decisive factor in shaping their consciousness. One such example is Salvador Sánchez Cerén. He grew up in the small town of Quezaltepeque, situated in a mostly rural area to the northwest of San Salvador. His mother was a market vendor and his father was a carpenter. Sánchez was one of nine siblings. "We were poor," he says,

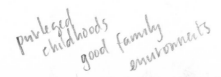
privileged childhoods
good family environments

but "not extremely poor . . . because the economic activities of my mother and father allowed them to maintain my nine siblings in a dignified state, not luxurious, but sufficient to provide us with an education and a minimum of material comfort." He credits his parents with "creating an environment of family unity that provided us with an ethical framework and in taking responsibility for the situations that arise in life." His perspective growing up was decidedly small-town. Visits to the capital city, with its "great movement of vehicles," represented "a totally different world." Nevertheless, Sánchez was decidedly unfamiliar with the day-to-day life of El Salvador's peasants. Not until his adulthood, while working as a teacher in rural areas, did he "come to know their reality." After attending junior high and high school in Quezaltepeque, experiences that he recalls with great fondness, Sánchez left home to become a teacher. He had the privilege of attending the premier teacher-training school, the Escuela Normal Alberto Masferrer.[16]

The comandante memoirists who choose not to comment on their upbringing, or even necessarily to discuss the economic position of their families, reveal that they had disproportionate access to education and that they were often raised with a Christian-derived expectation of service to others. Nidia Díaz, a high-ranking commander in the PRTC, tells a story of disproportionate educational opportunities and a Christian upbringing that instilled in her the expectation of service.[17] José Luis Merino of the FAL and Raúl Mijango of the ERP both describe growing up in relative poverty, such that they had to begin working early in their lives, but both of them make clear that they too had educational opportunities and eventually they attended the University of El Salvador. Mijango describes his family during his childhood as "happy and sociable," and even after the death of his father at a young age, which put financial strains on the family: "the sense of joy may have diminished, but the overall happiness did not."[18] Arquímedes Antonio Cañadas of the ERP provides comparatively few details about his family background and childhood, but one thing is clear: he had access to books and an education such that he developed what he calls a "reading addiction."[19]

The Original Status Quo, or the Incorrect, Improper Order of Things

After opening their memoirs with descriptions of their happy youths and positive family upbringing, the comandante memoirists arrive at a moment in their lives when they discover that Salvadoran society is far more troubled than they realized. For some memoirists, this moment came early in life, usually because they were surrounded by politically active family members or friends. For others it came later, often when they arrived at university and found themselves surrounded by intellectually and politically engaged faculty and students. Salvador Samayoa is one the narrators who found politics late, because in his "relatively well-off family, politics was not a career option. . . . It was expected that one would make his way in some other career or profession."

Regardless of when the moment of awareness occurred, each author grants it a prominent position in her or his narrative structure and usually demarcates it with a distinct chapter or subhead. Schafik Hándal refers to it as "my awareness"; Sánchez Cerén labels it "Consciousness Awakening," as does Lorena Peña; and Juan Medrano refers to it as "Coming to Consciousness."[20] This moment in the narrative is decisive because it fulfills multiple purposes. On an individual level, it presents the author with a dramatic choice—either ignore the evidence of El Salvador's harsh reality and live a "normal" life, or embrace political activism and become a target for arrest, torture, and death. An unavoidable sense of drama hangs in the balance of the decision. In narrative terms, a political awakening allows the author to establish the original status quo. When the author realizes the reality of El Salvador's problems, she or he then has the opportunity to tell the story of El Salvador's past, which in turn establishes the flawed social order that legitimizes his or her decision to turn to radical militancy.

The memoirists' moment of political awakening is usually triggered by a specific event. Repressive action by the state's security forces against them or their friends is a common trigger, but education and being exposed to new ideas and new ways of thinking, whether in school or by associating with friends or family members, is the more common route to consciousness. Rarely do the authors situate themselves in a specific ideological camp at this stage in their story, nor do they attribute their awakening to Marxism-Leninism or to an exposure to the classic texts of Marx, Lenin, or other canonical leftist authors. Eduardo Sancho claims he and his fellow militants took up arms first and read Marx later.[21] A rare exception is Arquímedes Cañadas of the ERP, who in addition to the influence of his politically active older brother, Dennis, attributes his radicalism to reading works by Lenin, Trotsky, Che, and Marx.[22] Most of the authors credit their awakening to a socially engaged Christianity, or the inspiration of certain international events, like the Cuban revolution or the Vietnam War. If Fidel Castro or Che Guevera make an appearance in the narrators' stories at this point, they do so in abstract, nonspecific ways, more or less devoid of ideology, absent of any references to their distinct revolutionary theory. The memoirists usually describe Castro and Guevara simply as upstarts who proved to the world that a small country can have a big impact.[23] In short, the foundational reference points for the co-mandante memoirists tend to be local and personal.

Salvador Sánchez describes himself as uninformed and politically naïve when he graduated from high school in 1960, and he attributes his "awakening of political consciousness" to educational enlightenment at a teacher-training school. After high school, he entered the prestigious Normal Alberto Masferrer, where he encountered a "highly qualified faculty . . . [who] inculcated in me a vocational calling to be a teacher and also provided me with high quality training." As a consequence, "I began to discover what was going on in the country." When he began working as a teacher, he discovered that the only path to job security was by being subservient to the bureaucrats of the ruling military regime (PCN). When his fellow teachers began mobilizing to gain more autonomy in the mid-1960s, the state responded with repression and intransigence. Subsequently, Sánchez began to think differently about El Salvador, starting with his hometown of Quezaltepeque, which he says "as a youth, I didn't understand at all." But with his new interpretative framework, he began linking the poverty of the "hundreds of people sleeping in doorways" to the wealth of the local elites who had "their own country club and their exclusive social circle."[24]

Like Sánchez, Juan Medrano claims that "I was not very political when I entered the university in 1971." He too came from a humble background; his father was a small farmer in the San Miguel region, and he had to start working early in life. The older rural laborers he encountered instructed him about class exploitation, but "my politicization began . . . when I was in my first year at the university [UES]." In addition to getting to know fellow "students that were deeply involved in the creation of the guerrillas," he began to "read the great literary texts . . . [and] I further dedicated myself to reading books about the French, Mexican and Cuban Revolutions, as well as the independence of Venezuela and its foundation in Bolivarian ideals."[25]

Eduardo Sancho and Humberto Centeno attribute their politicization mostly to education. They grew up in more privileged homes than

Medrano and Sánchez, but they too claim that education was the main reason for their political awakening. Sancho credits his experience at the UES and groups like the Círculo Literario Universitario (University Literary Society) with showing him how to interpret El Salvador in a new way.[26] Centeno got an earlier start than Sancho, but he too attributes his politicization to a study group, one that he joined in high school. His involvement in that group led him to join the Movimiento Estudiantil Revolucionario de Secundaria (MERS), the high school students' association, which propelled him to participate in political demonstrations and eventually to affiliate as a militant activist.[27]

The army officer who joined the guerrillas, Marcelo Cruz Cruz, attributes his awakening to a combination of seeing human rights abuses and acquiring an educational framework to interpret them. The abuses in question occurred during El Salvador's war with Honduras in 1969. He claims that the Salvadoran army's treatment of the Honduran civilians in its occupied zones was "virtually the same 'barbarism' that the Hondurans were accused of committing against our countrymen." He claims that "the situation impacted me, and I came to realize that the army and its commanding officers . . . were not very reflective." When asked by his interviewer when he came to that realization, he admits that it was later, "after the war," not at the moment the abuses occurred. After the war, the army sent him to study in Mexico, and it was there, in the vibrant political and educational environment of early-1970s Mexico, that he began to think differently. "My experience there led me realize," he says, "that El Salvador's problems with poverty, misery, illiteracy, malnutrition and unemployment were not unique, but rather existed throughout Latin America."[28]

Many of the comandante memoirists credit their family environments with playing an important role in their politicization. Sanchez refers to his brother and uncle, who "spoke a lot about Fidel and the Cuban Revolution." He claims that one of his brothers was arrested and tortured for having "expressed sympathy for Fidel Castro's cause."[29] Similarly, Lorena Peña's father was politically active, going back to 1944, when as a young army officer he participated in the coup to overthrow General Martínez. Peña says she marched in demonstrations in high school that were repressed by security forces, and that as a result of her encounter with "this persecution I began to develop consciousness and clarity." Her brother responded to the repression by joining the nascent FPL guerrillas. Her father was imprisoned for nearly one year in 1972, accused of participating in the failed attempt to overthrow the military regime after the fraudulent presidential election. On the day of her high school graduation Peña went to visit her father in prison rather than pick up her diploma. This combination of experiences led her to become more radicalized, and soon she began entertaining the idea of becoming a militant. Her brother served as her recruiting contact for the FPL.[30]

Mauricio El Sólido of the FAL hails from an affluent family in Chalchuapa in western El Salvador and credits his brother-in-law, Victoriano García, with his political awakening. García had been an activist in various leftwing groups since the late 1960s and preceded El Sólido as a commander in the FAL. In an interview in April 2013, El Sólido praises García's passion as well as the depth and power of his arguments, which he sees as all the more impressive considering García's lack of formal education.

> Victoriano impacted me. He was the first person I heard speak with such passion and force about the need to incorporate oneself into the popular struggle and to take land from the wealthy. My then-conservative way of thinking was impacted . . . and the strength of his logic left me pensive, meditating on his responses. And I had to conclude: he is right.[31]

Raul Mijango of the ERP hailed from a more humble background than Peña and El Sólido, but he too links his political consciousness to his family. His father died when he was a boy, so he had to work when he was young. Many of his working-class family members belonged to unions, and his mother organized a study group. He began his political activism in the unions as a teenager, and if there was a moment of awakening for him, it was when his brother was murdered by the national guard as a suspected political activist. Upon returning from the funeral, Mijango and some of his union comrades began planning an attack on a local post of the national guard.[32]

Like Mijango, José Luis Merino of the FAL came from a poor background—a family of itinerant workers, some of whose members were involved in union politics. When his interviewer asks what awakened his revolutionary potential, Merino refers to working as a young man "given the difficult financial situation that my family faced," which put him in contact with union activists, starting with members of his own family.[33] Victoriano García, the passionate recruiter of Mauricio El Sólido, tells a similar story in a 2007 interview. "My family lived as planters for Dr. Roberto Bustamante, near Chalchuapa, and when the conflicts over agricultural reform began, the old man evicted us, and we had to move to the village. . . . I was around 16 or 19 years old. . . . We rented a room, paid 7 colones, and the seven of us lived there." García was introduced to politics by a friend of his uncle, Antonio González, who was a member of the Communist Party and the construction workers' union: "We were agricultural workers, we worked picking coffee, and so it was that they began to introduce me to the organization."[34]

Regardless of the source of their political awakening, be it friends, family, education, or a specific act of repression, the comandante narrators typically use it as the point of departure to engage with the broader history of El Salvador. That history takes the form of a brief narrative, or as snippets of historical factoids inserted into their personal narratives. In other words, the memoirists typically begin their stories at a personal level, and then expand outward once they arrive at their moment of political awakening. Their renditions of Salvadoran history become the original status quo that depicts society as deeply flawed and needing revolutionary restructuring.[35]

Most of the memoirists' historical reference points consist of the litany of failed democratization movements or mass mobilizations that were met with state repression and elite intransigence. Francisco Jovel, the ranking commander of the PRTC throughout the war, identified the dates he considers key to El Salvador's story of mass mobilization as "32, 44, 60, and the decades of the 70s and 80s."[36] Jovel is referring to the uprising and military massacre of 1932, the overthrow of General Martínez in 1944, the short-lived progressive coup in October 1960, and the widespread mass militancy of the 1970s and 1980s. Short of the occasional overzealous narrator who takes El Salvador's story all the way back to the Spanish conquest, most of the memoirists use the same dates as Jovel and start with 1932.[37]

Just like their civilian elite antagonists, the guerrilla comandantes see the events of 1932 as a metaphor for the broader whole of El Salvador before the civil war. But whereas the elites see it as evidence of leftist leaders taking advantage of humble peasants, the guerrilla commanders see it as evidence of intransigent elites presiding over an unequal society and allying with the military to use violence on a colossal scale in defense of the status quo. The words of Father Miguel d'Escoto, who wrote the prologue to Salvador Sánchez's memoir, capture the general sentiment, saying that General Martínez was the "representative and defender of oligarchic rights . . . who repressed the communist [electoral] victory in various departments and refused to allow the popularly elected officials to assume their offices." When "the population rose up with machetes and clubs," he says, "the bloody consequence of General Martínez's actions was a great massacre . . . one of the worst, if not the worst atrocity committed against a Latin American people struggling for their liberation."[38]

1932

Francisco Jovel adds another element on 1932 to the comandante's narrative when he claims that the uprising represented the first time urban radicals went to the countryside and brought peasants into a united mass front, which serves as a precursor to what he and the other guerrilla organizers see themselves as having done in the 1970s and 1980s. In his words, "our generation undertook something marvelous, going to the countryside, organizing the workers of the countryside; we were university students and we earned the confidence of the peasantry, gradually, without overwhelming them, so that they could understand our ideas and maintain their self-confidence."[39] The patronizing nature of Jovel's claim has two unintended consequences. First, it ironically lines up his narrative with that of the civilian elites, who accuse the guerrillas of turning formerly docile peasants into revolutionary militants. Second, it places the guerrilla leaders in a position superior to the masses of the countryside, which is something that rank-and-file narrators push back against (see chapter 6).

For the comandante narrators, the events of 1932 are symbolic and metaphorical, because none of them had personal experience with it, nor do any of them describe their parents as having been directly involved. However, when their stories arrive at the overthrow of General Martínez in 1944, many of the memoirists' describe their parents' involvement in those events as influential in shaping their political views. Lorena Peña, for example, makes a tongue-in-cheek reference to her family as her "strategic rearguard," and opens her memoir with her military father's opposition to Martínez: "[His] democratic convictions led him to join the failed coup against the Martínez dictatorship in 1944."[40] The downfall of Martínez inspired hope in the likes of Peña's father, but the conservative backlash in the coup of 1944 provides Peña and other narrators with yet another metaphor of entrenched interests doing whatever was necessary to preserve the status quo.[41] Schafik Hándal was actually old enough to be present in San Salvador as a teenage boarding school student during the mobilization against Martínez. He cites one of the mass strikes against Martínez as a pivotal moment in his own political consciousness, describing it as "an electric shock running down my spine."[42]

1944

When they get to the coup of 1960, the comandante memoirists portray it as a repeat of 1944. A group of progressive officers and civilians took control of the government amid promises of reform. They accomplished much while in power, but they lasted only three months before being overthrown by a group of officers espousing anticommunist conservatism. The events of 1960–1961 occurred just before most of the comandante memoirists were old enough to be politically aware, so they usually discuss them indirectly or through the experience of older family members.[43]

In the late 1960s and early 1970s, most of the comandante narrators were in their late teens or early twenties, just beginning to find their own political identities. It is usually at this point when their personal stories converge with the national story and the first-person of the narrative intermingles with the third-person events of the Salvadoran story. For a few of the more senior memoirists, like Schafik Hándal, the convergence point arrives earlier, but all of the narrators consider the 1960s and 1970 as decisive. They typically cite the teachers' strikes in 1968 and 1971 as important events in shaping their own consciousness.[44] They focus particular attention on the fraudulent presidential election of 1972, when the reigning military regime stole the victory from José Napoleón Duarte and then later invaded the UES.

In fact, if there is any one event that serves as the defining moment for all of the comandante memoirists, either in regard to their personal story or the nation's story, it is the election of 1972. Almost every one of them cites it as evidence that militant opposition was necessary. In the words of Carlos Rico, the electoral campaign had generated "euphoria and confidence" among the masses of Duarte supporters, whose work in the campaign had provided them with "an experience of combative mass action. . . . The defeat in the election was a watershed."[45] Such high hopes then produced a major crisis of confidence. According to Father David Rodríguez, a former Jesuit priest who joined the FPL in the mid-1970s, the 1972 election was a breaking point for him and many of his parishioners. He was working as a priest in the small town of Tecoluca at the time, and most of his parishioners supported Duarte as a byproduct of their Bible-based study groups and catechist training. "A great many problems occurred in 1972 when Duarte [and the Christian Democrats] won a lot of mayoral races, but they stole the election and sent him into exile. In Tecoluca the Christian Democrats won the mayoral race, but the [ruling] PCN imposed Atilio Cañas of the PCN upon us; the people despised him."[46]

José Luis Merino had by then been a member of the Communist Party for two years. He followed the party line and supported Duarte's candidacy and even "formed part of his security detail." He too looks back on the electoral fraud as a defining moment: "I had my first experience with hard-fought politics in the protest against the fraud of 1972."[47]

Most of the memoirists joined their respective organization within a year or two of the 1972 election. By the time of the next presidential election, in 1977, they had given up on electoral politics. Thus, the blatant fraud that the military government perpetrated in that election did not surprise them and rarely do they cite it as decisive in their own ideological evolution. Nevertheless, they often refer to it in their narratives as an important event because many mass voters still hoped electoral politics could stop the slide toward anarchy. The subsequent fraud and the military crackdown on opposition demonstrations served as a recruiting boon for the mass front organizations.[48]

The comandante memoirists use this compendium of historical episodes between 1932 and the late 1970s to establish the foundational status quo. They insist that the historical record proves that El Salvador suffered from a decrepit social structure that was defined by hierarchy and repression. The people who benefitted from that structure—oligarchic elites and military officers—were not going to give up without a fight, which left oppositional activists no choice but to take up arms. It is at this point in their stories that the comandante memoirists claim that their decision to become armed militants constituted an act of self-defense. What came first, they insist, was the repression of legitimate and peaceful requests for change. Militancy was merely a reaction to the repression. Most of the memoirists make this claim explicitly, and the example by Gersón Martínez is representative of the broader whole. As he puts it, "there always existed a generalized authoritarian militarism and in response to that there was popular discontent, dissatisfaction, protest and the popular struggle." He continues on to say that the repression and the intransigence, or what he calls the "counterinsurgency war," had been well underway before the first guerrilla organization had even formed."[49] After summarizing the situation between 1931 and 1981, Schafik Hándal expresses the argument of self-defense by saying simply that, "a revolutionary war was necessary to put an end to the dictatorship."[50]

Such a claim contrasts directly with the views of civilian elites and officers, who insist that the guerrillas attacked them first, because, after all, prewar society had been properly ordered, or at least it was in the process of becoming properly ordered by reformist military officers. They claim that the guerrillas acted preemptively and unjustly. As one member of the civilian elite, Orlando de Sola, puts it, after offering his summation of the nation's recent history, "I can take your eye out with a fork, if you know what I mean. When it comes to that, I believe in the right of self-defense. . . . When there is an imminent threat, I believe in acting."[51] Interestingly, the elite and officer memoirists use many of the same historical reference points as the guerrillas, including 1932, 1944, and 1972. But whereas the guerrillas see repression and the preservation of elite privilege, elites and officers see communist conspiracies and threats to the nation's core institutions—private property and/or the military.

The Militant Attack on the Improper Order

The first exposition that emerges from the original status quo is the memoirists' decision to join the guerrillas and take up the armed fight. That decision usually occurs in two stages. The narrators first join the guerrillas secretly but retain their public personas, and then later become fully clandestine militants. Most of the people who went on to become guerrilla commanders joined early, in the first half of the 1970s. For each of them, the decision to incorporate was momentous because it constituted a point of no return. At that moment a person became an enemy of the state and was targeted for elimination. The decision to become a guerrilla also meant that the individual in question agreed to defer to the guerrilla command structure, and in most cases to prioritize allegiance to the guerrillas over all other personal or professional ties, including spouses and children.

Recognizing the significance of the decision, each memoirist usually remembers precisely when he or she became a fully clandestine militant, giving those decisions due prominence in the narrative. For example, Gersón Martínez of the FPL says that "definitely, my passage into the guerrillas represented an irrevocable step forward along a growing continuum in defense of the majority's interests." He eventually became a recruiter and brought many people into the FPL, and says that "for each militant [the decision to affiliate] signified a change, a passage into a new life and a moral transformation."[52] Juan Medrano of the ERP remembers that "when they approached me about entering the guerrillas, I felt a combination of joy and worry, believing that it was the right decision but rife with uncertainty."[53] As an indication of the importance of the decision to become a clandestine militant, the memoirists often recall specific details of the moment when it occurred. Lorena Peña, for example, remembers the day in May 1973 when her brother recruited her into the FPL and she had her initial meeting with a ranking FPL member in a public park. "My first meeting," she recalls, "was with comrade Rafael Avalos, who years later was disappeared by the police."[54]

For all of their awareness of the ideological distinctions between the militant organizations, the memoirists reveal that when it came to deciding which organization to join, chance often played as much a role as measured assessment. Lorena Peña joined the FPL because her brother belonged to it and he recruited her. But her sister joined a rival organization, the ERP, because her boyfriend belonged to it.[55] Raúl Mijango says that when his initial guerrilla organization, the Organización Revolucionario de Trabajadores (ORT), and its armed wing the Fuerzas Revolucionarios Armadas del Pueblo (FRAP), dissolved in the late 1970s, each member was free to choose another organization. In theory, that moment offered each member the opportunity to choose an organization based upon his or her particular ideological orientation. But Mijango recalls that in his case, at least, he joined the ERP out of circumstance, because he happened to be acquainted with some of its members.[56] Arquímedes Cañadas describes a rather humorous scene in the early 1970s when he was first approached by guerrilla recruiters. They happened to be from the ERP, but he had no awareness of the ideological divisions within the left, and so he assumed that their leader was Salvador Cayetano Carpio of the rival FPL, because he was the only militant commander Cañadas had heard of at the time.[57]

Whatever the reasons for choosing one guerrilla organization over another, the comandante memoirists' decisions to become guerrillas opens up a series of complications and crises that drive their narrative forward into the latter years of the 1970s. One complication that permeates the memoirs is the fear of being captured by the state's security forces or by paramilitary death squads. Being detained by them meant almost certain torture and probable death, as evidenced by those who were captured and lived to tell their tales, or by those who were captured but did not survive and whose disfigured corpses sometimes turned up later. Often the bodies of captured guerrillas never reappeared, leaving survivors to imagine the worst about what their comrades endured before dying.

The sense of fear was particularly intense in the urban settings, before the fight went to the countryside, where the fighters at least felt more pro-

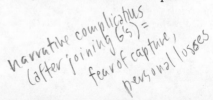

tected by the environment and their fellow guerrillas. In the cities in the 1970s, small guerrilla cells lived in isolation from one another in densely populated areas where one lapse in security, or simply one stroke of bad luck could tip off security forces and result in terrible consequences. In a 1997 interview, Ana Guadalupe Martínez summarizes the fear that accompanied incorporation into the guerrillas: "Everyone, leaders and rank-and-file members alike faced the prospect of being captured and disappeared during that period."[58] Eduardo Sancho recalls that "I was living in fear of death," although as a leader "I was unable to confess that." He elaborated on his sense of fear after describing the secret torture cells that existed in police stations and military barracks, and the types of tortures that were known to have been inflicted upon detainees: "Fear and terror invaded the psyche of urban guerrillas. . . . Nearby flashes of light caused anxiety attacks, and popping sounds that mimicked explosive charges sent tremors through one's bones, these were invisible wounds of the first years between 1972 and 1974, they went unaccounted but accumulated inside you."[59] Some of the narrators say they carried cyanide pills in case they were captured to avoid compromising their comrades under torture. If taken alive, they were expected to hold out for at least 48 hours before succumbing to the pain and confessing, in order to give their comrades time to take evasive action.[60] Juan Medrano sums up the consequences of not confessing to the police when one was detained: "horrible death."[61] Rubén Aguilar, a Mexican journalist who resided in El Salvador between 1980 and 1984 and worked undercover with the FPL, says he lived in constant fear. He describes going around unarmed, hiding your true identity, and not knowing if the police have discovered you and might pick you up at any moment, living "in constant fear."[62]

Almost every comandante memoirist carries the memory of at least one person close to him or her who was arrested and killed, usually after having been tortured. For Lorena Peña it was her brother, who was killed in an army raid on a safe house in August 1975. "I took the loss of my brother very hard," she says, "I wasn't able to say goodbye to him, I couldn't go to his funeral, I couldn't give any sign of mourning in the safe house where I was living; it was a clandestine mourning, shared only with comrades of my cell and not even with any of the other cells."[63] For Eduardo Sancho, it was Lil Milagro, who was held in detention for almost two years before being killed.[64] Similarly, most comandante memoirists have their own stories of encounters with security forces, either arrest and torture or a narrowly missed assassination attempt. Salvador Sánchez was arrested and detained for six months in 1978 for political activity. Raul Mijango relates two episodes in which he survived death. One of them occurred at a bus stop in the capital city where he was sitting alone waiting for a bus. An SUV drove by and one its occupants sprayed the bus stop with bullets, but "by luck and reflexes, I managed to escape."[65] Humberto Centeno offers enlightening comments on the psychological aspect of political activism, knowing that detention, torture, and death were possibilities. When an interviewer asks him if he was prepared for clandestine life, Centeno responds, "No, psychologically speaking. Look, we knew all too well that many members of the security forces had been trained as torturers." Although Centeno's comment references a later period in the conflict, in the mid-1980s when he was detained and tortured for his involvement in union activism in San Salvador, his description of the psychology of fear applies broadly to all of the memoirists throughout the duration of the struggle.[66]

After reading the countless descriptions of death and torture contained in the comandantes' life stories, a reader can't help but feel as if the memoirists who lived to tell their tales were statistical oddities. Everyone who joined the guerrillas ran the gauntlet of the state's security forces. The chances of survival were small, or at least they seem that way in the memoirists' narratives, especially in accounts by activists who joined their movement early and faced the risk of capture for many years. The memoirists who survived could just as easily have succumbed to the misfortune that cost so many of their comrades their lives. The lingering sense of fear and the repeated descriptions of death and physical abuse imbue their life stories with a macabre pall, despite the memoirists' strong belief in the merits of their actions and the legitimacy of their cause.

Another narrative complication that emerges from the memoirists' decision to join the guerrillas and become a clandestine militant is the negative impact on one's family life. For the safety of everyone involved—themselves, their family members, and their organizations—militants had to more or less sever ties with their families, unless their family members joined them in the struggle. Parents had to leave children, sons and daughters had to break off contact with their parents, and spouses had to be apart for years on end. In the words of Sánchez Cerén, "the stage of being clandestine was a huge sacrifice because we had to break relations with our parents and old friends and create a different life." Sánchez's immediate family joined him in his clandestine life, so at least he had them with him. But in the early stages, before his wife knew

148   The Awakening

of his involvement, he had to sneak around, hiding his activities from her, which sometimes required him sleeping elsewhere for multiple nights in a row, thereby raising suspicions and putting stress on their marriage.[67] That kind of familial stress, and the assumptions of infidelity that accompanied it, led Humberto Centeno's wife to reach a breaking point, when she told him that he had to choose between her and the party. Centeno chose the latter. He also had to endure the knowledge that his two teen-aged sons were imprisoned by the state's security forces for two years as retribution for his political activities.[68] Raul Mijango left behind a nine-months-pregnant wife, prompting her, like Centeno's wife, to ask him angrily, "Who are you married to first, your wife or the revolution?" Like Centeno, Mijango chose the latter, telling her, "I will not renounce the revolution."[69] Lorena Peña became pregnant shortly after she joined the guerrillas, forcing her to choose between being a mother and being a guerrilla. She chose the guerrillas, and she sent her son to live with her mother. She describes the feeling of having done so as "having one's arm, or head or foot cut off without anesthesia."[70] She only saw her son once per month thereafter, which strained their relationship forever after. Similarly, Marvin Galeas left behind a young child when he joined the guerrillas.[71] And Dagoberto Gutiérrez recalls that his decision to become a clandestine militant within the Communist Party resulted in "me leaving my family for the next 18 years. I didn't see my family for their own protection during those years I was clandestine."[72]

The memoirists recognize and usually lament the burdens that their political activism placed upon family members. A few of them describe the burdens in rather unaffected tones. Raul Mijango, for example, hardly expresses an emotion when he describes sending his wife a letter from the front saying that he wasn't coming home and that she was released from their marriage.[73] Similarly Marvin Galeas hardly mentions his child. It's not clear if Mijango and Galeas are emotionally detached or employ writing styles that depict them that way. Most of the memoirists express strong emotions when discussing the impact of their political activism on family members. They defend their decisions by saying that they were motivated by selflessness, by the decision to fight for a greater good, and thus invariably everyone had to make sacrifices. Nidia Díaz summarizes this sentiment when she rationalizes leaving her son behind.

The defense of principals and the social cost one pays because I had the opportunity to say "No, I'm going to take care of my son, or finish my profession, I lessen my participation and that's it." But no. First and foremost was the struggle and I have to continue ahead if I want a better future for my son. I have to give it to him.[74]

The comandante memoirists describe other challenges resulting from their decision to become a clandestine militant. For security reasons, they not only had to abandon past relationships, but also forego new ones. They lived in poverty, on the run, and under great pressure, all the while having to maintain a public persona that would limit suspicion.[75] Almost every one of the memoirists recalls long hours of seclusion in safe houses, either awaiting orders or hiding from authorities. "Clandestine life is difficult, full of limitations," says Raul Mijango. One of the most difficult aspects of clandestine life, he says, "is in regard to personal relationships." Militants were prohibited from having intimate relations without anyone outside the confidence of the organization, and Mijango remembers the mandate being especially challenging for young men like him, who were "in the prime of life." Men outnumbered women in the organizations by a large margin, and so Mijango recalls the experience of waiting for a prospective girlfriend to come along as akin to waiting at a bank in a long line that never moves. Mijango also recalls the experience of living in one safe house as being "closed in for entire days, leaving only at night, eating the rations of food that the leader bought from Kemal, a nearby eatery."[76] Similarly, Eduardo Sancho recalls being sequestered in a safe house on one occasion for fifteen days. "We never left during the light of day, nor did we lift a blind. . . . We had a five-pound jug of dried milk that we would mix up during those long days, without any books to read nor radio to listen to." Sancho goes on to note that the so-called founding pioneers, like him, had to leave everything behind, "girlfriends, university studies, a normal social life, parents, siblings, favorite readings, travel, clubs and childhood friends." He summarizes the experience by saying that "no one is prepared naturally to cope with those conditions."[77]

One way that the memoirists resolve these crises and challenges is by celebrating their friendships and the collective nature of the struggle. In this regard, the memoirs bring to mind the work of Elisabeth Jean Wood. In her study of insurgent collective action in El Salvador, she finds that people who supported the insurgency found "pleasure in agency," meaning they enjoyed being part of a collective endeavor, fighting for something bigger than themselves. In Wood's words, "pleasure in agency is the pleasure in together changing unjust social structures through intentional action."[78] Wood's subjects tended to be members of the rank and file, but the comandante memoirists express similar sentiments, drawing strength from having participated in a collective exercise.

Lorena Peña, for example, says she assuaged the guilt she felt for leaving her new son behind by reading revolutionary texts that defined motherhood in broader terms. She recalls a Mother's Day speech by Lenin in which he celebrated revolutionary mothers for their willingness to nurture humanity as a whole, rather than just their own family. "That text," Peña says, "consoled me and made me feel that I wasn't a terrible mother, but rather had assumed a historic and social maternity." Peña also recalls strong friendships with her fellow guerrillas and how they helped her navigate personal challenges. One Christmas holiday, Peña was alone in a safe house while neighbors all around her celebrated with friends and families. Two fellow guerrillas who were not in hiding at the time sacrificed dinner with their families to be with her that evening. "They taught me a magnificent lesson about solidarity," she writes.[79]

A key moment in most of the memoirists' celebration of collective action is their first armed operation. For most of them it consisted of a paradoxical blend of personal fear and collective triumph. They were nervous about going into combat, but they believed the operation symbolized the moment they and their fellow militants demonstrated a willingness to put their lives on the line to pursue justice and to become active agents in Salvadoran history. Carlos Rico opens his memoir with a description of his first armed operation with the ERP in 1972. It was the now well-known attack on a pair of national guardsmen outside a hospital in San Salvador that signified the beginning of the ERP's armed actions. "Upon receiving the order," he writes, "I began to shake, we were not playing around, the moment of truth had arrived, my military preparation left a lot to be desired, I was far from being a commando, but I had to go forward." The successful conclusion to that operation prompted the ERP to emit their inaugural communique to the public, declaring that "the peace of the rich has ended. The war of the people has begun."[80] For José Luis Merino of the FAL, his first armed action came later, in 1977. It consisted of "sabotaging transport," that is, burning busses as part of a public demonstration against the fraud of the 1977 presidential election. "My first experience was traumatic, I shook all over, my feet, my hands. . . . I was carrying a .45 caliber automatic pistol, and I stuck it in the ribs of a man to make him move. I was shaking, shaking. . . . I was barely able to control my nerves and prevent myself from shooting him."[81]

As part and parcel of their celebration of collective action, the memoirists exhibit an intense loyalty to their respective guerrilla organization, and they equate, often implicitly, their guerrilla faction with the masses of Salvadorans. They believe that their respective organization was the rightful leader in the fight for justice, and thus each narrator tells a similar foundational narrative in which taking up arms against the state is done for the masses.

Paradoxically, such organizational loyalty fuels the sectarianism that undermines a sense of collective purpose and shared sacrifice. By virtue of having joined a particular guerrilla organization, whether he or she did so intentionally or by chance, each memoirist inherently rejected the alternatives. The various guerrilla organizations were divided by ideology and strategy, and sometimes by the personalities of their leaders, and they competed with one another for recruits and resources, to say nothing of preeminence within the public's consciousness. Unavoidably, whenever memoirists extol the virtues of their respective organization, they disparage their rivals. José Luis Merino summarizes his understanding of the rivalry in the mid-1970s, saying that "at that time, there was no communication or coordination with the other four revolutionary organizations that would later go on to form the FMLN. We were alienated from one another." He goes on to say that "furthermore, we were enemies."[82]

Once the memoirists ended up in their respective organization, they received ideological training as to the virtues of their organization's ideology. Almost every memoirist speaks of a period of intense studying, reading and listening to lectures by their leaders. As Lorena Peña recalls, once she joined the FPL, a core part of her initial training consisted of "an intense political formation." In addition to reading and discussing a variety of canonical texts by Lenin and Marx, she and other recruits were required to read "the newspaper *El Rebelde* that was the official organ of the FPL. It educated us about service to the people, being loyal to the cause and being prepared to die for it."[83] Both Peña and Sánchez Cerén comment on the extended training sessions they had with the FPL's founder, Cayetano Carpio, who instructed them on ideological matters and on various aspects of guerrilla life. Peña says she "saw him as a father figure."[84] Sánchez Cerén recalls that "we read, studied and listened to lectures."[85]

A main focus for all the comandante memoirists, regardless of which organization they belonged to, was "*realidad nacional*" (national reality).[86]

That phrase appears repeatedly, in almost every memoir, and it reflects one of the memoirists' most fundamental propositions, namely that they were basing their distinct version of militant activism on a foundation of objective truth. As just one typical example of this type of debate, Schafik Hándal describes the Communist Party's dispute with the FPL, the breakaway faction led by his nemesis Salvador Cayetano Carpio. Hándal says that he and his fellow communists based "our conception on an objective analysis of the history of our country."[87] A basic goal of each guerrilla organization was to define objectivity for its members, to share it with anyone willing to listen, and to convince as many people as possible that their interpretation of reality was the correct one. To the extent that they paid the other guerrilla factions any mind, they contested their rivaling definitions of national reality.[88]

In time each of the memoirists rose to the ranks of leadership in their respective organization, and some even became trainers of newly incorporated members. Lorena Peña, for example, became a trainer within a couple years of her recruitment into the FPL. She helped organize the "*escuela de cuadros*" (recruit school), in which she and other teachers "provided instruction about national reality, the socio-economic formation of El Salvador, counterinsurgency strategy, Prolonged Popular War, mass fronts, military fronts, militia fronts and party construction."[89]

One goal of these training programs was for the leaders of each organization to ensure that their members shared a common ideological vision. They hoped that this vision would imbue the members with a sense of collective purpose and grant them the ability to agree on strategy and tactics. More cynical onlookers, including former guerrillas who abandoned the ranks, claim that the goal of the training was to indoctrinate the rank and file into the leaders' worldview and thus make them compliant followers.[90] Even the language of the loyalists could be interpreted to support that claim. For example, as Lorena Peña puts it, one objective of the classes was to ensure that "recruits would come to be part of our common vision and share our collective understanding about strategy and our approach to collective work."[91]

Naturally, one goal of achieving this common vision was to define the enemy, that is, the elites, the military, and the U.S. government. But invariably the training took the form of defining the rival guerrilla factions and explaining why their ideological approaches were wrong. These interorganizational critiques promoted factionalism, which emerges as one of the main crises and complications in the memoirists' narratives. The animosity between the PCS and the FPL was particularly intense, as evidenced by the narrative of the longtime PCS leader Schafik Hándal, who devotes an entire subsection of his memoir to disparaging the secessionist FPL founder and former secretary general of the PCS, Cayetano Carpio. In a subsection titled "Cayetano and his dogmatism," Hándal accuses Cayetano of being self-righteous and believing that his understanding of Marxism was more sophisticated than that of the other members of the PCS in the 1960s because he spent three years studying in the Soviet Union. Hándal says that he and his fellow party members who had stayed behind in El Salvador achieved a high level of competency in Marxism through self-study. Hándal offers a revisionist explanation for Cayetano's decision to split with the party in 1969 and eventually found the FPL. The standard narrative says that Cayetano broke from the PCS in opposition to the party's support for El Salvador's war against Honduras in 1969. But Hándal attributes the split to Cayetano's anger over being rejected as the party's leader. Hándal claims that the ranking members of the party resisted pressure to accept Cayetano as their leader from a Soviet diplomat who met with them in Costa Rica in 1969. It was in response to that rejection, Hándal claims, that Cayetano decided to break away.

The accuracy or inaccuracy of Hándal's claims is beside the point. The main thing to appreciate about his portrayal of Cayetano is that it demonstrates the level of animosity between two organizations nearly thirty-five years after their initial split in 1969, and more than twenty years after Cayetano's death in 1983. Hándal's personal animosity toward Cayetano is indicative of the broader institutional factionalism between the various organizations on the left. He shares similar, although less extensive, criticisms of the other three guerrilla factions: the ERP, the RN, and the PRTC.[92] Ironically, given Hándal's accusations of dogmatism against Cayetano, the longtime ERP leader, Joaquín Villalobos, directs the same accusation against Hándal, calling him an authoritarian leader and a constant conspirator focused on advancing his own political career. Villalobos's critiques of Hándal's conduct during and after the war, ironically mimic the elites' and officers' standard criticism of communists, as relentless conspirators. Referencing his twelve years of working with Hándal on the FMLN's general command, Villalobos describes him as the ultimate conspirator. Hándal's organization, the Communist Party, and its armed wing, the FAL, were militarily insignificant in Villalobos's assessment, and so to make up for their deficiencies, Hándal devoted his energies to jockeying for position within the FMLN and to presenting himself before the public as the FMLN's lead spokesperson. Meanwhile, Villalobos says he and the other commanders were busy fighting a war. Villalobos laments not having worked harder to keep Hándal in check. He took to calling Hándal "Ayatollah Hándal" during Hándal's bid for the presidency in 2004.[93]

Carlos Rico of the RN says that these factional divides assumed international dimensions. Each organization sought out international allies and often criticized its rivals before them in hopes of monopolizing international support. As just one example, Rico mentions the competition in the mid-1970s in Costa Rica between the FPL and the RN for support from the Costa Rican left.[94] Schafik Hándal refers to interfactional competition between the five guerrilla organizations for arms and supplies coming from international sources in the months leading up to the first offensive in 1981.[95]

Even though the memoirists sometimes demonstrate an intense awareness of rival organizations and their ideological differences, their narratives exhibit a highly paradoxical trait: they go for long stretches without mentioning their rivals, thereby portraying themselves and their particular organizations as the main protagonists in the story. As just one example, Carlos Rico was affiliated with a group of young militants who founded the ERP, but he doesn't mention the FPL until page seventy-seven of his memoir; and even then gives it only a passing reference. Curiously, factional divides defined Rico's early militancy. He broke from the founding group of the ERP and joined the ORT, and later joined the RN when it broke from the ERP in 1975. Yet, his memoir makes it seem as if a major rival organization, the FPL, was nonexistent. In particular, at the decisive moment in 1971–1972 when the ERP and ORT were forming, he makes no mention of the FPL as an option or even a factor in his and his comrades' decision-making.[96] He says nothing about the Communist Party either, until the war breaks out in earnest in 1980 and 1981. Similarly, Lorena Peña of the FPL rarely mentions the other guerrilla organizations throughout her narrative of the 1970s, making only passing references to them under special circumstances, like the ERP's decision to assassinate Roque Dalton in 1975.[97]

Even in the narrow geographical confines of El Salvador, the memoirists demonstrate that the rival organizations could be oblivious of one another. Before the war moved out to the countryside in earnest after 1981, the theater of battle was small. It consisted mostly of urban areas, particularly the capital city of San Salvador, which at the time was a modest-sized city of fewer than one million people. At any given moment between three and six distinct militant organizations were operating simultaneously, and they were carrying out similar missions—robbing banks, kidnapping elites, seeking recruits, setting up safe houses, issuing communiques, and trying to establish themselves as the leading opposition organization. There was only so much money, so many recruits, and so many opportunities to go around, and yet the memoirists rarely discuss the rival organizations as direct competitors for those resources. Herein, the memoirs reveal a highly paradoxical quality of leftist factionalism in the 1970s: it was simultaneously all-important and irrelevant.

In addition to competition between the various guerrilla organizations, the memoirists describe factions existing within each organization. Sometimes these clashes were caused by competition for leadership positions or personality disputes. Carlos Rico identifies one clash as being the consequence of a rivalry between "the interior and the exterior," that is, between those comrades inside El Salvador, who believed they were "running the risk of losing their lives or being captured and tortured," and those "outside," who worked in international circles and lived more "comfortable lives." As a leader of the RN's logistics and supply chain Rico spent a lot of time abroad and belongs to the "exterior" group, and while he expresses sympathy toward the views of his comrades inside El Salvador, he nonetheless considers their criticisms to be discriminatory and invalid.[98]

More fundamentally, the memoirists claim that internal rivalries originated in members' divergent interpretations of *realidad nacional* and took the form of differing opinions about strategy and tactics. The existence of these internal rivalries is no surprise; after all, each organization came into existence by rejecting or breaking from a prior organization. So within each of them it is natural that factions and fault lines continued to exist, threatening yet more secessionism. Lorena Peña and Salvador Sánchez both comment on the emergence of an internal dispute in the FPL in 1975 over the relationship between the vanguard leadership and the rank-and-file followers. Peña says that "when the great debate ended, various recruits quit the party, convinced that we were defeated."[99] Salvador Sánchez comments on a similar dispute within the FPL a few years later, when some affiliated members of the mass front organizations "took positions contrary to the armed struggle," which went against the FPL's fundamental goal of toppling the regime militarily.

One consequence of this dispute was a growing ideological divide between the FPL's two ranking leaders, Salvador Cayetano Carpio and Mélida Anaya Montes, which ended in homicidal tragedy a few years later.[100] Raúl Mijango relates a similar situation at roughly the same time within his initial organization, the ORT/FRAP. Its members disagreed with one another over the future of armed conflict. But instead of trying to resolve their dispute and maintain their organization, the members decided to dissolve and allow themselves to affiliate with other organizations.[101]

One of the most notorious internal disputes within the guerrilla organizations occurred in the ERP in 1975 and culminated in the assassination of the poet Roque Dalton.[102] Because of the notoriety of Dalton's execution, most every one of the memoirists with ties to the ERP comments on the events. The consensus is that Dalton got caught in the middle of a series of complicated disputes between the various leaders of the ERP over ideological and tactical issues. The end result is that a particular faction opposed to Dalton gained the upper hand and decided that he had to be eliminated. They accused him of various things, including being an agent for the CIA, which ironically is the same accusation that the Communist Party directed against the members of the ERP for embarking on revolutionary militancy in the first place. Newly released CIA documents prove that accusation to have been false, although while Dalton was imprisoned in El Salvador in 1964, an agent for the CIA met with him on two occasions and tried to convince him to become an asset in exchange for his freedom; Dalton refused.[103] The faction that opposed Dalton's killing then broke away from the ERP and formed the RN. Juan Medrano stayed with the ERP throughout the crisis and believes that Dalton's death was a decisive moment in the history of the guerrillas. "Looking at the events in hindsight," he says, "Dalton's death undermined our leaders' legitimacy and made it difficult for us to advance a collective struggle with a shared vision about politics and military strategy." He claims that Dalton's death "not only sealed the political divide, but also placed a vendetta on our organization."[104] Both Medrano and Schafik Hándal claim that when members of the RN issued a communique condemning Dalton's killing, the leadership of the ERP targeted RN leaders for assassination. Medrano says he was sent on a mission to assassinate a particular leader, Dr. Víctor Amaya, who was a former friend. He managed to avoid carrying out the order by contacting another leader in the ERP and getting permission to abort the mission.[105]

The killing of Dalton highlights a major challenge that each of the guerrilla organizations faced, namely balancing a vertical chain of command in a fight against authoritarianism while simultaneously trying to encourage open discussion within the ranks and protect the organization from legitimate threats, like infiltrators and spies. Carlos Rico comments on this issue specifically in regard to his decision to leave the ERP in its early stages, accusing its leaders of exhibiting traits consistent with "typical bourgeois military authoritarianism."[106]

The threat of infiltrators was real, and whether or not an organization could root them out carried life or death consequences. Juan Medrano says that a security lapse in the ERP in the 1970s allowed the police to raid sixteen of the organization's twenty safe houses in San Salvador.[107] As another example, José Merino describes how, during the early days of union organizing in the late 1960s, the owners of a factory that was being targeted by the union planted a spy in one of the secret cells; he gave the names of the cell members to the owners who then fired all of them.[108]

But as Dalton's execution illustrates, the issue of protecting the organization from spies was open to abuse. It could be manipulated by insecure leaders in the midst of factionalist disputes to eliminate rivals and secure their positions. Almost every one of the memoirists acknowledges that a major challenge before the Salvadoran left in its formative years in the 1970s up to the outbreak of war in 1980 and 1981 was its propensity to factionalize and engage in internecine disputes. Francisco Jovel of the PRTC comments on this issue in an interview in which he contrasts El Salvador's left and right, saying that "the right appreciated the importance of unity more than the left. . . . The right understood that survival depended on unification, whereas leftists could not see the need for unification as part of their quest for power."[109] Similarly, Carlos Rico says that his experience of going through the factionalized dissolution of the ORT in 1975 showed how "we committed a common error of Latin American leftists by dividing ourselves . . . which resulted in tense moments, with each faction convinced of the righteousness of its ideas."[110]

Consistent with their criticisms of rival organizations, the comandante memoirists remain loyal to their own organization. They tend to speak about it in uniformly positive terms, and they defend its actions and policies over time. This demonstration of loyalty is no surprise; after all, they were leaders in their organizations and thus they have strong incentives to cast things in a positive light. Their loyalty remains true even for those memoirists who were sanctioned by higher-ranking leaders. For example,

Lorena Peña was sanctioned by the leadership of the FPL in the late 1970s for conduct in her personal life. She broke off a romantic relationship with another FPL leader, who happened to be a peasant, and so she was accused of harboring bourgeois pretensions. As punishment, she was not allowed to fraternize with, or even speak to men for six months. Peña considers her punishment strange, and in hindsight sexist, but she admits that at the time her feminism was too undeveloped to fully grasp its significance. Despite her displeasure with the sanction, she accepted it and remained loyal to the FPL for the remainder of her life.[111] Something similar occurred with Juan Medrano of the ERP. He too was sanctioned, although later than Peña, partly for personal reasons and partly due to his leaders' authoritarian tendencies. He disagreed with the sanction, but accepted it and remained in the organization, eventually returning to a leadership position. He is willing to criticize the ERP, not only for his sanction, but also for things like the assassination of Roque Dalton. But for the most part, he speaks highly of the ERP and remains loyal to it and its leaders.[112]

As part and parcel of their loyalty to their organizations, the comandante memoirists portray their relations with their rank-and-file members as harmonious, and they extend that harmony outward to the civilian masses. As one example, Juan Medrano of the ERP describes the relationship that he and some other guerrilla commanders from urban areas developed with the peasants of Morazán while recruiting in the region. "Little by little, the peasants (*campesinos*) befriended us," he says. "They opened their minds and hearts to us, to the point that we became their spiritual, moral and political consultants."[113] Like Francisco Jovel and his comments about the relationship between leftist leaders and rural masses in the 1932 uprising, Medrano offers this description without any apparent awareness that such a claim might reveal a hierarchical perspective, in which the urban educated leadership sees itself as superior to the rural recruits.[114]

As the comandantes' narratives approach the formal beginning of the civil war in 1980 and 1981, they begin to resolve some of the prevailing crises and complications by celebrating the guerrillas' accomplishments. After all, the guerrilla organizations started from scratch in the early 1970s and achieved many things in a decade or less. Their founders had little training, and many of them were not yet old enough to have graduated from college. Nevertheless, they built militant organizations from the ground up, virtually in isolation, with moderate assistance from friendly foreign governments.[115] "We built our guerrilla force from nothing," says Salvador Sánchez. "It was a formidable task."[116] They learned how to acquire and deploy weaponry, build up cash reserves to bankroll their operations, set up impressive supply chains, recruit hundreds into their organizations, and garner the support of hundreds of thousands of their fellow citizens, many of whom joined one of the mass front organizations. By the late 1970s, the guerrillas were beginning to contest the state's monopoly on violence. Even though many guerrillas died in the process and they remained outmanned and outgunned, they were becoming forces to be reckoned with. Carlos Rico injects a sense of pride in his memoir about his and his comrades' accomplishments just prior to the formal outbreak of war.

> The armed revolutionary movement came into existence as a historical necessity; born out of nothing, lacking in experience, devoid of politico-military training, we had to learn everything bit by bit, through trial and error . . . including how to steal taxis and requisition other vehicles, always trying to avoid harming the general population in the process, and later recuperating weapons and robbing banks. It was a growing wave of activities, not just one, two or three isolated events, but many of them, some of which resulted in the loss of brave revolutionary comrades.[117]

Nonetheless, by the end of the 1970s, none of the guerrilla factions had the capacity to defeat the Salvadoran military and overthrow the state alone. United, they at least stood a fighting chance. Thus, the creation of the FMLN in late 1980 becomes a major expository episode in the comandantes' narratives. All of the prior crises and complications seem to funnel into that moment, when the disparate guerrilla forces unite and channel their collective energies into plans for the final offensive in January 1981. Almost all of the memoirists organize their narratives around this moment, in a manner similar to Salvador Sánchez, whose chapter subheadings go from "Unity of the FMLN" to the "Final Offensive of 1981."[118] Indeed, the moment of unification typically marks the midway point in most of the memoirs, as it did for Carlos Rico, who arrives at it on page 175 of his 430-page memoir, describing the united front as "having gone through a long road full of sectarianism, vanguardism and bad times, but the process had advanced and we arrived at the point of having awareness about the need to integrate ourselves into a revolutionary union."[119] However, as we are about to see in the next chapter, the memoirists also show that factionalism remained a lingering issue through-out the war, as the failure to overthrow the dictatorship in 1981 gave way to more than a decade of brutal and incessant fighting.[120]

Conclusion

The main argument in the comandante memoirists' narrative is that prior to the civil war El Salvador was defined by an unjust and improper social order that desperately needed a revolutionary overhaul. To establish this foundation, the memoirists first have to get beyond their relatively happy childhoods. Most of them came from well-adjusted, middle- or lower middle-class families in urban areas with access to education. Even those who hail from more modest backgrounds had disproportionate access to education and other opportunities. The satisfaction they derive from their childhoods establishes a paradoxical parallel with their elite antagonists, in that both of them portray something about El Salvador's past as good and proper. It is due to the comandantes' political awakening, usually as a consequence of their educational opportunities, that they became aware of El Salvador's reality. By choosing then to follow their conscience and become political activists, the memoirists unleash a series of crises, com-plications and resolutions that drive their narrative forward toward the civil war. The crises include, among other things, the negative impact on family lives, the personal challenges faced by living a secret life, and the fear of being captured and tortured by the state's security forces or para-military bands. The memoirists meet these crises and complications with resolutions, such as the pleasure of collective action, the accom-plishments of the guerrillas and the eventual unification of the guerril-las in preparation for the 1981 offensive.

5   The Reckoning

Guerrilla Comandantes during and after the Civil War

As they take up the civil war in 1980 and 1981, the comandantes' life stories continue to employ the same collectively shared narrative structure as before. Their stories about the war and the postwar era are chronologically organized as they pass through a series of crises, complications, and resolutions. The narrators divide this phase of their stories into four periods: 1981–1983; 1984–1989; 1989; and 1989 to the present. These divisions correspond to the rising and falling fortunes of the guerrillas.

The first period, 1981–1983, represents hope and potential resolution. The guerrilla factions unite and launch a major offensive with the goal of seizing control of the state. They lose that battle, but over the next three years they stand up to the Salvadoran army and push it out of nearly 25 percent of Salvadoran territory.

The next period, 1984–1989, constitutes a crisis. Unable to defeat the Salvadoran army outright, the guerrillas are forced to downsize their units and resort to smaller, hit-and-run tactics, making the prospect of total military victory unlikely.

The third period, the year 1989, is defined by a remarkable turnaround, a second "final offensive" in which the guerrillas stunningly occupy portions of the capital city for up to two weeks. Once again, the offensive fails, but the guerrillas score a broader victory. The Salvadoran government and its U.S. benefactor are forced to accept their inability to defeat the guerrillas, and the guerrillas gain enough traction in the offensive to assure that some of their most pressing demands, namely democratization and the overhaul of the state's security forces, will be achieved by war's end. The 1989 offensive represents the main climax in the memoirists' narrative.

The final period, 1989 to the present, comprising the peace accords and the postwar era, constitutes the resolution, denouement, and new status quo. The memoirists find postwar El Salvador to be a mixed bag. All of them are relieved the war is over, and most of them celebrate the achievements of the peace accords. But some find the new status quo lacking: a rich minority still dominates the economy, and despite a functioning democracy, the conservative ARENA party wins the first three presidential elections after the war. Nevertheless, as leaders of the insurgency, the memoirists are inclined toward an optimistic assessment of the war and its outcome. Their optimism contrasts with the views of their rank and file, whose postwar lives tend to be defined more by hardship.

Within each of these four time periods, a variety of mini crises and resolutions unfold that create a constant ebb and flow between the broader narrative trends and specific events in the narrators' lives. For example, the period between 1981 and 1983 may be defined by a sense of hope and potential resolution, but within it the memoirists recall various crises, like ongoing factionalism, which sometimes had murderous consequences. As another example, the period from 1984 to 1989 is generally described as a time of demoralization and crisis, but during that phase the memoirists point to notable victories, like the kidnapping of President Duarte's daughter and the exchange of her for nearly one hundred imprisoned comrades.

The First Offensive and Guerrilla Ascendency, 1981–1983

Even though the memoirists now know that the 1981 offensive failed and that they endured eleven more years of grueling war, they imbue their descriptions of the initial phase of the war with hope and optimism. In narrative terms, they resolve some lingering crises and challenges from the prewar era. Throughout the 1970s, the memoirists faced tremendous obstacles to building up their respective organizations' capacities, not only because of heightened repression by the state's security forces, but also because of their own factional disputes. But by the latter half of 1980, their hard work is beginning to pay dividends. The various guerrilla factions manage to set aside their differences enough to form a united front, the FMLN, in October 1980. Together, the factions begin planning for a nationwide offensive in January 1981. The hope is that the offensive will mimic events in neighboring Nicaragua in July 1979, where the Sandinistas received broad popular support during a final military push against the Somoza dictatorship.[1]

The memoirists recall that in the months leading up to the founding of the FMLN, their insurgency faced headwinds. Despite their organizations' growing capacity and a rising surge in mass mobilization, highlighted by a massive march in San Salvador in January 1980, the regime stood firm and the guerrillas remained divided. A military coup by younger progressive officers in October 1979 and the announcement of a series of sweeping reforms, including a land reform and the purging of abusive officers, failed to end the repression. The Communist Party was the lone radical organization to back the coup, while the four militant guerrilla organizations at the time—the FPL, the ERP, the RN and the PRTC—either rejected it as a counterinsurgent ploy or withheld support to see how it was going to turn out. One of the FPL commanders at the time, Gersón Martínez, captures the pessimistic assessment of the coup when he later describes it in a post-war interview as "being purely counterinsurgent, with a clear agenda: undermine the guerrillas, take the water away from the fish, take the water away from the guerrillas, take away the guerrillas' mass support."[2] Even though the other three guerrilla organizations shared Martínez's opinion, the coup deepened their factional divide as each of their respective leaders interpreted it through their distinct ideological lens. According to José Luis Merino of the PCS/FAL, the coup resulted in "communication between the revolutionary organizations, but their relations were ultimately weakened due to their divergent interpretations of the event."[3]

Lorena Peña says that factional discord continued to define the left, as evidenced by her description of a meeting between Schafik Hándal of the PCS and Salvador Cayetano Carpio of the FPL just weeks prior to the October 1979 coup. Cayetano was in Cuba recuperating from a medical procedure and Peña accompanied him. Hándal happened to be in Cuba at the same time and arranged to see Cayetano. The two former allies had hardly seen one another in the ten years since Cayetano split with the PCS and formed the FPL. Hándal's purpose in arranging the meeting was to inform Cayetano that the PCS was ready to take up arms and join the fight, so the meeting could have been a relatively joyous one. According to Peña, Cayetano received the news coldly and the two men barely spoke. "It was a brief visit," she says, "they said good-bye, and Schafik [sic] left."[4]

Amid such discord, the memoirsts claim that it took the pressure of outsiders to bring the factions together and create a united front. The memoirists universally credit the Cubans, and especially the personal interventions of Fidel Castro, with encouraging the five guerrilla organizations to realize that they were stronger united than divided. Ironically, the organization that most closely adhered to the Cubans' insurrectionary model of revolution, the ERP, was at odds with the Cuban government over the assassination of Roque Dalton in 1975. Dalton had been living in exile in Cuba prior to joining the ERP and he had been in good standing with the Cuban government. According to Juan Medrano Guzmán of the ERP, it was only the demonstrable success of the ERP in the field that forced the Cubans to accept its merits and include it in the revolutionary front.[5]

Not surprisingly, a mere act of unification in late 1980 did not eradicate years of distrust, and the memoirists recall lingering factionalism. Even up to the last moment before the FMLN was formally announced, the RN threatened to withdraw.[6] Carlos Rico of the RN reveals that after unification, guerrillas half-jokingly used the term "*cinquismo*" (the five, or "five-ism") to refer to their alliance. Whenever a public event required the presence of the FMLN, each organization insisted that one of its delegates be present, not necessarily to project a united front before the world, he claims, but "because of the distrust among the alliance."[7] Similarly Salvador Sánchez recalls that "within our shared conceptualization of armed struggle, unity was far from complete, and the theme of unity was a topic of eternal discussion." He says that the leadership of the FPL, under Cayetano's guidance, wanted to hold the top position within the movement, much to the chagrin of the other four organizations, especially the ERP, which considered itself superior to the FPL militarily. Regardless of the formal unification that constituted the FMLN, the five factions retained a lot of autonomy throughout the war. As Salvador Sánchez puts it, "the fact of the matter is that each one of the five organizations was in charge of its own military force, social networks and geographic territory."[8]

Amid the ongoing distrust, the comandantes recall their organizations and the members of their mass front organizations facing intensifying repression by the state's security forces and paramilitary death squads. Lorena Peña describes the situation in early 1980 as a chaotic swirl or "*un hervidero*" (swarm).[9] In addition to high-profile events like the murder of Archbishop Romero in March 1980, as many as 1,000 people were dying each month in military-related violence. Peña offers a concise picture of the scale of the repression when she describes the situation in and around the city of Santa Ana, where she was posted in 1980:

In Santa Ana City a death squad emerged and was operating indiscriminately, attacking one social sector after another. One week only students' bodies appeared, the next week market vendors, the next tailors, the next nurses and the next workers. When I would travel from Santa Ana to Chalchuapa or some other city, I was constantly distressed by the scenes of death along the way, decapitated and dismembered bodies . . . incredible. And government troops were everywhere.[10]

It wasn't the members of the guerrilla organizations who suffered the most in the face of such repression. Certainly some of them fell prey to death and torture, but they were protected by their organizations' security structures. By contrast, the masses who marched in the streets on a regular basis, often at the behest of guerrilla leaders as part of their membership in the mass front organizations, exposed themselves to the regime's deadly wrath. The state tried to exploit this fact at the time, and both the elite and the officer memoirists continue to do so in their narratives (see Chapters 2 and 3) by accusing guerrilla leaders of duping the masses and leading them to slaughter in order to make martyrs out of them.[11] The comandante memoirists dismiss those accusations, but still they debated the morality of encouraging unarmed masses to enter into the regime's line of fire. The comandante memoirists recall that debates over this issue inspired factional disputes within and between the various guerrilla organizations.[12]

The comandante memoirists claim that despite the repression, their resolve hardened. With each new massacre, torture victim, or disappeared person they believed the regime was revealing its true nature and bringing on its own downfall. The unification of the left in late 1980 and the launching of the "final" offensive in January 1981 constitute inspiring moments and points of pride for the memoirists. They find pleasure in the collective exercise of moving to a full offensive, and they celebrate the accomplishments of the preceding months that made it possible. Peña recalls that in the face of the gruesome repression, she and her fellow comrades retained "a high morale and we dedicated ourselves to our missions to recuperate arms . . . and prepare for the January offensive."[13] José Luis Merino says that his "personal experience at the beginning of the war . . . was intense and complicated," but above all else, he says, "from that seed of activity grew a great military force that became a model throughout Latin America."[14] Similarly, Juan Medrano recalls an analogy that "Santiago" (Carlos Consalvi), the main voice of Radio Venceremos, used on the eve of the 1981 offensive to describe the FMLN: "five organizations like five fingers on a hand, united and closing themselves into a strong fist to deliver a crushing blow to the dictatorship of this country."[15] And Carlos

Rico celebrates "the people's organization . . . their mystique, their combative morale, the psychological preparedness to fight."[16]

In the face of such celebratory emotion, the memoirists face a crisis with the defeat of the offensive. At the time, they had to accept the ugly truth that they lacked weaponry and preparation. Lorena Peña comments on the lack of weaponry relative to the number of fighters, and also on the lack of radios. She says the guerrillas had to rely on human couriers to communicate with one another.[17] Most distressingly, the guerrillas lacked the necessary linkages to the urban masses to inspire them to rise up in support of their offensive. As Juan Medrano summarizes, "inexperience, lack of weapons and above all else, the lack of participation on the part of the general populace prevented us from launching a genuine insurrectional offensive, like in Nicaragua."[18]

The defeat of the January offensive also meant that the guerrillas had to set aside hope for a quick victory and prepare for a longer slog. In the wake of their defeat, they more or less surrendered the urban areas to the government and retreated to their strategic rearguards in the countryside, particularly in northern Chalatenango, northern Morazán, and San Vicente. While they still hoped for a victory in the near future, they realized they were now in the midst of a protracted rural insurgency at the front of a peasant-based army.

With this recognition came personal challenges for the memoirists. Francisco Mena, the army captain who deserted the government and joined the ERP in the midst of the 1981 offensive, recalls the sense of disaffection he felt leaving his fellow soldiers in the army and then having to face them as an enemy. At one instance during the chaos of the offensive, he recalls passing by a roadblock guarded by members of the elite airborne unit that he once belonged to. "That was terrible for me," he says. "Not only did I know most of the airborne troops, but also most of the pilots." He also laments having to leave behind his family and expose them to potential repercussions of the regime. In fact, his brother was captured by one of the paramilitary death squads and subjected to months of torture before the guerrillas managed to arrange for his release in exchange for one of its high-profile prisoners.[19]

Mena was facing for the first time what the other comandantes had been confronting for many years—familial alienation and fear of reprisal. Still, though, all of them recognize that the situation in early 1981 meant a long war in the countryside with even more sacrifice. "What a shit I am," Mijango recalls saying to his wife at the time. "How cruel life has been for you because of me!"[20] That kind of self-criticism and emotional expressiveness sets the comandantes apart from both the elites and the officers.

Even though most of the comandantes had been training and working as armed militants for many years, almost all of them hailed from the cities and they had spent most of their lives in urban areas. Transitioning to the countryside was no easy feat for them, and they duly recall the challenge in their memoirs. They comment on the physical demands of hiking into the guerrilla controlled zones, the change in diet, and the difficulty of sleeping outside, sometimes in rainstorms with only a thin plastic sheet for protection. Francisco Mena of the ERP says he lost thirty-five pounds in the first few weeks of his incorporation.[21] Dagoberto Gutiérrez of the PCS/FAL says that his "first night in a guerrilla encampment was like nothing else." He describes himself as "an urban middle-class lawyer" and recalls that first night in the countryside as consisting of "a lot of hunger and rocks here, in the back . . . and, later, snakes."[22] Salvador Sánchez describes the process as "a total change: living far away from one's family, in camps, eating and drinking only when there is enough to go around for everyone, sleeping out in the open."[23] For Eduardo Sancho, transitioning from the "clandestine circle [in the city]" to the "theater of rural war in 1981" signified "innumerable changes of residences beneath trees, stone fences, abandoned homes and caves dug into hillsides."[24]

The focus the memoirists place on this transition to the countryside highlights a basic fact about the Salvadoran guerrillas: the comandantes were mostly urban, educated, and relatively affluent, whereas the fighters and sympathizers consisted mostly of illiterate, poor peasants. The memoirists demonstrate awareness of this dynamic, although they don't see it as a problem. Rather, they emphasize the unity within the guerrillas' ranks and celebrate the merging of the urban and rural sectors into a collective force. As just one example, Lorena Peña of the FPL says in a 2010 interview that the FPL conceived of itself at the time as "a hegemonic alliance of proletarians between urban workers and peasants."[25] Peña expresses this view as part of a description of the factional disputes within the guerrillas, indicating that the FPL considered its proletarian identity and internal unity as setting itself apart from the other organizations, which supposedly lacked the ability to establish ties to the peasantry. Her quote reveals that the leadership of the FPL saw no divide between its urban and rural members. Instead, leaders who hailed from affluent, urban areas were expected to abandon their bourgeois pretensions by "proletarianizing" themselves, venturing into the countryside, and finding common cause with the peasantry, which was part and parcel of the FPL's Prolonged Popular War strategy.[26] Even though the other four organizations did not necessarily share the FPL's ideology, they too believed that their respective army was defined by a healthy alliance between urban and rural sectors.

As a reflection of this belief, all of the comandante memoirists, regardless of which faction they belonged to, express their indebtedness to the peasantry for teaching them how to survive in the countryside and for working collectively in pursuit of a common goal. Francisco Mena Sandoval makes such a comment about the people of Morazán in regard to their contribution to the guerrillas' medical practices.

> We learned a great deal from the [peasant] comrades in general. There was no doubt that we found ourselves in the greatest University of Humanity in the world—the revolution. We witnessed things that would never have occurred outside of it: Young, illiterate women learning how to read and becoming part of the medical brigades, and when they were most needed, they responded with total efficiency, including times when there was no doctor around but they still had to perform complex abdominal surgery or perform amputations, and on many occasions they saved comrades' lives. . . . The doctors benefitted greatly from their knowledge of local herbs and the traditional medical customs of the peasantry.[27]

Lorena Peña credits the peasants for their "initiative," their general "peasant way of being," and for showing her "a marvelous world." She says she "learned how to start fires, walk at night without a light and take baths in beautiful rivers."[28] Peña's comment reveals that as part and parcel of their bond with the rural folk, the comandantes came to feel a great fondness for the countryside and its natural beauty. In the same paragraph that he comments on the challenges of his first night in the countryside, Dagoberto Gutiérrez describes waking up to "the beauty of the coffee-growing lands and the surrounding volcanoes." He continues on to say "the countryside is a marvelous experience. For the guerrilla, the countryside is a cradle, and just this single aspect could provide material for many books."[29] And Lorena Peña similarly recalls the impression that the "immense, starry nights" made on her. "The scenes were almost psychedelic, with thousands of fireflies turning themselves on and off."[30] With these appeals to El Salvador's natural beauty, the urban comandantes evoke a romantic nationalism similar to that of their elite counterparts (see Chapter 2), striking another ironic parallel with them.

The comandante memoirists celebrate the peasantry and emphasize the common bond that they believe they had with them. However, contrary to their apparent intentions, the memoirists demonstrate that they conceptualized rural folk hierarchically. Whenever they describe fellow guerrillas who happen to hail from the countryside, they are sure to note their rural origins, or they preface their reference to them by labeling them as a *campesino* (peasant). The comandantes do this especially when the person in question happens to hold some type of leadership position. A few examples will suffice to demonstrate the broader trend. Salvador Sánchez describes the leadership of the Bloque Popular Revolucionario (BPR), one of the mass front organizations in the mid-1970s, as consisting of "Mélida [Anaya Montes] . . . and Apolinario Serrano Polín, who was a peasant leader of that era."[31] Sánchez's discourse demonstrates that he believes that Mélida Anaya needs no designation as an urbanite, but Apolinario Serrano must be identified as a *campesino*. Similarly, when Francisco Mena Sandoval recalls some of the leaders of the BRAZ units in the early stages of the war, he describes them as "all peasants, warriors not by vocation, but by conviction."[32] Notably, Mena never designates himself, or the other commanders of the BRAZ who hailed from the cities as *urbanos* (urbanites). Carlos Rico includes the testimony of Fidel Recinos (Raúl Hercules) in order to share with his readers some descriptions of the RN's rural front around the Guazapa volcano. Recinos was one of the RN's main field commanders, and while Rico doesn't specifically label him with the term "*campesino*," what makes Recino's story stand out in Rico's narrative is his peasant origins and the fact that he grew up in the same area where he was commanding troops during the war.[33]

On rare occasions, the comandante memoirists hint at being aware of a divide between themselves and the peasant members of their organizations. Lorena Peña recalls a period when she was serving as a field commander in the San Vicente region: "In this front there were only about thirty of us from the capital city. Everyone else was a campesino." She says that to "talk about the city was unwelcome, as being something to do with the bourgeoisie."[34] Similarly, Raúl Mijango recalls an incident in which some of the rural-based fighters played tricks on some of the urbanites because, in their opinion, "the people from the city go around thinking they are so smart, but in fact they can't march or fight worth a damn."[35] Medrano points out that when he was tasked with setting up training schools in northern Morazán, "the majority of the students were campesinos but the instructors all came from cities."[36] But these types of insights by the comandantes are rare. Most notably, none of the comandante memoirists suggest that their members might have been discontented with their leadership.[37]

The crisis of losing the first offensive in January 1981 is quickly assuaged by the memoirists' descriptions of the guerrillas' successes over the next three years. They managed to create a large standing army consisting of brigade-size units and special-forces teams that could match the Salvadoran military in open combat. Just a few of its victories include the Battle of Moscarón in Morazán in 1982, attacks on the barracks of the Third Brigade in San Miguel in 1983 and on the Fourth Brigade in Chalatenango in 1984, and the destruction of most of the Air Force's planes and helicopters in an attack on the Ilopango Airbase in January 1982.[38]

Most significantly, during the first three years of the war, the guerrillas pushed the Salvadoran army out of roughly 25 percent of national territory, and not surprisingly, the memoirists are very proud of this accomplishment. They did this through a steady, step-by-step process starting from small zones of control and attacking one government stronghold after another, pushing out the soldiers, civilian militias, and/or paramilitaries (see chapter 1). Gersón Martínez describes this process as analogous to "the country being converted into a leopard skin, with small spots controlled by the guerrillas being converted rapidly into a tiger skin, with fangs."[39] Schafik Hándal equates it to dancing a tango, with the rival sides moving back and forth in geographic space.[40] The comandante memoirists readily acknowledge that the army could return to any of its lost areas whenever it wanted, but only through massive invasion forces that proved unsustainable for more than a few days or weeks at a time.[41] All the while, the guerrillas built up a vast network of support inside El Salvador, a highly organized international diplomatic effort, and an intricate logistical network that managed to keep its standing units on the battlefield.

The memoirists are proud of these accomplishments, and most of them recall thinking at the time that they had a chance of winning the war outright. When asked by an interviewer after the war if "there was ever a moment when the possibility of a Nicaragua-like triumph seemed real," Ana Guadalupe Martínez responds, "Yes, at the beginning." As evidence she refers to the massive popular demonstration against the regime in January 1980, when she says as many as 300,000 people marched in opposition to the government "in a small country like ours, with six million inhabitants and a capital city of only one million."[42]

Juan Medrano, Raúl Mijango, and Francisco Mena all helped train the combat units of the ERP, and each of them speaks with pride about their accomplishments. As a typical example, Mena says that "with the development of the special forces teams, many military victories, and the training of the new recruits in 1982 and 1983, we nearly managed to defeat the Salvadoran army."[43] The memoirists take particular pride in pointing out that almost none of them were formally trained as soldiers. As Salvador Sánchez puts it, "little by little we were transforming ourselves from union activists to military experts."[44] José Merino was placed in charge of the FAL's combat units. He acknowledges that they were much fewer in number than their counterparts in the FPL and the ERP, because the FAL got a much later start on militancy, but he is proud of their overall accomplishments:

> We sabotaged telephone poles, electrical substations . . . and even the hydroelectric dams, which the military considered essential and so it guarded them with battalions that resided there permanently. We did the same with army units; we began by attacking small National Guard posts in outlying municipalities and ended up attacking entire brigades; we could ambush small patrols of four or five soldiers and wipe out entire battalions in open combat.[45]

An explicit celebration of the combat capabilities of the FMLN is the 2008 history of the BRAZ units, *Brigada Rafael Arce Zablah ¡Misión Cumplida!*, based on testimonies by former members who shared their stories with Héctor Ibarra Chávez, a Mexican intellectual and activist and a fellow member of the ERP.[46]

Carlos Rico was tasked with organizing the RN's supply chain from his clandestine base in San Salvador. His responsibilities included accumulating stores of cash, arranging dozens of safe houses, vehicles, and fake identifications, and setting up supply networks that could move people and goods into and out of the country, and within the country as needed.[47] By any standard of measure, it was a massive undertaking, and his memoir makes evident the skills he needed to accomplish his goals, to say nothing of doing so under the threat of torture and death. His memoir often reads like a spy thriller, which suggests that he injected some artistic license into his narrative. Nevertheless, he describes such things as jetting around with briefcases full of cash and going undercover as a wealthy businessman to meet with contacts at expensive restaurants in San Salvador. Ultimately, Rico expresses the pride he feels in his accomplishments. In describing one particularly difficult mission, he concludes by saying "the logistics functioned perfectly, all of the war material arrived to its destination; we managed to move large quantities of material, including dried milk, vitamins, soap and other necessary items, and this time we made an exponential leap in the quality of our goods, including new armaments." Rico admits that he enjoyed his work: "Of course, I liked my work, and it was fun to overcome the danger with audacity."[48]

Similarly, Eduardo Espinoza was a medical doctor in the FPL and was put in charge of organizing its field hospital. Like Rico, Espinoza faced tremendous hurdles. He had to train staff members, keep medicines and supplies on hand, perform complicated surgeries—often under enemy fire—and set up triage stations and a hospital capable of picking up and moving on a moment's notice. He describes many episodes of *guinda* (flight) in which patients were carried through the countryside in slings over the shoulders of porters, usually at dark and barely ahead of an army invasion. But he takes great pride in having delivered all of his patients to safety and never allowing the hospital to fall into enemy hands: "We didn't lose a single patient, nor a single member of our brave and experienced team." Other points of pride for Espinoza revolve around his staff's homespun solutions to complicated medical problems, like weighing things with a scale made of bamboo, making sterilized saline solution with a still, and keeping blood and medicine chilled without electricity by using ammonium nitrate.[49] Santiago (Carlos Consalvi) offers a similar expression of pride in the peasant fighters in the ERP in northern Morazán who did things like run Radio Venceremos's signal through barbed wire fences to avoid detection by U.S. spy planes and warships.[50]

Apart from all the combat and death, the comandante memoirists remember the pleasure of experiencing a version of the new society they hoped to create after victory. In the rearguard areas, especially in the northern zones of Morazán and Chalatenango departments, weeks sometimes passed by without major military encounters. As Peña describes it, "the army couldn't venture into our zones very easily, knowing that if they did they would get hit hard, ambushed and maybe even annihilated."[51] During the lulls, Sánchez says "a period of tranquility set in that gave us the opportunity to set up schools for politico-military training."[52] In their zones of control, the guerrillas established many of the trappings of a normal society, including schools and courts, in which they not only castigated rule breakers, but also registered births, marriages, and deaths. They organized social events with music and dancing, and they tried "at all cost, amidst so much tension and tragedy, to create space to be a normal human being," says Peña. For her part, she recalls assembling "an important collection of orchids that took a lot of work on my part, until the army burnt the hillside where I was cultivating them during one of its invasions."[53] These various achievements arguably explain why many of the comandante memoirists devote disproportionate space to this initial phase of the war, between 1981 and 1983, compared to later periods.

However, the memoirists know now that a military victory would not happen by 1983, and they inject foreboding premonitions into their descriptions of the first three years of the war. One way they do so is by focusing on factional tensions within and between their respective organizations. Even after two or three decades away from the events, the memoirists describe their rival organizations with an array of nitpicking criticisms and disparaging comments that suggests a longstanding commitment to organizational identity. Juan Medrano uses the oft-cited term "born conspirators" to describe members of the Communist Party, implying that they were better at maneuvering for position within the FMLN than they were at fighting the enemy.[54] Similarly, Medrano's comrade in the ERP, Raúl Mijango, criticizes the PCS/FAL for coming to militancy late, only after members of the other organizations had paid dearly for their activism in the preceding years. As he puts it, "while we were fighting and dying in El Salvador, they were studying abroad." He also criticizes the PRTC for its lack of fighting will, and its main commander, Roberto Roca [pseudonym for Francisco Jovel], with being more concerned with looking the part of a guerrilla than with fighting like one.[55] Medrano of the PCS/FAL returns the insult to the ERP, accusing its members of undermining the FMLN's war effort during the 1981 offensive out of political selfishness. He claims the PCS had convinced the leader of the progressive officers, Colonel Majano, to join the insurrection. Medrano claims that the PCS arranged for Majano to be picked up by ERP operatives, but they failed to show up because they didn't want Majano to supplant their own contact in the military, Captain Francisco Mena Sandoval.[56]

Nitpicking comments aside, the memoirists recall that substantive issues still divided the guerrillas. Lorena Peña, for example, describes the FPL's opinion of the ERP in the early stages of the war, saying that "the ERP wasn't worth anything." By contrast, she says the FPL had the proper ideological line: "We represented the proletariat!"[57] In other words, Peña is saying that the FPL believed itself to be the only organization capable of bringing about a true social revolution. Carlos Rico contributes to this aspect of the narrative by claiming that the RN was the only organization in the FMLN committed to genuinely negotiating with the government to end the war. Rico claims that most members of the other organizations, especially the FPL and the ERP, manifestly opposed the idea. He criticizes them, saying that "among the leaders of the FMLN, triumphalist militarism predominated."[58]

José Luis Merino of the PCS/FAL says that coming out of the failure of the 1981 offensive, each organization was quick to blame the others for the defeat: "We all saw in the other ones the responsibility for the failure to achieve victory."[59] He goes on to say that such distrust slowed down decision-making and hindered the FMLN's ability to launch coordinated attacks. "We conducted some joint operations between two or more organizations," he says, "but the FMLN consisted of five organizations, each with their respective political commissions, high commands and military forces." He cites the example of the assault on the town of Cinquera in 1983 by combined forces of the FPL and the FAL as revelatory. When the combatants for the two organizations gathered, "We were sullen." He goes on to say, "It was noticeable we were together, but apart. We didn't want to mix forces."[60] He claims that ultimately the experience of fighting together in Cinquera created the first bonds of comradeship between members of the two organizations that lasted for years thereafter. But the notable point of his story is that their members were totally estranged from one another for the first three years of the war. Raúl Mijango claims that units of the FPL forcefully evicted some ERP supporters from one of its zones in Chalatenango department, calling them "petit bourgeois adventurers." He says the FPL considered them "almost equivalent to government spies," and for this they "were subjected to varying pressures to leave the area." He also points out that the decision to launch a follow-up offensive in 1982 was solely the ERP's decision and that only the RN agreed to participate in it. The FPL apparently called the decision an act of petit bourgeois adventurism and supposedly a FAL hospital refused initially to accept ERP wounded because of its opposition to the offensive.[61] Juan Medrano claims that in 1981 the leaders of the ERP believed that the FPL hoarded the best munitions for itself and refused to share them with the other organizations.[62] Medardo González of the FPL says that Cayetano Carpio and other leaders in the FPL's command discussed pulling their organization out of the FMLN in the wake of the failure of the 1981 offensive owing to the presence of so-called reformist tendencies in the other four organizations.[63]

One of the most demonstrable expressions of factionalism inside the guerrillas was the murder and suicide of the two top-ranking commanders in the FPL, Mélida Anaya Montes and Salvador Cayetano Carpio, in Managua in April 1983. Although the events remain debated, the consensus opinion among the memoirists is that the FPL was divided into two factions over a variety of strategic and ideological issues.[64] Anaya headed one faction that was supposedly less doctrinaire and more open to doing things like negotiating with the enemy, whereas the other was led by Cayetano Carpio and was more doctrinaire and committed to maintaining the strategy of a prolonged popular war. After a series of meetings, Cayetano Carpio supposedly felt the organization slipping from his control, and so in a fit of desperation he ordered some of his men to murder Anaya, which they did by stabbing her nearly one hundred times with an ice pick. Then, two days later, seemingly unable to live with what he had done, Cayetano Carpio took his own life while sitting at his desk in his office.

The episode delivered a blow to the entire FMLN, and each of the memoirists recalls being affected by it, regardless of their organizational affiliation. They all recognize Cayetano Carpio as a pathbreaking leader and as the most widely recognized Salvadoran guerrilla. He was sometimes referred to as the "Ho Chi Minh of Latin America." Naturally, the episode had its deepest impact on the memoirists of the FPL, most of whom had close personal relations with both Cayetano Carpio and Anaya. Since most of the FPL memoirists happen to have been allied with Anaya, they tend to hail her in their memoirs, although they try to avoid alienating the memory of Cayetano Carpio, because he remains highly regarded in some circles.[65] One indication of the sensitivity of the matter is Lorena Peña's terse response to an otherwise sympathetic interviewer who pressed her with questions about Cayetano Carpio and the murder and suicide: "Is this interview about me or Marcial [Cayetano Carpio]?" she asks.[66] The central place that the murder/suicide of Anaya and Cayetano plays in the memoirists' narratives serves as a foreboding predictor of more trouble on the horizon.

Crisis: Downsizing and Dispersion, 1984–1989

In late 1983 and early 1984, both the guerrillas and the Salvadoran army implemented sweeping strategic changes that altered the course of the war, reflecting a transitional shift into what the FPL comandante, Medardo González, calls "the second stage of the war."[67] Each side downsized their fighting units and focused more on hit-and-run tactics. The guerrillas changed from a "war of position" to a "war of movement," and began focusing their striking power on infrastructure, hoping to bleed the state to death. The army also turned to smaller-sized units, both to avoid a repeat of the massive human-rights catastrophes of the first three years of the war and to match the guerrillas' agility. These changes, largely a consequence of renewed financial support from the United States, brought the war to a stalemate. The guerrillas could not advance any further, and although the military moved away from the brink of collapse, it couldn't dislodge the guerrillas. José Luis Merino, who was serving as a military commander of the FAL at the time of the strategic shift, recalls the change from his perspective on the battlefield. "We would be totally exhausted and they would bring in fresh troops," he recalls. He continues on to say that "their rotation of troops combined with support from the Air Force and artillery quickly began getting the better of us; they would call in planes and helicopters and begin attacks with the Air Force and artillery such that they were able to establish fixed positions from which they could launch incursions into our zones of control."[68]

The shift in strategy represents a major crisis for the memoirists. As leaders, they were responsible for implementing the new policy, but even they have a difficult time portraying it as anything other than depressing. Francisco Mena is an exception to this. He describes the shift in positive, or at least neutral terms, but he wrote his memoir before the war officially ended, so for propaganda reasons he probably had no other choice.[69] The rest of the memoirists, writing with less immediate political exigency, depict a different reality. They describe the strategic shift as dashing their hopes for a quick military victory and taking away much of the joy they had come to feel from belonging to a large, collective process. As Lorena Peña puts it, the strategic change revealed that "the war was going to last much longer than we had thought and it would still take many years for us to achieve our final objective."[70]

José Luis Merino says the change took a psychological toll on him and his fellow combatants. They had been used to living and operating in large groups, where they felt relatively secure and enjoyed some modest comforts, such a regular meals and the ability to sleep under a roof, whenever possible. Downsizing meant that troops were reorganized into small units, sometimes as few as six fighters, who were sent into the field on their own, often for long stretches at a time, without immediate access to supply lines. Whereas the guerrillas once took pride in finding the enemy and fighting it, now they were avoiding contact and relying heavily on mines for self-defense. In Merino's words, "the decentralization meant not having a roof to sleep under at night, the need to be become self-sufficient in the field under hard conditions, a great vulnerability to surprise attacks, . . . and the danger of being exposed by the local population . . . as a result of the enemy's counterintelligence operations."[71]

The memoirists recall that the change in strategy was particularly impactful for the ERP's troops, who considered themselves to be the best fighters in the FMLN. Raúl Mijango was commanding some of those troops at the time and he says that the change "resulted in a loss of morale for hundreds of combatants and dozens of leaders." He goes on to say that "some combatants began to surrender in combat, others deserted, taking with them their arms and equipment."[72] Hándal claims that some mid-level commanders refused initially to implement the new orders because it meant a decline in their prestige and no longer having troops under their command.[73]

The change in strategy produces a variety of crises and complications in the comandantes' stories. One crisis was an apparent short-term reliance on forced recruitment. Some of the memoirists claim that in the midst of the strategic shift and the decline in morale, they worried about the flow of future recruits. So, ironically, as they were downsizing their forces, some factions apparently began to conscript in certain geographic areas, which they present as a depressing contrast to the overabundance of fighters they had at the beginning of the war. José Luis Merino of the FAL claims that the situation in 1983 and 1984 caused the FMLN's high command "to order forced recruitment, which we called 'patriotic recruitment,' and which damaged profoundly the FMLN's standing in society." He says that the policy "was terrible from a human perspective," and he describes being personally affected by watching mothers beg the recruiters to take them instead of their sons or daughters. He also says it was a military failure, because most of the new recruits deserted the first chance they had.[74]

Lorena Peña too says that some forced recruiting occurred at this precarious stage, but she insists that it was done by lower-level commanders without approval from the FPL's main leadership, and once the latter found out about it, they ended it.[75] In the ERP zones in northern Morazán, the policy was seemingly not meant to recruit fighters into the standing ranks, but rather to train the entire civilian population as militia members. The supposed objective was to disperse the guerrillas' fighting and survival capabilities, but as various ranking ERP comandantes describe it, the policy was a failure because most of the civilians interpreted it as forced recruitment and they either resisted the training or emigrated out of the zone.[76]

Various memoirists from the ERP recall that at about the same time as the strategic shift, their organization began creating new units of special-forces fighters comprised of boys around the ages of twelve or thirteen, drawn from the ranks of orphans who had sort of fallen into the guerrilla encampments by default. These units were the so-called Samuelitos, and Raúl Mijango claims that he was put in charge of training them.[77] Mijango does not question the morality or wisdom of using children as soldiers. However, Lorena Peña addresses the issue to defend the guerrillas' tactics. Noting that the guerrillas' critics have chastised them for using child soldiers, she responds by saying that it was the army who created the legions of orphans through its scorched-earth policies. She refers to the specific case of an orphan named Carlitos, a boy who had been accompanying the guerrillas. The army captured him, brutally tortured him, and left his mutilated body in a field. Peña asks metaphorically of her critics: "How could people know the scale of the holocaust that we were living?"[78] Nevertheless, it's difficult to read the descriptions of children being trained to kill as anything other than another example of a crisis in the memoirists' rendition of the strategic shift in 1983 and 1984.

Another crisis for the comandante memoirists in this second phase of the war is the enemy's growing air power. The military's command of the skies had always been a point of fear and consternation for the memoirists, but until 1984, its impact was less severe. After all, a guerrilla commando unit had destroyed much of the Air Force in early 1982. But between the strategic shift and a freshly supplied Air Force, air power took on ever-greater meaning. Small, isolated guerrilla units may have been less easy to find from the sky, but they were also more vulnerable when they were found, because they were less able to defend themselves against fast-moving air strikes that could drop troops almost anywhere.[79] Sánchez comments on this dynamic among his descriptions of the strategic shift, saying that "confronting the army's capacity for air transport was not easy, because they had the advantage of surprise and also it gave them a psychological edge over us and our civilian supporters."[80] Indeed, the military could claim that its new tactic resulted in the capture of at least one guerrilla commander, Nidia Díaz of the PRTC in 1985. Most of the memoirists endured at least one airborne attack, and they describe the fear and chaos that accompanied it. Juan Medrano says "the helicopters were a dark spot for us during the war." He describes two surprise helicopter attacks on the ERP's command center, one in the early stages of the war and another in 1986. In both instances, the ERP leadership barely escaped and suffered many casualties.[81]

A related crisis during this second phase of the war was the capture of other high-ranking comandantes. In addition to Nidia Díaz, who was captured with a cache of documents in her backpack, Miguel Castellanos of the FPL was captured at almost the same time in a separate mission.[82] Unlike Díaz, who refused to collaborate with her captors and suffered various abuses as a result, Castellanos betrayed his comrades and became a high-profile government informant.[83] He was a particularly valuable asset at the time of his capture because he was heading up the FPL's entire front around San Salvador, and thus he knew many of the FPL's urban cadre and the locations of various safe houses around the capital city. Lorena Peña says that his treason delivered a heavy blow and caused "enormous problems."[84] Among the many comrades who were captured and killed as a consequence of Castellanos's treason was Peña's father, Felipe. In the aftermath of Castellanos's capture, Lorena Peña was transferred from the "Frente Paracentral" in San Vicente to Guazapa to rebuild the San Salvador front. The FPL exacted retribution by assassinating Castellanos in 1989.[85]

The capture of Díaz and Castellanos and the military's growing skills in intelligence-gathering and infiltration create narrative crises for the comandantes. The presence of spies among the civilian population and traitors in the guerrillas' ranks had always been a point of concern, as demonstrated by Carlos Rico's description of the debilitating impact on the RN's Guazapa front due to army spies within the ranks.[86] But the strategic shift in 1983 and 1984 made the guerrillas' ranks even more susceptible to army infiltration. As José Luis Merino describes it, the guerrilla leaders' decision to disperse their troops invariably resulted in more contact between combatants and civilians under less controlled circumstances. A guerrilla unit of four or five fighters might show up in a small town, often at night, to conduct political work or shop at a local store. Each interaction carried with it the potential to expose the guerrillas to the enemy's intelligence-gathering networks. The civilians they encountered might be spies for the army, and sometimes individual guerrillas were confronted by government soldiers, usually members of PRAL units, who sometimes tried to coerce or cajole the guerrillas into become government assets. Merino details the complex and time-consuming counterintelligence tactics that the guerrillas had to employ in hopes of lessening the impact of the infiltration. He admits that in some cases combatants were executed as traitors.[87]

Merino does not make it clear whether the executions he refers to occurred only within his organization, the FAL, or throughout the FMLN more broadly. Regardless, his reference to the execution of traitorous combatants raises the specter of one of the guerrillas' most severe narrative crises during the second phase of the war, the internal purges within the FPL led by Mayo Sibrián. As revealed by the investigative reporting of former guerrillas Geovani Galeas of the ERP and Berne Ayalá of the FAL, starting around 1986, Sibrián, who had been placed in charge of the FPL's front around San Vicente, oversaw a wave of terror that resulted in the torture and death of many hundreds of FPL combatants and sympathizers. The pretext for his actions was counterintelligence operations. He supposedly believed, as apparently did other high-ranking leaders within the FPL, that the Frente Paracentral had a major infiltration problem. Sibrián was either charged with the task of resolving the problem or he took it upon himself to do so. In either case, a lot of people suffered greatly as a result of his actions. The overwhelming majority of victims were seemingly innocent of treason, and few, if any, of the victims were given a hearing to defend themselves.[88]

Most of the comandante memoirists remain silent about Mayo Sibrián and the purges in the FPL. Admittedly, Galeas and Ayalá did not publish their findings until 2007, and so some of the memoirists, especially those who were not in the FPL, may not have known about the events. However, some leaders of the other organizations, such as the ERP's Raúl Mijango and Juan Medrano, claim that they had heard of Sibrián's activities during the war, and that the issue was raised with leaders of the FPL during a meeting of the FMLN high command. In Medrano's opinion, Sibrián's actions should be placed in the context of the morale crisis that began with the strategic shift in 1984. He reasons that in the midst of doubts about the guerrillas' prospect for victory, Sibrián "began to see the ghosts of infiltrators all around him."[89] By some accounts, ranking members of the FPL were aware of the situation, even though the extent of their knowledge and their personal involvement in it are open to debate. Nevertheless, neither Salvador Sánchez Cerén, the main commander of the FPL at the time, nor Lorena Peña, who had been in command of the San Vicente region prior to Sibrián's arrival, mention anything about him or the purges in their memoirs, which were published in 2008 and 2009, respectively. Peña responds to the issue later, in a 2010 interview, when her interviewer presses her on the matter, but she deflects the question, saying simply that she had been transferred out of the region prior to Sibrián's arrival.[90]

As a result of these types of crises and complications in the second phase of the war, a sense of malaise hangs over the memoirists' narrative at this juncture. Those narrators who remain loyal to the FMLN after the war typically dedicate the fewest number of pages to this section of their story. Almost all of the narrators punctuate their portrayal of this era with descriptions of illness and feelings of despair that did not appear in the prior era. For example, Juan Medrano says that "the worry and tension that I was feeling caused me to suffer from psychosomatic illnesses. But in 1984 and 1985 I suffered from a genuine case of gastritis."[91] Schafik Hándal's description of this phase of the war is punctuated by deep criticisms of the ERP and its leader Joaquín Villalobos, whom he accuses of ordering unilateral military actions that were unwise and counterproductive and that had the singular goal of promoting Villalobos's position. Hándal even portrays some of the ERP's acts as being akin to "terrorism," and he is angry that the rest of the FMLN had to absorb the public relations fallout from the ERP's activities.[92]

Those memoirists who broke with the FMLN after the war tend to see this era as emblematic of the entire guerrilla effort, and thus, not surprisingly, they devote a disproportionately large number of pages to it. Marvin Galeas is one such example, and in his memoir he highlights various episodes from this period that he sees as symbolic, such as a case from 1988 when he says ERP leaders executed a sixteen-year-old combatant for treason. Galeas says the young man was broken-hearted over a girl and in his anguish he threatened to reveal the guerrilla's position to the army so it could be bombed and he could have his revenge on the girl. Galeas describes the situation as absurd, that leaders had the authority to "decide whether people will live or die" when the causal variable is a teenager's mood swings. He claims that he knows of dozens of victims who suffered similar fates. It was episodes like those, he claims, that led him to reconsider his ideological views and begin the process of rejecting the guerrillas as the war wound down to a close. And it is the prominence that he gives to these critical assessments that demonstrate the narrative importance of this second phase of the war for someone like him.[93]

Like Galeas, Berne Ayalá broke with the FMLN and has devoted most of his time in the postwar era to disparaging his former comrades. Most of the examples that he uses for his denunciations come from this second phase of the war. His journalistic collaboration with Geovani Galeas on the Mayo Sibrián case is just one example. In his second memoir, *Entre Marilyn Monroe y la revolución*, published in 2010, Ayalá uses his personal experiences leading troops for the FAL after 1984 to capture the malaise that he believes was hanging over the second phase of the war. Early in the memoir he summarizes his opinion of the guerrilla's cause by referring to guerrilla recruits who "wanted to make a revolution, but had no clue that they would end up in a degenerate revolution."[94]

Ayalá was given a low-level command position just as the guerrillas implemented their strategic shift. Subsequently, he spent most of the rest of the war leading small bands of troops around central and western El Salvador. He was not yet twenty years old when he was given the command, and most of his troops were younger than him. He says that it is absurd to think that groups of four to six armed teenagers traipsing around the countryside constitute a viable war strategy. Most of them were more interested in listening to rock music and pursuing girls than advancing the cause of social change. The isolating and harsh conditions under which they lived did little to alter their perceptions. In one of his many portrayals of his combatants' outlook, he says "can you imagine a young man of eighteen or twenty years of age . . . sleeping outside like an animal every night who comes across a young woman smelling of flowers, man, he's going to desert and go with her."[95]

Ayalá's writing style can make him seem impetuous. He makes unsubstantiated accusations against his superiors, and he seems more interested in portraying himself with detached indifference and demonstrating his knowledge of popular culture than in grappling with the issues in all their complexity.[96] Nevertheless, Ayalá possesses astute skills of narration and he captures the feeling of discontent that typifies other memoirists' descriptions of the second phase of the war. For example, when describing his first command assignment, he says that he was "coming to learn one of the most important lessons of the war: solitude, abandonment, isolation and a sense of impotence in a terrain lacking in mountains facing an enemy that was more numerous and better armed than we were." One of

Ayalá's more cynical themes revolves around the guerrillas' relations with civilians. Rather than being harmonious and mutually beneficial, Ayalá portrays them as hardly different than the relationship between civilians and the army. He claims that when he hears the phrase "*el pueblo*" (the people), rather than feeling inspired by a sense of collective struggle, he feels "his stomach turn." To Ayalá, "*el pueblo*" meant spies ready to divulge the location of guerrilla encampments "as a gift to the army."[97]

For all the doom and gloom that typifies the comandante memoirists' portrayal of the second phase of the war, they also find cause for celebration. They may have been subjected to an intensifying air war, but they became more effective at shooting down helicopters, even before they introduced surface-to-air missiles in 1990.[98] Juan Medrano says "the army's air tactics were a nightmare for us, but we became a nightmare to the Air Force as well."[99] Eduardo Linares claims proudly in an interview that "in Chalatenango we brought down three helicopters only with sharpshooters."[100] The guerrillas' offensive strikes may have been fewer and farther between than during the first phase of the war, but when they struck they usually did so effectively. For example, in one of its missions, the FMLN attacked the Mariona prison complex and released a host of detained comrades, some of whom had been held there for years. The flight from the prison occurred under heavy enemy fire, which gives Merino the opportunity to make a prideful observation about the guerrillas' constitutional fortitude. Hardened criminals had joined the guerrillas in the flight, but they were "crying, trembling and wetting their pants under the bombardment," whereas teenage guerrillas, some of whom were not even combatants, remained stoic and even "made fun of them."[101]

In another successful mission, FAL troops kidnapped President Duarte's daughter Inés on the streets of San Salvador in 1985 in response to the army's capture of Nidia Díaz and Miguel Castellanos. They managed to whisk her out of the capital and transport her to the Guazapa front before the army could respond. The FMLN then negotiated her release in exchange for nearly one hundred detained guerrillas, including Nidia Díaz, and safe passage to Cuba for another one hundred gravely wounded combatants.[102]

Above all else, the comandante memoirists celebrate the simple fact that despite their troubles between 1984 and 1989 they didn't give up. Eduardo Sancho believes that "the most important offensive of the war" occurred during this middle phase. It was the army's "operativo Domingo Monterrosa," a year-long offensive between 1987 and 1988 that had as its goal the mortal wounding of the guerrillas. He claims that its failure cemented the guerrillas' resilience.[103]

Strategic changes and increased U.S. aid aside, the basic nature of the conflict did not change. The army had to expend precious resources guarding strategic positions throughout the entire country while simultaneously trying to maintain a strong offensive capability. By contrast, the mobile and well-armed guerrillas could stay one step ahead of the army's main combat units and pick and choose their battles. José Luis Merino summarizes the state of affairs when he says the FMLN "established a strategic and tactical equilibrium despite the enemy having tens of thousands of troops." He goes on to say that "the army was obligated to be everywhere and thus it was weak throughout, and we decided when and where we would strike."[104] Compared to the first phase of the war, when the army was unable to stay in guerrilla-controlled zones for more than a few weeks, or even a few days, during the second phase of the war, it could stay there for months at a time. The counterinsurgency plan Unidos Para Reconstruir (United for Reconstruction), which was launched in January 1986, was built upon the premise of government troops remaining in an occupied zone for extended periods and winning the hearts and minds of the civilian population while there. Operation Fénix on the Guazapa volcano in 1986 was a manifestation of the plan. But the guerrillas simply left the targeted zones in advance of the army, and then returned when the army could no longer sustain itself.[105]

Lorena Peña reveals the unflagging determination of her troops in describing their response to the military incursions on Guazapa in 1986 and 1987. The logical choice in the face of the overwhelming military force was to retreat to the rearguard deep in Chalatenango Department to the north, and sometimes they did that. But on more than one occasion, Peña claims they chose the alternative option of moving forward toward the capital city to hide on the slopes of the San Salvador volcano, essentially sitting on the army's back doorstep. Sometimes she and her troops were so close to the urban areas they could see the lights of people's television sets through the windows in their homes. They usually had to remain in their hiding place on the volcano for many days at a time, avoiding detection, waiting for the army to leave Guazapa. All the while they had to remain silent and they could not light fires for cooking. "We were like ghosts," she writes, "and the people didn't see us, or at least they pretended not to."[106] Each of these stints on the San Salvador volcano was hard, but the guerrillas survived to fight another day. The flights to San Salvador predict the beginning of the third phase of the war, the second final offensive in November 1989, when troops from Guazapa would once again position themselves near San Salvador, but this time with the intention of overrunning the city.

Climax: The 1989 Offensive

The period from 1984 to 1989 functions as a depressing narrative dip between two highpoints—the first phase of the war between 1981 and 1983 and the second final offensive in November 1989. The offensive is compared frequently to the Tet Offensive in Vietnam in 1969, because both were military failures but public-relations victories. In each case, the guerrillas' adversaries had been writing them off, and in both cases the guerrillas launched a massive, surprise offensive that struck deep into their enemies' rearguard position. José Luis Merino summarizes the army's portrayal of the FMLN leading up to the offensive: "It had come to the point that they were giving this image of the FMLN as more or less defeated, that we had broken up into small, isolated groups, and that only the comandantes were desperately clinging on to hope of victory."[107] Schafik Hándal recalls that the army refused at the time to use the term "war" to refer to the conflict or to acknowledge the FMLN as a legitimate "army."[108]

The basic plan for the offensive was to attack most of the country's major cities. The centerpiece of the offensive was a multipronged assault on the capital city of San Salvador. The guerrilla leaders hoped the civilian population would respond to the offensive better than it had done in January 1981. The total number of guerrilla troops involved in the offensive is difficult to determine, but they probably numbered between 3,000 and 5,000, which would have represented most of the guerrillas' combat troops at the time.[109] The offensive wasn't exactly an all-or-nothing gamble, proven by the fact that the guerrillas failed to topple the government but survived to fight the war to a negotiated settlement. But the offensive was a major risk that consumed most of the guerrillas' fighting and logistical capabilities. Not only did the guerrillas have to train and supply a majority of their combatants, but also move them to the immediate environs of the cities without revealing themselves to the enemy. Furthermore, they had to establish supply lines that could function during the fighting so that their troops would not be isolated and cut off from food, ammunition, and medical care. Eduardo Sancho summarizes the scale of the task: "We had been preparing for the '89 offensive since May in order to get armaments into the capital city, quietly transfer two thousand fighters to the edge of the capital to attack it from three sides; moreover we had to mobilize and concentrate more than four thousand fighters throughout the entire country prior to 'D-day.'"[110]

Indeed, during the offensive, the guerrillas successfully struck most of the larger urban areas. The attack on the capital city of San Salvador lasted approximately two weeks and involved intense, house-to-house fighting against some of the army's elite units, like the Atlacatl Battalion. The army effectively stalled the guerrillas' advance, but it could not dislodge them from the city without resorting to bombing the poorer neighborhoods on the northern edge of the city where the guerrillas had holed up. A large, but undetermined number of civilians died during the bombardments. During their retreat, the guerrillas overran the exclusive neighborhood of Colonia Escalón, which forms the city's upper edge on the San Salvador volcano. For the first time during the war, elites witnessed combat firsthand. José Luis Merino describes the scene, somewhat coldly, as "oligarchic families . . . fleeing with their suitcases, with luggage on their backs, running through the streets. . . . This was the moment I felt that the armed forces were their most disorganized."[111]

Ultimately, the offensive did not generate the mass uprising that the guerrillas had hoped for. The guerrillas once again failed to inspire enough support in key areas, or at least they failed to create conditions that would have incited untested urban civilians to dive into battle against the heavily armed and notoriously brutal Salvadoran military. This lack of support is a difficult pill for the memoirists to swallow, but they acknowledge their failure, albeit sometimes assuaging themselves by criticizing the civilian population.[112] Carlos Rico of the RN, for example, accepts that the FMLN "had not constructed the backbone of insurrection in the cities [by 1989]." But then he delivers a stinging criticism of the urban citizenry when he says they "are like fifteen-year-old girls who have to be wooed constantly; if you leave them alone for even a little while, they'll go with any random guy from the neighborhood." He goes on to contrast them with peasants who bore "the weight of the war for all those years on their shoulders."[113]

The fact that the guerrillas actually managed to carry out the offensive is a point of great pride for the memoirists. After all, for the previous five years they had been operating in smaller units, largely on the defensive, hiding behind mine fields and concentrating their attentions on "fighting against infiltration and helicopter disembarkations," as Ayalá puts it.[114] Now they were going on the offensive, and not just any offensive, but an all-out, nationwide assault that had as its ostensible goal the end of the regime. In the process, they were taking the fight to the enemy in the capital city. Dagoberto Gutiérrez captures the sense of pride when he says in a 2011 op-ed piece that "before us, no other guerrilla organization on the continent had encircled its capital city."[115] Similarly, Roberto Cañas, a member of the guerrilla's negotiating team for the RN, uses the 1989 offensive to celebrate the FMLN's capabilities: "When they write the history of guerrilla movements in Latin America, even in the world, one will see the profound military and political capabilities of the FMLN."[116]

It is unclear if the guerrillas' leaders believed that the true objective of the November offensive was to defeat the regime, rather than simply boost their position at the bargaining table.[117] Either way, most of the memoirists acknowledge that the offensive proved that a military victory for either side was unlikely, and thus the war would have to end through negotiation. As Merino puts it, despite failing militarily "we had managed to break the military will of our enemy and make them realize the necessity of dialogue . . . as part of a negotiation."[118] Lorena Peña comments with pride on the guerrillas' ability to survive and their various military accomplishments, including "attacking and wiping out battalions," but she has to admit that just as the guerrillas didn't give up, "neither did the military surrender."[119]

Resolution, Denouement, and the New Status Quo: After the 1989 Offensive

The 1989 offensive represents the climax of the comandantes' stories, and most every one of them constructs his or her story in a way that places the offensive atop a rising crescendo.[120] Thereafter, the narrative descends downward, into resolution and denouement, comprised of the peace negotiations and the steady march toward the accords that ended the war in January 1992. The postwar era then constitutes a new status quo, bringing the narrative full circle from the original status quo before the war. After narrating the climax of the 1989 offensive, most of the memoirists end their stories relatively quickly. The post-1989 portions typically account for less than 10 percent of the memoirs' total pages. And some of the memoirists, like Carlos Rico, barely mention the postwar era at all, choosing instead to simply stop their stories with the end of the war.

Typically, the memoirists bundle the events after the 1989 offensive into a collective whole and discuss them en masse. This strategy makes sense because the concluding events are interrelated—negotiations produce the peace accords, which in turn set the parameters for postwar society. The memoirists tend to build their descriptions of those events around three categories: politics, militarism, and economics. Under politics, the main issue is democratic reform and the FMLN's transition from guerrilla army to political party. A subset of this category is the resurgence of factionalism within the left and the breaking apart of the FMLN alliance. Under the military category, the central concern is the future of the Salvadoran military and the extent to which it would accept reforms. A subset of this category is the issue of reconciliation and accountability, namely if war crimes would be addressed and adjudicated. Finally, under economics, the main question is the nature of the postwar economy and whether it would be structured any differently than before the war.

After the 1989 offensive, the war trudged on for two more years while negotiations inched toward a mutually agreeable solution. Sometimes heavy fighting erupted, such as during a guerrilla offensive in November 1990, but military engagements mostly decreased as both sides approached a negotiated settlement.[121] One of the guerrillas' main accomplishments during this phase of the war was to introduce surface-to-air missiles, and in narrative terms the missiles become an expository celebration. The missiles helped shift the balance of power, or, in the words of Juan Medrano, "they produced a new equilibrium in tactical terms," because they made the military's advantage in the air more tenuous.[122] As Salvador Sánchez puts it, the guerrillas had already "forced the enemy to fly higher, and then later when we acquired missiles and the technical knowledge to use them, we were able to shoot down airplanes."[123] It had been a hotly contested issue for many years as to whether the guerrillas were going to acquire surface-to-air missiles.[124] Their strategic importance was obvious, and the U.S. government had made it clear that the appearance of missiles in El Salvador would be interpreted as a threatening escalation on the part of the socialist block. It is for this reason, seemingly, that the guerrillas waited so long to use them. The comandantes claim that they acquired the missiles from multiple sources, including China, Russia, and, ironically, the U.S.-backed anticommunist Contras in Nicaragua, who sold them on the black market. Carlos Rico reveals how important the missiles were to the guerrillas' war effort by concluding his memoir with a description of the process of turning them over to the United Nations as evidence of the guerrillas' commitment to peace. As he puts it, "we knew that the missiles were a very delicate issue, something that needed to be handled with great care."[125] Raul Mijango claims that the missiles were valuable to the ERP in negotiations because they allowed it to bargain for a larger financial settlement to help its veterans' transition to postwar life.[126]

Some of the main guerrilla comandantes, including some of the memoirists, had already left El Salvador prior the 1989 offensive to guide the FMLN's international diplomatic efforts.[127] When negotiations became the primary concern after 1989, most of the memoirists left El Salvador. For those comandantes who had been leading troops in El Salvador, the transition from fighter to diplomat was, in Lorena Peña's words, "a drastic change."[128] Juan Medrano of the ERP describes the process of "entering the city (Managua) after so many years of living in the mountains; it was as big shock."[129] Suddenly the memoirists are no longer wearing fatigues in the countryside facing bombardment, but rather dressing in civilian clothes in the peaceful environs of cosmopolitan international cities, talking with the same people, or at least their representatives, whom they had just been fighting against on the field. All the while, the war continued on back home, where their comrades continued to fight and die on the battlefield. Roberto Cañas comments specifically on the sensation of sitting across from his enemies after a decade of war. He notes that in a small country like El Salvador, the battle lines were invariably personal, because "everyone knew everyone else one way or another, whether through ties of family, friends or school." Thus, he says, "the act of sitting down to talk with someone you had been fighting to the death against was a very difficult, tense situation."[130]

The negotiations were not easy. "The dynamic of our work in Mexico was very intense," recalls Peña.[131] Sancho describes the long days of negotiating, moving step-by-step toward an agreement. "Some days are exhausting," he says, "each participant has his own temperament, and there's simultaneously a big hurry and no hurry."[132] Even though most of the participants in the negotiations believed that the war could not be won militarily, the two sides had major disagreements. Cañas claims that one of the difficulties was the two sides' divergent sense of sacrifice. The government representatives complained that all the guerrillas had to do was stop fighting and surrender their weapons, whereas they felt they were expected to "change many things."[133] According to Peña, the guerrillas went into negotiations with a mandate from their supporters, who "desperately wanted an end to the war, but also demanded that changes take place in society, politics, justice and democratization."[134] In other words, the guerrilla negotiators had to end the war but also accomplish some of their original goals in the process.

By all accounts, the longest and most intense debates revolved around the future of the military, and especially the rewriting of the constitutional provisions that defined the army's existence. According to Salvador Samayoa, a member of the negotiating team from the FPL, the guerrillas' initial plan was to abolish the military altogether. But when that position became untenable, they scaled back and accepted a variety of reforms, including the downsizing of the army, the elimination of its most repressive sectors, and a restructuring of the national police to include former guerrillas in its ranks.[135] Notably, the guerrillas made no headway on economic matters, which meant that the neoliberal status quo under the incumbent ARENA party survived into the postwar era.[136]

Yet another delicate component of the negotiations revolved around accountability for human rights abuses during the war. The two sides agreed to establish a U.N.-sponsored truth commission, which assembled a relatively quick overview of the conflict. But no provisions were made for the prosecution of war crimes or for anyone to be held accountable for their actions before or during the war.[137]

In addition to differences between the FMLN and the government, each side had to deal with its own divisions. As described in Chapter 3, General Vargas, a member of the government's negotiating team, claims that many of his fellow officers consider him a traitor for having participated in the negotiations and for surrendering too much. Similar divisions existed within the FMLN, often falling along organizational lines. Salvador Samayoa, who was then with the FPL, claims that a contingency within the FMLN feared negotiating from a position of military weakness. He claims that the defeat of the Sandinistas in Nicaragua in 1990 created a lot of concern, particularly within the ERP, because it relied heavily on Nicaragua as a strategic rearguard. ERP leaders, and Joaquín Villalobos in particular, worried about their military capacity after the Sandinista loss and wanted to delay negotiations to regain the initiative.[138]

Eventually all parties arrived at an agreement and the war ended with the signing of the peace accords in Mexico City in January 1992. The memoirists universally celebrate the achievement. Salvador Samayoa claims that one of the most important aspects of the accords was the agreement to allow guerrilla combatants and their families who had been displaced from their rural homes to retain the lands they had occupied in the interim. Even though most of those lands were of meager economic potential, Samayoa says that if those people had faced the prospect of being evicted from them and thrust into the migratory labor pool, many of them would have kept on fighting.[139]

In assessing the end of the war and the postwar era, the memoirists ask themselves many questions: Was the war worth it? Did we accomplish our goals? Has postwar society lived up to our expectations? They seldom pose those questions explicitly, but they are clearly attempting to answer them. Broadly speaking, the memoirists view the war effort and postwar society in positive terms. After all, as guerrilla commanders who directed the insurgency, they have an incentive to portray their efforts as having accomplished something.

First and foremost, the memoirists defend the legitimacy of the war. Peña concludes her memoir by referring to the guerrillas' cause as "liberationist and humanist."[140] Eduardo Espinoza says that those who took up arms for the guerrillas "did not do it for a love of fighting or to impose suffering on one's neighbors or out of petty ambitions to possess power." Rather, he insists, "We were driven by a profound love for humanity."[141] Salvador Sánchez says he was similarly guided to become a revolutionary by his "loyalty to an ethic of shared sacrifice."[142] Ana Guadalupe Martínez uses her experience as a medical student to justify the guerrillas' war effort, saying that in her observations of "the lack of health in the general population and witnessing people having such a hard time getting a response about their health-care needs drove me to participate in the revolutionary struggle."[143]

When the comandante memoirists celebrate postwar society, they focus on two main byproducts of the war: democratization and the reformation of the military. They may have failed to achieve their original goal of seizing control of the state and restructuring society from the seat of power, but the memoirists emphasize their ability to reform the military as delivering on one of their main promises. As Juan Medrano puts it, "the demilitarization and the creation of conditions to construct a democracy became the foundational aspects of the negotiations and allowed us to complete the Accords."[144] Even Marvin Galeas agrees with Medrano on this point:

> In these 13 years the country has changed a lot. Debate has displaced combat as the form of settling political differences and as a way of

gaining power. The secret prisons are things of the past. The most diverse voices and ideologies can express themselves with total freedom. Those things that were said under one's breath before can be expressed out loud.[145]

Often the memoirists equate the end of the war so closely with democratization and military reform that they make them synonymous, as does Roberto Cañas when he discusses the negotiating process: "The price that it [the government] had to pay to get us to turn in our arms was to assure that conditions existed such that after the signing of the Peace Accords the process of transitioning to democracy would begin."[146]

The memoirists' personal lives provide another source of narrative resolution in the postwar era. Most of them live in relative material comfort after the war, or at least they enjoy the privilege of having options available to them. Before the war, most of them lived in educated, urban, and relatively affluent surroundings, and they typically return to similar circumstances after the war. Many of them retain leadership positions within the FMLN, and some serve as representatives in the National Assembly. Even those who have stayed away from politics, or have split with the FMLN, usually end up fine, such as Eduardo Sancho, who returned to writing and took a position at a Salvadoran university, and Joaquín Villalobos, who took a position at Oxford University in England and later served as a consultant for various governments on issues of intelligence-gathering and counterinsurgency.[147]

This is not to say that the memoirists haven't faced hardships in the postwar era. The transition to a "normal" life after so many years of war was not easy. The memoirists describe struggle with family reunification, domestic instability, uncertain careers, lingering health problems, the memory of lost loved ones, and even ongoing threats and assassination attempts. Lorena Peña comments on the difficulty of going from the youngest child in her family before the war to its matriarchal leader after the war, "responsible for this family." Her son, who she barely knows, returns from exile, and she has to answer a lot of hard questions: Where are we going to live? . . . What do I have to allow me to start building this new life? . . . How are the children going to go to school in El Salvador?" Meanwhile, she is a target of a failed assassination attempt outside her home by unknown assailants.[148] Similarly, Nidia Díaz describes two assassination attempts against her in 1994, the onset of health problems, and the challenges of reuniting her family after the war, including a son who had spent the war in exile.[149] Juan Medrano comments on a knee injury he sustained in 1984 that by the end of the war "had become unsustainable because the bones were so unstable that I was falling down."[150]

Nevertheless, the memoirists demonstrate that amid their hardships they have options. Nidia Díaz served two terms as an FMLN deputy in the National Assembly; after leaving office she received a scholarship to study constitutional law at a Salvadoran university.[151] Peña too went back to college, "as therapy," she says. She describes enjoying "being among young people who were working and studying, struggling to understand my assigned readings, prepping for exams, adopting an academic discipline and conducting research projects in the countryside."[152] These descriptions of opportunities stand in marked contrast to the experiences of rank-and-file actors (see Chapter 6), whose postwar experiences tend to be more bleak and marked by a lack of opportunity. One of the rare examples of a comandante referring directly to the distinct challenges faced by his or her members is from Medardo González of the FPL. In the midst of describing his own troubles in transitioning from the war to civilian life, he says that "I need to acknowledge that as hard as that step was for us leaders, it was harder for the thousands of our combatants."[153]

Marvin Galeas picks up this issue of the separation between guerrilla leaders and their fighters. Focusing on his own organization, the ERP, he accuses its leaders of abandoning their followers at the end of the war. He uses the specific case of the ERP's congress in 1992, shortly after the war was over, to highlight his claim. The congress represented an opportunity for all the members of the ERP to gather together in the wake of the peace accords and look to the future. Rather than a moment of celebration, the congress "was a suicidal moment," says Galeas. The leaders stood before their rank-and-file members unable to hide some basic facts: "We had not taken power as in Cuba and Nicaragua. Thus, we had not acquired public jobs or plots of land to be doled out. We had not expropriated factories and businesses to be transferred collectively over to the workers." Galeas accuses the leaders of failing to live up to the promises they had made throughout the war, "that they had repeated thousands of times that they would achieve victory or die trying." Galeas claims that ERP leaders, particularly Joaquín Villalobos, ordered their followers, in traditional military fashion, to accept their "social-democratic" platform, which Galeas claims was a far cry from the utopia they had supposedly promised. Galeas says the rank and file were demoralized, not only by the content of the platform, but also by the manner in which the leaders tried to impose it on them, mandating from above, as if the war was still going on, rather than working from below, in a more genuinely democratic fashion. The consequence, says Galeas, was "the evaporation of the ideological and moral glue that had held them together."[154]

Any criticism coming from Galeas needs to be read through the lens of his ideological shift to the right after the war. He throws a lot of questionable accusations at the ERP's leaders, such as saying that they masked their ideologically moderate roots during the war to inspire their fighters with Marxist-Leninist utopianism. Furthermore, he criticizes ERP leaders for failing to appreciate that their members sacrificed a lot to become guerrillas, like learning a trade that could have served them after the war. But such a criticism fails to acknowledge that one of the reasons poor people joined up with the guerrillas in the first place was because of the lack of such opportunities, which even Galeas admits.[155]

Nevertheless, Galeas's criticisms reveal something that the comandante memoirists know all too well: that postwar El Salvador is not the society they had envisioned. Like Galeas, they too have plenty of reasons to be pessimistic and uncertain. But acknowledging this pessimism puts them in a precarious situation. How can they legitimize the war effort and simultaneously acknowledge that postwar society is lacking? As leaders of the insurgency, they directed the guerrilla campaign and promised to create a better society in the process, and thus their credibility as leaders depends on selling the war as having been worthwhile.

One strategy that the comandante memoirists employ to account for the problems in postwar El Salvador is to blame their enemies. If inequality and poverty remain rampant in postwar El Salvador, then it's because selfish elites still have power and block programs that could alleviate people's suffering. In the words of Nidia Díaz in 2007, "We no longer have 14 families, but we now have seven economic power groups who enrich themselves at the expense of massive poverty and the expulsion of our labor force."[156] However, advancing that argument comes at a cost, because portraying one's enemies as strong is synonymous with portraying oneself as weak.

A classic example of this dilemma is the memoirists' descriptions of postwar politics. On the one hand, they celebrate the democratic reforms they helped create. But they are forced to accept the electoral dominance of the rival ARENA party in the first three presidential elections in 1994, 1999, and 2004. Nidia Díaz captures the essence of the dilemma when she says, once again in 2007, "So if you ask me what has happened in the

15 years since the singing of the Peace Accords, I would say that we have made advances in terms of democratization; however, three years ago these advances began to stagnate." Díaz then offers a feeble explanation: "There is stagnation, and democracy does not advance, not only due to a weakening of the institutions created by the Peace Accords, but also due to the regression of institutions that have forgotten the spirit in and for which they were created—for example, the National Civil Police."[157] In these few statements, Díaz embodies the complicated and sometimes schizophrenic attempt by the guerrilla memoirists to simultaneously validate the war effort and celebrate its accomplishments while admitting that postwar society is fraught with problems. Those memoirists who have shared their stories after 2009 find hope in the FMLN's victories in 2009 and 2014, but those victories are hardly unbridled successes. The first FMLN president, Mauricio Funes, was an outsider to the FMLN and it was widely rumored that he made a lot of secret deals with wealthy conservatives to win the election.[158] The presidency of Salvador Sánchez is racked by security concerns, brought on by the breakdown of a gang truce and a skyrocketing homicide rate. It is not uncommon to hear Salvadorans who lived through the civil war say that they feel like war has returned.[159]

A crisis parallel to the conservatives' electoral dominance is the resurgence of factionalism within the left. As we saw earlier, the memoirists recall that factionalism was a predominant feature of their organizations' existence before the war and during the first phase of the war. After the strategic shift in 1984, the intensity of the factional disputes seems to have subsided as the various guerrilla organizations arrived at a sort of equilibrium during the prolonged campaign. At least they rarely mention the issue of factionalism during the latter half of the war.[160] Instead, they emphasize the sense of unity in keeping the guerrilla struggle alive, as Salvador Sánchez does when he comments on the "importance of unity" at the end of his memoir, saying that "unity is a necessity of first order in any revolutionary strategy, especially in a country so dominated by a dictatorial structure."[161] But in the transition to peace, the factional disputes flared up again, like an unhappily married couple that stays together for their children and then gets divorced after the children leave home.

The defining characteristic of postwar factionalism is the emergence of an unofficial alliance between the more ideological doctrinaire members of the FPL and the PC against moderate members, who mostly belonged to the RN, ERP, and PRTC. The former come to be known as the *ortodoxos* (orthodox) and the latter as the *renovadores* (renovators). Juan Medrano describes the split in the context of the 1999 presidential election as a "debate within the FMLN between its social-democratic side, also called the renovators, represented by a majority of the members of the FPL and the PRTC, and the orthodox members of the PCS and some segments of the FPL."[162]

It is ironic that elements of the FPL and the PC would ally with one another given their bitter split in the 1970s and the strong discord that existed between their leaders Schafik Hándal and Cayetano Carpio.[163] However, like brothers who fight against one another until a common enemy comes along, the FPL and the PC realized that their dispute was one of degree, not of kind. In other words, most of the two organizations' members remained Marxist-Leninists, and their dispute during the 1970s was over how to apply Marxist-Leninist thinking to the situation of El Salvador, not whether Marxism-Leninism was valid. The PC's decision to join the militancy in 1979 and 1980 paved the way for the two organizations to realize their ideological similarities and their collective differences from the other three organizations in the FMLN.

This recognition is revealed in the memoirs by the FPL and PC memoirists praising one another's organizations and leaders. One such example was the battle of Cinquera in 1983 when the PCS/FAL and FPL coordinated an attack for the first time since the start of the war.[164] Another example is the FPL leaders praising PC/FAL leaders, mainly Schafik Hándal. Loreña Pena exhibits this tendency when she describes Hándal's skills during the peace negotiations: "I have never met a person who followed his convictions more energetically, or exhibited such passion in pursuing the cause of the people and demonstrated such breadth and depth of knowledge about social and political affairs."[165] Such praise of Hándal and the Communists is notably absent in the memoirs by former members of the ERP, RN, and PRTC; when they do mention Hándal, they do so critically.[166]

Indeed, most members of the RN, ERP, and PRTC were ideologically moderate. They had hardliners in their ranks who would later find common cause with the *ortodoxos*, but they tended to be secondary leaders or members of the rank and file. Carlos Rico comments on the ideological disputes within the RN between moderates, like him and Eduardo Sancho, and hardliners saying that "discontent and different ideologies existed, there was a tendency [by hardliners] to accuse a petit bourgeoisie of having taken over control of the RN and imbuing it with a social-democratic orientation."[167]

For the most part, the leadership of the RN, ERP, and PRTC was democratic socialist rather than Marxist Leninist. If the leaders of those organizations employed a Marxist-Leninist rhetoric before and during the war, they seem to have been done so at least partly out of Cold War exigencies, rather than strict ideological conviction. At least this is what Juan Medrano of the ERP claims when he says that "the early leadership [of the ERP] was naïve about international politics, and we believed that adopting the ML [Marxist-Leninist] banner would confirm our revolutionary credibility."[168] Eduardo Sancho builds on this premise when he summarizes the tensions within the FMLN over the final peace negotiations, saying that "during the '80s, a traditionally leftist sector of the RN accused us of being CIA collaborators and traitors for our social-democratic position in Europe and before the U.S. Congress in 1981."[169]

The moderates and hardliners remained roughly evenly matched throughout the first two presidential cycles after the war, even though the FMLN's candidates for those elections, Rubén Zamora in 1994 and Facundo Guardado in 1999, came out of the moderate wing. A large contingent of moderates left the party in the wake of the 1994 electoral loss, led by Joaquín Villalobos and other leaders from the ERP and RN. They had attempted to found a new, moderate alternative to the FMLN, but it failed dismally, and thereafter most of them pursued careers outside politics. As the debate heated up for the 2004 presidential election, the *ortodoxos* gained the upper hand. Led by Schafik Hándal, they expelled a number of their moderate rivals from the party, including the 1999 presidential candidate Facundo Guardado.[170] That expulsion, combined with the failure of Hándal's presidential bid in 2004, deepened the fissures. The alienation of some of the moderates has led them to affiliate with the conservative opposition, such as working as op-ed contributors for the notoriously conservative newspaper, *El Diario de Hoy*.[171] Some of them, like former ERP comandante Ana Guadalupe Martínez, even backed the ARENA candidate in the 2009 election.[172]

These factional disputes consume a predominant portion of the memoirists' postwar attention. They constitute a narrative crisis in the new status quo. The factionalism during the war may not have resulted in the FMLN's defeat, although it may have cost it an early victory, but the memoirists seem to believe that the resurgence of factionalism after the war took a major toll on the left's ability to compete with the right electorally. In describing the situation, the narrators' prose often turns acrimonious. As described earlier, Joaquín Villalobos took to calling PCS leader Schafik Hándal "Ayatolá Hándal" as his *ortodoxo* wing consolidated its hold over the FMLN in 2002.[173] Raúl Mijango stayed in the FMLN longer than some of his ERP counterparts, but he too eventually renounced his affiliation in the midst of the *ortodoxos'* rise in 2002. He accused Hándal and the other *ortodoxo* leaders of authoritarianism, saying that after he renounced, "many party members were afraid and thus they chose to close their ears, shut their mouths, endorse aberrations, tolerate injustice, and assume a servile stance, sacrificing their militancy so they could remain on the list of possible candidates for whatever post, or at least to avoid being expelled."[174]

Those on the *ortodoxo* side have similarly strong opinions about their moderate rivals. Lorena Peña accuses some of the former comandantes who left the party, including Joaquín Villalobos and Ana Guadalupe Martínez, whom she names specifically, of abandoning their political and moral consciences to "provide veiled justifications for the army's and the death squads' genocidal practices during the 1970s and 1980s." She says that after the signing of the peace accords "I was prepared mentally to struggle against the oligarchy and the rightwing sectors," but "I had not been prepared for the surge in doubts, sabotages, confusion and division within out ranks, from within the FMLN."[175] José Luis Merino uses words like "treason" and "contamination" to describe the actions of the moderates within the party. He says the FMLN's presidential candidate in 1999, Facundo Guardado, "championed rightwing causes, and for that the masses rejected him."[176]

The former PCS/FAL comandante, Dagoberto Gutiérrez, presents another side of the factional divide, having broken with the FMLN after its first presidential victory in 2009. He spent much of the war on the Guazapa front and remained loyal to the FMLN throughout the factional disputes and presidential defeats after the war. But as a member of the *ortodoxo* line, the reemergence of the moderate renovadores in the 2009 election was too much for him to bear. Gutiérrez broke with the FMLN and formed a new party that would adhere to the more traditional principles of the defunct communist party. In the process of clarifying his political ideals, he makes the bold claim that the FMLN never really existed.

Did the FMLN ever exist? No. What existed? Five organizations. The FMLN was a political accord between five different organizations.

Apart from that, there was nothing. Nothing more existed! All that really existed was the political commissions of each of the five organizations.

Gutiérrez may be employing a purposefully hyperbolic rhetoric, but the content of his message is clear—more committed leftists like him recognized that many of their allies in the FMLN differed ideologically. Thus, according to him, the FMLN was nothing more than a necessity of the war, "a political accord between communists, anticommunists and noncommunists."[177]

The factional disputes take on such a prominent role in the memoirists' narrations that much of their discussion of the postwar era is defined by them. For example, the memoirists universally celebrate the achievement of democratization, but then the moderate wing of the FMLN contextualizes that success negatively by lamenting the authoritarian tendencies of their *ortodoxo* rivals. As just one such example, Rubén Aguilar, of Mexico, who fought with the FPL for four years before resigning in the face of its leaders' intransigence, says that "it is a good thing that the guerrillas did not win the war . . . [because] El Salvador would have been a repeat of the disaster that occurred in Nicaragua," referring to the Sandinista's authoritarian-style political system.[178]

Although they seldom discuss economics in their memoirs, differing opinions about economic policies stand at the core of the memoirists' ideological differences. Admittedly, most all of the memoirists subscribe to some variation of what Salvador Sánchez hails as the "The redistributive and socially-oriented state," but beyond that, they disagree over fundamental issues like the extent of state invention in the economy and the appropriate amount of market-oriented reforms.[179] Nevertheless, they all tend to find lacking the neoliberal model that the ARENA party installed in the aftermath of the war. They say that one of their main failures was their inability to force their adversaries to place economic structures on the bargaining table. While they all share that opinion, the *ortodoxos* tend to be more vocal in their criticisms of ARENA's economic model, taking the opportunity to critique capitalism in a more sweeping rhetorical style. Lorena Peña, for example, refers to the "savage capitalism" that characterizes the postwar economy, and she refers to neoliberalism as a "new slavery."[180] Salvador Sánchez places postwar El Salvador in a broader continental pattern in which "capitalists assume control over the system and give private enterprise the lead role, rolling back past achievements of workers, attacking their organizations and imposing a process of neoliberal globalization."[181]

A final factional issue that arises in the postwar era is that of gender equity. The memoirists, male and female alike, make almost no mention of gender issues during the war. The female memoirists seem to believe that as comandantes they escaped the gender hierarchy that typified Salvadoran society at the time. Also, as comandantes they have a vested interest in promoting the guerrillas' image of being egalitarian organizations committed to equity in all areas. If the narrators remain loyal to the FMLN, they tend to carry this issue forward into the postwar era, as Nidia Díaz does when she hails the FMLN's record on gender equity, saying "the FMLN is the party that has the most women in politics, due to the policy that stipulates that women must be represented by a minimum of 35 percent in the decision-making organizations."[182] But in the aftermath of war, the limits of gender equity begin to arise, with Lorena Peña taking a lead role on the issue. Peña basically describes herself as becoming a feminist after the war, and experiencing a feminist awakening in a manner similar to her militant political awakening in the early 1970s. She attributes her awakening partly to some of the postwar policies, like the FMLN's land transfer program, in which no women appeared on the lists of recipients, and the fact that the peace accords "did not even include one comma specifically for women."[183] This awakening to gender rights compels Peña to look back on the guerrillas during the war with a more jaundiced eye, saying that things like her 1979 sanctioning, in which she was disallowed from speaking privately with men for six months, was probably sexist.[184]

Conclusion

The civil war is the most significant event in the comandante memoirists' lives. The scale of the conflict made it an unavoidable watershed for them and for the nation as a whole. Most of the comandante memoirists had become politically active as teenagers, and thus they were still young adults when the war began. They spent their formative years locked in confrontation and combat. They often found the war horrifying, like when close friends or family members disappeared or suffered unspeakable tortures. But at times they found it fulfilling, even glorious. They discovered a community amid the struggle, and they drew strength from the belief that they were fighting for a greater good. Rarely do they celebrate the violence that comes with militarism. Rather, they portray it as an unavoidable necessity in the face of relentless repression and a refusal by conservative stakeholders to accept change. At some point in their lives, each memoirist decided, as Salvador Samayoa had, that "one could only combat that form of repression by the state with equally militaristic measures."[185]

The memoirists had been preparing for war for many years, and they see it as the logical consequence of the nation's long and conflict-ridden history. However, the duration of the war surprises them, and therein lies the basis for the memoirists' roller-coaster narrative. They open on a high note, with a sense of hope and pride in the war's initial phase between 1981 and 1983. Despite losing the first offensive in 1981, their organizations rebounded quickly and ascended militarily, pushing the Salvadoran army to the brink of collapse. Even knowing in hindsight the war's long duration, the memoirists infuse their descriptions of the first phase with a sense of possibility and hope for a successful end to the conflict.

When victory eluded them by late 1983 and their enemy emerged stronger and more ready to endure a protracted struggle, the memoirists enter a downward cycle. They had to downsize their units and revert to hit-and-run tactics. Rather than seeking out their enemy and facing it, they avoided contact and took a more defensive stance. Morale in the ranks dropped, and some guerrillas even abandoned the field. Meanwhile their enemy enhanced its ability to strike at them, between its bolstered air force and increased intelligence capabilities. This downward cycle lasted nearly five years, which sets the stage for the dramatic upturn in the memoirists' narrative, the 1989 offensive. Seemingly down and out, the guerrillas struck back and forced their adversaries to reframe the narrative of the war. After describing that climactic phase, most of the memoirists quickly resolve their narratives in a closing section that covers the negotiations, the peace accords, and the making of a new, postwar status quo.

The comandante memoirists have a strong incentive to portray postwar El Salvador in positive terms. As commanders they directed the war effort and they were responsible for convincing people that the war needed to be fought and that the gains were worth the many sacrifices. Thus, most of the memoirists put a positive spin on the postwar era, although not without lamenting things like the resurgent factionalism within the left and the absence of more deeply structural reforms coming out of the peace negotiations.

6 Orders Are Orders

The Rank and File

. . . .

El Salvador's militant opposition rested its legitimacy on the premise that the ruling regime was repressive and intransigent. One of the most effective ways to prove that claim was to share the stories of people who experienced personally the regime's abuse. A classic example of this sharing was done by Rufina Amaya, the lone survivor of an army massacre in the hamlet of El Mozote in northern Morazán Department in December 1981. The interviews she granted about her experience in El Mozote played an immeasurably important role in exposing the regime's brutality. Her story was disseminated through various media outlets, both domestic and international, including the guerrillas' clandestine radio station, Radio Venceremos.[1]

The formal term for the life story of someone like Rufina Amya is "*testimonio*," (testimonial). A short, working definition of *testimonio* is a narrated life story of a marginalized person, usually told orally to an outside intermediary who has the contacts and credibility to publish the story, after editing it or organizing it into a reader-friendly format. By most definitions, a *testimonio* carries with it a politicized call for social change. In the words of Werner Mackenbach, a noted testimonial scholar, *testimonio* is a "direct and authentic cultural expression of the working class and the peasantry, especially in pursuit of recuperating a literary realism, meaning the history of the popular sectors in a colloquial discourse."[2] Most scholars also define testimonials as nonfictional, despite the term "literature" that is often used to describe them, meaning that notwithstanding the problems of recall that might afflict one's attempt to remember past events, the content of a *testimonio* represents an earnest attempt to narrate one's life story as it actually occurred.

Almost all of the life stories being evaluated in this chapter come in the form of *testimonio*, and thus the narrators are called "testimonialists," a term used interchangeably with narrators, subalterns, and rank and file. The narrators are a heterogeneous lot: they hail from varying regions of the country—some from cities, most from the countryside; some are more destitute than others; some are literate and some are not; and they represent varying ages and genders. But the one thing they have in common is belonging to subaltern El Salvador—the mass of poor, mostly rural folk. Almost all of the testimonial narrators were former guerrillas or guerrilla sympathizers.

These narrators are united into a memory community by the common qualities of their narratives and their collective differences from the narratives of the other memory communities. It is not the testimonial format of their stories that unites them, nor their shared position on the bottom rung of El Salvador's socio-economic ladder. Because almost all of the rank-and-file narrators were former guerrillas or guerrilla sympathizers, I have organized the bulk of this chapter around a comparison between their narrations and those of the guerrilla comandantes in the prior two chapters. It should be no surprise that the memories of these two communities exhibit some common themes. For example, the testimonialists portray the war as an act of self-defense and they highlight the repression and abuse committed by their adversaries.

But the rank-and-file narrators differ from the guerrilla comandantes in pronounced ways. They ignore things that the comandantes consider important and highlight things the comandantes downplay. For example, the rank-and-file narrators do not have fond memories of an idyllic prewar life that they overcame in a political "awakening." Most of them portray the onset of the war as a continuation, albeit a particularly brutal variant, of the hardships and struggles they endured prior to the war. They demonstrate indifference to the comandantes' chronology, ideology, and factionalism. They also reveal the darker side of the war, describing episodes the comandantes choose to exclude. And perhaps most importantly, the rank-and-file narrators often portray the comandantes in unflattering terms, thereby situating them discursively closer to the elites and officers.

A notable feature of this chapter is the inclusion of two testimonials by former army soldiers. The number of soldier testimonies available at the present time is minute, but their existence constitutes an important component of the collective memory of subaltern El Salvador. The soldiers may have fought against the rank-and-file guerrillas during the war, but they narrate their experiences more like them than their former army officers.

The Sources

Before and during the civil war, testimonial life stories played an important role in revealing the oppressive conditions of day-to-day life for most Salvadorans. In sharing their stories, the testimonial narrators challenged the hegemonic storyline being propagated by the country's rulers, namely that El Salvador was healthy and functional, or that it was on its way to becoming that way thanks to good leadership by reform-minded military officers. Because they questioned the status quo, testimonial narrators sparked the ire of the country's rulers, who viewed them as a threat and sought to limit the distribution and impact of their stories. In fact, most testimonials had to be published outside of El Salvador first, and anyone caught with a testimonial in his or her possession risked being identified as an enemy of the state.

Despite, or perhaps because of those conditions, El Salvador produced some important, even canonical examples of *testimonio*, most notably *Miguel Mármol: los sucesos de 1932*, first published in Costa Rica in 1972. It tells the story of a labor activist in the 1920s who cofounded the Communist Party in 1930 and survived a military firing squad during the crackdown in 1932.[3] Another early example is *Don Lito de El Salvador*, the story of a peasant from the rural environs of Suchitoto who became politically active in the late 1970s. He told his story to the Salvadoran academician, María López Vigil, who first published the story in Spain in 1982 and then reissued it in El Salvador in 1987.[4] Other commonly cited examples include the memoirs/autobiographies of three guerrilla commanders, Salvador Cayetano Carpio, Ana Guadalupe Martínez, and Nidia Díaz, published in 1967, 1980, and 1988, respectively.[5] Each of their stories revolves around being jailed and abused by the military. Scholars have long cited them as examples of *testimonio* because they exude political urgency and a call for justice. However, by some standards, these three works diverge from the definition of *testimonio* because the narrators were part of the so-called revolutionary elite.[6] All three of them were literate and wrote their own narrations; they didn't deliver them orally to someone else, and no intermediary guided them to publication on their behalf.[7] Regardless of such debates, the fact remains that testimonial-like narrations played an important role in El Salvador prior to 1992 because they provided a rare outlet for a counterhegemonic narrative.

Given testimony's importance to El Salvador before and during the civil war, it is somewhat ironic that the number of testimonies that have appeared since the end of the war far surpasses the number that existed before it. At least five or six times as many testimonies have appeared since 1992, comprising many thousands of pages of text. The testimonies come in diverse formats, from stand-alone books centered on one person's life to book-length compilations that contain multiple people's stories, as well as various interviews on websites and blogs. An example of the single-volume format is the 300-plus-page *testimonio* of Lucio Vásquez (Chiyo), a former combatant with the ERP who told his story to the French-Salvadoran journalist Sebastián Escalón Fontan. Another well-know and oft-cited example of a single-volume is *Hear My Testimony* by Maria Teresa Tula, who told her story to the U.S. academic Lynn Stephen. In the world of Salvadoran *testimonio*, these single-volume works are less common than compilations, which contain anywhere from half a dozen to fifty or more life stories. A few examples of these are *Mothers in Arms* (2010); *El Salvador, el soldado y la guerrillera* (2008); *De la memoria nace la esperanza* (1997)—translated as *Like Gold in the Fire* (1999); *Tomamos la palabra* (2001), and *Río de la memoria* (2011).[8] Most of them follow the standard testimonial format in that the narrators related their stories orally to literate, well-connected outsiders who edited the stories and oversaw their publication.

Some of the compilations include the life stories of people who do not qualify as members of the rank-and-file memory community and whose narratives place them elsewhere. For example, the compilation *Mothers in Arms* contains the narrations of five women, three rank-and-file guerrillas, and two guerrilla commanders—Nidia Díaz and Marisol Galindo. All five of the interviews were collected by volunteers from the SHARE Foundation, whose objective was to acquire stories revolving around issues of gender and motherhood. Indeed, the five subjects are united by those topics. But the narratives of the latter two diverge significantly from the former three, and thus I have placed them in the comandante memory community. Even the interviewers recognized their subjects' incongruities, as seen when they ask, "Could Nidia the comandante ever truly be a peer with Claudia the conscripted cook?" They go on to observe that after the war "Nidia has armed bodyguards around her because of assassination attempts . . . [but] that is not an issue for the likes of Claudia and Julia."[9]

I draw attention to this disjuncture in *Mothers in Arms* to explain why I utilize the sources as I have. It is not the format of a given narrative that determines which memory community, if any, a narrator belongs to, but rather it is the content and nature of the narrative. In regard to the narrators in *Mothers in Arms*, despite the appearance of their stories in the same publication and their commonality around gender issues, I separate them out, with the stories of the three rank-and-file actors being analyzed in the present chapter and the other two narrations in the prior two chapters. A comparable example is the life story of José Luis Merino, which appears as a single volume, *Comandante Ramiro*. Merino is a former field commander for the PCS/FAL, and his narration places him in the comandante memory community, even though he delivered his story in a classic testimonial-like way, by telling it orally to an outside intermediary, the Cuban intellectual Roberto Regalado, who then edited the narration and oversaw its publication.

What is to be made of the fact that almost all of the narrators that comprise the rank-and-file community originate from former guerrillas or guerrilla sympathizers? First and foremost it means that we have virtually no published life stories from the literally millions of poor and marginalized Salvadorans who remained neutral toward the guerrillas or opposed them, including the tens of thousands or hundreds of thousands of young men who cycled through the military as soldiers or who belonged to one of the government-sponsored paramilitary organizations. The scale of this silence is tremendous, and it might reveal a lot about the internal culture of the military and its emphasis on closing ranks around sensitive issues. At least this is the explanation that one low-level officer gave in Chapter 3 to explain why so few officers have written memoirs.[10] Still, it is remarkable that out of so many former soldiers, so few life stories have appeared. Thus, the volume *El Salvador, el soldado y la guerrillera*, by Oscar Martínez Peñate, is especially important, because it includes testimonies by two former soldiers and places them alongside testimonies from former guerrillas.[11]

This absence of narrations by former soldiers and politically conservative or politically unaligned poor people probably also reveals something about the politics of testimonials and the interpretive orientation of the interlocutors who gather them. By most definitions, testimonials advance a politicized call for justice, which means exposing the ills of society and calling for structural change. Potential narrators who hold a contrary view by supporting the status quo, regardless of the fact that they are poor and marginalized, do not fit most definitions of testimonialists, and thus they may not generate as much interest on the part of testimonial gatherers or the publishing houses that print testimonial collections.[12]

If a large number of these now-absent voices were to suddenly appear in El Salvador's public sphere, then a question for the present study would be whether the rank-and-file memory community as it exists currently in this chapter would remain intact, or if it would need to be separated out into more numerous and differentiated communities, perhaps based on ideological orientation. At least for now, I am setting the precedent of intermixing them by including the two former soldiers' narratives alongside the narratives of former guerrillas and guerrilla sympathizers. I do so because I believe their narratives are more similar than different and thus contribute to the making of a common memory community.

As a final comment on sources, a standard trait of Salvadoran testimonials is that they typically lack explanations as to the origins, context, or purpose of the narration. The North American academician Kathleen Logan noted this issue in her review of ten testimonial collections from across Latin America. She says that the works fail to discuss "either the context or the methodology of taking the testimonies." She goes to say that "this failure diminishes the effectiveness of the accounts because the reader lacks sufficient information to evaluate the testimonies or to appreciate their broader context."[13] Logan's lament applies well to the Salvadoran case. As just one glaring example, Oscar Martínez makes no reference to when, where, or under what circumstances the narrators in his important compilation, *El Salvador, el soldado y la guerrillera*, shared their stories with him.

Furthermore, on those rare occasions when the interviewers do discuss their role in the narrative process, they tend to present themselves as neutral conduits who simply collected the stories and transmitted them to readers in pure or "truthful" form. For example, the two Spanish intermediaries who assembled the testimonials for *Like Gold in the Fire* say that they transcribed the interviews word-for-word and "all we did was structure the accounts, put the events in chronological order and inject a rhythm which would make easier reading."[14] Pierre André Blondy, in writing the prologue to Martínez's *El Salvador*, makes a similar claim, saying that Martínez's narrations "are written as they were given and as dictated by the facts; there is no fiction or literary recreation in here."[15]

These claims of neutrality are problematic. Scholarship on *testimonio* has shown that the people who gather and/or edit them for publication often play an influential role in affecting the nature of the narration, not only by guiding the interview when it was occurring, but also later, during the editing process, while preparing the narrative for publication.[16] A rare exception to the norm is *Hear My Testimony,* by Maria Teresa Tula. The intermediary of that testimony, the U.S. academician Lynn Stephen, discusses the context of the interviews and the nature of the relationship between herself and Tula in the editing process.[17]

Similarities with the Comandantes

Once again, almost all of the life stories by rank-and-file narrators come from former guerrillas or guerrilla sympathizers. Most of them are by people who incorporated into the guerrillas as combatants, radio operators, or cooks. The rest are by people who did not officially incorporate into the guerrillas, usually older men and women, but who were sympathetic to them and often had family members in their ranks. Not surprisingly, then, rank-and-file narrators share some common memories with guerrilla comandantes.

The first and foremost point of convergence between the testimonial narrators and the comandante memoirists is the belief that the war was an act of self-defense. Romeo Valle, a narrator whose *testimonio* appears in Martínez's collection *El Salvador,* summarizes this sentiment when he says "it was the oligarchy through the government and the army that obligated us to take up arms to defend ourselves . . . fighting for our lives and freedom . . . and to change the unjust conditions that prevailed at the time."[18] Most of the narrators offer a similar refrain, and those few who do not do so explicitly advance the cause of self-defense implicitly, through the chronology of their narration. They begin with descriptions of abuse by elite landowners or soldiers, then they describe their embrace of militancy as a survival mechanism.

Virginia Nery, a one-time day laborer on a cotton plantation whose *testimonio* appears in the collection *Rio de la memoria,* offers a typical example of this narrative structure. She begins by describing the hardships of picking cotton, including low pay, punitive fines for small offenses, arbitrary firings, and poisoning from insecticides. In that environment, one of her sons incorporated into the guerrillas in 1980 and was killed in combat soon thereafter. She says that before leaving for the guerrilla camp her son told her, "Mama, I see that you do not eat. You give us your food and you do not eat."[19] Another example is provided by Lucio Rodas, another laborer in that same cotton-growing region, who describes the traumatic arrival of cotton. "Before the cotton growers came," he says, people got by "in this region working their small plots of land." But when the cotton growers arrived "everything became critical." They acquired all the land and "they didn't let us have even a chicken, much less cow, because they would be killed by the insecticide being sprayed by planes to protect the cotton from pests." As a consequence, "we began to organize."[20]

The narrators describe so many cases of violence and repression perpetrated against them, their families, or their communities, including massacres, torture, disappearances, and sexual abuse, that it is impossible to provide anything more than a cursory representation in this chapter. Chiyo describes various members of his family, including his mother, being killed in an army massacre in the region of northern Morazán.[21] "Margarita," whose narration appears in the collection *Y la montaña habló*, says she was raped by police officers while in prison.[22] One of the radio operators in Oscar Martínez's compilation *El Salvador* describes listening to an intercepted army radio transmission as soldiers castrated an old man on a roadside.[23] Roberto Guardado, whose narration appears in the compilation *Like Gold in the Fire*, says that he was scarred for life as a child because he saw his father being beaten savagely by soldiers during an interrogation.[24] Narrators in rural areas describe recurrent *guindas* (flights) in the night to escape repression, which resulted in additional misery and death, including the occasional suffocation of infants to prevent their crying from alerting nearby soldiers.

The foundational premise behind the narrators' appeal to self-defense is that the repression and violence preceded their militancy. It was only in response to the deplorable conditions under which they were living and unprovoked violence by the military and/or its paramilitary allies, that the narrators responded with mobilization, at first peacefully and then militantly. One source that makes this claim with heart-rending descriptions is *La semilla que cayó en tierra fértil*, a collection of roughly fifty testimonials from residents in ten Christian base communities in peri-urban neighborhoods around the capital city of San Salvador. The narrators follow a common pattern by first describing the deprivations afflicting their communities: poverty, state violence, a lack of education, a lack of healthcare, and so on. They say that when they began gathering to discuss these issues, usually within the context of Bible-based discussion groups, the security forces reacted swiftly and brutally. In the words of one narrator, María de Jesus, from the Tutunichapa neighborhood, "for the authorities, our meeting was not religious, but subversive." She says the security forces enlisted local residents to serve as *orejas* (spies). All it took was one accusation from an *oreja* and a person would disappear. As the repression intensified, paramilitary death squads preyed upon the communities. Various narrators describe the terror they felt as masked men showed up at people's homes in the middle of the night and ushered select people away, who were then never seen again, or who showed up dead soon thereafter, with signs of gruesome torture. The narrators describe the difficulty they faced in forming responses to these attacks. They were already living on the margins and had few resources to provide them with options. Further organization wrought more repression, but if they decided to abandon their homes and flee, where would they go, and what would they do when they arrived there? For some narrators, the options were clear: continue to be preyed upon or join the militant opposition.[25]

In the face of such innumerable hardships, the testimonial narrators draw strength from some of the same sources as their comandante counterparts—their communities and a shared sense of struggling together to improve society. Ismael, one of the narrators in the collection *Like Gold in the Fire*, captures this sentiment in his description of the time he was wounded in combat and thought he was going to die, but drew inspiration from the righteousness of the cause and the collective nature of the fight. As he puts it, "I knew why I was fighting. . . . To fight for what you believe in and die for it is definitely worth it. I always supported the revolution as much as I could. . . . I know that I'm poor and that we're fighting for the poor."[26] María Chichilco, whose *testimonio* appears in *El Salvador: por el camino de la paz,* says that in the face of the military's scorched-earth policies "the organization encouraged me to make it." She describes life in the guerrillas as "full of limitations, terrible, but also full or realizations; it was beautiful . . . to share something together like that! We fought for an ideal that has yet to die."[27] Romeo Valle, from Oscar Martínez's compilation *El Salvador,* celebrates the widespread nature of the opposition movement, saying that "all of those who struggled in El Salvador wanted to establish a democracy in place of war, and among those of us who participated were men, women, boys, girls and the elderly."[28] And Carlos Bonilla, whose *testimonio* appears alone under the title *Los años perdidos,* expresses a similar sentiment about his fellow combatants, saying that "the feeling of loyalty for your friends and your sense of brotherhood with them continues to grow as you faced those extreme circumstances."[29]

In fact, some of the testimonial collections grow directly out of community members' purposeful intent to share the story of their collective

struct to the handwritten margin notes

some -purposeful community efforts to record / share histories of collex struggle

pride

struggle. The compilation *Tomamos la palabra* is one such example. It originates with a group of women in one of the Christian base communities in northern Morazán. The women decided, as they describe it, to "put pencil to paper and begin to write the history of our lives, which is also the history of the Salvadoran people."[30] Some of them are illiterate, so they tell their stories to their literate children who dictate them. The collections *Like Gold in the Fire* and *Río de la palabra* are two other collections that were inspired by members of particular communities. In the case of *Like Gold in the Fire*, the two Spanish intermediaries who collected the interviews say that the community decided who would be interviewed.[31]

In addition to drawing strength from their collective endeavors, the testimonialists share in common with the comandante memoirists pride in their accomplishments. By becoming involved in the guerrillas, either directly or in a supporting role, they feel they took charge of their lives and worked toward something worthy and substantial. The narrator "Margarita" in the collection *Y la montaña habló* says that despite paying heavy personal costs for her involvement, "I feel proud for having participated. I think I was very responsible, that at the moment the need arose, I went to the mountains."[32] Chiyo describes the satisfaction he feels for having carried a wounded comrade to safety during combat: "In the midst of that combat, I'm proud to be able to say that 'I carried him out of there when he was wounded.' . . . These things are priceless." Chiyo also takes pride in the guerrillas' overall ability to stand up to an adversary that was better equipped and more numerous. "Each combatant was outnumbered ten or fifteen to one, and their soldiers had better arms and were transported around in trucks, received three meals per day and whenever they needed it they had the support of artillery and air power. But the quality of a [guerrilla] combatant was on a different plane than a government soldier."[33] In *El Salvador, por el camino de la paz*, the narrator Luis Caravantes celebrates the guerrillas' achievements in the war, saying that "at a personal level, I fought for 19 years to achieve change. I believe it was necessary to continue fighting for everything we achieved along the way."[34]

Another notable commonality between the rank-and-file testimonials and the comandantes' memoirs is the inclusion of personal details in their narrations. The comandantes' self-portrayals are much more rounded than the mostly flat descriptions provided by the civilian elites and officers. The comandantes describe their hopes and fears, and they discuss intimate details about their lives. The rank-and-file narrators do so to an even greater extent. Chiyo, for example, describes his first sexual encounter as a nervous sixteen-year-old, and the feelings of self-doubt he experienced as the result of being an illiterate peasant while his girlfriend was older and educated.[35] Carlos Bonilla reveals his feelings of helplessness and guilt when he was confronted with situations beyond his control that prevented him from saving his family.[36]

Many testimonialists, especially the female narrators, address issues relating to the most intimate issues of sexuality and gender relations. One source that does so in particular detail is the collection of testimonials by female guerrillas, *Y la montaña habló*, suggesting that the two outside coordinators of the project, Cristina Ibañez and Norma Vásquez, prioritized the issues of gender and sexuality in their questions, although neither of them say so explicitly. Margarita was one of their sources, and she reveals in her interview that she was raped by police officers and admits that the trauma affected her subsequent ability to bond emotionally with men. She says when she first arrived to the guerrilla camp as an eighteen-year-old that she was promiscuous and remained emotionally distant from her partners. When a fellow guerrilla tried to rape her, she fought him off at first, but later went to him and became his girlfriend and had a child with him. She says she didn't understand at the time why she would do such a thing, but later realized that it was a probably a consequence of her rape trauma. She confesses that between unwanted pregnancies and various violent, hierarchal experiences with sex, "the war has left me with a sexuality that is not very attractive."[37] Margarita's willingness to share that level of personal detail is exceptional, but hardly atypical from most of the rest of the rank-and-file narrators. Collectively, they stand apart from the members of the other three memory communities in their willingness to grant readers access to their innermost feelings.

Margarita's narration reflects the fact that a distinct subset of female narrations exist within the rank-and-file memory community. In addition to the collection in which Margarita's narration appears, *Y la montaña habló*, a few other female-centered compilations include *Mothers in Arms*, *Tomamos la palabra* and *Mujeres de la guerra*, to say nothing of single-volume narrations like *Hear My Testimony* by Maria Teresa Tula. These female narrators raise issues distinct from their male counterparts, such as motherhood, sexual violence, and gender hierarchy, not only in society generally, but also within the guerrillas' ranks specifically. These differences have the potential to divide the rank-and-file community along gender lines into two distinct memory communities. But by my reading of the sources, these gendered differences are of degree rather than of kind. The overarching structures of the women's narrations closely resemble that of the men's and collectively stand out as distinct from the other memory communities; thus the rank-and-file memory community should remain, at least presently, united along gender lines.[38]

Finally, the testimonial narrators share with the comandantes a tendency to frame their lives around personal issues rather than ideology, party affiliation, or political organization. Lynn Stephen, the interlocutor of Maria Teresa Tula's narration, observes this dynamic in her study of *testimonio*, saying that "they [testimonialists] do not usually begin from the viewpoint of a political party, revolutionary movement, or specific grassroots organization, but from their own personal history."[39] Stephen attributes this quality specifically to female narrators, but I found her description to apply equally well to male testimonialists. The rank-and-file narrators rarely reference figures like Marx, Lenin, or Che, and even when they describe themselves becoming politically conscious and/or politically active, they eschew ideological issues and organizational affiliations.

Admittedly, some of narrators closely link their stories to a particular organization and refer to it frequently. Maria Teresa Tula is one such example. The organization Co-Madres takes on central importance in her life and she cites it often. Similarly, other testimonial narrators identify with specific affiliations, usually a guerrilla organization, and reference it by name throughout their narrations. But as will be demonstrated below in greater detail, they generally ignore ideological debates and factional issues, choosing instead to focus on their own personal experiences and the interpersonal relations that make up their social milieu. The comandantes do much the same in the early parts of their narrations, but as they get further into their stories, they focus increasingly on their particular organization and its distinct ideological orientation.

Divergences with the Comandantes

Notwithstanding the commonalities that exist between the rank-and-file testimonies and the comandante memoirs, the divergences in their narrations are pronounced. Chiyo offers a comment that captures the essence of the difference. In the midst of describing his experiences as a combatant for the ERP, he distinguishes between guerrillas who joined by choice and those who joined by necessity.

> Most of the guerrilla comrades had really borne the brunt of the repression, including having had family members killed. We had many reasons to fight. But there were some other comrades for whom the war was not such a necessity. They hadn't felt the mistreatment of the army as we had and they had incorporated as a result of consciousness raising. They, who had not had family members murdered, were less able to stand up to the strong sanctions that were doled out for so-called ideological deviations.[40]

In this quote, Chiyo is not referring to the comandantes, but rather to some of his fellow rank-and-file combatants who he says were not well suited to endure the hardships of life as a guerrilla, especially sanctions by their commanders. He claims that the guerrillas who joined out of choice, meaning that they did so due to a political awakening or ideological conversion, were less equipped to handle the challenges, whereas members like him, who affiliated because they were compelled to by the loss of their homes or families to army massacres, were more stalwart when it came to dealing with adversity.

Even though Chiyo's statement is directed at fellow combatants, it applies aptly to the differences between the rank-and-file and the comandantes more generally. The difference is not that the comandantes were fickle and lacking in passion; they were not. Rather, the difference is that most of the comandantes fall into Chiyo's category of guerrilla-by-choice, and consequently they narrate the war differently than testimonialists like Chiyo. In general, testimonialists came to the struggle through lived experiences with repression and hardship, whereas most of the comandantes reveal in their narrations that they came to the struggle first by learning about the hardships in the lives of people like Chiyo, and then making the decision to become politically active as a consequence. As a reminder, a decisive stage in most every one of the comandantes' memoirs is the moment of "awakening" that led them to become politically active. Typically, the awakening occurs as a result of learning that their relatively happy, affluent childhoods and their access to educational opportunities were not the norm for most Salvadorans. Once they discovered this reality, they had to decide whether they were going to ignore it or dedicate their lives to changing it.

By contrast, the testimonialists rarely refer to a moment of awakening. Most of them describe their incorporation into the guerrillas not as a choice that came as a consequence of education, but rather as a need to survive in the midst of limited alternatives. Carlos Bonilla serves as an example. He came from a poor peasant family that got caught up in the political turmoil of the late 1970s. In Bonilla's case, his family was actually apolitical, and if anything slightly disinclined toward the guerrillas. Bonilla's testimonial opens with an unflattering portrayal of the guerrillas arriving to his village and acting like abusive thugs, forcibly conscripting him into their ranks over the pleading objections of his mother. Bonilla ended up fighting with the guerrillas, which he repeatedly calls "ironic" given his initial encounter with them. In the process of explaining why he stayed with the guerrillas, Bonilla distinguishes between having the option to "accept" (aceptar) the situation and being obligated to do so—"having to accept it obligatorily."[41] He says that he realized he had to choose between three options: flee the country; enlist in the army; or remain with the guerrillas. Admittedly, he could have chosen one of the first two options, and he explains that the main reason he chose the latter was because he intuited that the status quo was unjust and that elites and the government were responsible for it. Generally, his testimonial lacks any reference to a distinct political awakening or a period of consciousness raising. Rather, he presents the war and his participation in it as another stage in a series of hardships in his life. His narration lacks the before-an-awakening/after-an-awakening juxtaposition that defines the comandantes' narrations.

Chiyo's story functions similarly to Bonilla's. He was not yet ten years old when the war began in 1981, and by then he had lost most of his family, including his mother, to military repression. His father and his surviving older siblings joined the guerrillas, and by virtue of having nowhere else to go, with the exception of fleeing to a refugee camp in Honduras, he tagged along with the guerrillas and eventually becoming a combatant. Chiyo naturally had antipathy for the army and the government because of what happened to his family, so it was unlikely that he would have joined the army or supported the government. But like Bonilla, he does not describe a political awakening that led to his decision to stay with the guerrillas. Instead, his incorporation into the guerrillas was something that was forced upon him by circumstances of repression and death and that represented the best of some bad alternatives at the time.

Chiyo is somewhat distinct from other testimonial agents in that he describes his childhood in positive terms, even though his family was poor and struggled to make ends meet. He speaks with reverence of his familial relations and the environment of northern Morazán, using words like "beautiful" and "magical" to refer to such things as his father's work routine and going mushroom picking with his siblings. But Chiyo recognizes that he is probably predisposed to view his childhood nostalgically because he lost most of his family. He says that if he could, he would "resurrect my family and return to our village and live as we had before." Beyond that notable exception, Chiyo's story follows the typical pattern of other testimonial narrators. War was not an option; rather, it was an unavoidable reality that imposed itself upon him, forcing him to choose between fighting and fleeing. However strong Chiyo's commitment to the guerrillas' cause became, and indeed it became extremely strong, he never articulates a distinct ideological position. Instead, he is motivated by a fairly immediate rationale: the army massacred his family, he had few alternatives but to fall in with the guerrillas, and thus when he became old enough fight, he picked up a rifle and did so.[42]

These themes of prewar hardship and lack of choice appear constantly throughout the testimonials. The number of examples is far too large to provide anything more than cursory review here, but one more example can further reveal the broader trend. Niña Dolores (a pseudonym) in Gorkin, Pineda, and Leal's *From Grandmother to Granddaughter*, says "I was born with nothing, and all I've got now is nothing. That's my life, start to finish. Don't ask me why—that's just the way it's been for me." She goes on to portray her childhood as devoid of play because she had to work as soon as she was able: "You didn't fool around, play games, or any of that. . . . Soon as you could work, help out, you did. It wasn't like you had a childhood at all. At least, I didn't." In the face of that kind of description, the guerrilla commanders' stories of their childhoods stand apart and share a narrative conjuncture with the elites. When Niña Dolores describes the beginning of the war, she does so in a passive voice, reflecting her lack of power over the situation: "It was about in '80 or '81 that the war came here to Cabañas." She "wanted no part of it," but eventually found herself incorporated into the guerrillas as a cook and she served with them on two different occasions.[43]

Rank-and-file narrators commonly describe the onset of the war in passive language. Like Niña Dolores, they say such things as "the moment *onset of war— passive language*

arrived when the war began"; "the epoch of war arrived"; "then came the revolutionary process"; "I was trapped by the war"; and "when the war began."[44] These comments stand in stark contrast to those of the co-mandantes, almost all of whom narrate in an active voice, with them-selves, their comrades, or their organizations appearing as the subjects in sentences with active verbs showing them acting with purpose to plan and execute the war.

As just one example of this discourse, consider the narration by Man-uel Majano that appears in the in the testimonial collection *Río de la me-moria*. Majano incorporated into the guerrillas early and was more of a comandante than a classic subaltern testimonialist. Accordingly, when he describes the onset of the war, he uses the subjects "I" and "we" followed by active verbs: "We began to inculcate this value [liberation theology] such that the people were willing to struggle because they were being ex-ploited"; and, "I was responsible for the national commission of the masses. . . . We began to work."[45] Majano's narrative style mimics the co-mandantes' life stories and stands out as distinct from all the rest of the testimonial narrations in *Río de la memoria*.

The testimonial collections *Tomamos la palabra*, *Mothers in Arms*, and *Río de la memoria*, to name just three examples, contain recurrent tales of childhood hardship and a lack of choice when it came to the war. Fidencia Luna in *Tomamos la palabra* says she was raised by her grand-parents because "my parents were irresponsible and they didn't have the capacity to care for me." She says at the age of five "I began to work making tortillas. I earned 25 cents per day, working from six in the morning to six at night."[46] Similarly, Claudia Pérez in the same collection describes "a life growing up with a lot of enslavement. On various occa-sions I was punished cruelly by my mother and father." She continues on to say that "they came from a very poor background and they worked under similar conditions of castigation, and so I felt obligated to work very hard to make money and help them out." She eventually joined the guerrillas and spent six years with them, "not only as a cook, but also in military preparation." She describes a vague process of political awaken-ing when a family member who was with the guerrillas came to her house and "began to explain the situation of El Salvador." But ultimately she describes her incorporation into the guerrillas in fatalistic terms, saying that her family member made it clear that whoever lived in the area had to choose between the guerrillas or the army, because there was no safe middle ground.[47]

Another testimonialist, Julia Garcia, in *Mothers in Arms*, describes her incorporation into the guerrillas in 1981 as a consequence of living in a region in Usulután Department that the guerrillas happened to occupy: "Those of us who were left had no other option than to join the guerrilla forces. We had no other choice."[48] On occasion testimonialists express nostalgic happiness for the prewar era, but usually only because they find the postwar era to be worse, not because their lives before the war were ideal. As an example, Ruperto Castillo, whose narration appears in *Río de la memoria*, describes life before the war in positive terms, saying "our lives before the war were better, things were cheaper and more abundant. . . . Everything was easier." He makes these comments in the context of his low opinion of the postwar era, when "everything is difficult, staring with the dollarization of the economy. Now we are paid in colones and spend in dollars."[49]

A Raising of Consciousness?

My claim that testimonialists did not experience a consciousness-raising event like the comandante memoirists needs to be contextualized, because of course, many of them did, albeit in a particular way. Many poor people in El Salvador remained conservative and refused to join or support the guerrillas, and some fought actively against them in the army or progovernment paramilitary organizations. In the same way that the comandante memoirists describe themselves as going through a process of political awakening that caused them to move away from the apathy or conservatism of their peers, so too do the rank-and-file narrators who joined or supported the guerrillas set themselves apart from the poor who opposed the guerrillas and/or remained politically conservative. When the testimonialists make that comparison, they can sound a lot like the comandante memoirists experiencing a political awakening.

The testimonialists who embraced liberation theology are particularly inclined to describe their journey in awakening-like terms. As we saw in Chapters 4 and 5, many of the comandante memoirists attribute their political radicalization to an enlightened Christianity, so it is logical that the liberation theology-oriented testimonialists would echo them. Regardless of whether people are poor or affluent, they experience the transition to a liberationist theology similarly, by first recognizing the conservatism of the mainstream church and then purposefully rejecting it in favor of an alternative theology.

One example of a testimonialist describing this process is Evelin Romero, whose narration appears in *Rompiendo silencios*, a collection of narrations from the town of Villa el Rosario in Morazán Department. She hails from a peasant family that was steeped in conservatism, like most families around them. Romero attributes her family's conservative leanings largely to religious traditionalism, saying, "they [her family members] thought that the situation of inequality, between haves and have nots, was the will of God, that some illnesses were God's punishment, that children died of malnutrition because the Virgin Mary needed angels, and that destiny determined if life went badly or well." Romero had a different religious experience, thanks to her encounter with the young priest Miguel Ventura, who had been assigned to the area in the early 1970s. He introduced Romero to a new way of thinking that she says imbued her with a "new vision of reality, of life and of faith." The language she uses to describe her encounter with Ventura's teachings is reminiscent of the comandantes' descriptions of their political awakening. She says she went through a "process of consciousness formation," and that she "became aware of the reality in which we lived." She eventually joined the guerrillas and attributes her decision to her new consciousness, which "guided my actions during the military operations in Villa El Roario at the beginning of October 1980."[50]

A similar example is provided by Francisco López, whose story closely resembles Romero's. He comes from a religiously conservative peasant family in San Vicente Department, and he too was introduced to liberation theology by a young priest, "Chele David" [David Rodríguez]. The priest organized López and some of the other men into the "Caballeros de Cristo Rey" and provided them with catechist training, which became their opportunity to arrive at a new interpretation of reality through Bible-based teaching. López's description of that process is akin to an awakening. He says that "if I had not invested the time in the church, perhaps I would have become a National Guardsman. But I came to understand the Bible and to use it as a guide to orient myself."[51]

Even some of the testimonialists who do not attribute their support for the guerrillas to liberation theology describe a learning process that can sound like the comandantes' awakening. Luis, one of the testimonial agents in Michael Gorkin and Marta Pineda's *From Beneath the Volcano*, was a laborer on a plantation in the 1970s and admits that "I hadn't any political ideas or any knowledge about things." He goes on to say that "what helped open my eyes was one summer in the mid-70s when a group of organizers came along and started talking to us laborers."[52] In that same collection, Mari says that "during the war, we opened our eyes. Before that we lacked 'consciousness'—that's how we called it."[53]

From the collection *Mothers in Arms*, Morena Herrera describes growing up in a poor family in San Salvador and becoming politically active as a teenager in the 1970s. She describes a moment when a group of high school students demonstrating in front of the Ministry of Education were met with police repression. She says, "It was shocking to me! We students were asking for a very small thing and did not deserve such a brutal response. I started to understand that problems were not so simple when they were causing so much repression." She goes on to describe an enlightenment process that revealed to her the scale of the repression throughout the country. With each learning experience, she became more deeply committed to political activism, and she integrated herself further and further into opposition political circles, eventually becoming a guerrilla. As she puts it, "I continued getting involved more and more. I didn't stop."[54]

Notwithstanding these compelling examples, it is the exception rather than the norm when a testimonialist narrator sounds like a comandante experiencing an awakening. Taken collectively, the testimonials leave the overwhelming impression that the rank and file narrators came to activism and militancy differently than the comandante memoirists. Instead of learning about repression, they lived it, and their activism grew out of experience rather than education, as a logical step in an ongoing survival strategy rather than as a calculated decision. The war represented an extreme form of hardship, but almost every testimonial narrator describes it as part of a continuum with their past, rather than a radical departure. Even Morena Herrera, whose narration exhibits elements of an awakening, admits that "I do not remember that I thought much about what step was next. It was only a matter of taking action." She delivers this comment in describing her pathway to militancy, taking up arms out of pragmatic necessity. The community organization she belonged to was being subjected to police repression and "we had to take action to defend ourselves." She goes on to say, "First, we started to get armed with popular [political] weapons. Then we used homemade weapons, and little by little, we began organizing a militia movement."[55]

Descriptions like Herrera's emerge repeatedly from the testimonials. As another example, Inés Aviles in *El río de la memoria* says that she does not believe the war represented a radical break with the past, but rather an ongoing hardship in more intensified form. She incorporated into the guerrillas earlier than most, in 1973, when she was a thirty-year-old peasant living in the lower Lempa River region. "The war wasn't just the twelve years that they say," she says, "those twelve years were just the hardest ones."[56] Taken collectively, these examples reveal a different relationship to the war from the comandantes, who chose to go to war because they experienced a political awakening, compared to the testimonial agents who had war imposed upon them and who reacted to it with the tools before them.

This difference between choice and necessity should not be interpreted as a difference in autonomy or analytical capacity, as if the comandante memoirists acted with conscious intent and testimonial agents were passive people who were acted upon. Rather it reveals the differing logic of their respective positions in the midst of an unfolding societal trauma. People from affluent backgrounds who were not suffering from the deprivations of poverty and the abuses of authoritarian structures had to learn about those things and then decide to act upon their new-found knowledge. The testimonialists' pathway to activism often did not necessitate an intellectual awakening as such.

The testimonial agents were hardly passive or lacking in autonomous capacity. As Claudia Pérez puts it in her testimonial in *Tomamos la palabra*, "I don't know how to read or write. But I'll tell you that I have the ability to do anything."[57] Similarly, Romeo Valle begins his testimonial by saying that he has "limited ability to interpret and analyze things due to my low level of education," and then he unfolds a sophisticated analysis of the war and its legacy.[58] Even a cursory glance at the testimonial of Maria Teresa Tula reveals a person of tremendous fortitude with acute observational skills. And yet the description of her road to activism is typical of the other testimonials. She goes from being a politically naïve "working-class housewife" in Chapter 3 to a "Co-Madres activist" in Chapter 5, and in between lies not a political or ideological "awakening," but a "first political experience," when her husband was arrested during a strike at the factory where he worked. When Tula went to find him she witnessed the military beating and arresting people. The decisive moment in her narration comes when she witnesses a woman being beat by police and acts spontaneously: "So I turned to the group of women without knowing any of them and uttered the word '*compañeras*'—comrades—for the first time. 'Look *compañeras*,' I said. 'We have to make that soldier let go of that woman or he will kill her.' "[59]

An exceptional example is provided by Fidel Recinos's testimonial.[60] He grew up in a peasant family on the outskirts of the town of Suchitoto. He credits some outsiders to the region, a university student from San Salvador and a pair of priests, the Alas brothers, with helping him and his fellow peasants understand the cause of their poverty. But he says that he and a number of his fellow peasants decided independently to follow a militant path and join the guerrillas. He says that once they made that decision, they more or less vetted the various guerrilla organizations at the time to find the best fit for them. According to him:

> We began to seek out contacts in the FPL in Chalatenango and we managed to do so, but our problem with them grew out of their position, demanding that we should subordinate ourselves to them and therefore lose our identity totally. We made contacts with the ERP, and it was the same, they didn't understand that we were an organization with a defined political line, with a national perspective, or perhaps they just thought that we were naïve and inexperienced and that to be able to speak seriously about those matters you first had to put yourself in a subordinate position to them, so nothing came of our inquiries.[61]

Eventually, Recinos and his fellow militants settled on the RN. In so doing, they demonstrated a highly autonomous decision-making process in which they mapped out their own future and acted with purposeful intent in pursuit of their goals.

Academic research reveals that the experience of Recinos and his fellow peasants from Suchitoto was not exceptional, but rather occurred elsewhere throughout El Salvador. Pockets of peasant radicalism emerged in other areas in the early to mid-1970s, such as in northern Morazán and Chalatenango. In those areas, some peasants or peasant groups experienced a form of consciousness raising independent of the then-nascent guerrilla organizations. It appears that the liberationist wing of the Catholic Church played an important role in this process, particularly through catechist training seminars, which provided promising leaders in various communities the opportunity to learn how to think critically and to develop leadership skills. When they returned to their communities, some of their fellow community members joined them in the reflective process. In time, and usually in response to repressive violence by the state, they came to believe that militant self-defense was necessary. They began reaching out to the guerrillas at roughly the same time that the guerrillas were looking to move beyond their urban confines and build up support in the rural areas. Thus, according to scholarship, in a dialectical way, these two sides, the rural peasantry and the urban-based guerrillas, converged and nurtured a mutually beneficial relationship that became the foundation for El Salvador's armed insurgency that would sustain itself in the rural areas for the duration of the civil war.[62]   *misses Wood, Todd, etc*

Nevertheless, the fact remains that the overwhelming majority of testimonial narrations tell a different story from the findings of scholars and Recinos's narrative. Most rank-and-file narrators portray the war as an unavoidable reality, something that was imposed upon them, a hardship that had to be overcome, not unlike other hardships they had faced in their lives, albeit a particularly violent and catastrophic variant. Their narratives describe their participation in the war as a survival mechanism more than a consequence of consciousness raising and ideological evolution. What might explain this difference?   *summary of diffs*

Any answer to this question is speculative, but a likely explanation resides in the statistical realities of people's incorporation into the civil war. Simply put, the number of people who were political aware, politically active, or who had incorporated officially into a militant organization in the early to mid-1970s was a lot less than the number of people who were affected by the conflict and/or who incorporated into the guerrillas after 1980. The sheer scale of the conflict after 1980, especially in rural areas, was much greater than it had been before, owing in no small part to the military's sweeping campaigns in the countryside. Many more people were affected by fighting after 1980, and a significantly larger number of mobile, disaffected youth, including many orphans, suddenly came into existence and were available to be incorporated into the fighting. Furthermore, many of those people who became politically active in the early to mid-1970s faced death and disappearance for a longer period of time than those who incorporated after 1980, and thus by the end of the war, there were fewer of them around. When the process of gathering testimonials began to occur in earnest after 1992, it was statistically probable that a disproportionate number of the testimonial narrators would fit the description of a relatively young, not-necessarily-politically-aware peasant who experienced the war as an unavoidable reality that had to be reacted to and survived. By revealing the predominance of this narrative among the rank-and-file narrators, I am not advancing an objective claim about the history of mass mobilization in El Salvador. Rather, I'm showing what most of the rank-and-file narrations reveal when they   *methods-caveat* are read collectively and compared to the life stories of other memory communities.

Finally, this argument of guerrillas-by-necessity rather than guerrillas-by-choice should not be interpreted as evidence that the testimonial narrators conceived of the army and the guerrillas as equal alternatives. The narrators were not, "caught between two armies" that they had to choose between.[63] The extant sources make it manifestly clear that the narrators believe the army, the elites, and the government were responsible for their bad circumstances. Even though they are willing to criticize the guerrillas, sometimes harshly so, they considered the guerrillas and their cause as righteous compared to the other side. When they speak of the "war coming," they are referring to the increasing levels of violence perpetrated against people like them by the military and its paramilitary allies. When they faced the undesirable choice between fleeing and fighting, those who chose the latter were going to go to the guerrillas.

Many of the above examples reveal this fact, but an exemplary case is provided by the narration from Maria Cruz Carbajal in the collection *La semilla que cayó en tierra fértil*. She says that in the 1970s her husband worked for the Catholic Church distributing aid to needy families, especially those with malnourished children, and to pregnant women. Cruz claims that other families in the neighborhood who wanted the aid but did not qualify became angry with him, and so they informed the police that Cruz's husband was secretly a militant. She says that when the death squads came for her husband and her son, "they had no alternative but to go with the guerrillas."[64]

Historical Frames?

Another distinction between the rank and file and the comandantes is the use of history to frame the narrations. In short, the testimonial narrators typically do not include descriptions of Salvadoran history, beyond what they or their families experienced personally. As one typical example, Chiyo devotes only one paragraph to Salvadoran history out of more than three hundred pages of testimony. By contrast, almost all of the comandante memoirists dedicate substantial amounts of space in their stories to discussing history, often going back decades in time. The reason for this difference is not entirely clear, but one likely explanation is that testimonial narrators do not feel the need to justify their participation in the war. Since they did not necessarily choose to go to war, and they explain

[handwritten margin notes: caveat; Gs + FFAA not equal opps. selected Gs b/c more righteous (even if problems) Blame on mil/elites; not usual to include historical frames; maybe bc don't need to justify]

their involvement in the war as a logical reaction to events forced upon them—like an army massacre or some other form of oppression—they do not have to rationalize their existence as guerrillas. By contrast, the comandante memoirists seem to need to explain their choice to become militants and to either found or join a guerrilla organization. One way to do so is to marshal historical evidence that validates their decisions. In this regard, the members of the guerrilla comandante memory community have more in common with the members of civilian elite and officer communities, who also include many abstract historical references as part of justifying their ideological position and/or actions during the war.

Just as the testimonialists tend to disregard the history of El Salvador, so too do they ignore the comandante memoirists' chronological pattern for the war. As we saw in Chapter 5, almost every one of the comandantes divides the war into four phases: 1) the high point of 1981–1983; 2) the strategic shift and the low point thereafter, between 1984 and 1989; 3) the 1989 offensive and guerrilla resurgence; and 4) the negotiated settlement and the postwar era after 1992. By contrast, most of the testimonialists do not employ that chronological ordering in their narrations, instead depicting the war as a single chronological period. In part, this difference is explained by the fact that most testimonialists served in the war for only a fraction of the twelve years, whereas many of the comandante memoirists were in it for the full twelve years and much of the preceding decade as well. Thus, they tend to possess a broader institutional memory than their testimonial counterparts. But even those testimonialists who served for the duration of the war fail to narrate with chronological divisions. Chiyo is one such example. He was with the guerrillas for the entirety of the war, but throughout his more than three hundred pages of testimony he only includes fleeting references to such things as the strategic change in 1984 as a low point and the 1989 offensive as a highpoint.[65] For Chiyo the war is just the war, a rather unchanging and consistent experience. Rank-and-file actors like Chiyo were not involved in the broader strategic decision-making, and so even though they lived the consequences of those decisions, they do not frame their narrations around them.

Relations between Comandantes and the Rank and File

Another distinction between the rank-and-file narrators and the comandantes is the criticisms that the former direct against the latter. They may have fought on the same side during the war, but the members of the rank-

and-file community often describe their former comandantes in unflattering terms. They tend to portray them as akin to aloof bosses who were unwilling or unable to recognize the disgruntlement of their employees. By comparison, the comandantes depict their relations with the rank-and-file members as harmonious and based upon mutual respect. The comandante narrators sometimes make this claim overtly, especially when they are celebrating the peasantry for their help. Other times, they make the claim implicitly, or by default, with an unstated assumption that their regard for their organization as a whole, and the various homages they pay to the combatants and support staff reflects mutually shared feelings of support.

The rank-and-file narrators tell a different story, and Chiyo provides an emblematic example. On more than one occasion he uses the phrase "orders are orders" to describe occasions when he had to carry out an order he opposed. One example, among many that he cites, is seeing leaders send combatants into hopelessly lost battles that could only result in further death without hope for victory. Another example is when he was ordered to destroy illicit liquor stills belonging to local peasants because no alcohol was allowed in guerrilla-controlled zones. Chiyo says he felt badly for the peasants who had lost so much already and had managed to eke out a precarious living with the stills only to have comandantes come along and order their destruction.[66]

Broadly speaking, Chiyo sees the comandantes as residing in distinct spheres from the rank-and-file combatants. The comandantes were almost entirely outsiders to Morazán, usually urbanites from San Salvador, and he describes them as having little in common with the locals. He says that not only did they act differently, but also they were aloof and somewhat distant from the peasant locals, even when they were living and working alongside them in the camps. In his words, "the comandantes were all from urban areas," and "they were not like the rest of us comrades." He goes on to say that they "had better rifles and better uniforms," and that even though they were part of the camp, "their interactions with us were not intimate, and more distant." He says most of the leaders rarely smiled and their urban origins created a cultural divide with the rural combatants: "It was not the same talking with them as it was with a fellow comrade from the neighborhood." Chiyo cites a particular example when the main commander of the PCS/FAL, Schafik Hándal, came to their camp in Morazán and tried to deliver a rousing motivational speech to the combatants. According to Chiyo, the speech failed because he was much older and belonged to a different world than his listeners, so his attempts at humor and motivation fell flat.[67]

Chiyo occasionally offers respectful comments about his leaders, such as when he praises the main ERP commander, Joaquín Villalobos, for refusing to eat some chicken because there was not enough to go around for everyone else. He is notably respectful of the members of the Radio Venceremos team, who were not official "comandantes," but who were almost entirely urbanites and important figures in the guerrilla hierarchy. More typically, Chiyo is highly critical of the comandantes. He accuses the predominantly urban members of the political education teams of insulting rural people, calling them uneducated and ignorant. He says that talking to the girlfriend of a comandante was to risk your life. He relates examples of leaders abusing, even killing their girlfriends. He complains about leaders sanctioning rank-and-file members, often for spurious or arbitrary reasons. It was, as he puts it, all part of the "verticality of the guerrillas' structure, in which it was your role to follow orders and not to go around questioning things."

One way that Chiyo expresses his disregard for the guerrilla leadership is by sharing the story of a fellow combatant who deserted the guerrillas and joined the military, the ultimate treason that would produce a death sentence if the deserter was captured. But Chiyo shares the deserter's story without judgment, because he thinks he had been subjected to an arbitrary and unjustifiable sanction, and so he chose to pursue his only alternative—join the other side. After relating the deserter's tale, Chiyo then describes comandantes executing captured deserters, which has the discursive effect of creating sympathy for the accused and questioning the comandantes' actions. Chiyo also refers to the so-called Peche School, a sort of re-education camp where sanctioned guerrillas were sent for rehabilitation. He says that the leader of the school, "Peche," was notoriously abusive and that combatants frequently shared stories about goings-on at the school. Chiyo wonders if the comandantes knew what was going on, implying that if they did then they were complicit in the abuse, and if they did not then they were incompetent.[68]

One reason that Chiyo may have been inclined to view the comandantes in a critical light was his conflicted feelings around his brother's death. The comandantes failed to inform him when his brother had been killed in combat, and furthermore he later learned that his brother died because he had been sanctioned for seemingly dubious reasons, and as punishment

his commander ordered him to a particularly dangerous area of Usulután Department, where, sure enough, he was killed two weeks later. Chiyo
admits that he was angry about this. But Chiyo never abandons his political ideals or his support for the revolution. On various occasions he says
things like, "for me, the Revolution was sacred," and "it doesn't matter if
you were a member of the high command or the rank and file, you serve
the Revolution from wherever you are at." Thus, his criticisms of the comandantes can be interpreted as originating in his belief that they failed
to live up to their own revolutionary ideals.

Chiyo is especially critical of the comandantes after the war, who he
feels abandoned him and the other combatants in Morazán after "we had
watched their backs," because now they are "worried only about their positions of power in San Salvador." He says that some of the oppressive
comandantes, like those who physically abused their girlfriends, dare not
return to the region because they would face retribution. Chiyo harbors
special antipathy for Joaquín Villalobos, who he feels embodies the abandonment, both ideological and geographic. He relishes describing the
time Villalobos returned to Morazán after the war only to be met "with a
rain of eggs and tomatoes." On another occasion, while living in Mexico
after the war, Chiyo emphatically responds to someone informing him
that "your comandante" [Villalobos] is in town to deliver a lecture, saying, "My comandante? I have no comandante!"[69]

Like Chiyo, many of the other testimonial narrators include condemning accusations against the comandantes. Arnulfo, whose narration appears in the collection *Like Gold in the Fire*, portrays membership in the
guerrillas as akin to belonging to a gang in which the leaders were all-
powerful; once a person integrated, there was no getting out. Arnulfo
claims that his leaders in the ERP kept assigning him to dangerous and
isolating undercover operations in Honduras and Mexico that lasted
months at a time and left him feeling isolated and "hopeless." While on
those missions he found himself totally at the mercy of comandantes who
rejected his requests for reassignment: "They were blackmailing me
really." They eventually cast him out of the organization and cut him off
from his food and housing subsidy. He describes them as unwilling to be
flexible with the rank and file, even though someone like him wanted to
continue working for the guerrillas, simply in a different capacity, which
he claims he did despite his mistreatment. He describes his superiors as
acting like authoritarians, "if someone doesn't go with the flow, well, he's

a dissident. "I could see there was no internal democracy, and I told them if we were talking about democracy for the country we should practice it ourselves." He says, "They didn't like that. They couldn't take criticism."[70]

As another example, Romero Valle, who fought for the FPL, expresses sympathy for enemy soldiers because "all of the soldiers and guerrilla fighters come from the same sector of workers and campesinos." Normally, this sentiment would not constitute a criticism of guerrilla leaders, because they shared his opinion. But Valle places his comment within the context of saying that the comandantes abandoned the rank and file after the war as the FMLN "crumbled and disintegrated, and its leaders were bought off." Valle also talks about guerrilla leaders' penchant for abusive behavior, leaving rank-and-file members like him no option but "to see and hear, but to stay quiet about it." Valle is especially critical of the FPL's cult of personality around former comandante Salvador Cayetano Carpio. He says that even when Cayetano Carpio was alive, he realized that shouting slogans in battle like "¡Long Live Marcial!" was "a contradiction with what they had been taught and the next morning you find yourself realizing that it's no good."[71]

Mariana, whose narration appears in the collection of testimonials from women guerrillas, *Y la montaña habló*, says that male comandantes abused their authority by garnering sexual favors from female combatants. "I knew cases of abuse of power, male leaders who used their power to get what they wanted from female members; there were a lot of cases in which women had to comply, perhaps because of their difficult situation, such as if their children were under the party's authority."[72] In this regard, Mariana's testimony demonstrates how the rank-and-file narrations are united along gender lines. Even though she is describing a distinctly gendered experience, her ire is directed at comandantes, and therein her narration stands discursively united with her fellow male members of the rank-and-file memory community.

The Darker Side of the War

Just as the testimonial agents cast a pall over their leaders, so too do they discuss the less idealistic aspects of the guerrillas' war effort. As we saw in Chapters 4 and 5, the comandantes admit to the existence of traitors, the need for counterintelligence operations, forced conscription in 1984, and the generally messy nature of the war. But their portrayals of the war tend to stick to the positives, especially in regard to their relations with the rank-and-file members of their organizations, and the examples they use support the idealism of their cause, which ignores events that complicate the picture.

In contrast, the rank-and-file narrators discuss the guerrillas doing such things as assassinating and abusing people, conscripting involuntarily throughout the war, and engaging in internecine political conspiracies that cost people their lives. Mariana, a former urban commando whose factional affiliation is not clarified and whose *testimonio* appears in *Y la montaña habló*, captures this sentiment. She remains committed to the cause of social justice that compelled her to incorporate in the first place, but when she looks back upon the long arc of her time with the guerrillas, she says that her experiences taught her to "demystify things that I believed in and that were a real dream, and I now realize that the revolution, the party, the male comrades were not the rosy color that I imagined them to be." One dynamic that compels Mariana to make that comment is her belief that sexism was rampant within her organization: "I came to understand that in the revolution, men are as sexist and selfish as men in any other context."[73]

Another revealing example is provided by Luis in Gorkin and Pineda's *Beneath the Volcano*. In the example above, where he refers to himself as a politically naïve laborer on a plantation, Luis continues on to describe the involuntary methods that the nascent guerrillas employed to achieve their goals. He says that when the organizers came to the plantation and "started talking with the workers . . . 'Talking' isn't the right word, not for what took place that day." He says, "They came with masks on and they told us that we were to go on strike. I mean told us!" He describes them as "dead serious—if we didn't do that [strike] the whole bunch of us, we workers and the owners too, we'd all be shot. So of course we went along." Luis admits that the owners relented and agreed to the terms because they wanted to get the harvest in, but he reveals that the landowner then fled the country and so the next season there was no work to be had. Luis eventually incorporated into the FPL and fought for the entirety of the war. After describing the extensive abuses perpetrated by the military, he says "Did our side ever torture? Look, I'm not going to lie to you. We did too." He is quick to contextualize this claim by saying that "the Fuerza Armada was much more involved in torturing, much more brutal. But yes man (*si hombre*), we did some torturing too." Luis offers no specific examples to support his claim, although he says that what he describes is "no secret." Thus he may be referring to the known assassinations and kidnappings that guerrilla commanders admitted to during and after the war. But simply making the claim, and the straight-forward manner in which he says it, "*si hombre*, we did some torturing too," is completely absent from the comandantes' memoirs. That absence suggests that the comandantes are unwilling to raise issues that they think would cast a negative light on their leadership.[74]

A similar example is provided by Julia Garcia in the collection *Mothers in Arms*. She fought with the FPL and describes her incorpora-tion as involuntary and deceptive. Referring to the beginning of the war, she says "the FPL came to my house and obligated me to join their ranks, they promised to support my oldest sister and my mother who was blind as a consequence of the war. The FPL promised to provide the *canasta básica* [minimal daily food rations] for them, and they didn't do it." Garcia wanted to leave the FPL, but "I couldn't just leave the FPL and go home because then I would be a deserter, and they would kill me." Thus, she transferred her allegiance to another organization, the PRTC.[75] Chiyo describes witnessing episodes of forced recruitment by the ERP as early as 1982.[76] He also describes his experience of witness-ing guerrilla leaders torture and kill a government spy. In their life sto-ries, the comandantes do not necessarily deny that such acts happened, but if they mention them they pass over them quickly, providing minimal details.

Another topic that testimonialists discuss and that the comandante memoirists ignore is use of the refugee camps in Honduras as guerrilla rearguards. Officers focused on this issue in their criticisms of the guer-rillas, claiming that the guerrillas manipulated the international protec-tion of the United Nations and turned the refugee camps into safe havens and strategic rearguards (see Chapter 3). The comandantes either ignore the accusation, or specifically reject it as propaganda, saying that the camps were comprised of noncombatant refugees who had fled the mili-tary's scorched-earth tactics and that the guerrillas had little or no pres-ence there. The testimonialists offer an alternative perspective, claiming that the truth lay somewhere in between. They describe the camps as be-ing comprised primarily of noncombatant refugees, including many of their own family members, but also they say the guerrillas had a strong, even controlling presence there. They do not contradict the comandantes on this issue out of malicious intent or to side with the officers. Rather they seem unaware of, or unconcerned with the political implication of their descriptions, and so they bring it up regularly and at some length in their stories.[77]

A similar scenario plays out in the descriptions of the strategic rear-guard in Managua, where the FMLN had an external command structure. The comandantes portray it as a comfortable safe haven away from the daily bombings, where guerrilla leaders of all organizations could meet in peace without fear of being captured by the enemy. In particular, their descriptions do not portray Managua as a place of conspiracy or interne-cine fighting, with the unavoidable exception of the murder and suicide of the FPL's two key leaders, Mélida Anaya and Salvador Cayetano. But they present this as an isolated case rather than an institutional norm. When field commanders like Lorena Peña of the FPL or Juan Medrano of the ERP have the opportunity to go to Managua, their descriptions of it veer toward the idealistic.

They sound like Comandante "Fermín" of the FPL, who told one of his radio operators, upon sending her to Managua for medical treatment in 1984, that "Managua is different, you are going to forget about the bombs, the shooting and being constantly hunted." Upon arriving in Managua the radio operator found things to be very different. In her *testimonio*, she de-scribes staying in Managua for most of the rest of the war as a radio operator in a house that served as a guerrilla command structure. She describes the environment of Managua as defined by intrigue, petty in-fighting, and questionable practices, including assassinations of suppos-edly traitorous comrades. As she puts it, "Among the comrades who were living in Managua there prevailed social climbing, opportunism and envy, as well as an unpleasant work environment. . . . Conspiracies among those comrades was constant." She also insists that the FPL controlled a former plantation near the coast called "Pochomil," which functioned es-sentially as an execution site for comrades suspected of collaborating with the enemy: "We never saw again whoever was sent to this planta-tion of death; many were executed there." She summarizes her opinion of Managua saying that "some comrades lost their perspective about revolution" there.[78] Compared to the comandantes, the radio operator comes across in her testimonial like an unaffiliated outsider who bears witness, rather than an insider with a vested interest in guarding the organizations' image.

Just as the rank-and-file narrators discuss issues that the comandan-tes ignore, so too do they disregard things that the comandantes prize, namely organizational affiliation. The testimonialists do not normally view the guerrillas through a lens of organizational identity, and they pay little or no attention to the factional disputes that the comandantes obsess over. Carlos Bonilla, for example, refuses to malign the other organizations (he belonged to the FPL). He acknowledges that "their respective philosophies were perhaps distinct from those that guided my organization," but then insists that "it would be foolish to criticize someone for adhering to something they believe to be right and truthful and that appears to be as defensible a position as any other."[79] Similarly, Chiyo downplays organizational rivalries among the rank and file of the guerrilla organizations, brushing them off as something particular to the comandantes. He says "strong rivalries did not exist between the five organizations of the FMLN. Perhaps they did at the level of the comandantes, with their antagonisms, rivalries and distinct ideologies, but at the level of us combatants, I never felt that."[80] Another revealing example is provided by Mariana in her narration in the collection *Y la montaña habló*. Even though her testimonial is rather extensive, she never once mentions the specific organization to which she belonged, instead referring generically to "the struggle" and "the Front [FMLN]," as if organizational divisions didn't exist. Even when she speaks critically of her commanders because of what she perceives to be a culture of sexism and cases of sexual harassment, she still doesn't mention her organization by name and instead says she took her complaint to "leaders" in general.[81]

The reason that testimonial narrators tend to ignore organizational identity and factionalism would seem to be that they rarely chose their organization purposefully. Most of them explain that when they joined the guerrillas, they didn't weigh one group against another. They simply "went to the mountains," or "went to the camps," and joined whichever organization happened to have a stronghold in the region where they were. By contrast the comandantes often place ideological identity closer to the forefront of their decision-making, largely because they founded their own organizations in the midst of ideological discord. Exceptions to this rule exist, of course, as described in Chapter 4. Some comandantes joined their organizations for fickle reasons, such as the random variables that led the FPL commander Lorena Peña to join the FPL and her sister to join the ERP. Similarly, some peasants chose their organization with purposefulness and intent, as demonstrated by the example of Fidel Recinos, the militant peasant from Suchitoto. But these are exceptional cases; most comandantes reveal intentionality in their affiliation, and most rank-and-file narrators do not.

Finally, the rank-and-file narrators differ from the comandante memoirists in their portrayals of the postwar era. Whereas the comandantes express cautious optimism about the postwar era and generally emphasize the war's positive achievements, the testimonial agents are more pessimistic, about both the war's accomplishments and their own prospects. They criticize the comandantes for the way they negotiated the peace accords, and then for abandoning the rank and file after the war to pursue their own personal and political agendas. The narrators in the testimonial collection *La semilla que cayó en tierra fértil* pull no punches when it comes to assessing the comportment of the comandantes. María Cruz, a narrator from the San Ramón neighborhood, offers a typical example when she says, "the guerrilla leaders and the government left the country to meet and didn't give us any information about what they were doing. This saddened me, because I felt deceived."[82]

Another testimonialist, Julia Garcia, who fought with the ERP, complains in her narration that the comandantes abandoned the rank and file after the war. She says "the leaders only think about themselves and their families." But, as she claims, "we unite and pressure them to carry out the ideals and the struggle and to work to make our vision a reality after so much blood has been shed," revealing once again the rank and file's commitment to the revolutionary cause and its capacity for autonomous thinking vis-à-vis its former commanders.[83]

Niña Dolores echoes a similar refrain in her testimonial to Michael Gorkin, saying that guerrilla leaders promised the rank and file that "we're fighting to improve the lives of you who don't have anything . . . [and] when the war is over you'll get your due." But, according to Dolores, "it was just a dream." She calls the comandantes "the bosses of the guerrillas," and accuses them of using their position to get "their big houses and savings accounts in banks," whereas people like her got nothing: "Not me. I didn't get one centavo."[84] Joaquín, one of the former guerrillas whose *testimonio* appears in Gorkin and Pineda's *Beneath the Volcano* concurs with Dolores, saying that "the top command of the Fuerza Armada got paid off and, I hate to say it, some of our top people, like Villalobos, they got paid off real well too."[85]

The narrators also have broader and more generalized complaints about the failure of the war to achieve the things they set out to do. Sonia, one of the testimonialists in the collection *Y la montaña habló*, celebrates her time in the guerrillas and credits it with having given her the opportunity to mature as a person, and in particular as a woman. But then she says "I think we haven't achieved one tenth of the objectives that we sent out to achieve at the beginning of the war. . . . The poor are tired of being excluded."[86] Chiyo says that many of the former rank-and-file combatants discovered they had no prospects in northern Morazán after the war and so they migrated to the United States. He reasons that "if El Salvador can't provide one with opportunities, better to go wipe the ass of a gringo up there."[87]

The radio operator who criticized the FMLN command in Managua has similarly harsh things to say about the postwar era. She returned to El Salvador near the end of the war, and she and her husband continued to work on the behalf of the FPL in the urban environs of San Salvador. She admits that the end of the war produced an open environment in which she enjoyed an unprecedented degree of personal freedom. But after the war, she and her husband struggled to survive, especially in light of the ineffective reparation process, in which they had access to a small plot of land to become farmers, but the land was located in an arid, unproductive region and they received no technical or financial support to make it productive. She takes her personal experience and ties it into the broader experience of other poor people after the war, criticizing the war effort for failing to produce a better society:

> Up to the present day, I still do not know an El Salvador living in peace; children still die of malnutrition and lack of medicine; the national education system offers substandard academic training, from elementary school through university; there is no credibility in the justice system; and it's best we don't even discuss the legislative assembly, where the term "deputy" has acquired the connotation of an insult; national wealth remains concentrated in the hands of five oligarchic families; there is more violence, insecurity, corruption, and impunity today than before the armed conflict; it seems that the more things change the more they remain the same.[88]

She thinks conditions in El Salvador are as bad, if not worse than before the war.[89] And similarly, María David López, one of the narrators in the collection *La semilla que cayó en tierra fértil*, concurs: "In fact, my life has changed little since the end of the war."[90]

The Soldiers

[handwritten: —both Atlacatl   self-sens.   (?) why do other testim. narrate?]

Compared to the relative flood of narrations from rank-and-file members of the guerrillas, it is remarkable how few life stories we have from former soldiers or former members of the progovernment paramilitaries, especially in light of how many thousands of men rotated through those organizations during the war. A rare exception is provided by the Salvadoran academic Oscar Martínez Peñate in his collection, *El Salvador: el soldado y la guerrillera*. In addition to providing the stories of five former guerrillas, Martínez includes the life stories of two former soldiers, rank-and-file members of the notorious Atlacatl Battalion. In a pathbreaking move, he published the narrations alongside those of the guerrillas without attempting to categorize them differently. He suggests that despite being on opposing sides during the war, the soldiers share much in common with the former guerrillas: "The two have the same peasant origins, they belong to the same social strata in poor Salvadorans who lived in a different way, with childhoods defined by agricultural labor, limitations and deficiencies."[91] Indeed, these former soldiers' stories do share more in common in narrative terms with the former guerrillas than with the officers' stories in Chapter 3. Just as it is incorrect to group the rank-and-file guerrillas with the guerrilla comandantes, so too is it wrong to analyze these two soldiers alongside former military officers.

The two soldiers' narratives are quite long, comprising nearly 180 pages of text. Both belonged to the Atlacatl Battalion, with the first narrator being a regular soldier and the second a member of one of the battalion's special forces units. Both men seem motivated to clear their name by telling their stories. The first narrator speaks positively about the battalion, but mentions none of the battalion's well-known atrocities, even though he was a member for four years, between 1982 and 1986, when the battalion carried out some brutal counterinsurgency campaigns. The second source claims to have been part of the unit that assassinated the six Jesuit priests at UCA during the offensive of 1989. He clearly wants to downplay his role in the killings and shift responsibility to his superiors, of whom he is harshly critical. Thus, both of these testimonials need to be read within the context of their potentially self-serving motives. Nevertheless, they both represent revealing voices of subaltern El Salvador.[92]

[handwritten right margin: motives- self- serv.]

The first narrator is identified as Mauricio Bonilla Acosta, a pseudonym for a rank-and-file member of the battalion who hails from a rural area in Santa Ana Department.[93] He was conscripted in 1982 at the age of sixteen. He remained in the battalion for four years, the first two as a conscript and the second two as a volunteer enlistee. He was an infantryman who participated in numerous battles before losing a foot to a landmine in 1986. He received a discharge and was given a modest pension as a disabled veteran.

Bonilla's narrative structure is typical of the testimonials by other poor rural Salvadorans. He portrays his childhood as difficult, defined by work and family hardship. He was one of five siblings. His father abandoned them when Bonilla was young, and his mother died when he was fourteen. He was living with his grandmother when he was conscripted and had little education and few prospects. He says "we had to work from the age of six. . . . We had to because of the poverty." He describes living in homes with stick walls and cane-frond roofs, three of which burned down during his childhood.[94]

Bonilla does not demonstrate ideological commitment to the government, nor does he explain why the government deserved defending. He articulates support for the government's cause only one time, when explaining the army's mission to a captured guerrilla soldier. He recalls telling the captive that the guerrillas are "an armed insurgent force . . . against the system, and we are with the system." At the beginning of his *testimonio* he recalls the guerrillas' appearance in his home region in the late 1970s and describes them in negative terms, calling them terrorists and accusing them of robbing the local population and killing people, local landlords in particular. At another point he demonstrates resignation about class inequality, saying that "they say the army fights on the behalf of the rich, and perhaps that it is true, but the reality is that the rich are always going to exist, there will always be a boss and a subordinate, and while there have been thousands of wars, the difference between employers and employees continues to exist." No doubt his leftist adversaries would accuse him of suffering from false consciousness, of being unwilling to question the status quo that has him positioned at the bottom of the food chain. Nevertheless, these three brief references constitute the totality of Bonilla's ideological insights throughout his 120-page testimony. In other words, he offers little demonstrable ideological awareness, and instead seems resigned to his fate.[95]

This fatalistic worldview sets the stage for Bonilla's apathetic response to being conscripted, as if it were inevitable or unavoidable, even preferable to his limited alternatives. "It was as conflictive situation," he says, "and work in the countryside paid nothing, whereas at least in the barracks they paid better." The most emotion he expresses about being conscripted is when he says that he was relieved to have been picked up by an elite squad rather than an ordinary army unit because they paid better and he liked the way people responded to him as a member of the Atlacatl: "Everyone respected us." He says he was in the barracks for only two weeks before he was given his first payment of 225 colones, an amount that "I had never seen in all my life."[96]

Ultimately, Bonilla's testimonial is a tale of day-to-day toil and survival. He moves from one battle to the next and one hardship to another. His initial eighteen months of training was hard and dehumanizing. He claims he was forced to eat worms, dogs, and vultures. But he describes it all in unaffected terms, saying that he was obligated to follow orders and in the case of the food, at least "dog meat can be delicious if one knows how to cook it properly." When it comes to fighting guerrillas, Bonilla details many combat experiences, but mostly he describes long marches, hard labor, and hunger. For Bonilla, soldiering is a job, albeit one with higher risks than most others, but also higher pay. His overall approach to soldiering is summarized when he says "the most precious things to a soldier are his salary and his pass to leave the barracks." Bonilla is quite aware that soldiering is a poor man's job, and he takes special note of the time that the son of a relatively wealthy landowner from Chalatenango Department enlisted in the battalion: "All of us in the barracks were poor, and so when we saw someone who came from money it was strange, and we asked, Why don't you go to the military academy [to become an officer]?"[97]

Bonilla's wounding and his eventual discharge represent the climax and resolution to his narration. He prefaces the experience of stepping on a mine by commenting on the psychological aspect of combat: "You are a human being and some things are always present, fear, calamity, hunger and thirst; there are moments when you just wish you would get shot and killed so that at least you could get out of this place." The act of stepping on a mine and being discharged brings his story full circle, back to where he was before being conscripted—a poor young man with few prospects. He is disgruntled by the fact that wounded veterans like him "receive such a minimal pension." In response to his superiors' claim that at least "you got something," he says that "I did not agree with that." Eventually he acquires some training in electrical mechanics and finds a job in a machine shop, but now instead of being respected as a former member of the Atlacatl, he is feared, because people's perceptions are that "we were a den of assassins, badly raised people, disrespectful, thugs, drug addicts, and whatever else came to their minds."[98]

The second Atlacatl soldier who appears in Martínez's book goes unnamed and is identified simply as "an ex-commando," a member of one of the battalion's secretive and highly trained special forces unit who seems to have served between the mid-1980s and 1991. He reveals little about himself or his background prior to his incorporation into the battalion, beyond self-identifying as a member of "los de abajo" (the poor masses).

His narrative is shorter than Bonilla's, but it is also more targeted and bitter. The entire narrative is framed by his anger over the actions of his superiors after his unit completed the mission to kill the Jesuits in November 1989. He claims that he was standing guard below the Jesuits' residence by the university cafeteria and was not involved in the actual shooting, but he could see some of what transpired. He claims that shortly after returning from the mission, his superiors sold out the unit saying they had nothing to do with the murders. He claims that he and his fellow commandoes were arrested and imprisoned for three months, eventually being released on their own recognizance while the investigation proceeded. The excommando is irate with his superiors over this treatment and never forgives them. In one of his many denunciations of them he says "What they did was unjust, we had served, and they had told us many times that we were national heroes. . . . What we did for them we did against our will, we were obligated to do so."[99]

Naturally, the excommando's testimonial needs to be read in the context of his desire to clear his name in the Jesuit murders. Nevertheless, his anger toward his superiors turns him into something of a whistleblower, and he builds his narrative around exposing the Atlacatl's many crimes and abuses. Not only does he describe the battalion as being brutal with its enemies, but also of dehumanizing its own members, especially during training. Whereas Bonilla fails to offer any references to the Atlacatl's notorious misdeeds, the excommando produces a litany. As just one example, he describes the tortures that battalion members inflicted upon captured guerrillas during interrogations, including amputating body parts so that "they would die little by little." He says that during his training, his superiors brought in a captured guerrilla, killed him, made a large pot of soup out of his remains, and forced the recruits to eat it. He denounces his trainers by saying, "They were in charge of our care, but it was more like they were in charge of screwing us over." He offers many similar examples.[100]

After the fervor over the Jesuit case subsided, the excommando claims that his superiors unceremoniously discharged him and the other members of his unit: "They threw us out into the street as if we'd never served."[101] When they inquired after the war about a pension, they were told that they were not entitled to anything because as members of the special forces their identities had been kept secret, and so no record of their military service existed. He says he and his fellow unit members had no choice but to do the best they could in civilian life, which was disastrous for most of them, because they had little to build upon; they lacked land, jobs, and training. Like Bonilla, the excommando's testimonial comes full circle, with him being a poor person with few prospects after the war, just as he had been before it.

When the excommando summarizes his experience, he employs a class-based perspective, in which he portrays the officers as being in league with civilian elites to the detriment of poor people. As he puts it, "the millionaires and the army officials made us fight one another and the only people who died were the poor." He accuses his superiors of being liars, for "making us believe that we were fighting to defend the country and our families," but who actually used the war to enrich themselves, because "the war for the military leaders was a lucrative business." He concludes his testimony with regret for having served in the military, saying that nothing changed as a result of the war: "The poor are poorer and the only thing that has changed for them is the fact that the war has ended."[102]

In summary, the life stories of these two former Atlacatl soldiers exhibit many of the same traits as the testimonial narrations by rank-and-file guerrillas, with the exception of the side they fought on during the war. They are minimally educated, barely literate members of the poor masses who told their stories to an outsider interlocutor, who then published the narrations in a book. Even though they were soldiers who fought against the guerrillas, their life stories exhibit urgency about the hardships they endured. Therein, their stories can be read inherently as a call to political action, regardless of the ideological perspective, or lack thereof, that they exhibit.

Notably, the two soldiers share few, if any of the narrative structures of the officers in Chapter 3. They offer no historical context for the war, nor do they reference the military's supposed reforms prior to 1980 that the officers tout as proof of the guerrillas having been war mongers. The first source, Bonilla, seems neither concerned about, nor particularly aware of the broader context of the war. For him it's just another phase of his life typified by work and hardship. By contrast, the excommando speaks at greater length about the officers' explanations for the war, as well as their various crimes and misdeeds, because he is embittered and sees them as deceptively covering up their self-serving goals.

Conclusion

Rank-and-file actors constitute a distinct memory community in postwar El Salvador. Whether they are former guerrillas, guerrilla sympathizers, or army soldiers, their narrations share little in common with those of civilian elites, military officers, and guerrilla commanders. Former guerrillas and guerrilla sympathizers limit their narrations to their and their families' immediate experiences—they do not venture into El Salvador's past, like the comandantes do. Nor do they describe the war with the comandantes' chronological framing, most likely because they did not make strategic decisions and so they do not narrate their experiences through them. The rank-and-file narrators reveal the uglier side of the war, and they ignore things that the guerrilla comandantes emphasize, like organizational identity and factional disputes. The former rank-and-file guerrillas share much in common in narrative terms with the two former Atlacatl soldiers, who come from a similarly impoverished social position, and who tend to portray the war as more of an obligation than a choice.

Conclusion

· ·

No matter how much some Salvadorans might want to forget their civil war, they can't, or at least they can't collectively. The war has a ubiquitous, if sometimes unspoken presence, but it is always around, and it invariably shapes contemporary political debate, sometimes beyond the conscious awareness of its interlocutors. The amnesty law has prevented people from being prosecuted for their activities during the war, but many Salvadorans constantly ask themselves what happened during the war and who did what to whom.[1]

The life stories at the basis of the present study are discursive threads strung throughout El Salvador's new postwar public sphere. When these threads are woven together in the form of memory communities, they constitute the fabric of Salvadorans' collective consciousness about their civil war. The present study seeks to show that those threads exist, in the form of published texts, both in print and online. I do not try to prove where those threads came from, nor can I predict where they will go in the future. But I can reveal how they look here and now, as they crash back and forth into one another and construct meaning in people's minds in varying and unpredictable ways.

The Dutch academic and former FPL affiliate, Ralph Sprenkels, refers to these published life stories as "militant memories."[2] They are militant because they reference a conflictive past, but also because they are in conflict with one another today. The members of the four memory communities employ narratives that are mutually exclusive of one another. By providing different versions of history, they are competing with one another for the hearts and minds of the Salvadoran populace, just as the opposing sides had done during the civil war in the 1980s.

Sprenkels is justifiably pessimistic about the ability of life stories to provide a reliable account of the past. His pessimism extends from a belief that postwar El Salvador suffers from conditions that hinder society's ability to hold narrators accountable to their claims. These conditions include the absence of a well-grounded historiography of the civil war, the lack of autonomous institutions conducting research on the war, a judicial system lacking the authority to investigate people's activities during the war, and a political system that is dominated by two political parties (FMLN and ARENA) with vested interests in particular versions of the war. In light of such circumstances, Sprenkels says, "new historical narratives and perspectives may well gain currency in the near future, [but] El Salvador's political memory work is likely to remain polarized and subordinated to contemporary political interests." He concludes by insisting that when historical narratives are "submitted to the rhetorical requirements of militancy, history becomes virtually inseparable from propaganda."[3]

Indeed, the life story narrators that I have analyzed in the present study might be wrong; they might be lying, confused or forgetful. Or, they might be right; they may possess incredible capacities for recollection and they might be deeply invested in trying to relate the past as accurately as possible. Regardless, the simple fact is that each narrator provides an interpretation of the past and inserts it into the public sphere. The goal of the present study has been to document the narratives' existence and determine the extent to which they reveal particular patterns of recollection.

My central finding is that the life stories reveal the existence of four distinct memory communities, each with its own particular and highly uniform narrative. I've labeled the communities: civilian elites, military officers, guerrilla commanders and rank-and-file (testimonial) actors. These communities do not exist in public discourse in El Salvador, nor do their members demonstrate awareness of belonging to them as such. Therein, when the narrators set out to share their story, they did not do so with the intent of promoting or defending their particular community. They no doubt had certain conscious goals in mind, like settling old scores, avoiding future prosecution, promoting a political career, or perhaps simply preserving the past for posterity. Whatever their motives, what defines each narrator as a member of his/her memory community is the commonality of his/her narrative with all the other members of that community. The members of each group use narratives with similar styles and common content. They include many of the same historical references, and therein exclude other historical references. They portray the war, its causes and its aftermath in the same terms. They reveal a sense of self identity that bears much in common with the identities of the other members of their community, which stands in marked contrast to the members of the other three communities. Each narrator considers his/her narrative to be unique, a genuine effort at autonomous self expression.

Thus they would likely be surprised to learn how reductionist and common their narratives actually are.

The narratives of each community are defined by a unifying concept or theme. For the community of civilian elites, that concept is an unbridled defense of economic libertarianism and a sense that its members are a beleaguered, targeted minority. The members of this group subscribe to a particular brand of conservatism that is rooted in a belief that something rightfully belonging to them has been stolen, or is under threat of being stolen in the near future. Thus, they employ a highly militant rhetoric that calls for aggressive action to right past wrongs and avoid future injustices. A central component of this group's narrative is to claim that El Salvador once had a golden age, when hard-working entrepreneurs could make an honest living in a free-market without concern for government intervention or mass mobilization. The dates of that golden age vary slightly from one elite narrator to the next, but generally they all identify the 1960s as the time when things turned sour. It was then that reform-minded military officers holding political office began implementing social and economic reforms that elites believe targeted them and their possessions. Hence, the civilian elite memoirists are highly suspicious of the military, and in fact, they virtually eliminate the military from their descriptions of the war, as if twelve years of nearly daily combat with armed guerrillas never occurred.

The elites choose instead to highlight their own political activism, especially the founding of the ARENA political party. Their narratives suggest that their political activities were more important than the military's combat operations. This same sense of pride leads the elite narrators to imply that paramilitary deathsquads were justified to exist, because they represented civilians defending themselves when no one else would. Naturally, the elite narrators prefer to avoid references to paramilitary activities and they specifically look for opportunities to deny that they were involved in them. But some of them can't help but allow comments to slip through that defend paramilitaries' right to exist.

When it comes to describing the history of the civil war and its causes, the elite memoirists employ a highly selective narrative. They make no mention of unjust social conditions, or the existence of any form of systemic abuse, such as incarceration, torture or extralegal killing, except when it comes to the guerrillas' treatment of them. By claiming that El Salvador had a golden era when things were right and proper prior to the 1960s, they portray guerrilla leaders as social malcontents who were incapable of making it in a free economy so they resorted to demagoguery and theft in the form of revolutionary socialism to advance their personal interests. The elite memoirists harbor a similarly modest opinion of political leaders in the United States, even President Reagan. They describe Washington at best as a supporter of anti-elite reforms in El Salvador, and at worst as a beachfront for international communism in the western hemisphere. Broadly speaking, the civilian elite memoirists see themselves as an aggrieved minority, subjected to the expropriating tendencies of military reformers, ignorant U.S. policymakers and radical revolutionaries.

The unifying characteristic of the officers' memory community is a defense of the military as an institution and the desire to preserve its existence in the future. The officers do not portray Salvadoran history as having lost a once golden age. Rather, they describe El Salvador as having suffered from a variety of maladies that required active intervention by honest, dispassionate administrators like themselves, who could do what was best for the nation as a whole. As a result, the officers, most of who come from humble backgrounds, offer lukewarm assessments of the civilian elites. More often than not, they directly accuse elites of having created the conditions that allowed a radical guerrilla insurgency to take shape in the 1970s and 1980s. The officers share the elites' opinion about the guerrilla leaders, portraying them similarly as violent opportunists out for themselves. As part of that portrayal, the officers insist that the guerrillas had no justification to start the war because the military had been implementing the necessary reforms to fix the nation's problems. Naturally, the officers tend to describe the military as having fought the war honorably, and thus they too offer a highly selective version of it, making no mention of massacres or scorched-earth tactics. In regard to the military's internal structure, the officers portray their relations with rank-and-file soldiers as harmonious, defined by a shared commitment to achieving common nationalistic goals. Finally, the officers claim that they as individuals and the military as an institution were subjected to a civilian conspiracy at the end of the war, one in which the guerrillas and elites set aside their differences and united against the military in hopes of destroying it as a rival power. As for the United States, the officers share the elites' modest opinion of it. They appreciate U.S. aid, but they too believe that U.S. policymakers were ignorant outsiders who tried to impose their will on El Salvador and in the process hindered the military's ability to prosecute the war effectively.

246 Conclusion

The memory community of guerrilla commanders is defined by the be- lief that Salvadoran society necessitated restructuring and that guerrilla leaders needed to possess political power in order to carry out that re- structuring. Most of the guerrilla leaders come from relatively affluent backgrounds typified by solid family relations and educational opportu- nities. Most of them were university students when they incorporated into the guerrillas. Thus, their descriptions of their own histories and El Sal- vador's recent past tend to sound ironically similar to the civilian elites. They describe their childhoods in positive terms and even offer somewhat idyllic descriptions of El Salvador during their youth. It is only when they began to learn of society's injustices, usually as a result of their educa- tional opportunities, that they portray El Salvador in darker terms. But instead of lamenting the loss of a bygone golden era like their elite counter- parts, the guerrilla commanders exhibit something more akin to anger towards elites and officers for having stripped their innocence away from them.

In contrast to the elites and the officers, the guerrilla commanders of- fer a much more comprehensive description of El Salvador's past. They highlight acts of military brutality and elite exploitation, which is to be expected, because such events were a central component of their public- relations campaign during the war. It allows them to portray the war as an act of self-defense and their own actions as just and proper. Almost never do they admit to wrongful acts or bad decisions. As an extension of their positive self-assessment, they portray their relations with their rank-and-file combatants as harmonious, ironically similar to the way in which military officers portray their relations with their soldiers. The guerrilla commanders describe relations between the guerrillas and the broader civilian population as similarly harmonious. They also demon- strate strong allegiances to their particular guerrilla faction, suggesting that the FMLN was defined by a greater degree of factionalized identity than its leaders let on during the war.

The final community of rank-and-file actors, consisting almost exclu- sively of former guerrilla combatants and sympathetic civilians, is uni- fied by their search for greater opportunity in a more just society. They situate their life stories in a history of elite abuse and military repression, and thus, like the guerrilla commanders, they define the war as an act of self-defense. They document many cases of repression and abuse by elites and officers. However, the rank-and-file actors limit their narratives to events they or their families experienced personally, which contrasts with the guerrilla commanders, who tend to describe distant and disparate events that they did not see or experience. Notably, the rank-and-file narrators offer less celebratory descriptions of the guerrillas' war effort than the comandantes. They describe the comandantes in modest, even critical terms. Most of the rank-and-file actors came from rural areas and they describe the comandantes as urban outsiders who were aloof, domineering and sometimes abusive. The members of the rank-and-file community also tend to differentiate themselves from the comandantes as to their reasons for joining the war. Whereas the guerrilla commanders chose to become politically active, usually as a consequence of educational opportunities, most of the rank-and-file actors describe their journey to incorporation as driven by necessity and a lack of alternatives. They explain their pathway to militancy as rooted in personal loss, such as the torture or killing of a family member or the destruction of their home and livelihood. Notwithstanding their readiness to credit liberation theology and the organizational structures of the liberationist church as important to raising their political consciousness, the rank and file differentiates itself from the comandantes over the issue of being a guerrilla-by-choice vs. being a guerrilla-by-default. As a further elucidation of this point, I include in this memory group two testimonies from former army soldiers. Their narratives have more in common with their guerrilla adversaries than with their own officers, particularly in regard to their involuntary participation in the war.

· · · · ·

Published life stories are not the only site of remembrance in postwar El Salvador, but they are one of the most widely-used forms of expression. In the face of the existence of these four memory communities, and their mutually exclusive renditions of the war, one cannot help but wonder how stable postwar El Salvador can be, particularly in the face of so many destabilizing pressures, such as economic stagnation, gang violence, drug trafficking and out migration.[4] In his study of historical memory in post-Pinochet Chile, the historian Steve Stern sees a similar concern and asks, "How can one build a peaceful and ethical coexistence when society is populated by such different—and searing—remembrances?"[5] In the case of El Salvador, a hopeful sign is that most every life story narrator says that the suffering of the war was so profound that no one wants to return to it. And to date, despite its problems, El Salvador has had a succession of democratic elections and even one peaceful transfer of power between rival parties. After losing the first three postwar presidential elections, the FMLN won in 2009 and again in 2014, in the latter case with a former guerrilla commander leading the ticket.

The study of these life stories is important not only for revealing the communities that exist, but also for revealing the communities that might have existed. For example, one might have expected the guerrillas' narratives to be divided along the lines of their five organizational factions, or along ideological lines. The commanders demonstrate impressive loyalties to their respective faction, and they insult the leaders of rival factions, sometimes harshly. Those insults often follow the ideological lines that helped to divide the factions in the first place and that have taken on new life in the postwar era. One might also expect to see gender lines divide the comandantes' narratives.[6] But none of those possibilities emerge, leaving behind only a high degree of commonality in the comandantes' narratives.

For their part, the rank-and-file narrators more or less ignore factional and ideological divisions, and instead refer to the guerrillas in holistic terms. They describe their experience in both the war and the post-era era differently than their former comandantes, and often they have little complimentary to say about them.

The same situation applies to former army soldiers vis-à-vis their former commanding officers. Although the sample size is exceedingly small, one might expect their narratives to resemble those of the officers. But instead the soldiers' narratives look a lot more like those of their former enemies, the rank-and-file guerrillas.

One might expect the officers to be divided along one or more factional lines. They are not a homogenous lot; they subscribe to different ideologies, belong to rival *tandas,* and some of them personally despise one another. Furthermore, before and during the war their rivalries took the form of serious political machinations, including some episodes that had deadly consequences, such as the failed coup after the fraudulent presidential election in 1972. Yet, once again, these potential differences are subsumed by the commonalities of the officers' narratives, as each of them prioritizes the survival of the military above all else.

Finally, one might expect the former allies—civilian elites and military officers—to comprise a single memory community. Indeed, they have some common memories and share the same enemies in the form of leftist revolutionaries and their foreign allies, to say nothing of the United States government. But their narratives are more different than similar. They have divergent priorities and they see one another as rivals.

· · · · ·

The revelations contained in the life stories do not necessarily reveal anything about the objective reality of the civil war. Rather, they reveal the ways in which the narrators are remembering the war, or at least how they have chosen to narrate the war, and how they want other people to interpret it. Nevertheless, the discovery of these four memory communities provides some insights into the history of the war, suggesting that, among other topics, future scholars should consider looking deeper into the issue of factional divisiveness. Unity is a necessary component for any successful war effort, and indeed the two sides of the Salvadoran conflict promoted themselves as being highly unified. The life stories suggest that the face of unity during the war may have been masking some complicated and divisive fault lines that are manifesting themselves in particular ways in the postwar era.

Similarly, the revelations contained in the life stories, and in particular the discovery of the existence of four distinct memory communities, offers suggestive insights into postwar politics. As one example, consider the criticisms directed against the former guerrilla comandantes. Some surprising narrative synchronicities emerge among the various narrators that might have important political implications. The rank-and-file guerrillas' criticisms of their former comandantes converge fairly closely with the accusations directed at those same comandantes by civilian elites and officers. The latter portray the comandantes as conspirators who were out for their own ends and who fought the war from the comfortable confines of foreign hotels and luxury residences. Those criticisms can sound surprisingly similar to the rank and file's portrayals of the comandantes as aloof, sometimes abusive outsiders who had little in common with the combatants, who negotiated an end to the war without consulting them, and who then abandoned them for their own careers after the war. Ironically, the comandantes own narratives contribute to this synchronicity, as they say similar things about one another as part of their factional rivalries. Leaders of the other four organizations accuse the Communists and its leader Schafik Hándal as being born conspirators who were more concerned with jockeying for position within the FMLN than fighting the enemy on the field. The FMLN's division into rival camps after the war provides yet more opportunities for launching such critiques. The reformist *"renovadores,"* who come disproportionately from the ERP, the RN and the PRTC, use a similar rhetoric to critique the more hardline *ortodoxos,* whose members are drawn mostly form the PCS and the FPL.

This alignment of discursive allies reveals that a certain faction of the FMLN is confronting a lot of narrative pressure. This pressure could contribute, for example, to the ability of politicians within the conservative ARENA party, which includes some former high-ranking military officers, to garner support from poor, rural Salvadorans, and maybe even some former guerrilla combatants; they might find themselves aligned discursively against some former guerrilla comandantes. Similarly, such synchronicity could translate into difficulty on the part of the FMLN, or at least a certain faction therein, to expand or deepen its base of support within that same sector of the rural poor.

· · · · ·

By any standard of reasoned measure, some of the narratives are difficult to read, or to take seriously, because they advance outlandish and morally repugnant claims. I am referring here particularly to the narratives by some of the civilian elites and military officers. It is tragic and outlandish to claim, for example, that the guerrillas killed Archbishop Romero in March 1980 and the six Jesuit priests in November 1989. It is reprehensible to argue that what transpired in El Mozote in northern Morazán in December 1981 was anything other than a purposeful slaughter of 1,000 innocent and unarmed civilians by the Atlacatl Battalion under the direction of Colonel Domingo Monterrosa, who many military officers continue to identify as a hero.[7] It is equally repugnant to see those narrators whitewash, or simply ignore the sheer scale of the atrocities committed by the armed forces and the paramilitaries, who over the span of two or more decades murdered, tortured, raped and abducted untold tens of thousands of their fellow citizens. As an onlooker, it is tempting to dismiss the narrators of these claims as marginalized gadflies. Even if they are, the mere existence of their narratives in the public sphere necessitates analysis. But, in fact, these narratives are numerous and they are being read. One narration that makes some of the most reprehensible claims, David Panama's *Guerreros de la libertad,* is in its second edition.[8] Many of these narrators remain important public figures with active political careers. Ricardo Valdivieso was still serving in an official capacity in ARENA in the late 2010s. Colonel Sigifredo Ochoa Pérez was elected

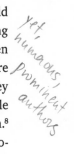

[handwritten marginalia: "1", "outlandish claims", "yet humous/ prominent authors"]

to the National Assembly for ARENA in 2012; and in the 2014 congressional elections, the names of Generals Zepeda, Corado and Vargas all showed up on ARENA's list of pre-candidates for deputy seats in the Assembly. Furthermore, the president of El Salvador for the term 2014–2020, Salvador Sanchez Cerén, the former head commander of the FPL, reveals nothing in his memoir about the brutal purges that occurred within his organization in the San Vicente region in the late 1980s.

· · · · ·

The four memory communities account for all but a few of the life stories that exist currently. The outliers are too few in number to constitute anything resembling a full-fledged memory community, but some of them could comprise "proto communities," or the early foundations of a future memory group. One such proto community is comprised of members of centrist or nonmilitant political parties. Contributory works would include: the memoir by Julio Adolfo Rey Prendes, a former high-ranking figure in the Christian Democratic Party; the account of the 1979 coup and subsequent reforms by Rodrigo Guerra y Guerra; and shorter interviews with Gerardo Le Chevalier, an activist in the Christian Democratic Party, and Víctor Manuel Valle, an activist within the *Movimiento Nacional Revolucionario* (MNR), a small progressive political party that formed part of the electoral coalition in the 1972 and 1977 presidential elections. An important precursor to these works is the 1986 autobiography by José Napoleón Duarte, co-founder and life-long member of the Christian Democratic Party and president of El Salvador between 1984 and 1989.[9]

These narratives by non-militant centrists do not fit into any of the four extant memory communities, but they do exhibit a hybrid quality, because they contain elements that appear in other communities' narratives. For example, the narrators tend to have a well-developed sense of historical chronology, which they use to contextualize their lives and justify their particular ideological position, like the civilian elites, the military officers and the guerrilla commanders. As just one revelatory example, José Napoleón Duarte, in his 1986 memoir, harshly chastises the military for murdering thousands of their countrymen in the 1932 uprising, but then simultaneously accuses the "Communist Indian Organizations" of "killing without mercy anyone serving or connected with the local well-to-do families." He then proceeds to make the highly spurious claim that "both sides killed tens of thousands of people" during the events, which situ-

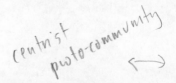

ates his narrative squarely in the argument-of-moral-equivalence trope, a central component of the narratives by civilian elites and officers.[10]

One aspect of the centrists' stories that resembles the narratives by civilian elites and guerrilla commanders is the description of their youths. For the most part, the centrist narrators come from relatively affluent, urban families and they had relatively happy, well-adjusted childhoods marked by educational opportunities and even international travel. Then they arrive at the moment, akin to the guerrilla commanders' consciousness raising, when they discover that their experiences are much different than the suffering and hardship that typified the lives of most Salvadorans. They hold the military regimes and the elites accountable for creating those conditions, and they describe themselves as becoming political activists in hopes of alleviating them. But whereas the guerrilla commanders translate their eye-opening experiences into radical politics and militant insurrection, the centrist narrators remain anti-communists, committed to the belief that conditions in the country can be improved through electoral politics and non-radical social reform. Throughout their chronological contexts, they celebrate any movement or organization that they see as having advocated for electoral democracy and non-radical social reforms.

When the narrators arrive to the late 1970s and the civil war, they find themselves in a complex and often paradoxical position. They had spent much of their political lives up to that point opposing dictatorial military rule, and they continue to harshly criticize the security forces and paramilitaries for the unrelenting abuses, including Rey Prendes listing the names of Christian Democratic party members who were murdered by the army or deathsquads.[11] But then in the face of an armed insurrection by militant guerrillas, the narrators are forced to portray the military as the bulwark of national defense and the sole element capable of preventing a communist takeover of government. Their descriptions of the guerrilla leaders tend to resemble those by the elites and officers, as incalcitrant hardliners on an illegitimate quest for power. But then they diverge from the standard officer narrative by dividing the officers along an ideological spectrum, picking out any of them who they can hold up as moderate advocates of social reform. Thus they celebrate events like the 1979 coup and its subsequent economic reforms, the 1982 and 1984 elections, and the military's strategic shift to a civic-action program in 1984 as proof of the existence of a moderate faction within the military. This stands out in distinct contrast to the officers themselves, even those who advocated for reforms. For example, Colonel Adolfo Majano titled his memoir "A Lost Opportunity," referring to the 1979 coup and subsequent economic reforms that he believed had the potential to avoid the civil war if only the intransigent elements on the right and the left would have allowed them work. But his narration does not deviate in any substantive way from the military hardliners he opposed, including his arch nemesis on the junta after the 1979 coup, General Jaime Abdul Gutiérrez.

A second potential proto community consists of liberationist Catholic priests. As contributions we have a short interview with Father David Rodríguez, a parish priest from the San Vicente region who chose to affiliate with the FPL guerilla front, an extended interview with Jon Cortina, a Jesuit at the UCA who avoided be killed in 1989, and the account by Father José Inocencio "Checho" Alas of Suchitoto, that covers a decade of heavy mobilizing prior to the war, 1968–1977. A notable precursor to those three works is the 1987 "testimonial" interview with Father Rogelio Ponseele, the Belgian priest who arrived to El Salvador in the mid 1960s and spent the entire war in the ERP's rearguard zone in northern Morazán.[12]

The priests' narratives exhibit even less of a demonstrable pattern than the centrist politicians because they are of such diverse types. The longest of them, Father Alas's memoir contains many first-person narrative elements, including a description of his abduction by security forces in 1970. But his overall narration remains focused on the impersonal story of peasant organizing in and around the municipality of Suchitoto during a specific window of time, 1968–1977. He provides no description of his own life before and after that period, and even much of his first-person narration fulfills the purpose of highlighting growing repression against the poor people of his community and their emerging response to it. Perhaps in that regard, Alas is revealing something that could be a foundational quality of liberationist priest narratives, the personal "I" at the center of the narration always telling the tale of a third-person community of the poor.

Like the centrist politicians, the liberationist priests' narratives exhibit hybrid qualities. They contain elements that are found in the guerrilla commanders and the rank-and-file actors. They tend, for example to come from relatively well-adjusted backgrounds, from affluent urban families who provided them with access to educational opportunities. Father Rodríguez, for example, mentions beginning his studies in Latin at the age of 11.[13] And then just like the guerrilla commanders and the centrist politicians, the priests describe a moment at which their naivety is dismantled by the discovery of the impoverishment of the greater mass of Salvadorans and the repression they are suffering at the hands of an abusive military regime. This discovery leads them to reorient their pastoral work towards the downtrodden, to embrace the so-called preferential option for the poor, which then puts them at odds not only with the military and the elites, but also with the conservative hierarchy of the Catholic Church, both in El Salvador and in Rome. The introduction of the conservative church into the broader narrative of the war is a distinct contribution by the priest narrators.

What distinguishes the priest narrators from the guerrilla commanders and the centrist politicians is the extent to which they keep the story focused on the poor, and usually on a very specific group of poor people for whom they served as pastor. For David Rodríguez it is the people in the zone of Tecoluca in San Vicente, for Father Alas it is the peasants around Suchitoto and for Rogelio Ponseele it is people living in the marginal neighborhood of Zacamil in San Salvador. The priests credit their own awakening to those people, and they essentially tell those people's story through the process of telling their own story. So even though the other priest narrators provide more comprehensive personal narratives than Father Alas, or at least they narrate with a broader arc of time and space, they adhere to the model that Alas exhibits above, namely subsuming the "I" to a third-person community of the poor. In the introduction to the interview with Father Cortina, the interviewer, Ralph Sprenkels, captures this element when he says that for Father Cortina, "the most important aspect of his pastoral work was always walking alongside the peasants, learning from them, and sharing their lives together."[14] That narrative component could emerge as the unifying theme of a future liberationist-priest memory community.

Other life stories exist that are too few in number to constitute even a proto community. They include a pair of memoirs by U.S. citizens who spent some portion of the war in El Salvador, one as a journalist and the other as an affiliate of the ERP guerrillas.[15] They also include a Salvadoran photojournalist who worked off and on in El Salvador throughout much of the war, and a Mexican internationalist who ended up with the ERP during the war.[16]

The members of the four memory communities and these few outliers that I have just described comprise the sum total of life stories that have appeared in El Salvador since 1992. This fact reveals that vast swaths of the population who lived through the war and potentially played important roles in it are completely absent from the current conversation. We have no life stories from non-conservative elites, U.S. military or diplomatic officers, conservative priests who opposed the liberationist turn, and most notably from the hundreds of thousands, or more likely millions of Salvadorans over the years who remained politically neutral or opposed to the guerrillas. With the exception of a miniscule number of soldiers' accounts, we also lack life stories from any of the tens of thousands, and probably hundreds of thousands of men who rotated through the Salvadoran army or any of its paramilitary or civil-defense allies. Only time will tell if these segments of the population begin to tell their stories and thereby enter into the narrative debate.

· · · · ·

Those Salvadorans who have chosen to tell their life stories seem to have been motivated by many of the same varied and complex issues that have led people in other countries to enter their life stories into the public sphere. Some of them are motivated by a sense of a past injustice or victimization that they believe has yet to be reconciled. They may believe that by telling their story they can help right a wrong, and perhaps in the process affect current and future policy. Some are inspired by pleasurable memories of the past, such as pride in their accomplishments, or the joy of having participated in collective action. Some are motivated by pure nostalgia, the simple pleasure of reminiscing about the past. Some are motivated by a need for personal therapy, a desire to come to terms with past traumas by talking or writing about them. Some are driven by self-promotion, to either defend their past actions or advance themselves in the present, especially in politics; and, indeed, many of the narrators coincidentally have pursued political careers before or after they published their narratives. The literary scholar Sylvia Molloy says that the act of telling one's life story, or "self-writing" as she calls it, "is a form of exposure that begs for understanding, even more, for forgiveness." And Iwona Irwin claims that the act of creating memory projects often comes with, or is inspired by self-justifying rationales, or perhaps unspoken needs. Some narrators are probably motivated by a combination of factors, and probably all of them, at some level, are motivated by factors of which they possess no conscious awareness.[17]

The motives behind the Salvadoran narrators can be summarized in a three-word alliteration: pleasure, pain and policy. Pleasure refers to the celebration of past accomplishments, or the joy of belonging to a collective movement. Pain refers to the loss of friends and loved ones or a sense of past injustice or victimization. Policy refers to the desire to narrate the past in hopes of affecting the present and/or future, which might include defending oneself against accusations of wrongdoing, or more generally deflecting criticisms from past policies, laws and/or political platforms. These three incentives can function independent of one another or as part of a mutually-reinforcing bundle.

Civilian elites find pleasure first and foremost in the fact that the guerrillas did not win the war, and even if they had to negotiate with them to end the war, they got what they wanted most—a free-market economy and sanctity for private property. They also got an amnesty law, which guarantees that they cannot be persecuted for crimes. Elite memoirists also think highly of ARENA, the political party they believe to best represents their interests. Those individuals who were directly involved in ARENA's founding, and who happen to be disproportionately represented by the memoirists, take great pride in ARENA's rapid and enduring success. They also cite the joy they felt in having been involved in a collective political action.

As for pain, elites believe they have much to remember. Dozens of them were kidnapped and assassinated by guerrillas, and much of the incentive to write their memoirs seems to originate in their desire to remember their fallen comrades or to attack the guerrillas for their human-rights abuses. They are also pained by the memory of the army and the U.S. government accusing them of causing the war by having hoarded wealth and abused their workers. The army, in particular, betrayed them in 1979 by backing the U.S. government's and the Christian Democrats' call for economic reforms. In those reforms, elites lost control over some of their land, export markets and banks. When those sectors were reprivatized in the 1990s and 2000s, some elites resent having been left out of the bonanza. They are usually the same elites who feel excluded by their political party, ARENA, and the new "neoliberal" leaders who oversaw the postwar privatization process.

As for policy, the elites want to insulate themselves from future prosecution and also to deflect accusations about their actions in the past. Orlando de Sola, for example, specifically denies being a sponsor of deathsquads in his interview.[18] They want to ensure that El Salvador stays true to its free-market foundation. They worry about the FMLN in power, and they demonstrate concern about the growing wave of demagogic leftwing governments throughout Latin America, like Chávez's Venezuela, Morales's Bolivia and of course Castro's Cuba. Some of them, like David Panamá and Orlando De Sola, also worry about neoliberalism and the new generation of conservative leadership. They are concerned that that ARENA is abandoning its nationalist populism and becoming an electoral machine designed to serve the interests of a few.

As for the officers, the pleasure incentive is defined primarily by their pride in having prevented the guerrillas from seizing control of the state. They and their institution held back a determined guerrilla insurgency for more than twelve years. They are also happy with the amnesty law that protects them from standing trial for suspected for crimes against humanity and other human rights violations.

On the pain front, the officers bemoan the military's failure to defeat the guerrillas on the battlefield; many wanted to keep on fighting, and only begrudgingly accepted a negotiated settlement. Many of them believe the military lost disproportionately at the negotiating table. Various sectors of the armed forces were dismantled in their entirety, and many dozes of officers were forced out of service under suspicion of human-rights violations. In contrast, their guerrilla adversaries were allowed to integrate fully into public life, and elites got to keep what they wanted most—private property and a free-market economy. The officers also, of course, lament the loss of the many thousands of their own soldiers and officers, who either fell in combat or survived into civilian life mangled bodies and damaged minds.

On the policy front, the officers want to protect themselves and their institution against investigation for actions during the war. As examples, both Orlando Zepeda and Camilo Hernández have been indicted by the court in Spain for participating in the assassination of the Jesuits in 1989. Both make clear in their respective memoir and interview that they want to counter those claims. Hernández confesses to participation in the conspiracy, but to a lesser extent than that claimed by the Spanish court, and he cites specifically the desire to receive "absolution in Spain" as the incentive to grant his interview.[19] Zepeda similarly insists in his memoir that the claim made by the Spanish court is unjust, because at the infamous meeting of the military high command where the order to kill the Jesuits was supposedly given, "not at any moment during the meeting were any people's names mentioned, much less those of the Jesuit priests."[20] In the face of calls from domestics and internationals alike that the amnesty law be repealed, the officers protest vigorously, saying that a deal was struck and it must be honored.[21] As a final policy incentive, the officers want to see the armed forces survive in perpetuity, and to that end they describe various threats lurking about that will require a strong and resolute military defense. As far as they are concerned, the civil war was simply one of many phases in the nation's history that threatened the military's survival, and so whether or not that war can be defined as a victory or defeat will be determined by whether or not the military survives into the future. In the words of General Orlando Zepeda, only "the future will tell who won and lost the war."[22]

As for the guerrilla comandantes, their pleasure derives from diverse arenas. They are proud to have been part of the guerrillas and to have joined up in a collective action in pursuit of social justice. They portray the guerrillas as pursuing noble goals and they cast themselves in the role of selfless actors willing to accept risk and sacrifice to be part of it. They also express pride in their accomplishments, namely from starting out as ill trained, underfinanced and outgunned upstarts in the early 1970s to legitimate contestants for state power inside of one decade.

The comandante memoirists take pride in their accomplishments during the war. They are quick to point out, as Joaquín Villalobos did in his 1982 interview with Marta Harnecker, that "we were . . . forced to solve the problem of learning military tactics in the daily clash with the enemy. We did not have a school where first the students graduated and then were taken to the theatre of operations."[23] The comandantes were mostly university students or union members before they joined the guerrillas, and the majority of the rank-and-file combatants were peasants. Together, in the face of overwhelming odds and nearly unbridled financial support for their Salvadoran government from the U.S., they built themselves into a formidable fighting force that could meet the Salvadoran army on the battle field and stand its ground. During the doldrums of 1984–1989, when they were not on the offensive as much, the comandante memoirists celebrate the fact that they survived and maintained the ability to launch the second offensive in 1989, and then fight the war to a negotiated settlement. Even though they failed to accomplish some of their main objectives at the bargaining table, they achieved a great deal, including democratization and the reformation of the military. They also celebrate particular accomplishments in their distinct arenas of responsibility, like Eduardo Espinoza's pride in the FPL field hospital, and Carlos Rico's similar expressions of pride in regard to his logistical achievements for the RN. Rico also admits to having really enjoyed his work for the RN, and despite the trauma of the war, "the years went by in a breath."[24]

On the pain front, the comandante memoirists lament the loss of friends and loved ones, the fear and trauma they experienced personally, and of being pursued by the state's security forces and paramilitary death squads, and of being targeted for detention, torture and/or death. They lament the factionalism that defined the guerrillas and weakened them through division rather than uniting them in strength. However, they also remain loyal to their distinct organizations and criticize the other guerrilla groups, therein, ironically, turning factionalism into a point of pride, because their loyalty to their group proves that they stayed true to their particular ideological perspective. They are saddened about failing to win the war outright, and they seem confused about their failure to inspire the general population to come out in the streets en masse and join them during the offensives in 1981 and 1989. They express grief over the strategic shift of 1984–1989 and all of its consequences. Their descriptions of that period tend to be as brief as possible and are characterized by an overshadowing pall.

On the policy front, the guerrillas have much less to hide than their elite and officer counterparts. Nevertheless, they distance themselves from, or at least they are sure to clarify their position regarding certain key events, like the assassination of Roque Dalton in 1975 and the kidnapping and/or assassination of various businessmen and elites throughout the 1970s. Juan Medrano's lament regarding the killing of Roberto Poma during a kidnapping attempt in 1977 is an example of the latter.[25] The comandante narrators occasionally respond to accusations by their adversaries, such as when Eduardo Sancho rejects claims made in the media at the time that the 1971 kidnap victim Ernesto Regalado showed signs of having been tortured by his captors. "This version is totally untrue," he says.[26] The comandantes defend the guerrillas' existence and their own decision for having participated in the insurgency by portraying the guerrillas' cause as just and their own motives as selfless. Therein, the comandantes legitimize the FMLN's right to exist as a political party and their own political aspirations. This is particularly true for those narrators who have remained loyal to the FMLN and have sought political office under its auspices. The memoir by Salvador Sánchez provides an obvious example of this expediency. He wrote his memoir on the cusp of becoming the FMLN's vice presidential candidate in the 2009 election. The shortest section in his book is the one devoted to the civil war, even though he was the top-ranking commander of the FPL between 1983 and 1992. His silence on this crucial period of his life suggests that he wants to avoid controversy in hopes of maximizing his political viability. Notably, both he and Lorena Peña fail to mention the case of Mayo Sibrián and the purges within the FPL, which makes Sánchez either a purposeful obfuscator or a somewhat inept leader who didn't know that one of his main commanders was killing people by the hundreds.[27]

As for the rank-and-file guerrillas, they express great happiness over their accomplishments during the war and the collective spirit that guided their cause. They believe that their fight was justified and that even if they didn't accomplish everything they set out to do, at least they had the strength to follow their convictions and stand up for themselves and their fellow countrymen. However, this subject represents a point of contention between the former guerrillas and the former army soldiers. The latter do not celebrate their service in the army nor the cause they fought for. Rather, they portray their participation in the war as obligatory, and not worth the personal pain they suffered as a consequence of it.

On the pain front, all of the rank-and-file narrators—former guerrillas and former soldiers alike—lament the tremendous suffering and trauma wrought by the war. They lost friends and family members, and they witnessed many of those deaths personally. Some of them were tortured or suffered debilitating injuries, and they know many people close to them who did as well. They lament the lack of substantive change in the postwar era. For all the pain and suffering that occurred, most of the narrators find themselves in the same situation as before the war, poor and with few prospects for a better future.

On the policy front, the former guerrilla narrators have the least to hide. Most of them believe that their participation in the war was just, and a matter of necessity. They readily describe the less rosy aspects of the guerrillas' war effort, and they even accuse the comandantes directly of sexism, poor leadership and selfish pursuits. The two former Atlacatl soldiers have more to hide. One of them patently ignores the battalion's well-documented abuses of civilians and enemy combatants, although he reveals quite a bit about the dehumanizing training process that he endured. The second one is much more anxious to spill the beans, almost like a whistle blower. But it is evident that he wants to divert blame away from him for his participation in the mission to kill the Jesuits, and that he harbors tremendous animosity for his former officers who he believes abandoned him and his fellow commandos after ordering them to carry out that mission.

. . . . .

The civil war in El Salvador was about killing people, seizing territory and competing for control over the state. But parallel to that was the war of words, the need to control the narrative of the conflict and in so doing to win over public opinion. Each of the two sides in the conflict, as well as the various factional divisions within each side, competed with one another to establish hegemony over people's minds. They wanted to convince as many people as possible, or at least more people than their rivals, that their explanation for the war was right. This battle for the narrative was waged on many fronts, life stories being one of them. Since the end of war in 1992, life stories have emerged as a main arena of conflict. The narrators of those stories are involved in an intense battle for control over the narrative of the war, even if the narrators themselves do not necessarily recognize their participation in it. Their stories, and the contrasting claims made therein, are playing themselves out in the discursive arena of El Salvador's postwar public sphere. In that space, the narrators are setting parameters for policy debates and for the definition of what it means to be Salvadoran in the aftermath of war.

Appendix

The Protagonists

Acosta Oertel, Mario. A wealthy landowner and minister of the interior under the ARENA governments after the war.

Alas, José Inocencio ("Checho"). A priest in Suchitoto in the 1960s and 1970s who embraced liberation theology and played a pivotal role in giving rise to Christian base communities and peasant activism in the environs of Suchitoto.

Anaya Montes, Mélida. A former leader of the teachers' union in the 1960s and early 1970s who incorporated into the FPL and became one of its top commanders. She was murdered in Managua in 1983, evidently upon the orders of the FPL's top commander, Salvador Cayetano Carpio.

Armando. A testimonial narrator whose life story appears in *Like Gold in the Fire*.

Arnulfo. A testimonial narrator whose life story appears in *Like Gold in the Fire*.

Aviles, Inés. A testimonial narrator whose life story appears in *Río de la memoria*.

Ayalá, Berne. A former guerrilla who has been an active writer and journalist investigator since the war's end.

Barahona, José Ramón. A wealthy businessman in the United States who hails from a poor family in El Salvador and who migrated to the United States in the 1960s.

Benavides, Guillermo. The army colonel who was commander of the military academy at the time of the killing of the Jesuits and apparently is the person who delivered the order to the unit to carry out the mission.

Bonilla Acosta, Mauricio. A pseudonym for a soldier in the Atlacatl Battalion whose testimonial narration appears in Oscar Martínez Peñate's *El Salvador*.

Bonillo, Carlos. A testimonial narrator whose life story appears as *Los años perdidos*.

Cabrera, Mario. A high-ranking leader in the labor and mass-front organizations who eventually affiliated with the ERP. Author of the memoir *Piruetas*.

Cañadas, Arquímedes Antonio. A high-ranking commander of the ERP who was captured by the military early in the war. Although he claims not to have betrayed his former comrades, the Salvadoran government eventually released him and U.S. intelligence agents ushered him into exile. Author of the memoir *Sueños y lágrimas de un guerrillero*.

Cañas, Roberto. An affiliate of the RN who was part of the guerrilla's negotiating team at the peace accords.

Caravantes, Luis. A testimonial narrator whose life story appears in *El Salvador: por el camino de la paz*.

Castellanos, Miguel. Alias for Napoleón Romero Garcia, a one-time high-ranking FPL comandante who was captured by the military in 1985 and accepted the government's offer of amnesty in exchange for intelligence on his former comrades, who then assassinated him in 1989.

Castillo, Ruperto. A testimonial narrator whose life story appears in *Río de la memoria*.

Cayetano Carpio, Salvador. Founder of the FPL who served as its main commander until his death in Managua in 1983, an apparent suicide.

Chávez Velasco, Waldo. A writer who served as a civilian apparatchik in the PCN governments of the 1960s and 1970s. Author of the memoir, *Lo que no conté sobre los presidents militares*.

Chichilco, María. A testimonial narrator whose life story appears in *El Salvador: Por el camino de la paz*.

Consalvi, Carlos Henríquez (Santiago). The main voice of Radio Venceremos.

Corado Figueroa, Humberto. A now-retired army general who was a member of the military academy's *"tandona"* class of 1969 and minister of defense between 1993 and 1995.

Cortina, Jon. A Jesuit at UCA in the 1980s who avoided being killed in 1989. A prominent scholar/theorist of liberation theology.

Cristiani, Alfredo. A wealthy coffee grower and businessman who became the first ARENA candidate to win the presidency (1989–1994). His rise to the heights of ARENA reflected a purposeful decision by ARENA founder Roberto D'Aubuisson to give his party a more moderate, probusiness appearance.

Cruz Carbajal, Maria. A testimonial narrator whose life story appears in *La semilla que cayó en tierra fértil*.

Cruz Cruz, Marcelo. A former army captain who joined the guerrillas early in the war and eventually served with the ERP in Morazán for most of the war.

D'Aubuisson Arrieta, Maria Luisa. Roberto D'Aubuisson's sister and a Catholic lay worker who embraced the liberationist theological wing of the Catholic Church, in contrast to her brother's rabid anticommunism.

D'Aubuisson, Roberto. A former army major, founder of the conservative political party ARENA, and failed presidential candidate in 1982 and 1984. A former head of military intelligence who was purged in the wake of the 1979 coup. Widely believed to have been involved in directing paramilitary activity during the war, including the death squad that killed Archbishop Romero.

De Sola, Orlando. Member of the wealthy de Sola family, and an early activist in ARENA.

Díaz, Nidia. A high-ranking commander in the PRTC who has remained active in FMLN political circles after the war.

Duarte, José Napoleón. A long-time leader of the Christian Democratic Party and president of El Salvador from 1984 to 1989.

Escalante, Luis. Member of a wealthy Salvadoran family and one-time head of the Banco Agrícola. He was kidnapped and held for ransom by guerrillas during the war.

Espinoza, Eduardo. A medical doctor in the FPL.

Flores Cruz, René Obdulio. A retired army sergeant who authored the memoir *Memorias de un soldado*.

Galeas, Geovani. A former guerrilla who has worked as an author and journalist, and who has collaborated closely with his brother, Marvin Galeas, on various conservative-leaning projects. Has also collaborated with another former guerrilla, Berne Ayalá, on some investigative reporting.

Galeas, Marvin. A former guerrilla who has worked as an author, blogger, and journalist after the war. An outspoken conservative since the war's end, Marvin has worked closely with his brother, Geovani Galeas. Author of the memoir *Crónicas de guerra*.

Garcia, José Guillermo. A now-retired army general who served as minister of defense from 1979 to 1984.

Garcia, Julia. A testimonial narrator whose life story appears in *Mothers in Arms*.

Gómez Zimmerman, Mario. A dermatologist who was kidnapped and held for ransom by guerrillas at the beginning of the war and who took up exile in Miami after being released in a police raid. Author of *Adelante Occidente* and the memoir *El Salvador: la otra cara de la guerra*.

González, Medardo. A high-ranking commander of the FPL.

Guardado, Roberto. A testimonial narrator whose life story appears in *Like Gold in the Fire*.

Guerra y Guerra, Rodrigo. A civilian political activist who was heavily involved in the 1979 coup and subsequent reforms. Author of the memoir *Un golpe al amanecer*.

Gutiérrez, Dagoberto. A high-ranking commander of the FAL.

Gutiérrez, Jaime Abdul. A retired army general and member of the military academy's class of 1957 as well as a member of the governing juntas between 1979 and 1982. Author of the memoir *Testigo y actor: una revisión de los antecedentes que nos han conducido a la situación actual de El Salvador*.

Hándal, Schafik. A longtime leader of the PCS and the ranking commander of its armed wing, the FAL, throughout the war. Remained a key leader of the FMLN after the war and ran unsuccessfully for the presidency as the FMLN candidate in 2004. Author of the memoir *Legado de un revolucionario: del rescate de la historia a la construcción del futuro*.

Hernández, Camilo. An instructor in the military academy in 1989. He knowingly lent out the AK-47 that was used to kill Jesuits.

Herrera, Morena. A testimonial narrator whose life story appears in *Mothers in Arms*.

Ismael. A testimonial narrator whose life story appears in *Like Gold in the Fire*.

Jovel, Francisco. Ranking commander of the PRTC for the duration of the war.

Kriete, Roberto. A businessman and airline magnate.

Le Chevallier, Gerardo. A political activist in the Christian Democratic Party.

Lemus, José María. A military officer and president of El Salvador between 1956 and 1960.

Linares, Eduardo. A high-ranking commander of the FPL.

López, Francisco. A testimonial narrator whose life story appears in *El río de la memoria*.

Lüers, Paulo. A former guerrilla with the ERP who has been an active blogger and columnist in the postwar era.

Luis. A testimonial narrator whose life story appears in *From Beneath the Volcano*.

Luna, Fidencia. A testimonial narrator whose life story appears in *Tomamos la palabra*.

Majano, Adolfo. A retired army colonel; member of the military's academy class of 1958; and member of the governing juntas between 1979 and 1980. A leader of the military's more reformist-oriented youth wing. Author of the memoir, *Una oportunidad perdida*.

Majano, Manuel. A testimonial narrator whose life story appears *Río de la memoria*. He incorporated into the guerrillas early and was more of a commander/leader than a classic rank-and-file testimonial agent.

Margarita. A testimonial narrator whose life story appears in *Y la montaña habló*.

Mariana. A testimonial narrator whose life story appears in *Y la montaña habló*.

Marín, Abraham. A retired army captain who served in the Atlacatl Battalion.

Martínez, Ana Guadalupe. A high-ranking commander in the ERP.

Martínez, Gersón. A high-ranking commander of the FPL.

Medrano Guzmán, Juan Ramón. A high-ranking commander of the ERP. Author of the memoir *Memorias de un guerrillero*.

Mena Sandoval, Francisco. A former army captain who joined guerrillas during the final offensive of 1981 and became a troop trainer for the ERP in northern Morazán for the duration of the war. Author of the memoir *Del ejército nacional al ejército guerrillero*.

Merino, José Luís. A high-ranking commander of the FAL. Author of the memoir/interview *Comandante Ramiro: revelaciones de un guerrillero y líder revolucionario salvadoreño*.

Mijango, Raúl. A high-ranking commander of the ERP. Author of the memoir *Mi guerra: testimonio de toda una vida*.

Montano, Inocente Orlando. A retired army colonel and former vice minister of public safety.

Nery, Virginia. A one-time day laborer on a cotton planation whose testimonial narration appears in the collection *Rio de la memoria*.

Niña Dolores. The pseudonym for a poor woman who narrates her life story in *From Grandmother to Granddaughter*.

Núñez, Monica. The pseudonym for the middle generation of three narrators from one wealthy family whose life story appears in *From Grandmother to Granddaughter.*

Núñez, Niña Cecilia. The pseudonym for the elder of three narrators from one wealthy family whose life story appears in *From Grandmother to Granddaughter.*

Núñez, Paulina. The pseudonym for the youngest of three narrators from one wealthy family whose life story appears in *From Grandmother to Granddaughter.*

Ochoa Pérez, Sigifredo. A retired army colonel; member of the military academy's *"tandona"* class of 1966; commander of the Fourth Brigade between 1982 and 1985; and member of the National Assembly for the ARENA party after the war.

Osorio, Óscar. A military officer and president of El Salvador under the auspices of the PND between 1950 and 1956.

Panamá, David. A wealthy landowner who was an early activist in the ARENA party. Author of the memoir *Los guerreros de la libertad.*

Peña, Lorena. A high-ranking commander of the FPL who has remained active in FMLN political circles after the war. Author of the memoir *Retazos de mi vida: testimonio de una revolucionaria salvadoreña.*

Pérez, Claudia. A testimonial narrator whose life story appears in *Tomamos la palabra.*

Ponce, Emilio. An army general who was the top-ranking member of the 1966 *"tandona"* class at the military academy; served as commander of the Third Brigade during the war and eventually went on to serve as minister of defense (1990–1993). He was head of the army's joint chiefs of staff during the second "final offensive" in 1989 when the Jesuits were murdered.

Ponseele, Rogelio. A Belgian priest who arrived to El Salvador in the mid-1960s. After receiving death threats for his work with poor communities in San Salvador, he chose to go the guerrilla-controlled zones in northern Morazán rather than return to Europe. He remained there for the duration of the war and has lived in El Salvador ever since. Subject of *Death & Life in Morazán: A Priest's Testimony from a War-Zone in El Salvador* by María López Vigil.

Recinos, Fidel. A peasant from the environs of Suchitoto in the early 1970s who became a high-ranking field commander in the RN throughout the war.

Rey Prendes, Julio Adolfo. A high-ranking figure in the Christian Democratic Party. Author of the memoir *De la dictadura militar a la democracia: memorias de un político Salvadoreño, 1931–1994.*

Rico Mira, Eduardo. A high-ranking commander of the RN who specialized in logistics. Author of the memoir *En silencio tenía que ser: testimonio del conflicto armado en El Salvador, 1967–2000.*

Rodas, Lucio. A testimonial narrator whose life story appears in the collection *Rio de la memoria.*

Rodríguez, David ("Chele David"). A Catholic priest from Tecoluca who subscribed to a liberationist theology and played a key role in promoting Christian base communities in his region. He eventually affiliated with the FPL guerrillas.

Romero, Evelin. A testimonial narrator whose life story appears in *Rompiendo silencios*.

Romero, Gaspar. Archbishop Oscar Romero's brother.

Romero, Julio. A military officer and president of El Salvador under the auspices of the PCN between 1962 and 1967.

Romero, Oscar. Archbishop of El Salvador between 1977 and 1980 and a leading figure of the liberationist wing of the church. Assassinated while saying mass in March 1980.

Samayoa, Salvador. A former affiliate of the FPL and a member of the guerrilla's negotiating team for the peace accords.

Sánchez Cerén, Salvador. Ranking commander of the FPL after the death of founder Salvador Cayetano Carpio in 1983. Vice president of El Salvador during the Funes administration (2009–2014) and president of El Salvador thereafter (2014–). Author of the memoir *Con sueños se escribe la vida: autobiografía de un revolucionario salvadoreño*.

Sánchez Hernández, Fidel. A military officer and president of El Salvador under the auspices of the PCN between 1967 and 1972.

Sancho, Eduardo. Ranking commander of the RN for the duration of the war. Author of the memoir *Crónicas entre espejos*.

Saravia, Alvaro. A member of the hit squad that assassinated Archbishop Oscar Romero.

Sibrián, Mayo. A high-ranking commander in the FPL and the main architect of the purges that occurred in the San Vicente region in the late 1980s. Assassinated by the FPL for his actions in 1991.

Sol Bang, Guillermo ("Billy"). A wealthy landowner, a founder of ARENA, and a kidnap victim of the guerrillas at the end of the war. Subject of the memoir/interview *Sol y acero: la vida de Don Guillermo Sol Bang*.

Sonia. A testimonial narrator whose life story appears in *Y la montaña habló*.

Tórrez, Adolfo. An ARENA party activist and private business owner.

Tula, Maria Teresa. A testimonial narrator who delivered her life story to U.S. academician Lynn Stephen. The story was published as *Hear My Testimony*.

Valdivieso, Ricardo. A wealthy landowner and one of the founders of ARENA. Author of the memoir *Cruzando El Imposible: una saga*.

Valle, Romeo. A testimonial narrator whose life story appears in Oscar Martínez's *El Salvador*.

Valle, Víctor Manuel. An activist in the MNR, a small progressive political party that formed part of the electoral coalition in the 1972 and 1977 presidential elections.

Vargas, Mauricio. A retired army general; member of the military academy's *"tandona"* class of 1966; combat commander in eastern El Salvador during the war; and a member of the government's negotiating team for the peace accords.

Vásquez, Lucio ("Chiyo"). A young combatant with the ERP in northern Morazán, who narrated his testimony as *Siete gorriones*.

Ventura, Miguel. A Catholic priest who subscribed to a liberationist theology. Arrived to the region of northern Morazán in the early 1970s and helped establish the foundation for Christian based communities, some of whose members would go on to form the backbone of the rural insurgency in the region during the civil war.

Vides Casanova, Eugenio. A retired army general; head of the Salvadoran Guardia Nacional (1979–1983) and minister of defense (1984–1988).

Vigil, Carlos Balmore. Army captain who gathered life stories from some fellow mid-level officers for the book *Soldados en combate*.

Villalobos, Joaquín. Ranking commander of the ERP for the duration of the war.

Von Santos, Herard. A now-retired army captain who served in the Atlacatl Battalion. Author of the memoir *Días de trueno*.

White, Robert. U.S. ambassador to El Salvador, 1977–1979.

Zepeda, Orlando. A retired army general; member of the military academy's "*tandona*" class of 1966; and vice minister of defense in the late 1980s. Author of the memoir *Perfiles de la guerra en El Salvador*.

Notes

Acknowledgments

1. Guerra y Guerra, *Un golpe al amanecer*, 13.

2. Consalvi, *Broadcasting the Civil War*.

3. Some works that have since appeared include Sprenkels, "Revolution and Accommodation"; Juárez, *Historia y debates*; Rey Tristán, *Conflicto, memoria y pasados traumáticos*; Hatcher, "On the *Calle del Olvido*"; Hernández Rivas, "Cartografía de la Memoria"; and Heidenry, "The Murals of El Salvador." Some works that have analyzed or employed life story sources include Sprenkels, "Roberto d'Aubuisson vs Schafik Handal"; Cortez Ruiz, "La memoria desde las élites"; and Galeas, *Héroes bajo sospecha*.

Introduction

1. The trial took place between 2012 and 2013 with final sentencing occurring on August 27, 2013. The key testimony by the prosecution's expert witness, Professor Terry Lynn Karl, occurred on January 8, 2013. The entire proceedings of the trial are contained on the website of the Center for Justice and Accountability (http://www.cja.org/article.php?list=type&type=518). For a concise journalistic summary of the sentencing, see Zabludovsky, "Salvadoran Linked."

2. http://www.cja.org/downloads/Montano_1.pdf, 29–30.

3. Beetham, *Politics and Human Rights*, cited in Richards, *After the Civil War*, 342. See also Gready, *Era of Transitional Justice*, and Ferrara, *Assessing the Long-Term Impact*. The United Nations conducted a hasty and heavily debated investigation at the end of the war that resulted in an important report that was published in 1993. See United Nations Commission, *From Madness to Hope*.

4. Jelin, *State Repression*, 44.

5. Steve Stern describes the competitive marketplace for memory in his study of collective memory in Chile after the overthrow of President Allende in 1973. See Stern, *Remembering Pinochet's Chile*, 107, and 124–25. See also McAllister and Nelson, *War by Other Means*.

6. For good overviews of the war, see Montgomery, *Revolution in El Salvador*; Byrne, *El Salvador's Civil War*; Stanley, *The Protection Racket State*; and Gordon, *Crisis política*.

7. See, for example, Guevara, Martínez and Murcia, "Entrevista con 'Chiyo'"; Dada, "Plática con Rubén Aguilar"; interview with Nidia Díaz, in Morgan and

Cargo, *Mothers in Arms*, 124–25; Gorkin and Pineda, *From Beneath the Volcano*; and Gorkin, Pineda, and Leal, *From Grandmother to Granddaughter*, 139–43, 158, 183, and 224.

8. Exceptions to this rule are the UN-sponsored truth commission and the forensic exhumation of victims from the 1981 massacre at El Mozote. See United Nations, *From Madness to Hope*; Danner, *Massacre at El Mozote;* and Binford, *The El Mozote Massacre.*

9. In fact, these contrasting approaches to the war can be found within families. See, for example, Gorkin, *From Beneath the Volcano*, which reveals differing relationships to the value of memory within one peasant family that had been involved in the war.

10. Stier, *Committed to Memory.* See also Gómez-Barris, *Where Memory Dwells*, 7.

11. For example, on documentary film, see Gould and Consalvi, *La palabra en el bosque*; on murals, see Heidenry, "The Murals of El Salvador" and the El Salvador Mural Archive at http://www.rachelheidenry.com/murals.php; on television, see Luz, "La epopeya de la guerra civil"; on museums see Hernández, "Cartografía de la memoria," and DeLugan, "Museums, Memory"; as an example of literature, see Galán, *Noviembre;* and on monuments see López Bernal, "Schafik Jorge Hándal."

12. Gómez, *Where Memory Dwells*, 8. For other discussions of the diverse source bases for memory studies, see Stern, *Remembering Pinochet's Chile*; and Atencio, *Memory's Turn.*

13. On life story scholarship, see Linde, *Life Stories.*

14. Ibid., 22.

15. Zepeda, *Perfiles de la guerra*; Corado, *En defensa de la patria.* Corado's source is complex because it would appear to have been written by a team of military researchers who had been tasked with the goal of telling the military's version of the war. I have a copy of the manuscript in draft form from 2007 that I was allowed to see while conducting research in the military museum and indeed it does not bear Corado's name as the sole author. Nevertheless, I include the work as a source for the present study because it appears in the public sphere as a physical book with Corado's name on it as the author of record and thus discursively contributes to the narrative debate, regardless of its actual authorship. An interview with Corado provides a narrative that is consistent with that found in the book. See Martínez and Arauz, "Entrevista con Humberto Corado." Similarly, in regard to Zepeda, I include it as a source because, like Corado, Zepeda was an important figure in the events he is describing and his book functions as a valuable contributor to the public debate, even if he keeps the story at more of a remove. Zepeda has also given personalized interviews. See, for example, Guevara, "Entrevista con el general Juan Orlando Zepeda."

16. Stern, *Remembering Pinochet's Chile*, 149–50.

17. Arauz and Vaquerano, "Plática con Gerardo Le Chevallier."

18. The foundational contribution is Dalton, *Miguel Mármol*. See also *testimonials* Hernández, *León de piedra*; López, *Don Lito de El Salvador*; Alegría, *No me agarrón viva*; Cayetano Carpio, *Secuestro y capucha*; Martínez, *Las cárceles clandestinas*; Díaz, *Nunca estuve sola*; and López Vigil, *Muerte y vida*.

19. The terms "public sphere" and "imagined community" are, of course, drawn from the works of Jürgen Habermas and Benedict Anderson. See Habermas, *Structural Transformation*; and Anderson, *Imagined Communities*.

20. For disturbing trends to the contrary, see Rauda, "El Faro denuncia," and Mackey, "A Salvadoran Writer."

21. For the Saca comment, see the interview with former guerrilla commander Nidia Díaz in Morgan and Cargo, *Mothers in Arms*.

22. See Richards, *After the Civil War*.

23. Byron, *Women, Revolution and Autobiographical Writing*, 4.

24. Paredes, prologue to *Cruzando El Imposible*, 2.

25. For an analysis of Habermas's concept of the public sphere, see Calhoun, "Introduction."

26. For an example of a Latin Americanist advancing this criticism of Habermas, see J. Wood, *Society of Equality*, 7–8.

27. See, for example, Barba and Martínez, *Like Gold in the Fire*; Consalvi, *El Río de la memoria*; Comunidades Eclesiales de Base del Norte de Morazán, *Tomamos la palabra*; and Consejo de Mujeres, *La semilla que cayó*. *(S) testimonials*

28. See Irwin-Zarecka, *Frames of Remembrance*. See also Jan Gross, *Neighbors*.

29. Irwin-Zarecka, *Frames of Remembrance*, 18.

30. For an example of someone who has used some life story evidence in pursuit of an objective rendering of the past, see Galeas, *Héroes bajo sospecha*.

31. See Scott, *Domination*. Models of interview-based research include the study conducted by Gould and Lauria regarding the events of 1932. See Gould and Lauria, *To Rise in Darkness*. Another example includes Jeff Gould's and Carlos Henríquez's study of peasant mobilization in northern Morazán in the early to mid 1970s. See Gould and Consalvi, *La palabra en el bosque*.

32. See Schacter and Coyle, *Memory Distortion*; and Schacter, *Seven Sins*

33. A particularly vivid example is provided by the former ERP commander Arquímedes Antonio Cañadas, *Sueños y lágrimas*.

34. A model of such scholarship is Sommer, *Foundational Fictions*. My own interpretation of Sommer's work can be found in Ching, Buckley, and Lozano-Alonso, *Reframing Latin America*, 210–13.

35. United Nations, *From Madness to Hope*.

36. Danner, *Massacre at El Mozote* and Binford, *The El Mozote Massacre*. See also, http://www.domingomonterrosa.info.

37. Galeas and Ayala, *Grandeza y miseria*.

38. See Garner, "The Tracks of an Author's, and a Reader's, Tears."

39. As two such examples, see Lindo Fuentes, Ching, and Lara, *Remembering a Massacre*; and Yuhl, *Golden Haze of Memory*. The first study charts the memories

and interpretations of a 1932 peasant uprising in El Salvador in the six or so de-cades after the event. Yuhl looks at white elite memories of slavery and race rela-tions in Charleston, South Carolina in the roughly eight decades after the end of the U.S. civil war.

40. Viterna, *Women in War*, 47.

41. For an emerging body of scholarship that makes this same claim, see Sprenkels, "Revolution and Accommodation"; Moodie, *El Salvador in the After-math of Peace*; Silber, *Everyday Revolutionaries*; and Wade, *Captured Peace*.

42. See Schacter, *Memory Distortion*.

43. Somers, "The Narrative Constitution of Identity," 606.

44. Straughn, "Review of Linde," 520. See also Jan Assmann, who says that memoires are peculiar to us as individuals and are simultaneously linked to the wider world. Assmann, *Religion and Cultural Memory*, 1–3.

45. Viterna, *Women in War*, 45.

46. Tilly, *Stories, Identities and Political Change*.

47. Jelin, *State Repression*, 12.

48. For one example of the relationship between identity and narrative around the issue of recruitment, see Viterna, *Women in War*.

49. On the issue of martyrdom and its relationship to memory, see Peterson, *Martyrdom and the Politics of Religion*; and Peterson and Peterson, "Martyrdom, Sacrifice, and Political Memory."

50. Molloy, *At Face Value*, 5.

51. McGrattan, *Memory, Politics and Identity*, 31.

52. Somers, "The Narrative Constitution of Identity," 629.

53. See Schroeder, "The Sandino Rebellion Revisited."

54. See Lindo Fuentes, Ching, and Lara, *Remembering a Massacre*.

55. Some excellent research exists on the issue of remembrances of the war, but their focus tends to be on postwar El Salvador more broadly than on collec-tive memory of the war specifically, and/or they don't rely much upon life stories as sources. See Sprenkels, "Revolution and Accommodation"; DeLugan, *Reimag-ining National Belonging*; Silber, *Everyday Revolutionaries*; Moodie, *El Salvador in the Aftermath of Peace*; Hatcher, "On the *Calle del Olivdo*"; Rey Tristán, Martín Alvarez and Juárez Avila, "The Limits of Peace"; Juárez, *Historia y debates*; Rey Tristán, *Conflicto, memoria y pasados traumáticos*; Sprenkels, "Roberto d'Aubuisson vs Schafik Handal"; Cortez Ruiz, "La memoria desde las élites"; Hernández Rivas, "Cartografía de la Memoria"; and Galeas, *Héroes bajo sospecha*

56. Scholars of Chile have taken a lead in this regard. See Stern, *Remembering Pinochet's Chile*; *Battling for Hearts and Minds*; and *Reckoning with Pinochet*; Gómez-Barris, *Where Memory Dwells*; Frazier; *Salt in the Sand*; and Ros, *Post-Dictatorship Generation*. On Brazil, see Atencio, *Memory's Turn*, Weinstein, *The Color of Moder-nity*; and Allier-Montaño, and Crenzel, *The Struggle for Memory in Latin America*.

57. As a small foray into this vast scholarship, see Irwin-Zarecka, *Frames of Remembrance*; Stier, *Committed to Memory*; and Wolfgram, *"Getting History Right."*

58. Hatcher, "On the Calle del Olvido."

59. Hatcher, "Mientras El Salvador Olvida."

60. For examples of those public attempts during the war, see, for example, Dixon and Jonas, *Revolution and Intervention*; Cayetano Carpio, *Listen Compañero*; Harnecker, *Con la mirada*; Karl, "Negotiations or Total War"; Perales, and Harnecker, *La estrategia de la victoria*.

61. Díaz, *Nunca estuve sola*; Martínez, *Las cárceles clandestinas*; and Cayetano Carpio, *Secuestro y capucha*. Other testimonials that appeared during the war but that have not received the same amount of critical analysis include Hernández, *León de piedra*; López, *Don Lito de El Salvador*; Alegría, *No me agarrón viva*; Carter, *A Dream Compels Us*; and Tula and Stephen, *Hear My Testimony*. For scholarly works that analyze testimony and give disproportionate attention to the first three works, see Padilla, *Changing Women, Changing Nation*, chapter 2; Byron, *Women, Revolution and Autobiographical Writing*, chapter 5; Craft, *Novels of Testimony*; Beverley and Zimmerman, *Literature and Politics*, chapter 7; and Treacy, "Woman, Guerrilla and Political Prisoner."

62. While sophisticated and important, the earlier studies on the war tended to reinforce this notion of unity more than later scholarship. See, for example, Grenier, *The Emergence of Insurgency in El Salvador*; Dunkerley, *The Long War*; Montgomery, *Revolution in El Salvador*; Byrne, *El Salvador's Civil War*; Pearce, *Promised Land*; Cabarrús, *Génesis de una revolución*; Baloyra, *El Salvador in Transition*; and Whitfield, *Paying the Price*. Héctor Lindo Fuentes and I assess the scholarship and cite the exceptions in the introduction to *Modernizing Minds in El Salvador*. For comparative scholarship, see Goodwin, *No Other Way Out*; Wickham Crowley, *Guerrillas and Revolution in Latin America*; Brockett, *Political Movements*; Mason, *Caught in the Crossfire*; Krujit, *Guerrillas*; and McClintock, *Revolutionary Movements in Latin America*.

63. On the war and its origins, see Viterna, *Women in War*; Stanley, *The Protection Racket State*; E. J. Wood, *Insurgent Collection Action*; Williams and Walter, *Militarization and Demilitarization*; Chávez, "Pedagogy of Revolution"; Juárez Ávila, *Historia y debates*; and Binford, "Grassroots Development," "Hegemony in the Interior," and "Peasants, Catechists and Revolutionaries." On the postwar era, see, for example, Sprenkels, "Revolution and Accommodation"; Moodie, *El Salvador in the Aftermath of Peace*; Silber, *Everyday Revolutionaries*; DeLugan, *Reimagining National Belonging*; and Wade, *Captured Peace*.

Chapter One

1. Stanley, "Review of *Emergence of Insurgency*," 215.

2. Described in Lindo Fuentes and Ching, *Modernizing Minds*, 3–6. For the 1961 census, see El Salvador, Asamblea Legislativa, *Memoria del primer congreso nacional*, 121–37. The figure regarding extraregional exports comes from

Bulmer-Thomas, *Political Economy*, 154. For education statistics, see Lindo Fuentes, "Schooling in El Salvador," 188–89.

3. For more about the land reforms, the emergence of the coffee economy, and the accompanying politics, see Lauria, *Agrarian Republic*; Lindo Fuentes, *Weak Foundations*; López Bernal, *Tradiciones inventadas*; Alvarenga, *Cultura y ética*; Acosta, *Los orígenes de la burguesía*; Ching, *Authoritarian El Salvador*; and Portillo, *La tenencia de la tierra*.

4. Williams and Walter, *Militarization and Demilitarization*, 16–17.

5. Ching, *Authoritarian El Salvador*. See also Lindo Fuentes, *Weak Foundations*; Colindres, *Fundamentos económicos*; Acosta, *Los orígenes de la burguesía*; Lauria, *An Agrarian Republic*; Alvarenga, *Cultura y ética*; Albiac, *Ricos más ricos*; and Pineda, "Los patriarcas de la oligarquía."

6. The political scientist Barbara Geddes shows how reformist movements can emerge from within a hierarchically structured patronage system, like that which existed in El Salvador leading up to the 1931 presidential elections. See Geddes, *Politician's Dilemma*, esp. chapter 4.

7. For more about the events of 1932, see Gould and Lauria, *To Rise in Darkness*; Lindo Fuentes, Ching, and Lara, *Remembering a Massacre*; and Ching, *Authoritarian El Salvador*, chapter 8.

8. From the poem "Todos," included originally in Dalton, *Las historias prohibidas del pulgarcito*. The original text reads: "Todos nacimos medio muertos en 1932. Ser salvadoreño es ser medio muerto." This particular translation is drawn from Dalton, Beverley, and Baker, "Poems," 76–77.

9. Stanley, *Protection Racket State*.

10. Hándal, *Legado*, 160.

11. Some standard bearers for comparative state development in Central American history are Williams, *States and Social Evolution*; Mahoney, *Legacies of Liberalism*; and Holden, *Armies Without Nations*.

12. In addition to Costa Rica, other cases of coffee-producing smallholders are Venezuela and the Dominican Republic. See Turits, *Foundations of Despotism*; Gudmundson, *Costa Rica Before Coffee*; Samper, *Generations of Settlers*; and Yarrington, *A Coffee Frontier*.

13. A standard bearer in the comparative study of Costa Rican democratization, although the comparison is with Guatemala, is Yashar, *Demanding Democracy*.

14. Hoselitz, *Industrial Development*. For more about Hoselitz's visit, see Lindo Fuentes and Ching, *Modernizing Minds*, 49–51; and Cárceres Prendes, "Discourses of Reformism," 79. For further analyses of the PRUD government and the era of the 1940s and 1950s in El Salvador generally, see Turcios, *Autoritarismo y modernización*; Guevara, "Military Justice"; Williams and Walter, *Militarization and Demilitarization*, chapter 3; Stanley, *Protection Racket State*, chapter 3; Holden, *Armies Without Nations*; and Castellaños, *El Salvador, 1930–1960*. For an insider's point of view in the form of a memoir, see Torres, *Los militares en el poder*.

15. Hoselitz, *Industrial Development*. The Lemus quote is drawn from an interview with the Salvadoran/Costa Rican academic, Jorge Cárceres Prendes. See Cárceres Prendes, "Discourses of Reformism," 79. For an analysis of modernization theory, see Gilman, *Mandarins of the Future*.

16. The Sol quote appears in Turcios, *Autoritarismo y modernización*, 48.

17. For more on Cerrón Grande, see Lindo Fuentes and Ching, *Modernizing Minds*, 211–22; Universidad Centroamericana, "Estudio de proyecto"; and Goodland, "Cerrón Grande."

18. For more on the teachers' movement, see Lindo Fuentes and Ching, *Modernizing Minds*; Almeida, *Waves of Protest*. For the life of one of the leading teacher organizers, Mélida Anaya Montes, see Perales and Villalta, *Ana María*.

19. For more on ORDEN, see Webre, *José Napoleón Duarte*; and Stanley, *Protection Racket State*. For references to the complex composition of ORDEN membership, see Todd, *Beyond Displacement*; and Silber, *Everyday Revolutionaries*.

20. The coup of 1979 and the reforms that followed in its wake are often portrayed as the last chance to have prevented El Salvador from sliding into civil war. See Campos, Rodolfo. *El Salvador entre el terror y la esperanza*; Guerra y Guerra, *Un golpe al amanecer*; Guerra, Tomás. *El Salvador, octubre sangriento*; and Lamperti, *Enrique Alvarez Córdova*. As just one exploration into repression by the state prior to the civil war, see the revelations in the so-called "libro rosado" and the "libro amarillo," Salvadoran government documents that contain evidence of the arrests and tortures of thousands of Salvadorans by the security forces in the 1970s and 1980s. On the libro rosado, see Valencia, "Los archivos secretos." On the libro amarillo, see http://unfinishedsentences.org/es/the-yellow-book/.

21. For some insights into some of these movements, see Parkman, Nonviolent Insurrection; Duarte, *Duarte*; Almeida, *Waves of Protest*; Huezo Mixco, et. al., *Coronel Ernesto Claramount Rozeville*; and Barba, "Los movimientos sociales."

22. Webre, *José Napoleón Duarte*.

23. See Lindo Fuentes, Ching, and Lara, *Remembering a Massacre*; and Gould and Lauria, *To Rise in Darkness*.

24. For more on these internal debates, see Lindo Fuentes, Ching, and Lara, *Remembering a Massacre*, chapter 5. For more on the electoral campaign of 1972, see Webre, *José Napoleón Duarte*; Duarte, *Duarte*, chapter 3; and Hernández Pico et al., *El Salvador*. See also Lara Martínez, *Del dictado*.

25. For more on the FUAR, see Partido Comunista de El Salvador, *45 Años de sacrificada lucha revolucionaria*, 14–15; Valle, *Siembra de vientos;* Menjívar Ochoa, *Tiempos de locura,* 27–29; Lamperti, *Enrique Alvarez Córdova;* Barba, "Los movimientos sociales"; and Hándal, *Legado*, 192–93.

26. For scholarly analyses on the origins of the FPL, see Alvarez, "Del partido a guerrilla"; Brockett, *Political Movements*; Menjívar Ochoa, *Tiempos de locura*, 28; and Krujit, *Guerrillas*. For primary evidence on the meaning and definition of the strategy of prolonged popular, see Cayetano Carpio, *Nuestras montañas*

son las masas; and the pro-Cayetano Carpio website, http://marcialteniarazon
.org/.

27. Beverley and Zimmerman make the claim that the Salvadoran left had a greater proclivity for factionalism than did its counterparts in Guatemala and Nicaragua. See Beverley and Zimmerman, *Literature and Politics*, 115–16.

28. ERP leader Joaquín Villalobos makes reference to literacy training in the parish of San Juan Opico under the tutelage of Father Alfonso Navarro, alongside another ERP founder, Rafael Arce Zablah. See Villalobos, "Homenaje a Rafael Antonio Arce Zablah." For good studies of the origins of the ERP, see Álvarez and Cortina Orero, "Genesis and Internal Dynamics"; and Gales, *Héroes bajo sosphecha*.

29. On the death of Dalton, see García and Espinoza, *Quién asesinó a Roque Dalton?* For a veiled response by Joaquín Villalobos, one of the main leaders of the ERP at the time, see Villalobos, "Review of *Revolutionary Movements*."

30. For more on the various factions of the left and the origins of the FMLN, see Álvarez, "Ideología y redes sociales." For an example of the personality clashes over the factionalism, see Schafik Hándal's vitriol toward Salvador Cayetano Carpio in *Legado*, 208–32.

31. See Chávez, "Pedagogy of Revolution"; Brockett, *Political Movements*, chapter 5; Binford, "Grassroots Development," "Hegemony in the Interior," and "Peasants, Catechists and Revolutionaries"; Guerra Calderón, *Asociaciones comunitarias*; Cárdenal, *Historia de una esperanza*; Sánchez, *Priest Under Fire*; and Gould and Consalvi, *La palabra en el bosque*.

32. Mainwaring and Pérez-Liñán, *Democracies and Dictatorships*, chapter 6.

33. See Mayorga et al., *El Salvador*; Montgomery, *Revolution in El Salvador*; Serpas, *La lucha por un sueño*; and Byrne, *El Salvador's Civil War*.

34. In his memoir, PCS/FAL commander Schafik Hándal claims that the 1981 offensive incited debate between the supporters of the FPL's Prolonged Popular War and the ERP's insurrectionist line, and that the reason the PCS supported the latter at the time was because the guerrillas lacked strategic rearguards in rural areas and in foreign countries and thus it was unclear how long they could hold out. See Hándal, *Legado*, 265. The FPL commander Medardo González writes in his memoir that the FPL leader at the time, Salvador Cayetano Carpio, considered withdrawing the FPL from the FMLN in the aftermath of the failed 1981 offensive. See González, Regalado, and Álvarez, *Memorias del camino*, 40.

35. Juan Medrano describes the offensive, including the intense battle for control of Usulután in *Memorias de un guerrillero*, 244–62.

36. The testimonialist Lucio Vásquez (Chiyo) offers insight into this very personal side of the war in Vásquez and Fontan, *Siete gorriones*.

37. For a good description of the guerrillas' ability to monitor the army's movements and stay one step ahead of it, see Consalvi, *La terquedad del izote*.

38. David Spencer has done some good research on the strategic aspects of combat in the Salvadoran civil war. See Spencer, *From Vietnam to El Salvador*

and *Strategy and Tactics*. As just a few of many sources shedding light on the Salvadoran military's abusive actions, including massacres of civilians, see Danner, *The Massacre at El Mozote*; Binford, *The El Mozote Massacre*; Lauria, "The Culture and Politics of State Terror"; Valencia, "Los archivos secretos"; and "Unfinished Sentences: La Quesara Massacre," http://unfinishedsentences .org/foia-la-quesera/.

39. Manwaring and Prisk, *El Salvador at War*; Waghelstein, "El Salvador"; Bosch, *The Salvadoran Officer Corps*; Bacevich et al., *American Military Policy in Small Wars*; Zepeda, *Perfiles de la guerra*; and Corado Figueroa, *En defensa de la patria*. For a reference to guarding agriculture plantations, see Von Santos, *Días de trueno*, 74.

40. United Nations, *From Madness to Hope*. For evidence on the La Quesara massacre that emerged after the United Nations report, see http://unfinished sentences.org/foia-la-quesera/. On El Mozote, see Danner, *The Massacre at El Mozote*; and Binford *The El Mozote Massacre*.

41. See Villalobos interview with Marta Harnecker, in Dixon and Jonas, *Revolution and Intervention*, 104.

42. See also Mainwaring and Prisk, *El Salvador at War*; and Bacevich et al., *American Military Policy in Small Wars*.

43. For more on the BRAZ, see Ibarra Chávez, *Brigada Rafael Arce Zablah*; and Mena Sandoval, *Del ejército nacional*.

44. For a good summary of the nature of the campaign of terror, see Lauria, "The Culture and Politics of State Terror." See also Valencia, "Los archivos secretos."

45. The strategic shift is discussed in Manwaring and Prisk, *El Salvador at War*; Waghelstein, "El Salvador"; and Sánchez Cerén, *Con sueños*, 169. For the issue of U.S. aid to El Salvador, see Quan, "Through the Looking Glass"; and Wheaton, "U.S. Strategies in Central America." For evidence of Bush's meeting with the military high command, see Thomas Pickering, U.S. Embassy, San Salvador, to U.S. Secretary of State, Washington, D.C., December 14, 1983, document no. 386 of NSA collection, "El Salvador: War, Peace and Human Rights, 1980–1994."

46. For more on the increased effectiveness of the Salvadoran Air Force, see Bacevich et al., *American Military Policy in Small Wars*, 31–33; and Peceny and Stanley, "Counterinsurgency in El Salvador."

47. Vickers, "The Political Reality," 32. See also Department of Social Sciences, Universidad de El Salvador, "An Analysis of Correlation of Forces."

48. ERP commander Raúl Mijango offers a good look into the morale problems of the ERP in the wake of the strategic shift in Mijango, *Mi guerra*. See also Hándal, *Legado*, 282–97.

49. Vickers, "The Political Reality," 29. See also Von Santos, *Días de trueno*, 69, for the effectiveness of this new use of air power.

50. Waghelstein, "El Salvador," 17.

51. José Luís Merino of the FAL provides detailed descriptions of the effectiveness of the air strikes and long-range patrols in Merino, *Comandante Ramiro*, 81–96; see also Hándal, *Legado*, 298.

52. Information report, U.S. Embassy, San Salvador, to Washington D.C., November 7, 1988, document no. 723 of NSA collection, "El Salvador: War, Peace and Human Rights, 1980–1994."

53. For more about the issue of corruption within the Salvadoran military, see Schwarz, *American Counterinsurgency Doctrine*, 17–22; and Bacevich et al., *American Military Policy in Small Wars*, 24–25. For a critical assessment of the one of the army's major offensives after 1984, which was designed to win over the hearts and minds of the local population, see Hernández Arias, *Fenix: cenizas de una operación estadounidense*.

54. For firsthand accounts of the fighting during the November offensive by combatants, see Marín, *Batallón Atlacatl*; Ayalá, *Entre Marilyn Monroe*, and *Al tope y más alla*. For more on the murder of the Jesuits, see Whitfield, *Paying the Price*; Doggett, *Death Foretold*; and Lasalle-Klein, *Blood and Ink*. For a firsthand account by a noncombatant, see the blog post by Bessy Ríos, "Hasta el tope, mis recuerdos y yo."

55. Interview with anonymous guerrilla, Perquín, March 17, 2008—former member of a surface-to-air missile team for the ERP in northern Morazán between 1990 and 1991. See also Sánchez Cerén, *Con sueños se escribe*, 157–67; and Arauz and Castro Fagoaga, "Plática con Francisco Jovel," 5. For more from the military's side, see Von Santos, *Días de trueno*, 68.

56. An interesting piece of evidence regarding the end of the Cold War and its implications for downsizing the conflict in Central America is the memorandum of a conversation between President George H. W. Bush and Eduard Shevardnadze, foreign minister of the Soviet Union, in the Oval Office on September 21, 1989. See document 8 of "The Shevardnadze File" at the National Security Archive, "Memorandum of Conversation between George Bush and Eduard Shevardnadze in Washington, September 21, 1989," http://nsarchive.gwu.edu/NSAEBB/NSAEBB481/docs/Document%208.pdf. My thanks to Knut Walter for directing this evidence to my attention.

57. For more on the negotiations and the end of the war, see Negroponte, *Seeking Peace in El Salvador*; Tulchin, *Is There a Transition*; Karl, "El Salvador's Negotiated Revolution"; Mayorga et al., *El Salvador; and Chávez*, "How Did the Civil War in El Salavdor End?; In his memoir, the FPL commander Medardo González laments particularly the FMLN's inability to place economic matters on the bargaining table. See González, Regalado, and Álvarez, *Memorias del camino*, 51–52.

58. I've heard Walter make this claim on various occasions, but the particular wording appearing here comes from a talk he delivered to a group of North American university students on March 19, 2008 in San Salvador.

59. The term *"casi nación"* appears in a reader comment by "Catalino P" on July 27, 2013, in Vaquerano and Lemus, "Plática con diputado Sigifredo Ochoa Pérez," 1.

60. Foley, "Laying the Groundwork," 76. See also Karl, "El Salvador's Negotiated Revolution." For information on the El Salvadoran postwar economy, see Segovia, *Transformación estructural*; Bull, "Diversified Business Groups"; Velázquez Carrillo, "La consolidación oligárquica neoliberal"; Haglund, *Limiting Resources*; Pelupessy, *The Limits of Economic Reform in El Salvador;* and Hinds, *Playing Monopoly.* For a pro-ARENA interpretation of the economy leading up to the end of the war, see Murray Meza, "The State of the Economy."

61. Anthropologist Ellen Moodie captured this pessimistic sentiment among Salvadorans in Moodie, *El Salvador in the Aftermath of Peace.* For similar takes, see Silber, *Everyday Revolutionaries*; and DeLugan, *Reimagining National Belonging.* See also Popkin, *Peace without Justice*; and Arnson and Olson, "Organized Crime in Central America." On the issue of homicide rates in El Salvador, see Archibald, "Homicides in El Salvador." For the issue of gangs and antigang policies by the government, see Van Der Borgh and Savenije, "De-securitising and Re-securitising"; and Holland, "Right on Crime?"

62. For a good overview of postwar elections, see Wolf, "Subverting Democracy"; Manning, *The Making of Democrats*, chapter 4; Córdova Macías and Ramos, "The Peace Process"; and Wade, *Captured Peace.* On the reforms in the military, see Walter, *Las fuerzas armadas*; and Foley, "Laying the Groundwork."

63. On post-war social movements, see Almeida, *Waves of Protest*; and Segovia, "Los movimientos sociales."

64. The United Nations Truth Commission identified D'Aubuisson as such. See United Nations, *From Madness to Hope.* For more on the death squads, see, for example, Molinari, "Escuadrones de la muerte"; and Majano, *Una oportunidad perdida.* The evidence that has been used to implicate D'Aubuisson in the assassination of Romero was captured with him when he was arrested in December 1980 by reformers in the military, led by Majano, who then passed the material to the U.S. Embassy; see Robert White, U.S. Embassy, San Salvador, to U.S. Secretary of State, Washington D.C., June 20, 1980, document no. 129 of NSA collection, "El Salvador: War, Peace and Human Rights, 1980–1994." See also the compelling *El Faro* interview with Alvaro Saravia, who admits to being part of the team that assassinated Romero, in Dada, "How We Killed the Archbishop." For a controversial piece of journalism that offers a muted, even sympathetic portrait of D'Aubuisson vis-à-vis these accusations, see Galeas, "Mayor Roberto." See also the *El Faro* interview with North American academic Terry Karl, in which she discusses her encounter with D'Aubuisson, in Martínez and Sanz, "Entrevista con Terry Karl." See also McGehee, "CIA Support of Deathsquads;" and Mazzei, *Death Squads or Self-Defense Forces.* In what has proven to be a remarkable piece of journalism, Craig Pyes, a reporter for the *Albuquerque Journal,* gained access to many of ARENA's founders in 1983. He wrote a revealing account in which his

sources praised the paramilitaries and virtually admitted their involvement with them. See Pyes, "Salvadoran Rightists." In an interview/personal conversation, the journalist Gene Polombo, who has been in El Salvador since the beginning of the war, told me on March 14, 2012 that Pyes's access was unprecedented and that his reports resulted in ARENA limiting its members' access to journalists. See also, Gilbert, "El Salvador's Death Squads."

65. See Call, "Democratisation"; Koivumaeki, "Business, Economic Experts"; Vickers, "The Political Reality"; Montgomery, *Revolution in El Salvador*; and Byrne, *El Salvador's Civil War*. For a primary-source look into the U.S.'s pessimistic assessment of D'Aubuisson, see Deane Hinton, U.S. Embassy, San Salvador, to U.S. Secretary of State, Washington D.C., December 15, 1981, document no. 241 of NSA collection, "El Salvador: War, Peace and Human Rights, 1980–1994."

66. For a good survey of U.S. funding during the war, see Quan, "Through the Looking Glass"; and Manning, *The Making of Democrats*, chapter 4. For more on FUSADES, see Foley "Laying the Groundwork"; and Johnson, "Between Revolution and Democracy." The reference to the new right is found in Johnson. See also Albiac, *Ricos más ricos*; Paniagua Serrano, "El bloque empresarial hegemónico salvadoreño"; and Pirker, "'La redefinición de la posible,'" chapter 4.

67. Zamora, *La izquierda salvadoreña*; Manning, *The Making of Democrats*, chapter 4. For more on ARENA's defeat in 2009, see Galeas and Galeas. *Las claves de una derrota.*

68. Villalobos's own professional activities after the war have provided his critics with plenty of ammunition, particularly his decision to become a consultant to the Mexican and Colombian armies on counterinsurgency strategies. See El Faro, "¿Dónde están los firmantes?"

69. See Puyana Valdivieso, "El proceso de selección"; Wade, *Captured Peace*; Zamora, *La izquierda salvadoreña*; and Córdova Macías and Ramos, "The Peace Process."

Chapter Two

1. Valencia and Martínez, "Plática con Orlando de Sola," Part 2. For more on this issue, see Rosenberg, "The Laboratory," chapter 4 in *Children of Cain*.

2. In fact much of the research of El Salvador's elites revolves around identifying them, compiling their family histories, and determining their business holdings, which reflects how little is known about them still. See Albiac, "Los ricos más ricos"; Velázquez, "La consolidación oligárquica"; and Pineda, "Los patriarcas de la oligarquía." Pineda's study is divided in three parts, only two of which seem to be posted on his home website (SIEP): http://www.ecumenico.org/leer .php/2575, and http://www.ecumenico.org/leer.php/2576. Fortunately, Marvin Galeas has posted all three on his blogspot: http://marvingaleas.blogspot.com; see the entries January 9, 2012 (part I), January 10, 2012 (part II), and January 12, 2012 (part III). See also Pineda, "El Salvador del siglo XXI," http://www.ecumenico

.org/leer.php/2568; and Paniagua Serrano, "El bloque empresarial." The foundational work remains Colindres, *Fundamentos económicos de la burguesía salvadoreña*.

3. For examples of this comparative analysis, see Wickham Crowley, *Guerrillas and Revolution*; and Goodwin, *No Other Way Out*.

4. For research on divisions within the right during the war, see Ramírez, "Militarismo, intelectuales y proyectos."

5. Robin, *The Reactionary Mind*, 4, 8, 25, 34, 36, and 98.

6. Robin has been criticized for lumping conservatives under too broad an umbrella and failing to distinguish between its multiple and often competing strains. See, for example, Lilla, "Republicans for Revolution."

7. See Lindo Fuentes and Ching, *Modernizing Minds*, chapters 1 and 2.

8. Abarca, "Estamos así por nuestro culpa," 9.

9. See Pyes, *Salvadoran Rightists*.

10. For narrative, see the classic studies by Chatman, *Story and Discourse*; and Bal, *Narratology*. For the specifics of narrative in historical studies, see White, *Tropics of Discourse*.

11. Robin, *The Reactionary Mind*, 9–10.

12. See Lindo Fuentes, Ching and Lara, *Remembering a Massacre*.

13. Middlebrook, *Conservative Parties*, 39.

14. Pyes, *Salvadoran Rightists*, 4.

15. The byproduct of their work, *From Grandmother to Granddaughter: Salvadoran Women's Stories,* was first published in translated form by the University of California Press in 2000 and reprinted in its original Spanish version in El Salvador as *De abuela a nieta* in 2003.

16. Gorkin, Pineda, and Leal, *From Grandmother,* 21–22, 32, and 38.

17. Ibid., 46 and 62–63.

18. Gómez Zimmerman, *El Salvador: Who Speaks for the People?*, 162. In the midst of working on that project, he wrote his treatise on Western history, *Adelante Occidente*, translated as *Power to the West*.

19. Ibid., 32, 33–34, 41, 45, and 65.

20. Ibid., 40 and 64.

21. Escalante Arce, *Sacrificios humanos*, 208–209.

22. Sarmiento, *Life in the Argentine Republic*. My analysis of Sarmiento's romantic nationalism can be found in Ching, Buckley, and Lozano-Alonso, *Reframing Latin America*, 189–92.

23. Gómez Zimmerman, *El Salvador: Who Speaks for the People?*, 29.

24. Valdivieso Oriani, *Cruzando*, 56–58 and 258.

25. Ibid., 89–95 and 244.

26. Carranza Bonilla and Chávez, *Las 100 historias*, 205.

27. Barahona's memoir was published in both English and Spanish. See Galeas and Barahona, *The Possible Dream*, and *El sueño possible*. Galeas and Sol Bang, *Sol y acero*.

28. Galeas and Barahona, *The Possible Dream*, 38, 40–41, and 89.

29. Ibid., 95–97.

30. Galeas and Sol Bang, *Sol y acero*, 26.

31. Ibid., 40 and 44.

32. For an analysis of earlier conservatives' uses of 1932, see Lindo Fuentes, Ching, and Lara, *Remembering a Massacre*; López Bernal, "Lecturas desde la derecha y la izquierda"; and Ramírez, "El discurso anticomunista."

33. The comments appeared originally in an editorial in the newspaper *Diario de Santa Ana* shortly after the insurrection and were reprinted in Méndez, *Los sucesos comunistas*. They were translated by Susan Greenblatt for Lindo Fuentes, Ching, and Lara, *Remembering a Massacre*, 336–37.

34. Galindo Pohl, *Recuerdos de sonsonate*, 35.

35. Escalante Arce, *Sacrificios humanos*, 16–17.

36. Gómez Zimmerman, *El Salvador: Who Speaks for the People?*, 34–37.

37. Guevara, "María Luisa d'Aubuisson Arrieta," 4.

38. Lindo Fuentes, Ching, and Lara, *Remembering a Massacre*, 358. See also López Bernal, "Lecturas desde la derecha y la izquierda"; and Ramírez, "El discurso anticomunista."

39. Gómez Zimmerman, *El Salvador: Who Speaks for the People?*, 105; Panamá Sandoval, *Los guerreros de la libertad*, 142.

40. Valdivieso Oriani, *Cruzando*, 199; Gómez Zimmerman, *El Salvador: Who Speaks for the People?*, 277–78.

41. Galeas and Sol Bang, *Sol y acero*, 193; Gómez Zimmerman, *El Salvador: Who Speaks for the People?*, 93.

42. Panamá Sandoval, *Los guerreros de la libertad*, 139.

43. Valdivieso Oriani, *Cruzando*, 180, 184.

44. http://marvingaleas.blogspot.com/. November 9, 2011, and October 21, 2011.

45. Gómez Zimmerman, *El Salvador: Who Speaks for the People?*, 73.

46. Panamá Sandoval, *Los guerreros de la libertad*, 76.

47. Gómez Zimmerman, *El Salvador: Who Speaks for the People?*, 115.

48. Panamá Sandoval, *Los guerreros de la libertad*, 76.

49. Gómez Zimmerman, *El Salvador: Who Speaks for the People?*, 22.

50. Gorkin, Pineda, and Leal, *From Grandmother*, 62.

51. Valdivieso Oriani, *Cruzando*, 199.

52. Gorkin, Pineda, and Leal, *From Grandmother to Granddaughter*, 37.

53. Pyes, *Salvadoran Rightists*, 36.

54. Gómez Zimmerman, *El Salvador: Who Speaks for the People?*, 26, 96, 97, and 198.

55. Guevara, "María Luisa d'Aubuisson Arrieta," 7.

56. Valencia and Arias, "Plática con Gaspar Romero," Part 2.

57. Gómez Zimmerman, *El Salvador: Who Speaks for the People?*, 78. A rare exception to this portrayal of Romero by civilian elites is provided by José Jorge

Simán, a member of the wealthy Simán family, who embraced Romero's liberationist message. See Simán, *Monseñor Oscar Arnulfo Romero Galdámez.*

58. Escalante Arce, *Sacrificios humanos,* 212.

59. Perhaps it is not coincidental that Martínez's economic program had been designed in part by Sol Bang's father. See Galeas and Sol Bang, *Sol y acero,* 8.

60. Gómez Zimmerman, *El Salvador: Who Speaks for the People?,* 56.

61. Panamá Sandoval, *Los guerreros de la libertad,* 23–24.

62. Gorkin, Pineda, and Leal, *From Grandmother,* 64–65.

63. Valdivieso Oriani, *Cruzando,* 152.

64. Gómez Zimmerman, *El Salvador: Who Speaks for the People?,* 61 and 69.

65. Ibid., 70.

66. Less vitriolic in his language regarding the 1979 coup is Mario Acosta Oertel, but his opposition to the coup leaders is implicit, because "it dispersed the organized political right," to which Oertel belonged. See Castro Fagoaga and Valencia, "Plática con Mario Acosta Oertel," 12.

67. Panamá Sandoval, *Los guerreros de la libertad,* 76.

68. Valdivieso Oriani, *Cruzando,* 72.

69. Gorkin, Pineda, and Leal, *From Grandmother,* 62.

70. Escalante Arce, *Sacrificios humanos,* 212–15.

71. Ibid., 221 and 228.

72. Gómez Zimmerman, *El Salvador: Who Speaks for the People?,* 48.

73. Panamá Sandoval, *Los guerreros de la libertad,* 157 and 174.

74. Gómez Zimmerman, *El Salvador: Who Speaks for the People?,* 13.

75. Escalante Arce, *Sacrificios humanos,* 21 and 257.

76. Galeas and Sol Bang, *Sol y acero,* 87.

77. Escalante Arce, *Sacrificios humanos,* 257.

78. Castro Fagoaga and Valencia, "Plática con Mario Acosta Oertel," 12.

79. Gorkin, Pineda, and Leal, *From Grandmother,* 80–81.

80. See Manuel, *Nightmare Revisited;* and Corr, U.S. Embassy, San Salvador, to U.S. Secretary of State, Washington, D.C., April 2, 1986, document no. 599 of NSA collection "El Salvador: War, Peace and Human Rights, 1980–1994."

81. Valencia and Martínez, "Plática con Orlando de Sola," Part 1. See Pyes, *Salvadoran Rightists,* 40, for reference to de Sola's loss of land.

82. Valencia and Martínez, "Plática con Orlando de Sola," Part 1.

83. Panamá Sandoval, *Los guerreros de la libertad,* 20, 37, and 60. For more on Panamá Sandoval, see his website, http://ernestopanama.com/escritores/.

84. Valencia and Martínez, "Plática con Orlando de Sola," Part 2.

85. Gómez Zimmerman, *El Salvador: Who Speaks for the People?,* 223.

86. Ibid., 61.

87. Valencia and Martínez, "Plática con Orlando de Sola," Part 3.

88. Gómez Zimmerman, *El Salvador: Who Speaks for the People?,* 189.

89. Valencia and Martínez, "Plática con Orlando de Sola," Part 2.

90. Panamá Sandoval, *Los guerreros de la libertad,* 86.

91. Gómez Zimmerman, *El Salvador: Who Speaks for the People?*, 156 and 166. Mario Acosta Oertel makes a similar claim, blaming the left for starting the fight, by saying "every action provokes a reaction; it's a law of physics." See Castro Fagoaga and Valencia, "Plática con Mario Acosta Oertel," 13.

92. Valdivieso Oriani, *Cruzando*, 89.

93. See Valdivieso Oriani, *Cruzando*; Panamá Sandoval, *Los guerreros de la libertad*; and Galeas and Sol Bang, *Sol y acero*.

94. Panamá Sandoval, *Los guerreros de la libertad*, 147–48; Galeas and Sol Bang, *Sol y acero*, 94–100.

95. Galeas and Sol Bang, *Sol y acero*, 203–62; see also Paulo Lüer's interview with Sol, September 26, 2011, http://columnatransversal.blogspot.com.

96. For a discussion of the broader privatization program, see, for example, Almeida, *Waves of Protest*; and Haglund, *Limiting Resources*.

97. Gorkin, Pineda, and Leal, *From Grandmother*, 39, 46, and 63.

98. Panamá Sandoval, *Los guerreros de la libertad*, 37, 199, and 202–14.

99. See United Nations, *From Madness to Hope*.

100. Galeas and Barahona, *The Possible Dream*, 108.

101. Gómez Zimmerman, *El Salvador: Who Speaks for the People?*, 142.

102. Galeas and Barahona, *The Possible Dream*, 56.

103. Galeas and Sol Bang, *Sol y acero*, 100.

104. Castro Fagoaga, "Plática con Adolfo Torrez," 7.

105. Panamá Sandoval, *Los guerreros de la libertad*, 159.

106. Castro Fagoaga, "Plática con Adolfo Torrez," 11.

107. Ibid., 57, 82, 142, 174, 193, and 195.

108. Robin, *The Reactionary Mind*, 57.

109. An additional outlet for Marvin Galeas is his blogspot, http://marvin galeas.blogspot.com/.

110. M. Galeas, *Crónicas de guerra*, 20, 31–32, 38–39, 50, 108–10, 271–72, and 277.

111. Marvin Galeas also criticizes people who turn "historical memory into a profitable business" by using the memory of people's deaths to their own gain, which, once again, is what he does in *Crónicas de guerra*. See M. Galeas, *Crónicas de guerra*, 128, 418, and 416.

112. M. Galeas, *Crónicas de guerra*, 20, 350–56, and 416–17.

113. As just one example of a leftist opinion of some of these commentators, see the blog with the picture of Ayalá, Villalobos, Geovani Galeas, and Lüers smelling ARENA's armpits, http://bastadecasaca.blogspot.com/2008/12/que -trabajito-mas-k-k-so-el-de-los.html.

114. G. Galeas, "Mayor Roberto D'Aubuisson"; Galeas and Sol Bang, *Sol y acero*.

115. See, for example, http://mayosibrian.blogspot.com/. The entry for September 22, 2008 is entitled, "Usted debe responder, Sr. Sánchez Cerén" [You must respond, Mr. Sánchez Cerén]. At the time Sánchez Cerén was running for vice president on the FMLN ticket for the 2009 elections. *Grandeza y misería* made

news in the United States. See Thomson, "A November Surprise?" For another website accompanying the publication of *Grandeza y miseria*, see http://informedeunamatanza.blogspot.com/. An example of the leftist response that claims Geovani Galeas admits that *Grandeza y miseria* was designed to promote ARENA's electoral bid can be found at http://bastadecasaca.blogspot.com/2009/03/geovani-galeas-confeso-que-grandeza-y.html.

116. G. Galeas, *Héroes bajo sospecha.*

117. Pyes, *Salvadoran Rightists,* 20.

118. M. Galeas, "De carne y hueso."

119. Lüers maintains a highly organized blogsite that includes all of his writings published in newspapers and other websites. For the critique of Marvin Galeas, see Lüers, "Carta a Marvin Galeas," June 25, 2009, http://columnatransversal.blogspot.com/2009/06/carta-marvin-galeas.html. For his defense of Marvin Galeas, see February 19, 2007; for his defense of Geovani Galeas's and Edwin Ayalá's work on *Grandeza y miseria*, see November 27, 2008.

120. http://columnatransversal.blogspot.com. For references to Lüers's arrival to El Salvador in 1981 and his political ideology, see January 14, 2008. For the quote about working for Altamirano and *El Diario de Hoy*, see September 8, 2011. For reference to his first column for *El Diario de Hoy*, see August, 30, 2007. For the criticism of *El Diario de Hoy* for authoritarian leadership before he started working for it, see September 19, 2005. For the reference to himself as a "sharpshooter," see February 20, 2010. For just one of the many examples of his ongoing criticisms of Sánchez Cerén, see January 18, 2010. For some examples of his criticisms of leftist governments throughout Latin America, see June 27, 2009, February 5, 2009, February 14, 2009, and March 13, 2008.

Chapter Three

1. Majano, *Una oportunidad perdida,* 150.

2. Flores Cruz, *Memorias de un soldado,* 119.

3. Duarte, *Duarte,* 97 and 106.

4. Interview with Mauricio Bonilla, in Martínez, *El Salvador,* 85.

5. My thanks to David Spencer for his insights on this matter and drawing my attention to the Arce quote.

6. Manwaring and Prisk, *El Salvador at War,* 216–18.

7. Vaquerano et al., "Plática con general Mauricio Vargas"; and Mauricio Vargas, interview by Jean Krasno. "Yale-UN Oral History Project: Central American Peace Process." San Salvador, June 20, 1997.

8. Zepeda Herrera, *Perfiles de la guerra,* 263.

9. Gutiérrez, *Message from the Vice President,* 1 and 6.

10. Among other complexities, it appears Gutiérrez was a CIA asset; see Stanley, *Protection Racket State,* chapter 5, esp. pages 137 and 144.

11. Manwaring and Prisk, *El Salvador at War,* 31.

12. Historian Héctor Lindo Fuentes relates an anecdote about a Salvadoran army officer at a conference in San Salvador memorializing the twenty-fifth anniversary of the 1979 coup by saying that he and other officers were shocked at seeing their Nicaraguan counterparts show up at the Salvadoran border penniless and desperate after Somoza's fall. See Lindo Fuentes, "Review of *Transnational Politics*," 805–6.

13. Duarte, *Duarte*, 97.

14. Manwaring and Prisk, *El Salvador at War*, 325. For the importance of Nicaragua, see the interview with Cruz Cruz in Ueltzen, *Conversatorio con los hijos*, 230; the interview with Garcia in Manwaring and Prisk, *El Salvador at War*, 31; Majano, *Una oportunidad perdida*; and Marín, *Batallón Atlacatl*, 17.

15. Central Intelligence Agency, "El Salvador: Performance on Certification Issues," July, 1983, document no. 347 of NSA collection, "El Salvador: War, Peace and Human Rights, 1980–1994." For more about the ideological divisions within the Salvadoran armed forces, see Corado Figueroa, *En defensa*, 160–61; Zepeda Herrera, *Perfiles de la guerra*, 37 and 77; Bosch, *The Salvadoran Officer Corps*; and the interview with General Woerner in Manwaring and Prisk, *El Salvador at War*, 56.

16. Interview with Cruz Cruz in Ueltzen, *Conversatorio con los hijos*; Mena Sandoval, *Del ejército nacional*.

17. Vaquerano et al., "Plática con general Mauricio Vargas," Part 1.

18. My thanks to David Spencer for insight on these issues.

19. Ambassador Robert White, U.S. Embassy, San Salvador, to U.S. Department of State, May 9, 1980, document no. 126 of NSA collection, "El Salvador: War, Peace and Human Rights, 1980–1994."

20. Majano, *Una oportunidad perdida*, 34, 97, 102, 150–51, and 203. For more on the claim about Majano being ready to join the ERP, see Marino, *Comandante Ramiro*, 59; and Hándal, *Legado*, 268. Majano makes no mention of this in his memoir, *Una oportunidad perdida*.

21. For a good description of the *tanda* system and the internal functioning of military politics, see Bosch, *The Salvadoran Officer Corps*.

22. Rostow, *Stages of Economic Growth*. For the history of the development of modernization theory, see Gilman, *Mandarins of the Future*.

23. Lindo Fuentes and Ching, *Modernizing Minds*.

24. Chávez Velasco, *Lo que no conté*, 18.

25. Majano, *Una oportunidad perdida*, 272.

26. Gutiérrez, *Testigo y actor*, 17, 182–83.

27. Corado Figueroa, *En defensa*, 106, 129, and 174.

28. Ibid., 84–85, 174, and 327. These paradoxical sentiments are evident in the interview that Corado granted to two reporters from *El Faro* in 2007. See Martínez and Arauz, "Entrevista con Humberto Corado."

29. Maykuth, "Battling for Hearts in El Salvador"; and Vaquerano et al., "Plática con general Mauricio Vargas," Part 3. A similarly vague appeal to mod-

ernization theory is offered by former President Molina in a brief but enlightening reflection on his record as a self-identified reformer; see Chávez Velasco, *Lo que no conté*, 179 and 183–84.

30. López, prologue to *En defensa*, by Corado Figueroa, 5. Corado exhibits a rhetoric that is almost identical to that of López in his 2007 interview for *El Faro*. See Martínez and Arauz, "Entrevista con Humberto Corado."

31. Manwaring and Prisk, *El Salvador at War*, 73–74.

32. Zepeda Herrera, *Perfiles de la guerra*, 314, 28, 29, and 314.

33. Chávez Velasco, *Lo que no conté*, 121.

34. Marín, *Batallón Atlacatl*, 15–17. See also Von Santos, *Días de trueno*, and Santos, *Soldados de élite*.

35. Zepeda Herrera, *Perfiles de la guerra*, 12.

36. Corado Figueroa, *En defensa*, 1.

37. Ibid.

38. Manwaring and Prisk, *El Salvador at War*, 373.

39. Marín, *Batallón Atlacatl*, 40–42 and 65.

40. Gutiérrez, *Testigo y actor*, 17, 76, and 172. Vaquerano and Lemus, "Plática con el diputado Sigifredo Ochoa Pérez," Part 3.

41. Zepeda Herrera, *Perfiles de la guerra*, 66, 239, and 242–44; Chávez Velasco, *Lo que no conté*, 154–57; and Corado Figueroa, *En defensa*, 255–58.

42. Chávez Velasco, *Lo que no conté*, 154–57.

43. Zepeda Herrera, *Perfiles de la guerra*, 29 and 31.

44. Corado Figueroa, *En defensa*, 220.

45. Vaquerano et al., "Plática con general Mauricio Vargas."

46. Marín, *Batallón Atlacatl*, 18.

47. Corado Figueroa, *En defensa*, 135.

48. Chávez Velasco, *Lo que no conté*, 164.

49. Corado Figueroa, *En defensa*, 151.

50. Gutiérrez, *Testigo y actor*, 141–46 and 158–61.

51. Corado Figueroa, *En defensa*, 105. See also Gutiérrez, *Testigo y actor*, 14–15.

52. Majano, *Una oportunidad perdida*, 340, 342, and 343.

53. Corado Figueroa, *En defensa*, 329.

54. Zepeda Herrera, *Perfiles de la guerra*, 19.

55. Manwaring and Prisk, *El Salvador at War*, 284.

56. Corado Figueroa, *En defensa*, 154.

57. Zepeda Herrera, *Perfiles de la guerra*, 15.

58. Guevara, "Entrevista con el general Juan Orlando Zepeda," 6.

59. Manwaring and Prisk, *El Salvador at War*, 44, 52, and 156.

60. The *tanda* that graduated from the military academy in 1966 is known as the "*tandona*" because it was a distinctly large class, roughly double the normal size. See Bosch, *The Salvadoran Officer Corps*. A list of the graduates and some descriptions of them and their respective honors can be found in an untitled Department of Defense Intelligence Information Report, 335-005-ES, November 14,

1966, document no. 373 of the NSA collection, "El Salvador: War, Peace and Human Rights, 1980–1994."

61. Zepeda Herrera, *Perfiles de la guerra*, 70.

62. Guevara, "Entrevista con el general Juan Orlando Zepeda."

63. Manwaring and Prisk, *El Salvador at War*, 215.

64. Zepeda Herrera, *Perfiles de la guerra*, 12.

65. Flores Cruz, *Memorias de un soldado*, 44.

66. Vigil, *Soldados en combate*. My thanks to David Spencer for insights on the Toyota promotion.

67. Corado Figueroa, *En defensa*, 174.

68. Manwaring and Prisk, *El Salvador at War*, 238.

69. Von Santos, *Días de trueno*, 27, 41, and 88.

70. Dada, "Entrevista con teniente coronel Camilo Hernández," Part 3 and Part 5.

71. Dada, "How We Killed the Archbishop."

72. For a similar example by one of the assassins of Father Rutilio Grande in 1977, see Santos, "Testimonio de uno de los asesinos."

73. Mauricio Vargas, interview by Jean Krasno. "Yale-UN Oral History Project: Central American Peace Process." San Salvador, June 20, 1997, 18.

74. Vaquerano et al., "Plática con general Mauricio Vargas," Part 1.

75. Marín, *Batallón Atlacatl*, 28 and 50.

76. Ibid., 92.

77. Vigil, *Soldados en combate*, 17 and 316.

78. Martínez and Arauz, "Entrevista con Humberto Corado."

79. Corado Figueroa, *En defensa*, 152–53, 155, 225, 236, 271, and 280–81.

80. Majano, *Una oportunidad perdida*, 221–32, 239, 260, 262, 265, and 273.

81. For another example of the argument of moral equivalence, see Martínez and Arauz, "Entrevista con Humberto Corado."

82. López, prologue to *En defensa*, by Corado, 8.

83. Corado, *En defensa*, 329.

84. Zepeda Herrera, *Perfiles de la guerra*, 311–12.

85. Vaquerano et al., "Plática con general Mauricio Vargas," Part 2.

86. A good description of this process can be found in Walter, *Las fuerzas armadas*.

87. Mauricio Vargas, interview by Jean Krasno. "Yale-UN Oral History Project: Central American Peace Process." San Salvador, June 20, 1997, 25. As an example of revelations relating to these abuses, see Valencia, "Los archivos secretos de la dictadura."

88. López, prologue to *En defensa*, by Corado, 9.

89. Corado, *En defensa*, 329.

90. Vaquerano et al., "Plática con general Mauricio Vargas," Part 2.

91. Mauricio Vargas, interview by Jean Krasno. "Yale-UN Oral History Project: Central American Peace Process." San Salvador, June 20, 1997, 16, 17, and 21.

92. Zepeda Herrera, *Perfiles de la guerra*, 248, 263, and 278–79.

93. Vaquerano and Lemus, "Plática con diputado Sigifredo Ochoa Pérez," Part 1.

94. López, prologue to *En defensa*, by Corado, 9.

95. Zepeda Herrera, *Perfiles de la guerra*, 299.

96. Vaquerano et al., "Plática con general Mauricio Vargas," Part 2.

97. Corado, *En defensa*, 141.

Chapter Four

1. Zepeda Herrera, *Perfiles de la guerra*, 13. Captain Herard Von Santos echoes Zepeda's sentiment in the prologue to the collection of war stories assembled by Captain Carlos Balmore Vigil, *Soldados en combate*, 8.

2. Guevara, "Entrevista con el general Juan Orlando Zepeda."

3. See Ladutke, *Freedom of Expression*, esp chapt. 2.

4. Francisco Jovel (Roberto Roca) describes the impressive output at the Universidad de El Salvador in 1971–1972 in Ueltzen, *Conversatorio*, 25. See also Medrano Guzmán, *Memorias*, 104. For an example of the challenges of early media distribution, see Cabrera, *Piruetas*, 183.

5. For a comprehensive analysis of the guerrillas' media-related activities, see Cortina Orero, "Comunicación insurgente." On Radio Venceremos, see Consalvi, *La terquedad del izote*. On Radio Farabundo Martí, the sister radio station to Radio Venceremos, see Leonard, *Ondas rebeldes*; and Escalona Terrón, *Radio Farabundo Martí*.

6. See Myer, *Underground Voices*; Martínez, *Las cárceles clandestinas*; Cayetano Carpio, *Secuestro y capucha*; and Díaz, *Nunca estuve*. Roque Dalton's renowned testimonial by communist party founder Miguel Mármol set the stage for the genre in 1972, detailing Mármol's narrow escape from a military firing squad during the military's suppression of the 1932 uprising. See Dalton, *Miguel Mármol*. Carlos Rico describes the way in which the ERP employed Martínez's memoir in international circles to garner sympathy and support for its cause. See Rico Mira, *En silencio*, 206.

7. Cabrera, *Piruetas*, 7.

8. Medardo Gónzalez of the FPL and Carlos Rico Mira of the RN are just two examples of narrators who more or less skip their childhoods and begin their stories with their involvement in political activism. See González, Regalado, and Álvarez, *Memorias del camino*; and Rico Mira, *En silencio*.

9. As one clear example, Mario Cabrera describes growing up in extreme poverty in San Salvador, but acknowledges the opportunities that he ended up having, such as working as a lifeguard, compared to *"obreros genuinos"* (real workers) in the countryside. See Cabrera, *Piruetas*, 109.

10. In addition to the examples below, see Márquez, "Francisco Valencia."

11. Peña, *Retazos de mi vida*, 23, 27, and 29.

12. Sancho, *Crónicas entre espejos*, 50 and 51. For a similar example from Francisco Jovel of the PRTC, who attended the University of El Salvador and whose father was a school director while he was growing up, see Arauz and Castro Fagoaga, "Plática con Francisco Jovel."

13. Arauz and Arias, "Plática con Humberto Centeno," Part 2.

14. The Samayoa quote is from his interview in Ueltzen, *Conversatorio*, 162; Gutiérrez's quote is from Martínez, Arauz, and Arias, "Plática con Dagoberto Gutiérrez," Part 1; and Hándal describes his childhood in *Legado*, 89–92.

15. Gutiérrez, "Carta a mi padre." Credit to Maria Mayo for finding and writing up this reference.

16. Sánchez, *Con sueños*, 28, 30, 39, and 50.

17. From Díaz's interview in Morgan and Cargo, *Mothers in Arms*, 39. See also the interview with Díaz in Phillips, "Nidia Díaz."

18. Mijango, *Mi guerra*, 37 and 39.

19. Cañadas, *Sueños y lágrimas*, 19.

20. Hándal, *Legado*, 92; Sánchez, *Con sueños*, 41; Peña, *Retazos de mi vida*, 29; and Medrano Guzmán, *Memorias de un guerrillero*, 36. See also González, Regalado, and Álvarez, *Memorias del camino*, 20.

21. Sancho, *Crónicas entre espejos*, 92.

22. Cañadas, *Sueños y lágrimas*, 20.

23. See Sancho, *Crónicas entre espejos*, 76; Nidia Díaz in her interview in Morgan and Cargo, *Mothers in Arms*, 39; Sánchez, *Con sueños*, 42.

24. Sánchez, *Con sueños*, 41 and 52. Cañadas also cites issues surrounding the teaching profession and his involvement in the teachers' strikes of the late 1960s and early 1970s as a high school student as being highly influential. See Cañadas, *Sueños y lágrimas*, 21–22.

25. Medrano Guzmán, *Memorias de un guerrillero*, 41–42.

26. Sancho, *Crónicas entre espejos*, 51–58.

27. Arauz and Arias, "Plática con Humberto Centeno," Part 2.

28. Cruz's interview appears in Ueltzen, *Conversatorio*, 223 and 226. The other army officer who joined the guerrillas, Francisco Mena Sandoval, sites similar military abuses, but against labor leaders within El Salvador. See Guevara and Sanz, "Plática con Emilio Mena Sandoval."

29. Sánchez, *Con sueños*, 42.

30. Peña, *Retazos de mi vida*, 34.

31. Servicio Informativo Ecuménico y Popular, "Entrevista con Mauricio El Sólido." Credit to Maria Mayo for finding and writing up this reference.

32. Mijango, *Mi guerra*, chapter 5.

33. Merino, *Comandante Ramiro*, 8–9.

34. Servicio Informativo Ecuménico y Popular, "Entrevista con Victoriano García." Unlike most former commanders, García provides very little detail about his entrance into political awareness, choosing to simply reveal the facts rather

than expand on the significance of his decision to engage in collective action. Credit to Maria Mayo for finding and writing up this reference.

35. See, for example, Cabrera, *Piruetas*, 97.

36. Servicio Informativo Ecuménico y Popular, "1932."

37. See interview with David Rodríguez in Ueltzen, *Conversatorio*, 263.

38. Sánchez, *Con sueños*, 20. See also Cabrera, *Piruetas*, 98.

39. Servicio Informativo Ecuménico y Popular, "1932." For other references to 1932, see Rico Mira, *En silencio*, 26–27; Peña, *Retazos de mi vida*, 51; and Merino, *Comandante Ramiro*, 26–28.

40. Peña, *Retazos de mi vida*, 17.

41. Centeno also discusses his father's involvement in the 1944 movement against Martínez. See Arauz and Arias, "Plática con Humberto Centeno," Part 2.

42. Hándal, *Legado*, 95.

43. For references to 1960, see Merino, *Comandante Ramiro*, 20; and Sánchez, *Con sueños*, 44–45, and 48–49.

44. Sánchez, *Con sueños*, 76–84; Rico Mira, *En silencio*, 25; Mijango, *Mi guerra*, 44; Peña, *Retazos de mi vida*, 30; Ana Guadalupe Martínez, interview by Jean Krasno. "Yale-UN Oral History Project: Central American Peace Process." San Salvador, June 21, 1997, 5; Guevara, "Entrevista con Gersón Martínez," Part 1; Cañadas, *Sueños y lágrimas*, 21; and González, Regalado, and Álvarez, *Memorias del camino*, 10.

45. Rico Mira, *En silencio*, 27. See also Mijango, *Mi guerra*, 53; interview with Nidia Díaz in Morgan and Cargo, *Mothers in Arms*, 39; Sánchez, *Con sueños*, 117–20; Guevara and Sanz, "Plática con Francisco Mena Sandoval"; González, Regalado, and Álvarez, *Memorias del camino*, 12.

46. Interview with Rodríguez, in Ueltzen, *Conversatorio*, 254.

47. Merino, *Comandante Ramiro*, 20.

48. Ibid., 40–41.

49. Guevara, "Entrevista con Gersón Martínez," Part 2. Carlos Rico opens his memoir with a similar discussion of the Salvadoran uprising as an example of "a just war as a legitimate defense," and he recognizes that his adversaries believed they were justified because they were supposedly defending "national sovereignty against international communist aggression." See Rico Mira, *En silenico*, 20. See also Cabrera, *Piruetas*, 11.

50. Hándal, *Legado*, 45.

51. Valencia, "Plática con Orlando de Sola," Part 2.

52. From an interview with Martínez in Ueltzen, *Conversatorio*, 136.

53. Medrano Guzmán, *Memorias de un guerrillero*, 47.

54. Peña, *Retazos de mi vida*, 42. See also Sancho, *Crónicas entre espejos*, 60 and 75; Sánchez, *Con sueños*, 94; and Mijango, *Mi guerra*, 42.

55. Arauz, Lemus, and Meza, "Plática con Lorena Peña." Part 2.

56. Mijango, *Mi guerra*, 102 and 109.

57. Cañadas, *Sueños y lágrimas*, 24–25.

58. Ana Guadalupe Martínez, interview by Jean Krasno. "Yale-UN Oral History Project: Central American Peace Process." San Salvador, June 21, 1997, 7.

59. Sancho, *Crónicas entre espejos*, 86 and 124.

60. The reference to cyanide is made by Rico Mira, *En silencio*, 61; and Sancho, *Crónicas entre espejos*, 122.

61. Medrano Guzmán, *Memorias de un guerrillero*, 94.

62. Dada, "Plática con Rubén Aguilar," Part 3; for another reference to the death squads see, Mijango, *Mi guerra*, 104–5.

63. Peña, *Retazos de mi vida*, 62.

64. Sancho, *Crónicas entre espejos*, 136.

65. Mijango, *Mi guerra*, 104.

66. Arauz and Arias, "Plática con Humberto Centeno," Part 1.

67. Sánchez, *Con sueños*, 95–97.

68. Arauz and Arias, "Plática con Humberto Centeno," Part 1.

69. Mijango, *Mi guerra*, 95–97, and 117.

70. Peña, *Retazos de mi vida*, 57.

71. M. Galeas, *Crónicas de guerra*, 99, 136, and 167.

72. Martínez, Arauz, and Arias, "Plática con Dagoberto Gutiérrez," Part 2.

73. Mijango, *Mi guerra*, 179.

74. Phillips, "Nidia Díaz," 39.

75. Sánchez describes how he and his family had to move around from house to house, all the while "trying to lead a normal-looking life that would call no attention to anyone." Sánchez, *Con sueños*, 98.

76. Mijango, *Mi guerra*, 85 and 98.

77. Sancho, *Crónicas entre espejos*, 80 and 85.

78. Wood, *Insurgent Collective Action*, 235.

79. Peña, *Retazos de mi vida*, 57 and 63. Similarly, José Luis Merino describes the support he received from his family members. Merino, *Comandante Ramiro*, 7.

80. Rico Mira, *En silencio*, 31 and 33.

81. Merino, *Comandante Ramiro*, 41–42.

82. Ibid., 42.

83. Peña, *Retazos de mi vida*, 53.

84. Arauz, Lemus, and Meza, "Plática con Lorena Peña," Part 2.

85. Sánchez specifically mentions Cayetano Carpio explaining to him the split between the FPL and PCS. Sánchez, *Con sueños*, 56 and 113.

86. Peña, *Retazos de mi vida*, 78; Mijango, *Mi guerra*, 50; Sanchez, *Con sueños*, 65 and 107; and Merino, *Comandante Ramiro*, 45.

87. Hándal, *Legado*, 244.

88. Merino accuses Duarte of losing touch with *realidad nacional* based upon his political decisions in the late 1970s. See Merino, *Comandante Ramiro*, 45. For Sancho's critique of Cayetano Carpio, see Sancho, *Crónicas entre espejos*,

128. For Juan Medrano's description of the internal disputes within the ERP and its leaders' collective dispute with the FPL over military strategy, see Medrano Guzmán, *Memorias de un guerrillero*, 69.

89. Peña, *Retazos de mi vida*, 78.

90. See, for example, M. Galeas, *Crónicas de guerra*; Prisk, *The Comandante Speaks*; Ayalá, *Entre Marilyn Monroe*; and Dada, "Plática con Rubén Aguilar."

91. Peña, *Retazos de mi vida*, 78.

92. Hándal, *Legado*, 208–32. For just one among many FPL critiques of the PCS's "electoralism," see González, Regalado, and Álvarez, *Memorias del camino*, 24.

93. Villalobos, "El ayatolá Hándal." For his part, a rebuke of Villalobos is provided by Arquímedes Cañadas, whose memoir leaves the lingering impression that Villalobos intentionally set him up to be captured by the Honduran military to eliminate him from the ERP. See Cañadas, *Sueños y lágrimas*, 274–78.

94. Rico Mira, *En silencio*, 131. He reveals that the relations with the various ideological factions in Nicaragua, Cuba, Panama and Mexico were equally fraught with rivalries, 131–46.

95. Hándal, *Legado*, 265.

96. Rico Mira, *En Silencio*, 66.

97. Peña, *Retazos de mi vida*, 84; Rico, *En silencio*, 179–96.

98. Rico Mira, *En silencio*, 155.

99. Peña, *Retazos de mi vida*, 60.

100. Sánchez, *Con sueños*, 114. Although debateable, and firmly rejected by some of Cayetano Carpio's supporters, the available evidence indicates that in the midst of a factional dispute within the FPL's command structure, Cayetano ordered the murder of Mélida Anaya Montes and then committed suicide soon thereafter.

101. Mijango, *Mi guerra*, 109–110.

102. On the death of Dalton, see García Dueñas and Espinoza, *Quién asesinó a Roque Dalton?* For an insider's veiled confessional, see Villalobos, "Review of Revolutionary Movements."

103. The *Washington Post* journalist Charles Lane reported on the revelations in these new documents. See Lane, "Reclutar, desertar o anular."

104. Medrano Guzmán, *Memorias de un guerrillero*, 21.

105. Ibid., 18–22, and 112–13; Hándal *Legado*, 251. See also Sancho, *Crónicas entre espejos*, 100–13; Rico Mira, *En silencio*, 39 and 103–15; and Alvarenga, *Roque Dalton*. Arquímedes Cañadas of the ERP says he was part of a hit squad sent out to assassinate RN leaders. See Cañadas, *Sueños y lágrimas*, 64.

106. Rico Mira, *En silencio*, 82.

107. Medrano Guzmán, *Memorias de un guerrillero*, 27.

108. Merino, *Comandante Ramiro*, 13.

109. Interview with Roca in Ueltzen, *Conversatorio*, 28.

110. Rico Mira, *En silencio*, 103.

111. Peña, *Retazos de mi vida*, 80–82; Arauz, Lemus, and Meza, "Plática con Lorena Peña," Part 4.

112. Medrano Guzmán, *Memorias de un guerrillero*, 295–309.

113. Ibid., 62.

114. Admittedly, though, on various occasions Medrano credits the peasantry with playing a more integrated role in shaping the organization and its views. He says the peasants' religiosity brought him back to his faith after he had put it aside during his years in the university studying Marxism. Medrano Guzmán, *Memorias de un guerrillero*, 130.

int'l connex

115. Many of the comandantes received some sort of training abroad, including José Luis Merino in the Soviet Union in 1974–1975. He notes that most of the members of his organization, the PCS/FAL, who received training abroad indeed ended up being comandantes, Merino, *Comandante Ramiro*, 23 and 32. Medrano went to Libya; see Medrano Guzmán, *Memorias de un guerrillero*, 173, and 180–90. Dagoberto Gutiérrez went to Vietnam: Martínez, Arauz, and Arias, "Plática con Dagoberto Gutiérrez," Part 2. Eduardo Linares went to both Cuba and Vietnam: Valencia, "Entrevista con Eduardo Linares." Miguel Castellaños went to Cuba: Prisk, *The Comandante Speaks*, 26.

116. Sánchez, *Con sueños*, 108.

117. Rico Mira, *En silencio*, 115 and 155.

118. Sancho, *Con sueños*, 132 and 137; Merino goes from "Birth of the FMLN," to "The 1981 Offensive." Merino, *Comandante Ramiro*, 48 and 57.

119. Rico Mira, *En silencio*, 176.

120. As one example, Schafik Hándal says in his memoir that much animosity and distrust remained when the FMLN was formed. See Hándal, *Legado*, 223.

Chapter Five

1. Medrano makes a direct comparison between the Nicaraguan offensive in 1979 and the January 1981 offensive in *Memorias de un guerrillero*, 202.

2. Guevara, "Entrevista con Gersón Martínez." Lorena Peña assesses the situation similarly: see Peña, *Retazos de mi vida*, 91.

3. Merino, *Comandante Ramiro*, 49. He also describes the PCS's hope to guide the coup, 49.

4. Peña, *Retazos de mi vida,* 82.

5. Medrano Guzmán, *Memorias de un guerrillero*, 200. See also Rico Mira, *En silencio*, 241–44; Peña, *Retazos de mi vida,* 83.

6. Rico Mira, *En silencio*, 212–14.

7. Ibid., 207.

8. Sánchez Cerén, *Con sueños*, 134–35 and 141; Peña reiterates this point in Arauz, Lemus, and Meza, "Plática con Lorena Peña," Part 3.

9. Peña, *Retazos de mi vida,* 91.

10. Ibid., 94.

11. Orlando Zepeda made this claim. See Guevara, "Entrevista con el general Juan Orlando Zepeda," Part 6. For a contemporary example from President Duarte in the mid-1980s, see Duarte, *Duarte,* 94.

12. For example, Salvador Sánchez comments on how he and Mélida Anaya discussed this issue and how it became a point of dispute within the FPL. See Sánchez Cerén, *Con sueños,* 114 and 187. Interestingly, José Luis Merino says that when he joined a mass front organization in the late 1960s, the youth wing of the *Partido Revolucionario 9 de Mayo* (PR-9M), he didn't know that it was a front for the Communist Party, which he later joined. See Merino, *Comandante Ramiro,* 9.

13. Peña, *Retazos de mi vida,* 95. See also González, Regalado, and Álvarez, *Memorias del camino,* 31.

14. Merino, *Comandante Ramiro,* 74.

15. Medrano Guzmán, *Memorias de un guerrillero,* 201.

16. Rico Mira, *En silencio,* 244.

17. Peña, *Retazos de mi vida,* 93 and 100.

18. Medrano Guzmán, *Memorias de un guerrillero,* 202.

19. Mena Sandoval, *Del ejército,* 246 and 294.

20. Mijango, *Mi guerra,* 118.

21. Mena Sandoval, *Del ejército,* 290.

22. Martínez, Arauz, and Arias, "Plática con Dagoberto Gutiérrez," Part 2.

23. Sánchez Cerén, *Con sueños,* 140.

24. Sancho, *Crónicas entre espejos,* 147. For similar descriptions, see Peña, *Retazos de mi vida,* 113; and Medrano Guzmán, *Memorias de un guerrillero,* 72.

25. Arauz, Lemus, and Meza, "Plática con Lorena Peña," Part 3.

26. For a clear expression of this from early in the war, see Alegría, *No me agarrón viva,* chapters 3 and 4. Salvador Samayoa relates an applicable example in an interview he gave early in the war explaining his decision to incorporate into the FPL. He describes himself as a petit-bourgeois intellectual, and then, using the parlance of the FPL at the time, he says he began to "proletarianize himself"; he encourages his fellow petit-bourgeois intellectuals to do the same. See Méndez Rodríguez, *Voices from El Salvador,* 67–68. Lorena Peña provides a related anecdote, saying that FPL leaders sanctioned her for the demise of her relationship with Dimas Rodríguez because he was a peasant and she was a petit-bourgeois intellectual. See Arauz, Lemus, and Meza, "Plática con Lorena Peña," Part 4; and Peña, *Retazos de mi vida,* 80–81.

27. Mena Sandoval, *Del ejército,* 297.

28. Peña, *Retazos de mi vida,* 115.

29. Martínez, Arauz, and Arias, "Plática con Dagoberto Gutiérrez," Part 2.

30. Peña, *Retazos de mi vida,* 115.

31. Sánchez Cerén, *Con sueños,* 88.

32. Mena Sandoval, *Del ejército,* 311.

33. Rico Mira, *En silencio,* 255–81.

34. Peña, *Retazos de mi vida,* 121.

35. Mijango, *Mi guerra*, 137–38.

36. Medrano Guzmán, *Memorias de un guerrillero*, 338.

37. See also Francisco Jovel's discussion of this in Arauz and Castro Fagoaga, "Plática con Francisco Jovel."

38. For a first-person account of this mission by one of the guerrilla participants, see the testimony by Comandante Sebastián (Carlos Aragón) in Yanes and Ellis, *Mirrors of War*, 134–36.

39. Guevara, "Entrevista con Gersón Martínez."

40. Hándal, *Legado*, 274–75.

41. For an explicit reference to this dynamic, see Sánchez Cerén, *Con sueños*, 156.

42. Olmo, "El Salvador: Ana Guadalupe Martínez."

43. Mena Sandoval, *Del ejército*, 305.

44. Sánchez Cerén, *Con sueños*, 145.

45. Merino, *Comandante Ramiro*, 74.

46. Ibarra Chávez, *Brigada Rafael Arce Zablah*. See also Consalvi, *La terquedad del izote*.

47. For a summary of his responsibilities, see Rico Mira, *Con silencio*, 304.

48. Ibid., 320, 330, 356, and 399. Lorena Peña offers a similar description of the scale and diversity of her responsibilities. See Peña, *Retazos de mi vida,* 114–15.

49. Espinoza, *Relatos de la guerra*, 43 and 46–52.

50. Consalvi, *La terquedad del izote.*

51. Peña, *Retazos de mi vida,* 115–16.

52. Sánchez Cerén, *Con sueños*, 155.

53. Peña, *Retazos de mi vida,* 119 and 115.

54. Medrano Guzmán, *Memorias de un guerrillero*, 71.

55. Mijango, *Mi guerra*, 125, 234, and 250.

56. Merino, *Comandante Ramiro*, 60. The story is also reiterated by PCS leader Hándal in *Legado*, 268.

57. Arauz, Lemus, and Meza, "Plática con Lorena Peña," Part 3.

58. Rico Mira, *En silencio*, 291.

59. Merino, *Comandante Ramiro*, 64.

60. Ibid., 77.

61. Mijango, *Mi guerra*, 139, and 155. Villalobos makes an oblique reference to this discord in his 1982 interview with Marta Harnecker. See Dixon and Jonas, *Revolution and Intervention*, 86.

62. Medrano Guzmán, *Memorias de un guerrillero*, 275.

63. González, Regalado, and Álvarez, *Memorias del camino*, 40.

64. See, for example, Beverley and Zimmerman, *Literature and Politics*, 140.

65. Arauz, Lemus, and Meza, "Plática con Lorena Peña," Part 4; and Sánchez Cerén, *Con sueños*, 185–96. As one example of a laudatory take on Cayetano Carpio, see the biography compiled and published online by the Centro de Documentación de los Movimientos Armados, *Comandante Obrero; and the website marcialtienerazon:* http://marcialteniarazon.org/.

66. Arauz, Lemus, and Meza, "Plática con Lorena Peña," Part 3.

67. González, Regalado, and Álvarez, *Memorias del camino*, 44.

68. Merino, *Comandante Ramiro*, 84.

69. Mena Sandoval, *Del ejército*, 338. On page 352 Mena criticizes his comrades who didn't understand the merits of the strategic shift.

70. Peña, *Retazos de mi vida*, 118. See also González, Regalado, and Álvarez, *Memorias del camino*, 43.

71. Merino, *Comandante Ramiro*, 87.

72. Mijango, *Mi guerra*, 258.

73. Hándal, *Legado*, 282.

74. Merino, *Comandante Ramiro*, 85.

75. Peña, *Retazos de mi vida*, 122.

76. Marisol Galindo of the ERP, who played a lead role in implementing the education component of the strategic shift among the recruits, explained this to me in a personal interview on March 23, 2008.

77. See, for example, M. Galeas, *Crónicas de guerra*, 226–28; Medrano Guzmán, *Memorias de un guerrillero*, 281–300; and Chiyo's interview, Guevara, "Entrevista con 'Chiyo.'"

78. Peña, *Retazos de mi vida*, 149.

79. Ayalá comments on this specifically, in *Entre Marilyn Monroe*, 256.

80. Sánchez Cerén, *Con sueños*, 184.

81. Medrano Guzmán, *Memorias de un guerrillero*, 343–52. See also Consalvi, *La terquedad del izote*, 240–42; and Ayalá, *Entre Marilyn Monroe*, 60, 127, 147, and 256.

82. President Duarte claims that the documents found with Nidia Díaz were highly important, see Duarte, *Duarte*, 354. See also the interview with Díaz and another PRTC comandante, Gilberto Osorio, who operated under Díaz's command, in Phillips, "Nidia Diaz." Osorio claims the documents were outdated and they were in the process of burning them when Díaz was captured.

83. See Prisk, *The Comandante Speaks*.

84. Peña, *Retazos de mi vida*, 129.

85. Another high-ranking comandante captured two years earlier was Arquímedes Cañadas, (pseudonym Alejandro Montenegro) of the ERP. But he was captured in Honduras while en route to Nicaragua. See Cañadas, *Sueños y lágrimas*.

86. Rico Mira, *En silencio*, 355 and 363.

87. Merino, *Comandante Ramiro*, 88–92. Eduardo Linares of the FPL describes an operation in 1985 when one of their fighters deserted and exposed their position to the army, much to the guerrillas' detriment. See Valencia, "Entrevista con Eduardo Linares."

88. G. Galeas and Ayalá, *Grandeza y miseria*. The first publication regarding the Sibrián situation was a piece in the online journal, *El Faro* by César Castro Fagoaga, "Mayo Sibrián."

89. Medrano Guzmán, *Comandante Ramiro*, 324.

90. Arauz, Lemus, and Meza, "Plática con Lorena Peña," Part 5.

91. Medrano Guzmán, *Memorias de un guerrillero*, 332. It was also at this time that Medrano suffered the sanction from ERP leadership, which he believes was unjustly meted out for having expressed dissent about military strategy. Another example is Rubén Aguilar leaving the FPL in late 1984 because he found the FPL leadership too dogmatic, even after the dust had settled from the Cayetano-Anaya murder-suicide incident. See Dada and Martínez, "Plática con Rubén Aguilar," Part 3.

92. Hándal, *Legado*, 297–301, and 336.

93. M. Galeas, *Crónicas de guerra*, 107–110. Galeas invests more space in his book to the early periods of the war, but he uses cases like this one in 1988 to solidify his alienation from the guerrillas.

94. Ayalá, *Entre Marilyn Monroe*, 43. For another account of the war by Ayalá, see *En el silencio de la batalla*.

95. Ibid., 95.

96. For example, he says guerrilla commanders sent combatants on suicide missions so they could steal their girlfriends. And he makes repeated references to the *"mentiras"* (lies) they told the rank and file. He also uses the term *"forzados"* (forced) to describe his incorporation, although it is not clear whether he means he was forcibly conscripted or that circumstances more broadly gave him no option. As for pop culture references, just one among many is his comparing a female cook to the Disney character Shrek. See Ayalá, *Entre Marilyn Monroe*, 49, 96, 171, and 239–40.

97. Ibid., 75 and 90. On page 258 he claims that the strategic shift killed off the first generation of guerrilla fighters.

98. Sánchez Cerén, *Con sueños*, 178 and 184.

99. Medrano Guzmán, *Memorias de un guerrillero*, 349.

100. Valencia, "Entrevista con Eduardo Linares."

101. Merino, *Comandante Ramiro,* 86.

102. Peña, *Retazos de mi vida,* 136–38; Merino, *Comandante Ramiro,* 102; President Duarte offers his version of this event in his memoir, *Duarte,* 241–68. See also the first-person testimonial/memoir by Américo Mauro Araujo in Servicio Informativo Ecuménico y Popular, "1985–2005."

103. Sancho, *Crónicas entre espejos,* 216 and 228.

104. Merino, *Comandante Ramiro,* 105.

105. See, for example, Hernández Arias, *Fenix: cenizas de una operación estadounidense.*

106. Peña, *Retazos de mi vida,* 139.

107. Merino, *Comandante Ramiro,* 115.

108. Hándal, *Legado,* 338.

109. RN comandante Eduardo Sancho claims that 6,000 fighters were involved, 2,000 in San Salvador and 4,000 throughout the rest of the country. See Sancho, *Crónicas entre espejos,* 253.

110. Ibid.

111. Merino, *Comandante Ramiro*, 114.

112. Naturally, Berne Ayalá focuses heavily on this failure. See Ayalá, *Al tope más alla*, especially 40.

113. Rico Mira, *En silencio*, 403. See also Merino, *Comandante Ramiro*, 102–3; and Olmo, "El Salvador: Ana Guadalupe Martínez."

114. Ayalá, *Entre Marilyn Monroe*, 125.

115. Gutiérrez, "22 años y la ofensiva se reanuda." See also Ana Guadalupe Martínez's description of the logistical effort for the offensive in Ana Guadalupe Martínez, interview by Jean Krasno. "Yale-UN Oral History Project: Central American Peace Process." San Salvador, June 21, 1997, 14–16.

116. Roberto Cañas, interview by Jean Krasno. "Yale-UN Oral History Project: Central American Peace Process, San Salvador June 19, 1997," 6.

117. For references to the debates over this issue and/or expressions of opinion one way or the other, see Ana Guadalupe Martínez, interview by Jean Krasno. "Yale-UN Oral History Project: Central American Peace Process." San Salvador, June 21, 1997," 18; Roberto Cañas, interview by Jean Krasno. "Yale-UN Oral History Project: Central American Peace Process, San Salvador June 19, 1997, 7–8; and M. Galeas, *Crónicas de guerra*, 73.

118. Merino, *Comandante Ramiro*, 119–20.

119. Peña, *Retazos de mi vida,* 198.

120. See, for example, González, Regalado, and Álvarez, *Memorias del camino*, 45. An exception to this is Berne Ayalá, who focuses heavily on the offensive in his writings, but from a more pessimistic perspective, focusing on the military failure caused by leaders' misconceptions and poor planning. See Ayalá, *Al tope más alla*, 72, for a summary comment.

121. See Peña, *Retazos de mi vida,* 191. Berne Ayalá strongly rejects the common assumptions that the FAL was only a secondary fighter within the FMLN. In his various venues he claims that the FAL was engaged in daily and heavy fighting, especially against the elite Atlacatl Battalion, on the southern slopes of Guazapa between the 1989 offensive and the end of the war. See Ayalá, *Al tope más alla*; and the transcribed conversation in 2007 between him, Geovani Galeas, and Captain (Ret.) Herard von Santos of the Atlacatl Battalion, originally posted on the now defunct website, CentroAmerica21, under the title, "Esclarecimiento de una acto de barbarie," http://web.archive.org/web/20090105233618/http://www.centroamerica21.com/edit/25-1/pguerra1.html.

122. Medrano Guzmán, *Memorias de un guerrillero*, 375.

123. Sánchez Cerén, *Con sueños*, 185.

124. For discussions within U.S. diplomatic circles over Schafik Hándal's threat to introduce missiles in 1987, see information report, U.S. State Department, Washington D.C., October 31, 1987, document no. 659 of the NSA collection, "El Salvador: War, Peace and Human Rights, 1980–1994."

125. Rico Mira, *En silencio*, 432.

126. Mijango, *Mi guerra*, 368–69. See also Sancho, *Crónicas entre espejos*, 212 and 252–54. Sancho says the guerrillas had the missiles during the final offensive in November 1989 but refused to use them because they were afraid of knocking down airplanes over populated centers.

127. See Krasnos's interviews with Ana Guadalupe Martínez, Schafik Hándal, Roberto Cañas, and Salvador Samayoa in the "Yale-UN Oral History Project"; and Medrano Guzmán, *Memorias de un guerrillero*, 383.

128. Peña, *Retazos de mi vida*, 181.

129. Medrano Guzmán, *Memorias de un guerrillero*, 391.

130. Roberto Cañas, interview by Jean Krasno. "Yale-UN Oral History Project: Central American Peace Process." San Salvador, June 21, 1997, 14.

131. Peña, *Retazos de mi vida*, 191.

132. Sancho, *Crónicas entre espejos*, 279.

133. Roberto Cañas, interview by Jean Krasno. "Yale-UN Oral History Project: Central American Peace Process." San Salvador, June 21, 1997, 14.

134. Peña, *Retazos de mi vida*, 189.

135. See Salvador Samayoa, interview by Jean Krasno. "Yale-UN Oral History Project: Central American Peace Process." San Salvador, June 19, 1997, 16. It offers an explicit reference to the guerrillas starting negotiations with a demand that the armed forces be abolished and then settling for reforms of the military. See also page 17 for references to the reforms of the National Police. See also Medrano Guzmán, *Memorias de un guerrillero*, 384.

136. Samayoa discusses the futility of the attempts to raise matters relating to land and economic structures at the negotiations. See Salvador Samayoa, interview by Jean Krasno. "Yale-UN Oral History Project: Central American Peace Process." San Salvador, June 19, 1997, 21; and Samayoa interview in Ueltzen, *Conversatorio*, 174–76. Francisco Jovel of the PRTC similarly laments this failure. See Arauz and Castro Fagoaga, "Plática con Francisco Jovel."

137. See Ana Guadalupe Martínez, interview by Jean Krasno. "Yale-UN Oral History Project: Central American Peace Process." San Salvador, June 21, 1997, 23; and interview with Nidia Díaz in Morgan and Cargo, *Mothers in Arms*, 41–42.

138. Salvador Samayoa, interview by Jean Krasno. "Yale-UN Oral History Project: Central American Peace Process." San Salvador, June 19, 1997, 13; and Schafik Hándal, interview by Jean Krasno. "Yale-UN Oral History Project: Central American Peace Process." San Salvador, June 19, 1997, 21. Juan Medrano comments on the heavy blow that the FSLN's electoral defeat in 1990 represented in *Memorias de un guerrillero*, 388. See also González, Regalado, and Álvarez, *Memorias del camino*, 46.

139. Salvador Samayoa, interview by Jean Krasno. "Yale-UN Oral History Project: Central American Peace Process." San Salvador, June 19, 1997, 21–22. Medardo González emphasizes the limited size and poor quality of the lands that were parceled out to peasants after the war. See González, Regalado, and Álvarez, *Memorias del camino*, 53.

140. Peña, *Retazos de mi vida,* 249.

141. Espinoza, *Relatos de la guerra,* 66.

142. Sánchez Cerén, *Con sueños,* 263.

143. Ana Guadalupe Martínez, interview by Jean Krasno. "Yale-UN Oral History Project: Central American Peace Process." San Salvador, June 21, 1997, 3.

144. Medrano Guzmán, *Memorias de un guerrillero,* 404. See also Merino celebrating the FMLN's electoral capacity in the postwar era, in *Comandante Ramiro,* 135; and González, Regalado, and Álvarez, *Memorias del camino,* 50.

145. M. Galeas, *Crónicas de guerra,* 416–17.

146. Roberto Cañas, interview by Jean Krasno. "Yale-UN Oral History Project: Central American Peace Process, San Salvador June 19, 1997, 14–15.

147. For a summary of the whereabouts of the signers of the Accords as of 2007, see El Faro, "¿Dónde están los firmantes?" in *El Faro,* January 15, 2007, http://archivo.elfaro.net/secciones/noticias/20070115/firmantes.html.

148. Peña, *Retazos de mi vida,* 204 and 208.

149. Interview with Díaz in Morgan and Cargo, *Mothers in Arms,* 46–48.

150. Medrano Guzmán, *Memorias de un guerrillero,* 396.

151. Interview with Díaz in Morgan and Cargo, *Mothers in Arms,* 46.

152. Peña, *Retazos de mi vida,* 220.

153. González, Regalado, and Álvarez, *Memorias del camino,* 49.

154. M. Galeas, *Crónicas de guerra,* 68–69 and 77–79.

155. Ibid., 78.

156. Interview with Díaz in Morgan and Cargo, *Mothers in Arms,* 40.

157. Ibid., 45.

158. As just one example see Lüers, "Carta al empresario y benefactor Nicolás Salume."

159. See, for example, Malkin, "El Salvador Cracks Down"; and Valencia, "Diez respuestas."

160. One exception is Carlos Rico Mira, who comments on the RN's need "to avoid confusions whenever crossing territory controlled by [the FPL]." See Rico Mira, *En silencio,* 413.

161. Sánchez Cerén, *Con sueños,* 256. See also Medrano Guzmán, *Memorias de un guerrillero,* 327.

162. Merino, *Comandante Ramiro,* 441.

163. Medrano describes the harsh critiques of Cayetano that Hándal made to him in 1981. See Medrano Guzmán, *Memorias de un guerrillero,* 274.

164. Merino, *Comandante Ramiro,* 80–81.

165. Peña, *Retazos de mi vida,* 237; see also page 213, where she praises Hándal alongside Mélida Anaya. Salvador Sánchez does the same for Anaya and Hándal in an October 2011 speech, "Palabras Acto de Juramentación de candidatos a Alcaldes, Alcaldesas, Diputados y Diputadas FMLN. XXVIII Convención de FMLN," posted on http://www.simpatizantesfmln.org/blog/?p=8836. See also González, Regalado, and Álvarez, *Memorias del camino,* 53.

166. Medrano Guzmán, *Memorias de un guerrillero*, 451–55.

167. Sancho, *Crónicas entre espejos*, 282. Medrano comments on these types of debates within the ERP in *Memorias de un guerrillero*, 307.

168. Medrano Guzmán, *Memorias de un guerrillero*, 190.

169. Sancho, *Crónicas entre espejos*, 276.

170. Medrano Guzmán, *Memorias de un guerrillero*, 441.

171. This includes Joaquín Villalobos and Salvador Samayoa, as well as Paulo Lüers, Geovani Galeas, and Marvin Galeas.

172. See Lüers, "Peces fuera del agua."

173. See Villalobos, "El ayatolá Hándal y el materialismo histérico." See also Olmo, "El Salvador: Ana Guadalupe Martínez."

174. Mijango, *Mi guerra*, 387.

175. Peña, *Retazos de mi vida,* 225–26.

176. Merino, *Comandante Ramiro*, 137. See also González, Regalado, and Álvarez, *Memorias del camino*, 61.

177. Martínez, Arauz, and Arias, "Plática con Dagoberto Gutiérrez," Part 4.

178. Dada and Martínez, "Plática con Rubén Aguilar," Part 3.

179. Sánchez Cerén, *Con sueños*, 273.

180. Peña, *Retazos de mi vida,* 222 and 235.

181. Sánchez Cerén, *Con sueños*, 261–62.

182. Interview with Nidia Díaz in Morgan and Cargo, *Mothers in Arms*, 45. In another interview, Díaz admits to facing some additional challenges as a female comandante during the war, although she generally tends to adhere to her overall positive portrayal of the guerrillas' position on gender equity. See Phillips, "Nidia Diaz."

183. Peña, *Retazos de mi vida,* 208.

184. Arauz, Lemus, and Meza, "Plática con Lorena Peña," Part 4.

185. See Samayoa interview in Ueltzen, *Conversatorio*, 161.

Chapter Six

1. For more about the dissemination of Amaya's original eyewitness *testimonio*, see Danner, *The Massacre at El Mozote*; Binford, *The El Mozote Massacre*; and Consalvi, *La terquedad del izote*, 81–91.

2. Mackenbach, "Realidad y ficción." See also Rodríguez, *Dividing the Isthmus*.

3. Dalton, *Miguel Mármol*.

4. López Vigil, *Don Lito de El Salvador*. For other early examples, see Hernández, *León de piedra*; and Alegría, *No me agarrón viva*. Although Alegría's work is focused on a guerrilla comandante, she includes interviews with poor Salvadorans that fit the criteria of testimonial. See also Carter, *A Dream Compels Us*.

5. Cayetano Carpio, *Secuestro y capucha*; A. G. Martínez, *Las cárceles clandestinas*; Díaz, *Nunca estuve sola*.

6. This term is found in Carillo, "Entre la historia."

7. For a look at this debate, see Beverley and Zimmerman, *Literature and Politics*, 190–93; and Tula and Stephen, *Hear My Testimony,* 225. Similar issues surround the novel *Un día de vida* (1980) by Manlio Argueta, which some scholars cite as an example of *testimonio,* while others do not.

8. Morgan and Cargo, *Mothers in Arms*; Martínez Peñate, *El Salvador, el soldado y la guerrillera*; Barba and Martínez, *Like Gold in the Fire*; Comunidades Eclesiales de Base del Norte de Morazán, *Tomamos la palabra*; and Consalvi, *Río de la memoria.*

9. Morgan and Cargo, *Mothers in Arms*, 92–93.

10. Flores Cruz, *Memorias de un soldado*, 119.

11. The collection of stories assembled by Captain Carlos Balmore Vigil, *Soldados en combate*, is something of an exception, because his sources are almost exclusively mid-level officers.

12. For the debate over the meaning and definition of "testimony," see Beverley and Zimmerman, *Literature and Politics*, 173, 177, and 178; Tula and Stephen, *Hear My Testimony*, 232; Mackenbach, "Realidad y ficción"; Zavala, "La nueva novela," 258; Logan, "Personal Testimony," 201, 207, and 208; and Cortez, "La realidad y otras ficciones."

13. Logan, "Personal Testimony," 204.

14. Barba and Martínez, *Like Gold in the Fire*, 16.

15. Pierre André Blondy, in Martínez Peñate, *El Salvador*, 1.

16. As just one example, in regard to Roque Dalton's role in shaping the final outcome of the *testimonio Miguel Mármol*, see Lindo Fuentes, Ching, and Lara, *Remembering a Massacre*.

17. Tula and Stephen, *Hear My Testimony*.

18. Martínez Peñate, *El Salvador*, 427.

19. Consalvi, *El río de la memoria*, 39.

20. Ibid., 24.

21. Vásquez, *Siete gorriones*, chapter 1.

22. Ibañez and Vázquez, *Y la montaña habló*, 39.

23. Martínez Peñate, *El Salvador*, 376–77.

24. Barba and Martínez, *Like Gold in the Fire*, 35.

25. Consejo de Mujeres Misioneras por la Paz, *La semilla que cayó*, 75–76. For an example of the problems afflicting the communities, see page 20, and for an example of the disappearances and tortures, see page 30.

26. Ibid., 43.

27. López Casanova, *El Salvador*, 21.

28. Martínez Peñate, *El Salvador*, 428.

29. Bonilla and Magaña, *Los años perdidos*, 63. For similar examples, see Vásquez, *Siete gorriones*, 115; and the narrations by Otilia and Leonardo, in Barba and Martínez, *Like Gold in the Fire*, 60 and 67.

30. Comunidades Eclesiales de Base del Norte de Morazán, *Tomamos la palabra*, 5.

31. Barba and Martínez, *Like Gold in the Fire*; and Consalvi, *El río de la memoria*. See also Consejo de Mujeres Misioneras por la Paz, *La semilla que cayó*.

32. Ibañez and Vázquez, *Y la montaña habló*, 41.

33. Vásquez, *Siete gorriones*, 168 and 267.

34. López Casanova, *El Salvador*, 68.

35. Vásquez, *Siete gorriones*, 253–55.

36. Bonilla and Magaña, *Los años perdidos*, 63.

37. Ibañez and Vázquez, *Y la montaña habló*, 42.

38. Ibañez and Vázquez, *Y la montaña habló*; Morgan and Cargo, *Mothers in Arms*; Comunidades Eclesiales de Base del Norte de Morazán. *Tomamos la palabra*; and Tula and Stephen, *Hear My Testimony*. See also Vásquez, Ibáñez, and Murguialday, *Mujeres—montaña*; and for a secondary study of female-centered testimonio, see Guzmán Orellana and Mendia Azkue, *Mujeres con Memoria*.

39. Tula and Stephen, *Hear My Testimony*, 226.

40. Vásquez, *Siete gorriones*, 193.

41. Bonilla and Magaña, *Los años perdidos*, 62.

42. Vásquez, *Siete gorriones*, 18, 19, 24, and 26. See also Guevara, Martínez, and Murcia, "Plática con 'Chiyo.'"

43. Gorkin, Pineda, and Leal, *From Grandmother to Granddaughter*, 139, 143, and 152.

44. Consalvi, *El río de la memoria*, 71, 76, and 93; Ibañez and Vázquez, *Y la montaña habló*, 9; Barba and Martínez, *Like Gold in the Fire*, 34.

45. Consalvi, *El río de la memoria*, 54–55.

46. Comunidades Eclesiales de Base del Norte de Morazán, *Tomamos la palabra*, 10.

47. Ibid., 35, 36, and 38.

48. Morgan and Cargo, *Mothers in Arms*, 25.

49. Consalvi, *El río de la memoria*, 95. For another example, see the narration by Claudia Pérez in Morgan and Cargo, *Mothers in Arms*. One of the compilers of *Mother in Arms* comments that she expected to see a more calculated decision to go to war on the part of her particular interviewee, but instead found that she was motivated by more immediate issues—reactive anger to a particular event. See Morgan and Cargo, *Mothers in Arms*, 98.

50. Rubio Serrano, *Rompiendo silencios*, 49 and 52; and interview with Miguel Ventura, April 16, 2008.

51. Consalvi, *El río de la memoria*, 65. For more on Father David Rodríguez, see Sánchez, *Priest Under Fire*. See also Doña Otilia's comment that as a result of Archbishop Oscar Romero's sermons "we began to be aware," in Barba and Martínez, *Like Gold in the Fire*, 22. See also references to a process of *despertar* (awakening) among the liberation theology-oriented narrators in Consejo de Mujeres Misioneras por la Paz, *La semilla que cayó*, 43 and 68.

52. Gorkin and Pineda, *From Beneath the Volcano*, 14.

53. Ibid., 99.

54. Morgan and Cargo, *Mothers in Arms*, 65 and 67. As another example, see the testimonial by Manuel Majano in which he expresses his opposition to his father's deference to landowners and his acquisition of an alternative, politicized consciousness, in Consalvi, *El río de la memoria*, 48–58.

55. Morgan and Cargo, *Mothers in Arms*, 67.

56. Consalvi, *El río de la memoria*, 81.

57. Comunidades Eclesiales de Base del Norte de Morazán, *Tomamos la palabra*, 41.

58. Martínez Peñate, *El Salvador*, 412.

59. Tula and Stephen, *Hear My Testimony*, 43.

60. Inteview with Fidel Recinos, June 19, 2009.

61. As recorded in Rico Mira, *En silencio*, 265.

62. See Chávez, "Pedagogy of Revolution"; Binford, "Peasants, Catechists and Revolutionaries"; and Gould and Consalvi, *La palabra en el bosque*. Gould advanced this thesis in the case of Nicaragua in *To Lead as Equals*.

63. See David Stoll's study of the Guatemalan civil war, *Between Two Armies*.

64. Consejo de Mujeres Misioneras por la Paz, *La semilla que cayó*, 56.

65. Ibid., 82–84. For references to the strategic shift in 1984 and the decline in morale, see pages 167 and 186–88. For references to the 1989 offensive as a highpoint, see page 257. Carlos Bonilla refers to the 1981–1983 period as a sort of highpoint, when the army had to fight the guerrillas straight up—see Bonilla and Magaña, *Los años perdidos*, 93. Another rare exception is provided by Luis Caravantes in López Casanova, *El Salvador*, 35–69.

66. Vásquez, *Siete gorriones*, 290–91 and 302–303.

67. Ibid., 213 and 215. He says that not until he was transferred to work with the Radio Venceremos team did he ever spend much time in the presence of urbanites.

68. Ibid., 156, 189–90, 192, 214, 238, 251, 253, and 282.

69. Ibid., 123, 233, 251, 302, 313, and 324. Chiyo distinguishes his opposition to his former comandantes from the likes of Marvin Galeas, whom he describes as "that ego that was always about me me me." See Guevara, Martínez, and Murcia, "Plática con 'Chiyo,' " 7.

70. Barba and Martínez, *Like Gold in the Fire*, 45. For similar claims from other members of the FPL, see Ward, *Missing Mila*.

71. Martínez Peñate, *El Salvador*, 412 and 429.

72. Ibañez and Vázquez, *Y la montaña habló*, 30.

73. Ibañez and Vázquez, *Y la montaña habló*, 34. Here, of course, is a narration that has the potential to divide the rank-and-file community along gender lines. Her criticisms of sexism come within the context of criticizing the comandantes, but her critique broadens discursively to include all men, regardless of rank.

74. Gorkin and Pineda, *Beneath the Volcano*, 14 and 34.

75. Morgan and Cargo, *Mothers in Arms*, 25.

76. Vásquez, *Siete gorriones*, 141.

77. See, for example, Luís in Gorkin and Pineda, *Beneath the Volcano*, 28; and Vásquez, *Siete gorriones*, 244–46.

78. Martínez Peñate, *El Salvador*, 397, 400, and 405. —> Managua as FPL intrigue, conspiracy

79. Bonilla and Magaña, *Los años perdidos*, 42.

80. Vásquez, *Siete gorriones*, 169.

81. Ibañez and Vázquez, *Y la montaña habló*, 30 and 33–34.

82. Consejo de Mujeres Misioneras por la Paz, *La semilla que cayó*, 62. The same claim is made by the narrator "El Negro," from the La Fosa neighborhood on page 39.

83. Morgan and Cargo, *Mothers in Arms*, 27–28.

84. Gorkin, Pineda, and Leal, *From Grandmother to Granddaughter*, 156.

85. Gorkin and Pineda, *Beneath the Volcano*, 68.

86. Ibid., 34.

87. Vásquez, *Siete gorriones*, 237; see also 308–12.

88. Martínez Peñate, *El Salvador*, 431.

89. As one other example, see the *testimonio* of Manuel, who comments on still lacking land after the war, in López Casanova, *El Salvador*, 84.

90. Consejo de Mujeres Misioneras por la Paz, *La semilla que cayó*, 39.

91. Martínez Peñate, *El Salvador*, 16.

92. Herard Von Santos, a memoirst and former officer in the Atlacatl Battalion, disputes the veracity of the second narration. See the post on his blogspot, "Soldado y Guerrillera," September 27, 2013, http://herard-elfusilylapluma.blog spot.com/search?updated-max=2013-10-08T11:57:00-06:00&max-results=7 &start=7&by-date=false.

93. For information about Martínez's use of pseudonyms, see Martínez Peñate, *El Salvador*, 17.

94. Ibid., 21.

95. Ibid., 36 and 85.

96. Ibid., 28 and 30.

97. Ibid., 39, 54, and 101.

98. Ibid., 123, 134, and 138.

99. Ibid., 166 and 180.

100. Ibid., 144 and 153.

101. Ibid., 170.

102. Ibid., 179 and 180.

Conclusion

1. For just a few examples, see Galeas, *Héroes bajo sospecha*; Galindo Doucette, "Silencios y tabúes"; and Flores García, "La caza del coronel Montano."

2. Sprenkels, "Roberto d'Aubuisson vs Schafik Handal," 1.

3. Ibid., 26–27.

4. See Sprenkels, "Revolution and Accommodation"; Moodie, *El Salvador in the Aftermath of Peace*; Silber, *Everyday Revolutionaries*; and DeLugan, *Reimagining National Belonging*.

5. Stern, *Remembering Pinochet's Chile*, 102.

6. For more on the issue of gender in the Salvadoran civil war and in postwar memory, see Padilla, *Changing Women*; Shayne, *The Revolution Question*; Viterna, *Women in War*; Kampwirth, *Women & Guerrilla Movements*, and *Feminism and the Legacy of Revolution*.

7. Vaquerano and Lemus, "Plática con diputado Sigifredo Ochoa Pérez," Part 2. On the complex politics of the memorialization of Monterrosa, see Alvarado, "$20 mil gastó gobierno de Funes." See also, http://www.domingomon terrosa.info.

8. Panamá Sandoval, *Guerreros de la libertad*.

9. Duarte, *Duarte*; Rey Prendes, *De la dictadura*; the interview with Valle appears in Ueltzen, *Conversatorio*, 56–74; and Guerra y Guerra, *Un golpe al amanecer*.

10. Duarte, *Duarte*, 33.

11. Rey Prendes, *De la dictadura*, 325–28.

12. The interview with Rodríguez appears in Ueltzen, *Conversatorio*, 245–68; Sprenkels, *Caminar con el pueblo*; Alas, *Iglesia, tierra y lucha campesina*; and López Vigil, *Muerte y vida*.

13. Ueltzen, *Conversatorio*, 11.

14. Sprenkels, *Caminar con el pueblo*, 3.

15. Frazier, *El Salvador Could be Like That*; and Brenneman, *Perquín Musings*.

16. Montecinos, *Arriesgar la vida*; and Ibarra Chávez, *Historias de barro*.

17. Molloy, *At Face Value*, 6; Irwin-Zarecka, *Frames of Remembrance*, 8; see also 60–116 for broader elaborations on this issue. See also Stern, *Remembering Pinochet's Chile*.

18. Valencia and Martínez, "Plática con Orlando de Sola."

19. Dada, "Entrevista con teniente coronel Camilo Hernández."

20. Zepeda Herrera, *Perfiles de la guerra*, 217.

21. See, for example, Santos, "Eliminar la amnistía no es ningún error"; Vaquerano et al., "Plática con general Mauricio Vargas"; González, "Sánchez Cerén."

22. Zepeda Herrera, *Perfiles de la guerra*, 299.

23. See Villalobos's interview with Marta Harnecker in Dixon and Jonas, *Revolution and Intervention*, 77–78.

24. Espinosa, *Relatos de la guerra*; Rico Mira, *En silencio*, 332.

25. Medrano Guzmán, *Memorias de un guerrillero*, 108–11.

26. Sancho, *Crónicas entre espejos*, 75.

27. Sánchez Cerén, *Con sueños*; Peña, *Retazos de mi vida*.

Bibliography

Document/Archival Collections

Library of Congress.
    "Mexican and Central American Political and Social Ephemera, 1980–1991,
    Central America, Salvadoran Revolutionary Pamphlets." Washington, DC:
    Library of Congress Preservation Microfilming Program, 1992.
National Security Archive (NSA), George Washington University.
    "El Salvador: The Making of U.S. Policy, 1977–1984."
    "El Salvador: War, Peace and Human Rights, 1980–1994."
North American Congress on Latin America (NACLA)
    "El Salvador." 30 microfilm reels, Wilmington, DE: Scholarly Resources, 1997.
        "The Shevardnadze File."
United Nations Document Center
    "Yale-UN Oral history Project: Central America."

Interviews

Anonymous former guerrilla, member of an ERP surface-to-air missile team,
    March 17, 2008, Perquín El Salvador, interview by the author.
Galindo, Marisol, March 23, 2008, Perquín, Morazán, El Salvador, interview by
    the author.
Polombo, Gene, March 14, 2012, San Salvador, interview by the author.
Recinos, Fidel, June 19, 2009, San Salvador, interview by the author.
Ventura, Miguel, April 16, 2008, Ciudad Segundo Montes, Morazán, El Salvador,
    interview by the author.
Walter, Knut, March 19, 2008, San Salvador, interview by the author.

Periodicals

Contrapunto (San Salvador, El Salvador)
Diario de Santa Ana (Santa Ana, El Salvador)
Diario1.com (San Salvador, El Salvador)
DiarioCoLatino (San Salvador, El Salvador)
El Diario de Hoy (San Salvador, El Salvador)
El Faro (San Salvador, El Salvador)

La Página (San Salvador, El Salvador)
La Prensa Gráfica (San Salvador, El Salvador)
New York Times (New York, New York, USA)

Published Sources

Acosta, Antonio. *Los orígenes de la burguesía de El Salvador: El control sobre el café y el Estado, 1848–1890.* Seville, Spain: Anaconga Libros, 2013.

Alas, José Inocencio. *Iglesia, tierra y lucha campesina: Suchitoto, El Salvador, 1968–1977.* El Salvador: Asociación de Frailes Franciscanos, 2003.

Albiac, M. Dolores. "Los ricos más ricos de El Salvador." *Estudios Centroamericanos (ECA)* 54, 612 (1999): 814–64.

Alegría, Claribel. *No me agarrón viva: La mujer salvadoreña en lucha.* Mexico City: Editorial Era, 1983.

Allier-Montaño, Eugenia, and Emilio Crenzel, eds. *The Struggle for Memory in Latin America: Recent History and Political Violence.* New York: Palgrave Macmillan, 2015.

Almeida, Paul. *Waves of Protest: Popular Struggle in El Salvador, 1925–2005.* Minneapolis: University of Minnesota Press, 2008.

Alvarado, Jimmy. "$20 mil gastó gobierno de Funes en informe que recomienda continuar el culto a Domingo Monterrosa." *El Faro*, January 12, 2015, http://www.elfaro.net/es/201501/noticias/16323/$20-mil-gast%C3%B3 -gobierno-de-Funes-en-informe-que-recomienda-continuar-el-culto-a -Domingo-Monterrosa.htm.

Alvarenga, Luis. *Roque Dalton: La radicalización de las vanguardias.* San Salvador: Editorial Universidad Don Bosco, 2011.

Alvarenga, Patricia. *Cultura y ética de la violencia: El Salvador, 1880–1932.* San José, Costa Rica: Editorial Universitaria Centroamericana, 1996.

Álvarez, Alberto Martín. "Del partido a guerrilla: Los orígenes de las Fuerzas Populares de Liberación Farabundo Martí (FPL)." In *Historia y debates sobre el conflicto armado salvadoreño y sus secuelas,* edited by Jorge Juárez Avila, 55–62. San Salvador: Universidad de El Salvador and Fundación Friedrich Ebert, 2014.

Álvarez, Alberto Martín, and Eudald Cortina Orero. "The Genesis and Internal Dynamics of El Salvador's People's Revolutionary Army, 1970–1976." *Journal of Latin American Studies* 46, no. 4 (November 2014): 663–89.

Anderson, Benedict. *Imagined Communities: Reflections on the Origin and Spread of Nationalism.* London: Verso, 1983.

Arauz, Sergio, and Mauro Arias. "Plática con Humberto Centeno." *El Faro*, March 7, 2010, http://www.elfaro.net/es/201003/el_agora/1305/.

Arauz, Sergio, and César Castro Fagoaga. "Plática con Francisco Jovel." *El Faro*, April 24, 2007, http://archivo.elfaro.net/Secciones/platicas/20060424 /Platicas1_20060424.asp.

Arauz, Sergio, Efrén Lemus, and Frederick Meza. "Plática con Lorena Peña." *El Faro*, May 3, 2011, http://www.elfaro.net/es/201104/el_agora/4025/.

Arauz, Sergio, and Ricardo Vaquerano. "Plática con Gerardo Le Chevallier." *El Faro*, January 10, 2010, http://www.elfaro.net/es/201001/el_agora/906/.

Archibald, Randal. "Homicides in El Salvador Dip, and Questions Arise." *New York Times*, March 24, 2012, http://www.nytimes.com/2012/03/25 /world/americas/homicides-in-el-salvador-drop-and-questions-arise.html ?_r=0.

Argueta, Manlio. *Un día en la vida*. San Salvador: UCA Editores, 1980.

Arnson, Cynthia, and Eric Olson, Steven Dudley, James Bosworth, Douglas Farah, and Julie López, eds. "Organized Crime in Central America: The Northern Triangle." Woodrow Wilson Center Reports on the Americas no. 29, November 2011, https://www.wilsoncenter.org/publication/organized -crime-central-america-the-northern-triangle.

Assmann, Jan. *Religion and Cultural Memory: Ten Studies*. Stanford: Stanford University Press, 2006.

Atencio, Rebecca. *Memory's Turn: Reckoning with Dictatorship in Brazil*. Madison: University of Wisconsin Press, 2014.

Ayalá, Berne. *Al tope y más alla: Testimonio de la guerrilla salvadoreña desde la ofensiva de 1989 a los acuerdos de paz*. 3rd ed. San Salvador: Cipitío Editores, 2005 [1996].

———. *En el silencio de la batalla: Un relato sobre la guerra civil salvadoreña*. San Salvador: Editorial Expedición Americana, 2014.

———. *Entre Marilyn Monroe y la revolución*. San Salvador: eXa Editores, 2010.

Bacevich, Andrew J., James D. Hallums, Richard H. White, and Thomas F. Young. *American Military Policy in Small Wars: The Case of El Salvador*. Institute for Foreign Policy Analysis Special Report. Washington, DC: Pergamon-Brassey's, 1988.

Bal, Mieke. *Narratology: An Introduction to the Theory of Narrative*. Toronto: University of Toronto Press, 1985.

Baloyra, Enrique. *El Salvador in Transition*. Chapel Hill: University of North Carolina, 1982.

Barba, Jaime. "Los movimientos sociales." In *Los movimientos sociales en sociedades posbélicas: La experiencia de El Salvador*, edited by Alexander Segovia, 33–60. San Salvador: FLACSO El Salvador, 2015.

Barba, Maribel, and Concha Martínez. *Like Gold in the Fire: Voices of Hope from El Salvador: War Exile and Return, 1974–1999*. Birmingham, UK: Nueva Esperanza Support Group, 1999. Published originally in Spanish as *De la memoria nace la esperanza*. San Salvador: Taller y Arte Gráfico, 1997.

Beetham, David. *Politics and Human Rights*. Oxford, U.K: Blackwell Publishers, 1995.

Beverley, John, and Marc Zimmerman. *Literature and Politics in the Central American Revolutions*. Austin: University of Texas Press, 1990.

Binford, Leigh. *The El Mozote Massacre: Anthropology and Human Rights*. Tuscon: University of Arizona Press, 1996.

——. "Grassroots Development in Conflict Zones of Northeastern El Salvador." *Latin American Perspectives* 24, no. 2 (March 1997): 56–79.

——. "Hegemony in the Interior of the Revolution: The ERP in Northern Morazán, El Salvador." *Journal of Latin American Anthropology* 4, no. 1 (1999): 2–45.

——. "Peasants, Catechists and Revolutionaries: Organic Intellectuals in the Salvadoran Revolution, 1980–1992." In *Landscapes of Struggle: Politics, Society and Community in El Salvador*, edited by Aldo Lauria and Leigh Binford, 105–25. Pittsburgh: University of Pittsburgh Press, 2004.

Bonilla, Carlos, and Jesús Magaña. *Los años perdidos: Vivencias de Carlos Bonilla—ex guerrillero de El Salvador*. Mexico: Jemcab Producciones, 2005.

Bosch, Brian J. *The Salvadoran Officer Corps & the Final Offensive of 1981*. Jefferson, NC: McFarland, 1999.

Brenneman, Ron. *Perquín Musings: A Gringo's Journey in El Salvador*. El Salvador: printed by author, 2013.

Brockett, Charles. *Political Movements and Violence in Central America*. New York: Cambridge University Press, 2005.

Bull, Benedicte. "Diversified Business Groups and the Transnationalisation of the Salvadorean Economy," *Journal of Latin American Studies* 45, no. 2 (May 2013): 265–95.

Bulmer-Thomas, Victor. *The Political Economy of Central America Since 1920*. New York: Cambridge University Press, 1987.

Byrne, Hugh. *El Salvador's Civil War: A Study of Revolution*. Boulder, CO: Lynne Rienner, 1996.

Byron, Kristine. *Women, Revolution and Autobiographical Writing in the Twentieth Century: Writing History, Writing the Self*. Lewiston, NY: Edwin Mellon, 2007.

Cabarrús, Carlos Rafael. *Génesis de una revolución*. Mexico: CIESAS, 1983.

Cabrera, Mario E. *Piruetas*. 2nd ed., San Salvador: Palibrio, 2012.

Calhoun, Craig. Introduction to *Habermas and the Public Sphere*. Edited by Craig Calhoun, 1–48. Cambrdige, MA: MIT Press, 1992.

Call, Charles T. "Democratisation, War and State-Building: Constructing the Rule of Law in El Salvador." *Journal of Latin American Studies* 35, no. 4 (November 2003): 827–62.

Campos, Rodolfo. *El Salvador entre el terror y la esperanza: Los sucesos de 1979 y su impacto en el drama salvadoreño de los años siguientes*. San Salvador: UCA Editores, 1982.

Cañadas, Arquímedes Antonio. *Sueños y lágrimas de un guerrillero: Un testimonio sobre el conflicto en El Salvador*. San Salvador: n.p, 2013.

Cárdenal, Rodolfo. *Historia de una esperanza: Vida de Rutilio Grande*. 3rd ed. San Salvador: UCA Editores, 2002.

Carranza Bonilla, José Manuel, and Ana Margarita Chávez Escobar. *Las 100 historias que siempre quise saber: Personas exitosas de El Salvador.* San Salvador: Editorial GTC, 2011.

Carrillo, José Domingo. "Entre la historia y la memoria—entrevista y revolución: Estudio de las elites políticas revolucionarias en Guatemala, 1960–1996." *Istmo* 2 (July–December 2001), http://istmo.denison.edu/n02/articulos/elites.html.

Carter, Brenda. *A Dream Compels Us: Voices of Salvadoran Women.* Boston: New Americas Press, 1989.

Castellaños, Juan Mario. *El Salvador, 1930–1960: Antecedentes históricos de la guerra civil.* San Salvador: Dirección de Publicaciones, 2001.

Castro Fagoaga, César. "Mayo Sibrián, el carnicero de la Paracentral." *El Faro,* January 15, 2007, http://archivo.elfaro.net/secciones/noticias/20070115/noticias3_20070115.asp.

———. "Plática con Adolfo Torrez." *El Faro,* August 21, 2006, http://archivo.elfaro.net/Secciones/platicas/20060821/Platicas1_20060821.asp.

Castro Fagoaga, César, and Daniel Valenica. "Plática con Mario Acosta Oertel, ex ministro del Interior." *El Faro,* October 23, 2006, http://archivo.elfaro.net/Secciones/platicas/20061023/Platicas1_20061023.asp.

Cayetano Carpio, Salvador. *Listen Compañero: Conversations with Central American Revolutionary Leaders.* San Francisco: Center for the Study of the Americas, 1983.

———. *Nuestras montañas son las masas: Salvador Cayetano Carpio-Comandante Marcial, documentos y escritos de la revolución.* Vienna: Corriente Leninista Internacional, 1999.

———. *Secuestro y capucha.* Quito: Editorial Conejo, 1982 [1967].

Centro de Documentación de los Movimientos Armados (CEDEMA). *Comandante Obrero: Salvador Cayetano Carpio.* 2nd ed. N.p.: CEDEMA, 2011, http://www.cedema.org/ver.php?id=4581.

Chatman, Seymour. *Story and Discourse: Narrative Structure in Fiction and Film.* Ithaca, NY: Cornell University Press, 1980.

Chávez, Joaquín. "How Did the Civil War in El Salvador End? . . . Not So Well." *American Historical Review* 120:5 (December, 2015): 1784–1797.

Chávez Velasco, Waldo. *Lo que no conté sobre los presidentes militares.* San Salvador: Indole Editores, 2006.

Ching, Erik. *Authoritarian El Salvador: Politics and the Making of the Military Regimes, 1880–1940.* South Bend, IN: University of Notre Dame Press, 2013.

Ching, Erik, Christina Buckley, and Angélica Lozano-Alonso, eds. *Reframing Latin America: A Cultural Theory Reading of the Nineteenth and Twentieth Centuries.* Austin: University of Texas Press, 2007.

Ching, Erik, Virginia Tilley, and Carlos Gregorio López Bernál. *Las masas, la matanza y el Martinato: Ensayos sobre 1932.* San Salvador, El Salvador: UCA Editores, 2007.

Colindres, Eduardo. *Fundamentos económicos de la burguesía salvadoreña.* San Salvador: UCA Editores, 1977.

Comité Central del Partido Comunista de El Salvador. *45 Años de sacrificada lucha revolucionaria.* 2nd ed. San Salvador: Publicaciones del Partido Comunista de El Salvador, 1976.

Comunidades Eclesiales de Base del Norte de Morazán. *Tomamos la palabra: Testimonios de mujeres de las Comunidades Eclesiales de Base del Norte de Morazán.* San Salvador: UCA Editores, 2001.

Consalvi, Carlos Henríquez. *La terquedad del izote: El Salvador, crónica de una victoria.* Mexico: Editorial Diana, 1992. Published in English as *Broadcasting the Civil War in El Salvador.* Translated by Charlie Nagle and Bill Prince. Austin: University of Texas Press, 2010.

——, ed. *El río de la memoria: Historia oral del Bajo Lempa, Zona Tecoluca.* San Salvador: MUPI, 2011.

Consejo de Mujeres Misioneras por la Paz (eds.). *La semilla que cayó en tierra fértil: Testimonios de miembros de las comunidades cristianas.* San Salvador: Consejo de Mujeres Misioneras por la Paz, 1996.

Corado Figueroa, Humberto. *En defensa de la patria: Historia del conflicto armado en El Salvador, 1980–1992.* San Salvador: Universidad Tecnológica de El Salvador, 2008.

Córdova Macías, Ricardo, and Carlos Ramos. "The Peace Process and the Construction of Democracy." In *In Wake of War: Democratization and Internal Armed Conflict in Central America,* edited by Cynthia Arnson, 79–106. Stanford, CA: Stanford University Press, 2012.

Cortez, Beatriz. "La realidad y otras ficciones: Visiones críticas sobre el testimonio centroamericano." *Istmo* 2 (July–December 2001), http://istmo .denison.edu/no2/articulos/testim.html.

Cortez Ruiz, Israel Enrique. "La memoria desde las élites: Un acercamiento a las memorias del conflicto armado salvadoreño en Salvador Sánchez Cerén y Ricardo Valdivieso Oriani." Paper presented at the XII Congreso Centroamericano de Historia, San Salvador, El Salvador, July 15–18, 2014.

Craft, Linda J. *Novels of Testimony and Resistance from Central America.* Gainesville: University Press of Florida, 1997.

Dada, Carlos. "Entrevista con teniente coronel Camilo Hernández." *El Faro,* June 6, 2011, http://www.elfaro.net/es/201106/noticias/4323/.

——. "How We Killed the Archbishop." *El Faro,* March 25, 2010, http://www .elfaro.net/es/201003/noticias/1416.

Dada, Carlos, and Oscar Martinez. "Plática con Rubén Aguilar." *El Faro,* December 17, 2010, http://www.elfaro.net/es/201012/el_agora/3125/.

Dalton, Roque. *Las historias prohibidas del pulgarcito.* Mexico: Siglo Veintiuno Editores, 1974.

——. *Miguel Mármol: Los sucesos de 1932 en El Salvador.* San José, Costa Rica: Editorial Universitaria Centroamericana, 1972. Published in English as

Miguel Mármol. Translated by Kathleen Ross and Richard Schaff. Willimatic, CT: Curbstone Press, 1987.

Dalton, Roque, John Beverley, and Edward Baker. "Poems." *Social Text* 5 (Spring 1982): 74–85.

Danner, Mark. *The Massacre at El Mozote.* New York: Vintage, 1994.

DeLugan, Robin. *Reimagining National Belonging: Post-Civil War El Salvador in a Global Context.* Tuscon: University of Arizona Press, 2012.

———. "Museums, Memory, and the Just Nation in Post-Civil War El Salvador." *Museums and Society* 13(3): 272–85.

Department of Social Sciences, Universidad de El Salvador. "An Analysis of the Correlation of Forces in El Salvador." *Latin American Perspectives* 14, no. 4 (1987): 426–52.

Díaz, Nidia. *Nunca estuve sola.* San Salvador: Editorial UCA, 1988. Published in English as *I Was Never Alone: A Prison Diary from El Salvador.* New York: Ocean Press, 1992.

Dixon, Marlene, and Susanne Jonas, eds. *Revolution and Intervention in Central America.* San Francisco: Synthesis, 1983.

Doggett, Martha. *Death Foretold: The Jesuit Murders in El Salvador.* Washington, DC: Georgetown University Press, 1993.

Duarte, José Napoleón. *Duarte: My Story.* New York: Putnam, 1986.

Dunkerley, James. *The Long War: Dictatorship and Revolution in El Salvador.* London: Junction Books, 1982.

El Faro. "¿Dónde están los firmantes?" *El Faro,* January 15, 2007, http://archivo .elfaro.net/secciones/noticias/20070115/firmantes.html.

El Salvador, Asamblea Legislativa. *Memoria del primer congreso nacional de reforma agraria.* San Salvador: Publicaciones de la Asamblea Legislativa, 1970.

Escalante Arce, Luis. *Sacrificios humanos contra derechos humanos: Relato del secuestro de un banquero salvadoreño.* 2nd ed. San Salvador: EDILIT, 1991 [1986].

Escalona Terrón, María Teresa. *Radio Farabundo Martí . . . en la memoria.* San Salvador: FundAbril, 2014.

Espinoza, Eduardo. *Relatos de la guerra.* San Salvador: Imprenta y Editorial Universitaria, 2007.

Flores Cruz, René Obdulio. *Memorias de un soldado.* San Salvador: by author, 2009.

Flores García, Víctor. "La caza del coronel Montano." *El País,* August 28, 2013, http://internacional.elpais.com/internacional/2013/08/28/actualidad /1377658665_012327.html.

Foley, Michael. "Laying the Groundwork: The Struggle for Civil Society in El Salvador." *Journal of InterAmerican Studies and World Affairs* 38, no. 1 (1996): 67–104.

Frazier, Joseph. *El Salvador Could Be Like That: A Memoir of War, Politics and Journalism on the Front-Row of the Last Bloody Conflict of the US-Soviet Cold War.* Ojai, CA: Karina Library Press, 2013.

Frazier, Leslie Jo. *Salt in the Sand: Memory, Violence and the Nation-State in Chile, 1890 to the Present*. Durham, NC: Duke University Press, 2007.

Galán, Jorge. *Noviembre*. Mexico: Planeta, 2015.

Galeas, Geovani. "Mayor Roberto D'Abuisson: El rostro más allá del mito." *La Prensa Gráfica*. Edición Especial, November 7, 2004.

———. *Héroes bajo sospecha: El lado oscuro de la guerra salvadoreña*. San Salvador: Athena, 2013.

Galeas, Geovani, and Edwin Ernesto Ayala. *Grandeza y miseria en una guerrilla*. 2nd ed. San Salvador: Centroamérica 21, 2008.

Galeas, Geovani, and Marvin Galeas. *Las claves de una derrota*. San Salvador: Editorial Cinco, 2009.

Galeas, Marvin. *Crónicas de guerra*. San Salvador: Editorial Cinco, 2008.

———. "De carne y hueso." *Diario de Hoy*, June 17, 2009, http://www.elsalvador .com/mwedh/nota/nota_opinion.asp?idCat=6342&idArt=3740533.

Galeas, Marvin, and Guillermo Sol Bang. *Sol y acero: La vida de Don Guillermo Sol Bang*. San Salvador: Editorial Cinco, 2011.

Galeas, Marvin, and José Ramón Barahona. *The Possible Dream: The Life of José Ramón Barahona*. Translated by Margaret Carson. San Salavdor: Colleciones Grandes Centoamericanos, 2007. Published in Spanish as *El sueño posible: La vida de José Ramón Barahona*. San Salvador: s.n., 2006.

Galindo Doucette, Evelyn. "Silencios y tabúes de la guerra de los 80," *Contracultura*, June 30, 2013, http://www.contracultura.com.sv/silencios-y -tabues-de-la-guerra-de-los-80.

Galindo Pohl, Raynaldo. *Recuerdos de sonsonate: Crónica del 32*. San Salvador: Tecnograf, 2001.

García Dueñas, Lauri, and Javier Espinoza. *Quién asesinó a Roque Dalton? Mapa de un largo silencio*. San Salvador: Indole Editores, 2010.

Garner, Dwight. "The Tracks of an Author's, and a Reader's, Tears." *New York Times*, March 27, 2012, http://www.nytimes.com/2012/03/28/books/wild-by -cheryl-strayed-a-walkabout-of-reinvention.html?pagewanted=all.

Geddes, Barbara. *Politician's Dilemma: Building State Capacity in Latin America*. Berkeley: University of California Press, 1996.

Gilbert, Laura. "El Salvador's Death Squads: New Evidence from U.S. Documents," Center for International Policy, March, 1994, http://www .ciponline.org/dethsqud.txt.

Gilman, Nils. *Mandarins of the Future: Modernization Theory in Cold War America*. New Studies in American Intellectual and Cultural History. Baltimore: Johns Hopkins University Press, 2004.

Gómez-Barris, Macarena. *Where Memory Dwells: Culture and State Violence in Chile*. Berkeley: University of California Press, 2009.

Gómez Zimmerman, Mario. *Adelante Occidente*. Miami: Editorial SIBI, 1988. Published in English as *Power to the West! A Study in Nomocracy*. Translated by Zusel Pordominsky. New York: Vantage, 1997.

——. *El Salvador: Who Speaks for the People?* Translated by Zusel Pordominsky. Miami: Editorial SIBI, 1989. Published in Spanish as *El Salvador: La otra cara de la guerra.* Miami: Editorial SIBI, 1986.

González, Douglas. "Sánchez Cerén: Hay presiones para derogar la Ley de Amnistia." *La Página,* January 20, 2012, http://www.lapagina.com.sv /nacionales/61276/2012/01/19/Sanchez-Ceren-Hay-presiones-para-derogar -la-Ley-de-Amnistia.

González, Medardo, Roberto Regalado, and Roberto Regalado Álvarez. *Memorias del camino para compartir: Entrevista con Medardo González, [alias] comandante Milton Méndez.* San Salvador: Editorial Morazán, 2010.

Goodland, Robert. "Cerrón Grande Hydroelectric Project: Environmental Impact Reconnaissance." Washington, DC: The World Bank, April 1973.

Goodwin, Jeff. *No Other Way Out: States and Revolutionary Movements, 1945–1991.* New York: Cambridge University Press, 2001.

Gordon, Sara. *Crisis política y guerra en El Salvador.* Mexico: Siglo Veintiuno Editores, 1989.

Gorkin, Michael, and Marta Pineda. *From Beneath the Volcano: The Story of a Salvadoran Campesino and His Family.* Tucson: University of Arizona Press, 2011.

Gorkin, Michael, Marta Pineda, and Gloria Leal. *From Grandmother to Granddaughter: Salvadoran Women's Stories.* Berkeley: University of California Press, 2000.

Gould, Jeffrey. *To Lead as Equals: Rural Protest and Political Consciousness in Chinandega, Nicaragua, 1912–1979.* Chapel Hill: University of North Carolina Press, 1990.

Gould, Jeffrey, and Aldo Lauria. *To Rise in Darkness: Revolution, Repression and Memory in El Salvador, 1920–1932.* Durham, NC: Duke University Press, 2008.

Gould, Jeffrey, and Carlos Henríquez Consalvi. *La palabra en el bosque* [*The Word in the Woods*]. New York: Films Media Groups, 2012. DVD, 57 min.

Gready, Paul. *Era of Transitional Justice: The Aftermath of the Truth and Reconciliation Commission in South Africa and Beyond.* New York: Routledge, 2011.

Grenier, Yvon. *The Emergence of Insurgency in El Salvador: Ideology and Political Will.* Pittsburgh: University of Pittsburgh Press, 1999.

Gross, Jan. *Neighbors: the destruction of the Jewish community in Jedwabne, Poland.* Princeton, NJ: Princeton University Press, 2002.

Gudmundson, Lowell. *Costa Rica Before Coffee: Society and Economy on the Eve of the Export Boom.* Baton Rouge: Louisiana State University Press, 1977.

Guerra Calderón, Walter. *Asociaciones comunitarias en el área rural de El Salvador en la década 1960–1970: Análisis de las condiciones que enmarcan su desarrollo.* San José, Costa Rica: CSUCA, Programa Centroamericano de Ciencias Sociales, 1976.

Guerra, Tomás. *El Salvador, octubre sangriento: Itinerario y análisis del golpe militar del 15 de octubre de 1979*. San José, Costa Rica: Centro Víctor Sanabria: Distribución de Ediciones Revista Respuesta, 1979.

Guerra y Guerra, Rodrigo. *Un golpe al amanecer: La verdadera historia de la Proclama del 15 de Octubre de 1979*. San Salvador: Indole Editores, 2009.

Guevara, Christian. "Entrevista con el general Juan Orlando Zepeda." *El Faro*, July 10, 2009, http://archivo.elfaro.net/dlgalp/contrainsurgencia/gjoc.asp.

———. "Entrevista con Gersón Martínez." *El Faro*, n.d., http://www.elfaro.net /dlgalp/contrainsurgencia/gm.asp.

———. "María Luisa d'Aubuisson Arrieta." *El Faro*, February 28, 2005, http:// archivo.elfaro.net/dlgalp/romero/R_D.asp.

Guevara, Christian, and José Luis Sanz, "Plática con Emilio Mena Sandoval, 'Manolo.'" *El Faro*, August 25, 2003, http://archivo.elfaro.net/secciones /Noticias/20030825/Platicas1_20030825.asp.

Guevara, Christian, Oscar Martínez, and Diego Murcia. "Entrevista con 'Chiyo.'" *El Faro*, November 22, 2004, http://archivo.elfaro.net/secciones /Noticias/20041122/Platicas1_20041122.asp#.

Gutiérrez, Dagoberto. "Carta a mi padre," *Servicio Informativo Ecumenico y Popular* (*SIEP*), December 3, 2012, http://ecumenico.org/article/carta-a-mi-padre/.

———. "22 años y la ofensiva se reanuda," *SIEP*, November 14, 2011, www .ecumenico.org/leer.php/2566#.

Gutiérrez, Jaime Abdul. *Message from the Vice President of the Revolutionary Government Junta of El Salvador*. San Salvador: Secretaría de Información de la Presidencia de la República, 1981.

———. *Testigo y actor: Una revisión de los antecedentes que nos han conducido a la situación actual de El Salvador*. San Salvador: Universidad Tecnológica de El Salvador, 2013.

Guzmán Orellana, Gloria, and Irantzu Mendia Azkue. *Mujeres con memoria: Activistas del movimiento de derechos humanos en El Salvador*. Bilbao: Hegoa, 2013.

Habermas, Jürgen. *The Structural Transformation of the Public Sphere: An Inquiry into a Category of Bourgeois Society*. Translated by T. Burger and F. Lawrence. Cambridge: Cambridge University Press, 1989.

Haglund, LaDawn. *Limiting Resources: Market-Led Reform and the Transformation of Public Goods*. University Park: Pennsylvania State University Press, 2010.

Hándal, Schafik. *Legado de un revolucionario: Del rescate de la historia a la construcción del futuro*. San Salvador: Ediciones Instituto Schafik Hándal, 2011.

Harnecker, Marta. *Con la mirada en alta: Historia de la FPL Farabundo Martí a través de sus dirigentes*. San Salvador: UCA Editores, 1993.

Hatcher, Rachel. "Mientras El Salvador olvida, Guatemala recuerda." *El Faro*, February 7, 2015, http://www.elfaro.net/es/201602/academico/17989 /Mientras-El-Salvador-olvida-Guatemala-recuerda.htm.

Heidenry, Rachel. "The Murals of El Salvador: Reconstruction, Historical Memory and Whitewashing." *Public Art Dialogue* 4, no. 1 (2014): 122–45.

Hernández, Alfonso. *León de piedra: Testimonios de la lucha de clases en El Salvador.* San Salvador: n.p., 1981.

Hernández Arias, Miguel. *Fenix: Cenizas de una operación estadounidenses.* CEDEMA, 1996, http://www.cedema.org/uploads/FENIX.pdf.

Hernández Pico, Juan, C. Jerez, E. Baltodano, I. Ellacuría, and R. Mayorga. *El Salvador: Año político, 1971–1972.* San Salvador: UCA Editores, 1973.

Hinds, Manuel. *Playing Monopoly with the Devil: Dollarization and Domestic Currencies in Developing Countries.* New Haven, CT: Yale University Press, 2006.

Holden, Robert. *Armies Without Nations: Public Violence and State Formation in Central America, 1821—1961.* New York: Oxford University Press, 2004.

Holland, Alisha. "Right on Crime? Conservative Party Politics and Mano Dura Policies in El Salvador." *Latin American Research Review* 48, no. 1 (Spring 2013): 44–67.

Hoselitz, Bert. *Industrial Development in El Salvador.* New York: United Nations, 1954.

Huezo Mixco, Luis, Carlos Pérez Pindea, Oscar Meléndez and Guillermo Cuéllar Barandiarán. *Coronel Ernesto Claramount Rozeville: Honor y compromiso.* San Salvador: Secretaría de Cultura de la Presidencia, Dirección Nacional de Investigaciones en Cultura y Arte, 2015.

Ibañez, Cristina, and Norma Vázquez. *Y la montaña habló: Testimonios de guerrilleras y colaboradores.* El Salvador: Las Dignas, 1997.

Ibarra Chávez, Héctor Angel. *Brigada Rafael Arce Zablah, ¡misión cumplida!: Una historia contada por sus protagonistas.* Mexico: Ediciones Expediente Abierto, 2009.

——. *Historias de barro y otros cuentos de la guerra en El Salvador: Memorias de un internacionalista.* Mexico City: Ediciones Expediente abierto, 2009.

Irwin-Zarecka, Iwona. *Frames of Remembrance: The Dynamics of Collective Memory.* New Brunswick: Transaction, 1994.

Jelin, Elizabeth. *State Repression and the Struggles for Memory.* London: Latin America Bureau, 2003.

Juárez Ávila, Jorge, ed. *Historia y debates sobre el conflicto armado salvadoreño y sus secuelas.* San Salvador: Universidad de El Salvador and Fundación Friedrich Ebert, 2014.

Kampwirth, Karen. *Women & Guerrilla Movements: Nicaragua, El Salvador, Chiapas, Cuba.* University Park: Pennsylvania State University Press, 2003.

——.*Feminism and the Legacy of Revolution: Nicaragua, El Salvador, Chiapas.* Athens: Ohio University Press, 2004.

Karl, Terry. "El Salvador's Negotiated Revolution." *Foreign Affairs* 71, no. 2 (Spring, 1992): 147–64.

——. "Negotiations or Total War: Salvador Samayoa Interviewed." *World Policy Journal* 6 (Spring 1989): 321–56.

Koivumaeki, Riitta-Ilona. "Business, Economic Experts, and Conservative Party Building in Latin America: The Case of El Salvador." *Journal of Politics in Latin America* 2, no. 1 (2010): 79–106.

Krujit, Dirk. *Guerrillas: War and Peace in Central America*. London: Zed Books, 2008.

Ladutke, Lawrence Michael. *Freedom of Expression in El Salvador: The Struggle for Human Rights and Democracy*. Jefferson, NC; McFarland and Co., 2004.

Lamperti, John. *Enrique Alvarez Córdova: Life of a Salvadoran Revolutionary and Gentleman*. Jefferson, NC: McFarland, 2006.

Lane, Charles. "Reclutar, desertar o anular." *Letras Libres* (October 2012): 60–65, http://www.letraslibres.com/revista/reportaje/reclutar-desertar-o-anular.

Lara Martínez, Rafael. *Del dictado: Miguel Mármol, Roque Dalton y 1932, del cuaderno (1966) a la 'novela-verdad' (1972)*. San Salvador: Editorial Universidad Don Bosco, 2007.

Lasalle-Klein, Robert. *Blood and Ink: Ignacio Ellacuria, Jon Sobrino, and the Jesuit Martyrs of the University of Central America*. Maryknoll, NY: Orbis Books, 2014.

Lauria, Aldo. *An Agrarian Republic: Commercial Agriculture and the Politics of Peasant Communities in El Salvador, 1823–1914*. Pittsburgh: University of Pittsburgh Press, 1999.

——. "The Culture and Politics of State Terror in El Salvador." In *When States Kill: Latin America, the U.S. and Technologies of Terror*, edited by Néstor Rodríguez, 85–114. Austin: University of Texas Press, 2005.

Leonard, Ralf. *Ondas rebeldes, ondas conformes*. San Salvador: Ediciones H. Boll, 1999.

Lilla, Mark. "Republicans for Revolution." *New York Review of Books* 59, no. 1 (January 12, 2012): 12–16.

Linde, Charlotte. *Life Stories: The Creation of Coherence*. New York: Oxford University Press, 1993.

Lindo Fuentes, Héctor. Review of *Transnational Politics in Central America*, by Luis Roniger. *Journal of Latin American Studies* 44, no. 4 (November 2012): 805–7.

——. "Schooling in El Salvador." In *Going to School in Latin America*, edited by Silvina Gvirtz and Jason Beech, 179–201. Westport, CT: Greenwood Press, 2008.

——. *Weak Foundations: The Economy of El Salvador in the Nineteenth Century*. Berkeley: University of California Press, 1990.

Lindo Fuentes, Héctor, and Erik Ching. *Modernizing Minds in El Salvador: Education Reform and the Cold War, 1960–1980*. Albuquerque: University of New Mexico Press, 2012.

Lindo Fuentes, Héctor, Erik Ching, and Rafael Lara. *Remembering a Massacre in El Salvador: The Insurrection of 1932, Roque Dalton and the Politics of Historical Memory*. Albuquerque: University of New Mexico Press, 2007.

Logan, Kathleen. "Personal Testimony: Latin American Women Telling Their Lives." *Latin American Research Review* 32, no. 1 (1997): 199–211.

López Bernal, Carlos Gregorio. "Schafik Jorge Hándal y la 'Unidad' del FMLN de postguerra: Entre la memoria y la historia." Paper presented at the 55th Congreso Internacional de Americanistas, San Salvador, July 12–17, 2015.

———. *Tradiciones inventadas y discursos nacionalistas: El imaginario nacional de la época liberal en El Salvador, 1876–1932.* San Salvador: Imprenta Universitaria, 2007.

———. "Lecturas desde la derecha y la izquierda sobre el levantamiento de 1932: Implicaciones político-culturales." In Las masas, la matanza y el martinato: ensayos sobre 1932, by Erik Ching, Virginia Tilley and Carlos Gregorio López Bernal, 187–220. San Salvador: UCA Editores, 2007.

López Casanova, Alfredo. *El Salvador: Por el camino de la paz y la esperanza: testimonios de excombatientes insurgentes.* Guadalajara, Jalisco, Mexico: Casa Cultural El Salvador, 1995.

López Vigil, María. *Don Lito de El Salvador: Habla un campesino.* San Salvador: UCA Editores, 1987. Published in English as *Don Lito of El Salvador.* Maryknoll, NY: Orbis Books, 1990.

———. *Muerte y vida en Morazán: Testimonia de un sacerdote.* San Salvador: UCA Editores, 2005 [1987]. Published in English as *Death & Life in Morazan: A Priest's Testimony from a War-Zone in El Salvador.* Translated by Dinah Livingstone. London: Catholic Institute for International Relations, 1989.

Lüers, Paulo. "Carta al empresario y benefactor Nicolás Salume." *Diario de Hoy,* March 29, 2009, http://www.elsalvador.com/especiales/2008/observador /PLuers120309.asp.

———. "Peces fuera del agua." *Diario de Hoy,* February 21, 2009, http://www .elsalvador.com/especiales/2008/observador/PLuers210209.asp.

Luz Nóchez, María. "La epopeya de la guerra civil salvadoreña llegará a la televisión en 2016." *El Faro,* December 5, 2014, http://www.elfaro.net/es /201412/el_agora/16307/La-epopeya-de-la-guerra-civil-salvadore%C3%B1a -llegar%C3%A1-a-la-televisi%C3%B3n-en-2016.htm.

Mackenbach, Werner. "Realidad y ficción en el testimonio centroamericano." *Istmo* 2 (July–December 2001), http://istmo.denison.edu/n02/articul os /realidad.html#texto16.

Mackey, Danielle Marie. "A Salvadoran Writer Goes Into Exile." *New Yorker,* February 24, 2016, http://www.newyorker.com/books/page-turner/a -salvadoran-writer-goes-into-exile.

Mahoney, James. *The Legacies of Liberalism: Path Dependence and Political Regimes in Central America.* Baltimore: Johns Hopkins University Press, 2003.

Majano, Adolfo. *Una oportunidad perdida: 15 de octubre 1979.* San Salvador: Indole Editores, 2009.

testimonio [handwritten marginal note]

Malkin, Elisabeth. "El Salvador Cracks Down on Crime, but Gangs Remain Unbowed." *New York Times*, August 11, 2015, http://www.nytimes.com/2015 /08/12/world/americas/el-salvador-cracks-down-on-crime-but-gangs -remain-unbowed.html?_r=0.

Manning, Carrie. *The Making of Democrats: Elections and Party Development in Postwar Bosnia, El Salvador and Mozambique*. New York: Palgrave Macmillan, 2008.

Manuel, Anne. *Nightmare Revisited, 1987–88: Tenth Supplement to the Report on Human Rights in El Salvador*. New York: Human Rights Watch, 1988.

Manwaring, Max, and Court Prisk, eds. *El Salvador at War: An Oral History of the Conflict from the 1979 Insurrection to the Present*. Washington, DC: National Defense University Press, 1988.

Mainwaring, Scott, and Aníbal Pérez-Liñán. *Democracies and Dictatorships in Latin America: Emergence, Survival, and Fall*. New York: Cambridge University Press, 2013.

Marín, Abraham Alberto. *Batallón Atlacatl: Génesis y ocaso*. San Salvador: UFG Editores, 2007.

Márquez, Carlos Mario. "Francisco Valencia: No maté en la guerra, pero lo habría hecho si me hubiera tocado." *Diario1.com*, October 9, 2014, http:// diario1.com/zona-1/2014/10/francisco-valencia-no-mate-en-la-guerra-pero -lo-habria-hecho-si-me-hubiera-tocado/.

Martínez, Ana Guadalupe. *Las cárceles clandestinas de El Salvador: Libertad por el secuestro de un oligarca*. Sinaloa, Mexico: Universidad Autónoma de Sinaloa, 1980.

Martínez, Carlos, and Sergio Arauz. "Entrevista con Humberto Corado, ex ministro de defensa." *El Faro*, March 6, 2006, http://archivo.elfaro.net /Secciones/platicas/20060306/Platicas1_20060306.asp.

Martínez, Carlos, Sergio Arauz, and Mauro Arias. "Plática con Dagoberto Gutiérrez." *El Faro*, August 29, 2010, http://www.elfaro.net/es/201008/el _agora/2340/.

Martínez, Carlos, and José Luis Sanz. "Entrevista con Terry Karl." *El Faro*, April 19, 2010, http://elfaro.net/es/201004/noticias/1531/.

Martínez Peñate, Oscar. *El Salvador, el soldado y la guerrillera: Historia y relatos de vida*. San Salvador: UFG Editores, 2008.

Mason, T. David. *Caught in the Crossfire: Revolutions, Repression and the Rational Peasant*. Lanham, MD: Rowman and Littlefield, 2004.

Maykuth, Andrew. "Battling for Hearts in El Salvador." *The Philadelphia Enquirer*, February 2, 1987, accessed on http://www.maykuth.com/Archives /salv87.htm.

Mayorga, Román, Salvador Sánchez Cerén, Pedro Nikken, Enrique Ter Horst, and David Escobar Galindo. *El Salvador: De la guerra civil a la paz negociada*. San Salvador: Ministerio de Relaciones Exteriores, 2012.

Mazzei, Julie. *Death Squads or Self-Defense Forces? How Paramilitary Groups Emerge and and Challenge Democracy in Latin America*. Chapel Hill: University of North Carolina Press, 2009.

McAllister, Carlota, and Diane Nelson. *War by Other Means: Aftermath in Post-genocide Guatemala*. Durham: Duke University Press, 2013.

McClintock, Cynthia. *Revolutionary Movements in Latin America: El Salvador's FMLN and Peru's Shining Path*. Washington, DC: United States Institute of Peace, 1998.

McCracken, Lyn and Theodora Simon. *Mujeres de la guerra*. El Salvador: SHARE El Salvador, 2012.

McGrattan, Cillian. *Memory, Politics and Identity: Haunted by History*. New York: Palgrave Macmillan, 2012.

McGehee, Ralph. "CIA Support of Deathsquads: El Salvador," October 9, 1999, http://www.serendipity.li/cia/death_squads1.htm#El.

Medrano Guzmán, Juan Ramón. *Memorias de un guerrillero*. Rev. ed. San Salvador: New Graphic S.A. de C.V., 2006.

Mena Sandoval, Francisco. *Del ejército nacional al ejército guerrillero*. San Salvador: Ediciones Arcoiris, 1990.

Méndez, Joaquín. *Los sucesos comunistas en El Salvador*. San Salvador: Imprenta Funes y Ungo, 1932.

Menéndez Rodríguez, Mario. *Voices from El Salvador*. San Francisco: Solidarity, 1983. Published originally in Spanish as *El Salvador: Una auténtica guerra civil*. San José, Costa Rica: Editorial Universitaria Centroamericana, 1980.

Menjívar Ochoa, Rafael. *Tiempos de locura: El Salvador, 1979–1981*. San Salvador: FLACSO/Indole Editores, 2008.

Merino, José Luís. *Comandante Ramiro: Revelaciones de un guerrillero y líder revolucionario salvadoreño*. Rev. ed. Mexico: Oceano Sur, 2011.

Middlebrook, Kevin. *Conservative Parties: The Right, Democracy and Latin America*. Baltimore: Johns Hopkins University Press, 2000.

Mijango, Raúl. *Mi guerra: Testimonio de toda una vida*. San Salvador: s.n., 2007.

Molinari, Lucrecia. " 'Escuadrones de la muerte': Grupos paramilitares, violencia y muerte en Argentina ('73–'75) y El Salvador ('80)." *Diálogos* 10, no. 1 (February–August, 2009): 91–116.

Molloy, Sylvia. *At Face Value: Autobiographical Writing in Spanish America*. Cambridge: Cambridge University Press, 1991.

Montecinos, Iván. *Arriesgar la vida . . . para fotografiar la muerte*. San Salvador: Editorial LIS, 2012.

Montgomery, Tommie Sue. *Revolution in El Salvador: From Civil Strife to Civil Peace*. 2nd ed. Boulder, CO: Westview Press, 1995.

Moodie, Ellen. *El Salvador in the Aftermath of Peace: Crime, Uncertainty and the Transition to Democracy*. Philadelphia: University of Pennsylvania Press, 2010.

Morgan, Betsy, and Caroline Cargo, eds. *Mothers in Arms: Conversations with Women Combatants in El Salvador/Madres in armas: Conversaciones con mujeres ex-combatients de El Salvador.* Philadelphia: Jaime Moffett Media Design and Production, 2010.

Murray Meza, Robert. "The State of the Economy." In *Is There a Transition to Democracy in El Salvador?*, edited by Joseph Tulchin, 105–25. Boulder, CO: Lynne Rienner, 1992.

Myer, Christina. *Underground Voices: Insurgent Propaganda in El Salvador, Nicaragua and Peru.* Santa Monica, CA: Rand, 1991.

Negroponte, Diana. *Seeking Peace in El Salvador: The Struggle to Resurrect a Nation at the End of the Cold War.* Basingstoke, UK: Palgrave Macmillan, 2012.

Olmo, Enrique del. "El Salvador: Ana Guadalupe Martínez, 'Comandante María,'" Iniciativa Socialists, www.inisoc.org/anagua.htm.

Padilla, Yajaira. *Changing Women, Changing Nation: Female Agency, Nationhood and Identity in Trans-Salvadoran Narratives.* Albany: State University of New York Press, 2012.

Panamá Sandoval, David Ernesto. *Los guerreros de la libertad.* Andover, MA: Versal Books, 2005.

Paniagua Serrano, Carlos Rodolfo. "El bloque empresarial hegemónico salvadoreño," *Estudios Centroamericanos* 57 (July–August 2002): 609–93.

Paredes Osorio, Richard. Prologue to *Cruzando El Imposible: Una saga,* by Ricardo Orlando Valdivieso Oriani. San Salvador: s.n., 2007.

Parkman, Patricia. *Nonviolent Insurrection in El Salvador: The Fall of Maximiliano Hernández Martínez.* Tucson: University of Arizona Press, 1988.

Pearce, Jenny. *Promised Land: Peasant Rebellion in Chalatenango, El Salvador.* London: Latin American Bureau, 1986.

Peceny, Mark, and William Stanley. "Counterinsurgency in El Salvador." *Politics & Society* 38, no. 1 (March 2010): 67–94.

Pelupessy, Wim. *The Limits of Economic Reform in El Salvador.* New York: St. Martin's, 1997. Inserted into chapter 1

Peña, Lorena. *Retazos de mi vida: Testimonio de una revolucionaria salvadoreña.* Querétaro, Mexico: Ocean Sur, 2009.

Perales, Iosu, and Marta Harnecker. *La estrategia de la victoria: Entrevistas a los comandantes del FMLN, Leonel González, Jesús Rojas, Ricardo Gutiérrez.* El Salvador: Ediciones Farabundo Martí, 1989.

Perales, Iosu, and Claudia Sánchez Villalta. *Ana María: Combatiente de la vida.* Querértaro, Mexico: Ocean Sur, 2012.

Peterson, Anna. *Martyrdom and the Politics of Religion: Progressive Catholicism in El Salvador's Civil War.* Albany: State University of New York Press, 1996.

Peterson, Anna, and Brandt Peterson. "Martyrdom, Sacrifice, and Political Memory in El Salvador." *Social Research* 75, no. 2 (2008): 511–42.

Phillips, Tracy. "Nidia Díaz: Guerrilla Commander." Ft. Belvoir Defense Technical Information Center, 1997, http://www.dtic.mil/cgi-bin/GetTRDoc ?AD=ADA394030.

Pineda, Roberto. "Los patriarcas de la oligarquía salvadoreña." *SIEP*, December 17, 2011, http://www.ecumenico.org/article/los-patriarcas-de-la -oligarquia-salvadorena/.

Popkin, Margaret. *Peace without Justice: Obstacles to Building the Rule of Law in Salvador*. University Park: Pennsylvania State University Press, 2000.

Portillo, Geraldina. *La tenencia de la tierra en El Salvador: La Libertad, 1897– 1901, Santa Ana, 1882–1884, 1897–1898*. Instituto de Estudios Históricos, Antropológicos y Arqueológicos, Universidad de El Salvador, 2006.

Prisk, Courtney, ed. *The Comandante Speaks: Memoirs of an El Salvadoran Guerrilla Leader*. Boulder, CO: Westview Press, 1991.

Puyana Valdivieso, José Ricardo. "El proceso de selección de los candidatos a diputados del FMLN: ¿Qué hay detrás de los candidaturas?" *Reflexión Política* 10, no. 20 (December 2008): 202–25.

Pyes, Craig. "Salvadoran Rightists: The Deadly Patriots." *Albuquerque Journal*, December 18–22, 1983.

Quan, Adán. "Through the Looking Glass: U.S. Aid to El Salvador and the Politics of National Identity." *American Ethnologist* 32, no. 2 (2005): 276–93.

Ramírez, Alfredo. "Militarismo, intelectuales y proyectos de país: Las derechas salvadoreñas en vísperas de la guerra civil (1972–1984)." Paper presented at the 55th Congreso Internacional de Americanistas, San Salvador, El Salvador, July 12–17, 2015.

Rauda Zablah, Nelson. "El Faro denuncia amenazas contra sus periodistas." *El Faro*, August 13, 2015, http://www.elfaro.net/es/201508/noticias/17263 /El-Faro-denuncia-amenazas-contra-sus-periodistas.htm.

Rey Prendes, Julio Adolfo. *De la dictadura militar a la democracia: Memorias de un político Salvadoreño, 1931–1994*. San Salvador: INVERPRINT, S.A. DE C.V., 2008.

Rey Tristán, Eduardo, and Pilar Cagiao Vila, eds. *Conflicto, memoria y pasados traumáticos: El Salvador contemporáneo*. Santiago de Compostela: Universidad de Santiago de Compostela, 2011.

Rey Tristán, Eduardo, Alberto Martín Alvarez, and Jorge Juárez Avila. "The Limits of Peace in the Case of El Salvador: Memories in Conflict and Permanent Victims." In *The Struggle for Memory in Latin America: Recent History and Political Violence*, edited by Eugenia Allier-Montaño and Emilio Crenzel, 165–82. New York: Palgrave Macmillan, 2015.

Richards, Michael. *After the Civil War: Making Memory and Re-making Spain Since 1936*. New York: Cambridge University Press, 2013.

Rico Mira, Carlos Eduardo. *En silencio tenía que ser: Testimonio del conflicto armado en El Salvador, 1967–2000*. San Salvador: Universidad Francisco Gavidia, 2003.

Ríos, Bessy. "Hasta el tope, mis recuerdos y yo." November 11, 2014, http:// losblogs.elfaro.net/repubuca743/2014/11/hasta-el-tope-mis-recuerdos-y-yo .html.

Robin, Corey. *The Reactionary Mind: Conservatism from Edmund Burke to Sarah Palin.* New York: Oxford University Press, 2011.

Rodríguez, Ana Patricia. *Dividing the Isthmus: Central American Transnational Histories, Literatures and Cultures.* Austin: University of Texas Press, 2009.

Ros, Ana. *The Post-Dictatorship Generation in Argentina, Chile and Uruguay: Collective Memory and Cultural Production.* New York: Palgrave Macmillan, 2012.

Rosenberg, Tina. *Children of Cain: Violence and the Violent in Latin America.* New York: William Morrow, 1991.

Rostow, Walt Whitman. *The Stages of Economic Growth: A Non-Communist Manifesto.* Cambridge: Cambridge University Press, 1960.

Rubio Serrano, Fina. *Rompiendo silencios: Desobediencia y lucha en Villa el Rosario.* Barcelona: REDS y MUPI, 2009.

Samper, Mario. *Generations of Settlers: Rural Households and Market on the Costa Rican Frontier, 1850–1935.* Boulder, CO: Westview Press, 1990.

Sánchez Cerén, Salvador. *Con sueños se escribe la vida: Autobiografía de un revolucionario salvadoreño.* Querétaro, Mexico: Ocean Sur, 2008.

——. "Palabras Acto de Juramentación de candidatos a Alcaldes, Alcaldesas, Diputados y Diputadas FMLN." XXVIII Convención de FMLN, October 10, 2011, http://www.simpatizantesfmln.org/blog/?p=8836.

Sánchez, Peter. *Priest Under Fire: Padre David Rodriguez, the Catholic Church, and El Salvador's Revolutionary Movement.* Gainesville: University of Florida Press, 2015.

Sancho, Eduardo. *Crónicas entre espejos.* Rev. ed. San Salvador: UFG Editores, 2004.

Santos, Carlos. "Eliminar la amnistía no es ningún error, General Vargas." *DiarioCoLatino*, June 19, 2009, http://www.diariocolatino.com/es/20090619 /opiniones/68099/Eliminar-la-amnist%C3%ADa-no-es-ning%C3%BAn -error-General-Vargas.htm?tpl=69.

——. "Testimonio de uno de los asesinos del padre Rutilio Grande." *Contrapunto*, March 20, 2015, http://www.contrapunto.com.sv/reportajes /testimonio-de-uno-de-los-asesinos-del-padre-rutilio-grande.

Sarmiento, Domingo. *Life in the Argentine Republic in the Days of the Tyrants: Or, Civilization and Barbarism.* New York: Collier Books, 1961.

Schacter, Daniel. *The Seven Sins of Memory: How the Mind Forgets and Remembers.* Boston, Mass: Houghton Mifflin, 2001.

Schacter, Daniel and Joseph Coyle. *Memory Distortion: How Minds, Brains and Societies Reconstruct the Past.* Cambridge, Mass: Harvard University Press, 1995.

Schroeder, Michael. "The Sandino Rebellion Revisited: Civil War, Imperialism, Popular Nationalism, and State Formation Muddied Up Together in the Segovias of Nicaragua, 1926–1934." In *Close Encounters of Empire: Writing the Cultural History of U.S.-Latin American Relations,* edited by Joesph,

Gilbert, Catherine LeGrand, and Ricardo Salvatore, 208–68. Durham, NC: Duke University Press, 1998.

Schwarz, Benjamin. *American Counterinsurgency Doctrine and El Salvador: The Frustrations of Reform and Illusions of Nation Building.* Santa Monica, CA: Rand, 1991.

Scott, James. *Domination and the Arts of Resistance: Hidden Transcripts.* New Haven, Conn: Yale University Press, 1990.

Segovia, Alexander. *Transformación estructural y reforma económica en El Salvador.* Guatemala: F & G Editores, 2002.

——. "Los movimientos sociales en El Salvador en la posguerra." In *Los movimientos sociales en sociedades posbélicas: La experiencia de El Salvador,* edited by Alexander Segovia, 63–97. San Salvador: FLACSO El Salvador, 2015.

Serpas, Jaime Roberto. *La lucha por un sueño: Antecedentes y crónicas completas de la guerra civil en El Salvador.* San Salvador: s.n., 2006.

Servicio Informativo Ecuménico y Popular. "Entrevista con Mauricio El Sólido," *SIEP.* April 14, 2013, http://ecumenico.org/article/ingrese-en-chalchuapa-y -en-1970-al-partido-comunis/.

——. "Entrevista con Victoriano García." *SIEP,* May 2, 2011, http://ecumenico .org/article/sigo-luchando-por-la-tierra-entrevista-con-victori/.

——. "1932: heroica y dolorosa página de nuestra historia . . . Síntesis de Ponencia de Francisco Jovel en Foro sobre el 32." *SIEP,* February 2, 2011, http://www.ecumenico.org/leer.php/2394.

——. "1985–2005: 20 años después de la captura de Inés Duarte," *SIEP,* October 16, 2005, http://www.ecumenico.org/leer.php/1799.

Shayne, Julie. *The Revolution Question: Feminisms in El Salvador, Chile, and Cuba.* New Brunswick, NJ: Rutgers University Press, 2004.

Silber, Irina Carlota. *Everyday Revolutionaries: Gender, Violence and Disillusionment in Postwar El Salvador.* New Brunswick, NJ: Rutgers University Press, 2011.

Simán, José Jorge. *Monseñor Oscar Arnulfo Romero Galdámez: Un testimonio.* San Salvador: printed by the author., 2007; available at http://www .untestimonioderomero.com/Libro/index.html.

Somers, Margaret. "The Narrative Constitution of Identity: A Relational and Network Approach." *Theory and Society* 23, no. 5 (October 1994): 605–49.

Sommer, Doris. *Foundational Fictions: The National Romances of Latin America.* Berkeley: University of California Press, 1993.

Spencer, David. *From Vietnam to El Salvador The Saga of the FMLN Sappers and Other Guerrilla Special Forces in Latin America.* Westport, CT: Praeger, 1996.

——. *Strategy and Tactics of the Salvadoran FMLN Guerrillas: Last Battle of the Cold War, Blueprint for Future Conflicts.* Westport, CT: Praeger, 1995.

Sprenkels, Ralph. *Caminar con el pueblo: Una entrevista con Jon Cortina.* San Salvador: Ediciones Populares: 2009.

———. "Roberto d'Aubuisson vs Schafik Hándal: Militancy, Memory Work and Human Rights." *European Review of Latin American and Caribbean Studies* 91 (October 2011): 15–30.

Stanley, William. *The Protection Racket State: Elite Politics, Military Extortion and Civil War in El Salvador.* Philadelphia: Temple University Press, 1996.

———. Review of *Emergence of Insurgency in El Salvador: Ideology and Political Will*, by Yvon Grenier. *Comparative Politics* 94, no. 1 (March 2000): 214–15.

Stern, Steve. *Battling for Hearts and Minds: Memory Struggles in Pinochet's Chile, 1973–1988.* Durham, NC: Duke University Press, 2006.

———. *Reckoning with Pinochet: The Memory Question in Democratic Chile, 1989–2006.* Durham, NC: Duke University Press, 2010.

———. *Remembering Pinochet's Chile: On the Eve of London, 1998.* Durham, NC: Duke University Press, 2006.

Stier, Oren. *Committed to Memory: Cultural Mediations of the Holocaust.* Amherst: University of Massachusetts Press, 2003.

Stoll, David. *Between Two Armies in the Ixil Towns of Guatemala.* New York: Columbia University Press, 1993.

Straughn, Jeremy. Review of *Life Stories: The Creation of Coherence*, by Charlotte Lind. *American Journal of Sociology* 101, no. 2 (September 1995): 518–20.

Thomson, John. "A November Surprise?" *The Washington Times*, November 9, 2008, http://www.washingtontimes.com/news/2008/nov/09/a-november -surprise-in-el-salvador/.

Tilly, Charles. *Stories, Identities and Political Change.* Boston: Rowman and Littlefield 2002.

Todd, Molly. *Beyond Displacement: Campesinos, Refugees and Community Action in the Salvadoran Civil War.* Madison: University of Wisconsin Press, 2010.

Torres, Fidel. *Los militares en el poder: Memorias.* San Salvador: Editorial Delgado, 2007.

Treacy, Mary Jane. "Woman, Guerrillera and Political Prisoner: Conflicting Identities in Salvadoran Memoirs." *Monographic Review/Revista Monográfica* 11 (1995): 347–59.

Tula, Maria Teresa, and Lynn Stephen. *Hear My Testimony. Maria Teresa Tula, Human Rights Activist of El Salvador.* Boston: South End Press, 1994. Published in Spanish as *Este es mi testimonio: María Teresa Tula, luchadora pro-derechos humanos de El Salvador.* San Salvador: Editorial Sombrero Azul, 1995.

Tulchin, Joseph, ed. *Is There a Transition to Democracy in El Salvador?* Boulder, CO: Lynne Rienner, 1992.

Turcios, Roberto. *Autoritarismo y modernización: El Salvador, 1950–1960.* San Salvador: Concultura, 2003 [1993].

Turits, Richard Lee. *Foundations of Despotism: Peasants, the Trujillo Regime and Modernity in Dominican History.* Stanford, CA: Stanford University Press, 2003.

Ueltzen, Stefan. *Conversatorio con los hijos del siglo: El Salvador del siglo XX al siglo XXI.* El Salvador: Editorial Milenio, 1994.

United Nations Commission on the Truth for El Salvador. *From Madness to Hope: The Twelve-Year War in El Salvador.* New York: United Nations Security Council, 1993.

Universidad Centroamericana. "Estudio de proyecto 'Cerrón Grande.'" *Estudios Centramericanos* no. 286–87 (August–September, 1972): 511–633.

Valdivieso Oriani, Ricardo Orlando. *Cruzando El Imposible: Una saga.* San Salvador: s.n., 2007.

Valencia, Daniel. "Los archivos secretos de la dictadura." *El Faro,* December 10, 2015, http://www.elfaro.net/es/201512/el_salvador/17578/Los-archivos -secretos-de-la-dictadura.htm.

Valencia, Daniel, and Carlos Martínez. "Plática con Orlando de Sola." *El Faro,* July 10, 2009, http://archivo.elfaro.net/secciones/platicas/20090710 /Platicas1_20090710.asp.

Valencia, Ricardo. "Diez respuestas que ayudan a comprender por qué las maras colapsaron el transporte público." *El Faro,* July 31, 2015, http://www .elfaro.net/es/201507/noticias/17237/Diez-respuestas-que-ayudan-a -comprender-por-qu%C3%A9-las-maras-colapsaron-el-transporte -p%C3%BAblico.htm.

——. "Entrevista con Eduardo Linares." *El Faro,* n.d., http://archivo.elfaro.net /dlgalp/contrainsurgencia/el.asp.

Valencia, Roberto, and Mauro Arias. "Plática con Gaspar Romero," *El Faro,* August 8, 2011, http://www.elfaro.net/es/201108/el_agora/5019/.

Valle, Victor. *Siembra de vientos: El Salvador, 1960–1969.* San Salvador: CINAS, 1993.

Van Der Borgh, Chris, and Wim Savenije. "De-securitising and Re-securitising Gang Policies: The Funes Government and Gangs in El Salvador." *Journal of Latin American Studies* 47, no. 1 (February, 2015): 149–76.

Vaquerano, Ricardo, and Efren Lemus. "Plática con diputado Sigifredo Ochoa Pérez." *El Faro,* July 24, 2013, http://www.elfaro.net/es/201307/platica /12703/.

Vaquerano, Ricardo, Daniel Valencia, Diego Murcia, and Mauro Arias. "Plática con general Mauricio Vargas." *El Faro,* January 24, 2010, http://www.elfaro .net/es/201001/el_agora/977/.

Vásquez, Lucio (Chiyo), and Sebastián Escalón Fontan. *Siete gorriones.* San Salvador: MUPI, 2012.

Vásquez, Norma, Cristina Ibáñez, and Clara Murguialday. *Mujeres—montaña: Vivencias de guerrilleras y colaboradoras del FMLN.* Madrid: Horas y Horas, 1996.

Velázquez Carrillo, Carlos. "La consolidación oligárquica neoliberal en el salvador y los retos para el gobierno del FMLN." *Revista América Latina* 10 (2011): 161–202, http://yorku.academia.edu/CarlosVel%C3%A1squezCarrillo /Papers/855959/_La_Consolidacion_Oligarquica_Neoliberal_en_El_Salvador_y _los_Retos_para_el_Gobierno_del_FMLN_.

Vickers, George. "The Political Reality After Eleven Years of War." In *Is There a Transition to Democracy in El Salvador?* edited by Joseph Tulchin, 25–57. Boulder, CO: Lynne Rienner, 1992.

Vigil, Carlos Balmore. *Soldados en combate.* San Salvador: N.p, 2013.

Villalobos, Joaquín. "El ayatolá Hándal y el materialismo histérico." *El Diario de Hoy,* January 26, 2005, http://www.elsalvador.com/noticias/2005/01/26 /editorial/edi4.asp.

——. "Homenaje a Rafael Antonio Arce Zablah," *El Diario de Hoy,* September 28, 2005.

——. Review of *Revolutionary Movements in Latin America: El Salvador's FMLN and Peru's Shining Path,* by Cynthia McClintock. *Journal of Latin American Studies* 32, no. 2 (May 2000): 586–88.

Viterna, Jocelyn. *Women in War: The Micro-processes of Mobilization in El Salvador.* New York: Oxford University Press, 2013.

Von Santos, Herard. *Días de trueno.* San Salvador: s.n., 2006.

——. *Soldados de élite en Centroamérica y Mexico.* San Salvador: s.n. 2008.

Wade, Christine. *Captured Peace: Elites and Peacebuilding in El Salvador.* Athens: Ohio University Press, 2016.

Waghelstein, John. "El Salvador: Observations and Experiences in Counterinsurgency, an Individual Study Project." Carlisle Barracks, Pennsylvania, Army War College, Senior Officers Oral History Program, 1985.

Walter, Knut. *Las fuerzas armadas y el acuerdo de paz: La transformación necesaria del ejército salvadoreño.* San Salvador: Fundación Friedrich Ebert, 1997.

Ward, Margaret. *Missing Mila, Finding Family: An International Adoption in the Shadow of the Salvadoran Civil War.* Austin: University of Texas Press, 2011.

Webre, Stephen. *José Napoleón Duarte and the Christian Democratic Party in Salvadoran Politics, 1960–1972.* Baton Rouge: Louisiana State University Press, 1979.

Weinstein, Barbara. *The Color of Modernity: São Paulo and the Making of Race and Nation in Brazil.* Durham, NC: Duke University Press, 2015.

Wheaton, Philip. "U.S. Strategies in Central America." In *Revolution and Intervention in Central America,* edited by Marlene Dixon and Susanne Jonas, 236–54. San Francisco, CA: Synthesis Publications, 1983.

White, Hayden. *Tropics of Discourse: Essays in Cultural Criticism.* Baltimore: Johns Hopkins University Press, 1978.

Whitfield, Theresa. *Paying the Price: Ignacio Ellacuría and the Murdered Jesuits of El Salvador.* Philadelphia: Temple University Press, 1994.

Wickham Crowley, Timothy. *Guerrillas and Revolution in Latin America: A Comparative Study of Insurgents and Regimes Since 1956.* Princeton, NJ: Princeton University Press, 1991.

Williams, Philip, and Knut Walter. *Militarization and Demilitarization in El Salvador's Transition to Democracy.* Pittsburgh: University of Pittsburgh Press, 1997.

Williams, Robert. *States and Social Evolution: Coffee and the Rise of National Governments in Central America.* Chapel Hill: University of North Carolina Press, 1994.

Wolfgram, Mark. *"Getting History Right": East and West German Collective Memories of the Holocaust and War.* Lewisburg: Bucknell University Press, 2011.

Wolf, Sonja. "Subverting Democracy: Elite Rule and the Limits to Political Participation in Post-War El Salvador." *Journal of Latin American Studies* 41, no. 3 (August 2009): 429–65.

Wood, Elizabeth Jean. *Insurgent Collective Action and the Civil War in El Salvador.* Cambridge: Cambridge University Press, 2003.

Wood, James. *The Society of Equality: Popular Republicanism and Democracy in Santiago de Chile, 1818–1851.* Albuquerque: University of New Mexico Press, 2011.

Yanes, Gabriela, and Keith Ellis. *Mirrors of War: Literature and Revolution in El Salvador.* New York: Monthly Review Press, 1985.

Yarrington, Doug. *A Coffee Frontier: Land, Society and Politics in Duaca, Venezuela, 1830–1936.* Pittsburgh: University of Pittsburgh Press, 1997.

Yashar, Deboarah. *Demanding Democracy: Reform and Reaction in Costa Rica and Guatemala, 1870s–1950s.* Stanford, CA: Stanford University Press, 1997.

Yuhl, Stephanie. *A Golden Haze of Memory: The Making of Historic Charleston.* Chapel Hill: University of North Carolina Press, 2005.

Zamora, Ruben. *La izquierda salvadoreña: partidaria salvadoreña: Entre la identidad y el poder.* San Salvador: FLACSO, 2003.

Zepeda Herrera, Juan Orlando. *Perfiles de la guerra en El Salvador.* San Salvador: New Graphics, 2008.

Theses and Dissertations

Cáceres Prendes, Jorge. "Discourses of Reformism: El Salvador, 1944–1960." Ph.D. diss., University of Texas, Austin, 1994.

Chávez, Joaquín. "Pedagogy of Revolution: Popular Intellectuals and the Origins of the Salvadoran Insurgency, 1960–1980." Ph.D. diss., New York University, 2010.

Cortina Orero, Eudald. "Comunicación insurgente y proceso revolucionario en El Salvador, 1970–1992." Ph.D. diss., Universidad de Santiago de Compostela, 2015.

Guevara, Aldo. "Military Justice and Social Control: El Salvador, 1931–1960." Ph.D. diss., University of Texas, Austin, 2007.

Hatcher, Rachel. "On the Calle del Olvido: Memory and Forgetting in Post-Peace Public Discourse in Guatemala and El Salvador." Ph.D. diss., University of Saskatchewan, 2015.

Hernández Rivas, Annette Georgina. "Cartografía de la memoria: Actores, lugares y prácticas en El Salvador de posguerra, 1992–2015." Ph.D. diss., Universidad Autónoma de Madrid, 2015.

Johnson, Kenneth. "Between Revolution and Democracy: Business Elites and the State in El Salvador During the 1980s." Ph.D. diss., Tulane University, 1993.

Pirker, Kristina. "'La redefinición de la posible': Militancia política y movilización social en El Salvador, 1970–2004." Ph.D. diss., National Autonomous University of Mexico, 2007.

Ramírez, Alfredo. "El discurso anticomunista en El Salvador de las derechas y el estado como antecedente de la guerra civil en El Salvador, 1967–1972." B.A. thesis, National University of El Salvador, 2008.

Sprenkels, Ralph. "Revolution and Accommodation. Post-Insurgency in El Salvador." Ph.D. diss., Utrecht University, 2014.

Websites and Blogs

Andrew Maykuth Online, http://www.maykuth.com/.
Basta de Casaca!, http://bastadecasaca.blogspot.com/.
The Center for Justice & Accountability, http://www.cja.org/.
Centroamerica21, http://www.centroamerica21.com (now defunct).
Centro de Documentación de los Movimientos Armados, http://www.cedema.org/.
Columna Transversa, Achivo de las Columnas de Paolo Lüers, http://columnatransversal.blogspot.com/.
David Ernesto Pánama's blog/webpage, http://ernestopanama.com/escritores (now defuct).
Domingo Monterrosa Info, http://www.domingomonterrosa.info/.
Eduardo Sancho's blog/webpage, http://eduardosancho.com/sancho (now defunct).
The El Salvador Mural Archive, http://www.rachelheidenry.com/murals.php/.
El Torogoz, http://eltorogoz.net/.
Herard Von Santos's blog/webpage, http://herard-elfusilylapluma.blogspot.com/.
Hunnapuh: Comentarios, http://hunnapuh.blogcindario.com/.
Informe de una Matanza, http://informedeunamatanza.blogspot.com/.
Istmo: Revista virtual de estudios literarios y culturales centroamericanos, http://istmo.denison.edu/.

Marcialtienerazon, http://marcialteniarazon.org/.

Marvin Galeas blog, http://marvingaleas.blogspot.com (now defunct).

Marxist Internet Archive, http://www.marxists.org/.

Mayo Sibrian: El Carnicero de las FPL, http://www.mayosibrian.blogspot.com/.

Serendipity: CIA Support of Death Squads, http://www.serendipity.li/cia/death
_squads1.htm#El

Servico Informativo Ecumenico y Popular (SIEP), http://www.ecumenico.org/.

Simpatizanesfmln, http://www.simpatizantesfmln.org/blog/?p=8836/.

Unfinished Sentences: El libro amarillo, http://unfinishedsentences.org/es/the
-yellow-book/.

Unfinished Sentences: La Quesara Massacre, http://unfinishedsentences.org
/foia-la-quesera/.

Index

Fundación Salvadoreña para el Desarrollo Económico y Social (Salvadoran Foundation for Economic and Social Development, FUSADES), 51–52

Funes, President Mauricio, 52–53, 94

Galeas, Geovani, 92–94, 181–82
Galeas, Marvin, 73, 90–93, 149, 182–83, 194–95
Galindo, Marisol, 299 (n. 76)
Galindo Pohl, Reynoldo, 70–71, 81
gang violence, in postwar El Salvador, 13, 50, 196
García, Gen. José Guillermo, 102, 116
García, Julia, 219, 232, 235
García, Victoriano, 140
Gómez Zimmerman, Mario, 58, 64–65, 72–79, 84
González, Medardo, 175, 194
Grande, Father Rutilio, 88, 124
Guardado, Facundo, 198–99
Guardado, Roberto, 210
Guatemala, compared to El Salvador's memory of war, 22
Guerra y Guerra, Rodrigo, 252–53
guerrilla warfare: as executed by the Salvadoran guerrillas, 39–49, 171–74; as a merging of urban and rural, 223–24. *See also* comandantes
Guevara, Che, 38, 138
Gutiérrez, Dagoberto, 135, 149, 168–69, 188, 199–200
Gutiérrez, Gen. Jaime Abdul, 100–103, 106, 113, 116, 254

Hándal, Schafik, 104, 144, 250, 278 (n. 34); recognizing reformist efforts by military regimes, 30; animosity towards Cayetano Carpio, 39, 153–54, 164; upbringing, 135–36; political awakening, 137, 142–43; on Dalton assassination,

157; on 1983/4 strategic shift, 178, 182; as postwar leader, 197–99; as distinct from peasantry, 227–28
Hernández, Col. Camilo, 17, 120–21, 258
Hernández Martínez, Gen. Maximiliano, 106–7, 141–42; as interpreted by officer narrators, 112–14; overthrow in 1944 as a narrative subject, 142
Herrera, Morena, 221
historical frames, 225–27
Honduras: as migration site for landless Salvadorans, 26; war with El Salvador in 1969, 37, 103, 139, 154; as site of UN refugee camps during the war, 116, 216, 232
Hoselitz, Bert, 32–33
human rights: as relating to U.S. policy in El Salvador, 45; as subject of elite criticism, 80–82; as a subject of officers' narrations, 115–17

Indians: and ethnic conflicts over land, 27–28; absence of in Costa Rica, 31–32; and rebellion of 1932, 252
indigenous. *See* Indians
industrialization, 26, 32
infiltrators, within the guerrillas ranks, 158, 180–82
insurrectionist strategy. *See* Ejército Revolucionario del Pueblo
Ismael (testimonial narrator), 211

Jesuit priests of the UCA: trials relating to suspected assassins, 2; dramatization of, 3; assassination of, 120–23, 237, 240–42, 251; critiques by the right relating to Oscar Romero, 77, 88–89, 113
Joaquín (testimonial narrator), 235
Jovel, Francisco, 141–42, 158–59, 174

Valle, Romeo, 209, 211, 222, 230
Valle, Victor Manuel, 252
Vargas, Gen. Mauricio, 1–2, 100, 103, 108, 119, 122, 126–29, 251
Vásquez, Lucio (Chiyo), 210, 225–26, 236; on the issue of guerrillas by choice, 214–17; criticisms of comandantes, 227–30; on ignoring guerrilla factionalism, 234
Ventura, Miguel, 220
Vides Casanova, Gen. Eugenio, 100, 115, 119
Vigil, Capt. Carlos Balmore, 98, 113, 118, 123

Villalobos, Joaquín, 52, 92, 193, 228–29, 235, 295 (n. 93); interview with Marta Harnecker in 1982, 43–44; critiques of Schafik Hándal, 154–55, 198–99
Von Santos, Capt. Herard, 119–20

Walter, Knut, 28, 49
White, Robert, 117
Wood, Elisabeth Jean, 150–51

Zamora, Rubén, 198
Zepeda, Gen. Orlando, 5, 17, 100, 109, 112, 115–18, 126–28, 130, 251, 258–59